European Economic History

E. Damsgaard Hansen

European Economic History

From Mercantilism to Maastricht and beyond

Copenhagen Business School Press

European Economic History

© *Copenhagen Business School Press*, 2001
Printed in Denmark
Set in Plantin and printed by AKA-Print, Aarhus
Cover designed by Kontrapunkt, Copenhagen
Book designed by Jørn Ekstrøm
1. edition 2001
ISBN 87-630-0017-2

Distribution:
Scandinavia
Munksgaard/DBK, Siljangade 2-8, P.O. Box 1731
DK-2300 Copenhagen S, Denmark
phone: +45 3269 7788, fax: +45 3269 7789

North America
Copenhagen Business School Press
Books International Inc.
P.O. Box 605
Herndon, VA 20172-0605, USA
phone: +1 703 661 1500, fax: +1 703 661 1501

Rest of the World
Marston Book Services, P.O. Box 269
Abingdon, Oxfordshire, OX14 4YN, UK
phone: +44 (0) 1235 465500, fax: +44 (0) 1235 465555
E-mail Direct Customers: direct.order@marston.co.uk
E-mail Booksellers: trade.order@marston.co.uk

To
Milène, Nelly and Eric

Preface

There were two reasons for me to write this book – a modest one and a second, a little less so.

The modest reason was that I hoped to learn from the very process of its writing. This has indeed been fulfilled. Although the fog covering both the remote and the recent past has not entirely lifted, it has been dispersed somewhat. By the recent past, I mean the years since the Second World War. Here the process of writing has helped me bring order to personal memories and experiences primarily concerning European integration.

The less modest reason for writing the book was the hope that it may prove helpful to others. Older readers might use it to find consistency for their thoughts and feelings about a period that they have lived through themselves. Younger readers might, hopefully, find the book valuable as a way to acquaint themselves with European economic history as part of their education or their work. This book was initially written in relation to my work as a teacher of economic history. However, as work with the manuscript progressed, it acquired the character of a revisiting of the past and gained a degree of reflection beyond the scope of a textbook.

The book concentrates on the six original member-states of the EC, the Benelux countries, France, Germany, and Italy, as well as Great Britain, the Scandinavian countries, Spain, and Portugal. In addition to them, references are made in most tables to Austria, Finland and Switzerland. The USA and Japan are also drawn into the exposition due to their importance to the economy of Western Europe. It might have been proper to confine the title to Western Europe, considering that only little mention is made of Central and Eastern Europe. However, during most of the 1900s, direct economic relations between countries of the Communist bloc and the countries of Western Europe were few and far between, whereas the relations examined in this book are mainly based on the conditions and traditions of Western Europe. Special sections and chapters deal with the history of individual countries under the heading "National developments". Those sections may provide exchange students with an introduction to the economic history of their host country.

A leading theme of the book is the development of international economic cooperation in the 1900s, including European integration since World War Two. However, to fulfil the requirements of the CEMS-programme (Community of European Management Schools), which offers an international Masters of Business Administration qualification, the period of the first breakthrough of early industrialism has been included. It is recommended that courses concentrating on recent economic history should include the period from 1914 to 1945 in order to give a better understanding of the aims and means of international economic policy in the post-war years.

In the early 1990s, when I started giving lectures on economic history, including the history of European integration, it was the outcome of an early personal field of interest. In 1949, while still a secondary school pupil, I dared to make a visit to the Danish Ministry of Foreign Affairs and asked for information concerning the Marshall Plan. I can no longer remember the contents of the documents I received. I did, however, remember and recognize the rooms when, after obtaining a Masters Degree in Economics, I was installed in the very same place 8 to 9 years later. During the following years, I worked in the Danish foreign service with matters concerning our agricultural exports in the first years of the European Economic Community, the formation of the European Free Trade Association (EFTA), questions related to the GATT, and Nordic cooperation. By far the most interesting work was provided by the opportunity to serve as secretary to the Danish negotiating team when Denmark, in the wake of Great Britain, negotiated for membership of the EEC in 1961-63. After the French "non" to the British application, I had the chance to work for the Danish permanent mission to the United Nations in New York, and this included participation in a session of the General Assembly. After this, I served for a shorter period as an economic counsellor at our Embassy in Washington DC; all in all, eight interesting years.

For family reasons I then left the foreign service, and shortly afterwards found myself teaching economics at the Copenhagen Business School. This background may have had an impact on my, I hope, modest use of terms and expressions from economic textbooks.

I thank the Economics Faculty of the Copenhagen Business School and the Institute of Economics for their support. The present volume is a shortened and adapted edition of a prior Danish edition. The re-writing and translation turned out to be a far greater job than I had anticipated. I thank those who assisted me. What remains of doubtful reasoning, erroneous conclusions and outright errors may all be attributed to

E. Damsgaard Hansen.

Contents

List of tables

Introduction

Why another book on economic history? The answer can be stated briefly: because history gets longer and new aspects of our past engage our interest as time goes by. Four such areas will be mentioned below:

- rapid internationalization of the world's economies along with the growing importance of global and regional international organizations,

- development of European integration within the framework of the EC/EU,

- the influence of external developments on European integration including foreign policy and security matters,

- the change around 1973 in the economic climate after more than twenty years of high growth.

Each of those topics is dealt with separately and in great detail, but not in one and the same exposition. The aim of the present work is thus to bring together these topics in a broad presentation of recent European economic history. Since the author's background is in one of the minor EC-countries, the problems and struggles within the EC can be said to be viewed "from the sideline". To this should be added a fifth, related point:

- existing books tend to place the main emphasis, by far, on the three greatest economies of Western Europe throughout history, the British, the German and the French, with the result that the remaining countries tend to disappear deep into the footnotes.

This problem has been dealt with for the separate periods through descriptions of "national developments". Besides Great Britain, France

and Germany, these include Belgium, Denmark, Italy, the Nether-
lands, Norway, Portugal, Spain and Sweden – to which are added the
United States and Japan. Furthermore, most tables include Austria,
Finland, and Switzerland.

Part I describes the conditions that had to be fulfilled to enable the
breakthrough of industry to take place in the 1700s and the early
1800s. The point of departure consists in the observation of the simple
fact that without the possibility for mass-distribution and mass-sale of
products there will be no possibility for mass production. To this
should be added that without mass-demand for products, there would
be no possibility for mass sales. These were made possible through the
existence in Western Europe of a society where wide sections of the
population had the means to fuel the necessary mass-demand. Further
conditions for mass sales were fulfilled by the existence of the necessary law and order, in the broadest sense, to ensure the fulfilment of
contracts and the security of merchants involved in long distance
trade. Another aspect, which is emphasized, is the conscious use of
economic policy by the mercantilists as a tool in the formation of the
state by giving society a common identity. The endeavours of Louis
XIV of France – other heads of state could be mentioned as well – to
promote an internal uniformity through business law, fiscal policy and
currency systems, makes one think of the present European Community. In this respect, the idea of creating an internal market is not new,
although present day results outstrip by far the results of the age of
Louis XIV.

Part II deals with the period between early industrialization and the
First World War, from 1750 to 1914. The complexity of the industrial
breakthrough is analyzed as an interrelation between process and
product innovation promoted by the natural sciences in its later stages.
The 1800s, for instance, saw improvements in the means of communication with railways, steamships, the telegraph and telephone as leading examples. One aspect of this was a rapid internationalization of
economies from the second half of the 1800s onwards. Throughout a
major part of this period, from the mid-1870s to 1914, there existed a
system of stable, almost fixed, exchange rates combined with a system
of free capital movements which, in important respects, reminds us of
the present day EMU. Although, it should be noted, the liberal structure of society and a far smaller public sector diminished the entire
scope of economic policy.

The years 1914-45, dealt with in *Part III*, can be seen as another Thirty Years War with a built-in pause. The treatment of the period is split up into three chapters under the headings: "Ten years of war, 1914-18 and 1939-45", "Eleven years of bungling, 1918-29" and "Ten years of crises, 1929-39". The overall impression of the years 1914-45 is summarized in the words: "a period of bad experiences".

The best thing that could be said about the bad experiences is that they were made useful. This is a main theme of *Part IV*, covering the period 1945-73. It begins by describing some major aspects of the history of international organizations, dealing especially with the League of Nations and the United Nations. A comparison of the two organizations, reflecting the different degrees of mutual responsibility for the world economy, provides better evidence than lengthy explanations of the changes in attitude to the international economy between 1919 and 1945. This is followed by a review of the efforts in the wake of the Second World War to abolish the economic restrictions inherited from the years of crisis and war, including the work by the OEEC which was set up under the aegis of the Marshall Plan. The 1950-73 period has been called a "golden age", characterized by exceptional economic growth, although there were substantial differences between the countries of Western Europe. The growth factors are analyzed, as are the differences in the growth rates.

Part V deals with European integration during the years of high growth. A basic point of the analysis is that there should be no separation between the concerns and motives behind foreign policy and security considerations on the one hand and matters concerning economic integration on the other. This was indeed the case with the creation of the European Coal and Steel Union in the early 1950s as well as the setting up of the Treaty of Rome later on in the 1950s. To prevent discrimination in trade between the countries of Western Europe, an initiative was taken by Great Britain to set up a free trade area among the OEEC-countries. The initiative failed due to Franco-British disagreement. A smaller European Free Trade Association, EFTA, was established instead. It was not until 1973 that a partial solution to the problem of discrimination was found when Britain and two other countries joined the EC, this move being supplemented by the establishment of a free trade arrangement between the EC and the remaining EFTA countries.

As a way of analizing integration processes, different types of integration are mentioned: confederal as opposed to federal integration and sectoral as opposed to general integration, including foreign policy and security matters. This constitutes an analytical framework consisting of four "boxes" which can be used to describe trends in the process of integration. As far as matters dealt with by the EC (the ECSC, the EEC and EURATOM) are concerned, there has been a movement towards increased sectoral, federal integration. As far as foreign policy and security matters are concerned, there has been a tendency towards increased confederal integration under the auspices of the European Council. A one-dimensional characteristic of overall development is impossible and should not be attempted.

Part VI, covering the years after 1973, starts with the dramatic rise in oil prices. At the beginning, the rise was blamed for the lowering of the growth rates and the increase in unemployment. It was later realized that the oil crisis should be considered as a catalyst to a process, which was already underway. A comparison between the economic development since 1973 with the preceding twenty or so years does not present a pretty picture: growth rates halved and unemployment went up by four to five times. Comparisons to periods before the golden years give a more favourable picture. The British economist and historian, Angus Maddison, has argued that the years after 1973 come out as "second best". At least, this is the case for some countries. It was the golden period from 1950 to 1973 that was the exception to the rule with its extraordinary growth rates. The conclusion is, as far as those years are concerned, that the major problem in Western Europe was not that growth rates had been halved, but that 17 million out of a labour force of 170 million have remained out of work. The economic setback of the oil crisis primarily meant a halt to the dynamics of European integration, marked by failed plans like the Werner plan presented in 1970 outlining the creation of a an economic and monetary union. It was not until the mid-1980s, that it was realized that national schemes were insufficient to overcome the economic problems of Western Europe, and that the process of integration began to regain speed. This was reflected in the Single European Act, followed by the Maastricht Treaty of 1992. Once again, external developments, this time the collapse of the Communist bloc, had speeded up the process of integration. The end of the 1990s saw the EC/EU facing two major problems, the realization of the third stage of the EMU and the extension of the Community towards the east.

Part I
The background to industrialization

The term "industrial revolution" is not precise and will, on the whole, be avoided. Considered as a revolution, the so-called industrial revolution was a slow and lengthy affair. Some authors place it as early as 1750, others in the first quarter of the 1800s. Adam Smith's famous example, the production of pins, which he used in his "Wealth of Nations" published in 1776 at a time when, according to traditional accounts the revolution had reached its peak, does not leave one with the feeling that he was witnessing an industrial revolution. Had that indeed been the case, such a well-informed observer of his time would probably had chosen an example with more smoke and steam.

Rather than considering the introduction of highly mechanized production as a beginning, it seems more reasonable to view it as an intermediate stage. The fact that the industrial breakthrough has attracted so much concern and interest, at the expense of the background to this breakthrough, is undoubtedly due to the fact that those preconditions are far more difficult to observe than the smoke of factory chimneys in Manchester and Birmingham.

Four basic conditions that must be fulfilled are:

1. agriculture must be able to produce a surplus of food,
2. a physical and institutional framework suitable for mass distribution must exist,
3. mass production techniques have to become current knowledge,
4. such technique must be superior under current price relations.

These four requirements mean, expressed in other terms, that it must be possible for part of the population to work in other areas than agriculture, and that it must also be possible to undertake mass distribution combined with mass production based on mechanical, non-animal power. The industrial breakthrough was itself based on this latter mechanical aspect, which was by far the most spectacular. In consequence, this aspect attracted the lion's share of interest among historians and economists.

The fulfilment of the first condition – the existence of a food surplus – is not new. Ancient Rome was a metropolis with one million inhabitants or more. Points 2 and 3 were also, at least partially, fulfilled in the days of the of the Roman Empire. Grain was shipped from North Africa to Rome in large quantities and water-mills and windmills were known power sources. There were, however, serious problems with the last of the four points; namely, that any given mechanical technique had to prove its superiority under existing price conditions. The steady supply of cheap labour in the form of slaves diminished any interest in labour-saving production methods, at least for as long as the Roman empire could ensure a constant supply of slaves as the result of military supremacy in its border conflicts.

Chapter 1, *A short historical introduction*, describes the development of agriculture in Northern Europe after the fall of the Roman Empire. This period is characterized by a movement of the economy to the north. In addition to the Mediterranean economy, a new northern economic grouping was in the making. Here, just as in the south, it was water that kept the economy together; the North Sea, the Baltic and the streams and rivers running out into the two seas. Chapter 2, *The growth of trade, 1200-1500*, describes Mediterranean trade, Nordic trade and trade between the two areas. Special attention is given to the refinement of the institutional framework behind this growing trade. Here we might speak of a "commercial revolution" as a precondition of the "industrial revolution" which appeared six to seven hundred years later. Chapter 3, *Commercial Capitalism I, 1500-1750, Politics and institutions*, has, as its leading theme, an analysis of the economic and political philosophy of the period known as mercantilism. The similarity between the state-building policy of the mercantilists and present day attempts within the European Community is pointed out. Chapter 4, *Commercial Capitalism II, 1500-1750, Changes in the balance of power*, starts by describing the voyages of discovery, the temporary rise of Portugal and Spain to a leading position, followed by the movement of the economic centre of gravity of Western Europe. This was first to the Netherlands and then, at the end of the period, across the English Channel to Great Britain.

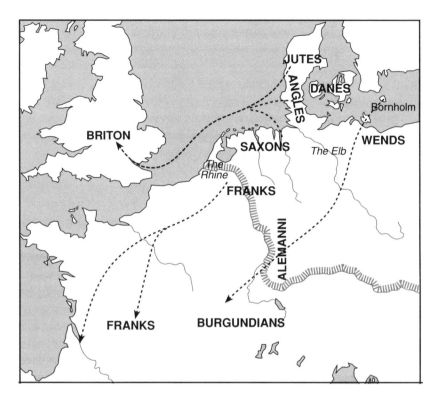

Fig. 1: The border regions of the Roman Empire to the north-east are indicated by shading to the east of the Rhine and to the north of the Danube. The Great Migrations directly connected to the fall of the Western Roman Empire took place around the year 400. Burgundians, coming from the Baltic area, pushed down from the upper Rhine to the west of the Jura Mountains, reaching the area of present-day Burgundy. The Franks, coming from what was to become north-western Germany, the Netherlands and Belgium, made their way towards the south-west. About the year 500, a kingdom, Franconia, was founded, unifying the advancing Franks with the indigenous Gallo-Roman population. This meant that the connections with Roman culture and its economy were maintained. With the establishment of Franconia, there is thus a direct line to the new empire of Charlemagne (768-814) and the Holy Roman Empire, set up as a successor to the Roman Empire.

Similarly, around the year 400, another flow of migrants sailed across the North Sea from Jutland, Schleswig, Holstein and Friesland. In Britain, they forced the Celts westwards, destroying what was left of the presence of the Romans. From the year 700, there were at first raids, then the establishment of Vikings from Norway and Denmark. In the year 1066, William the Conqueror appeared – since when no foreign army has invaded Britain. From the north of the Danube, the Alemannis pressed southwards towards what is now present-day Austria and the German speaking part of Switzerland.

Chapter 1

A short historical introduction

The Middle Ages, the millennium between year 500 and year 1500, has traditionally been considered a period of obscurity and decay in the history of Europe. This applies to culture as well as to the economy. Preceding the gloom there was Ancient Rome with its classical culture and antique buildings. After it came the artistry and banking of Florence, the discoveries made from Genoa, Cadiz and Lisbon. As well as the traditional "dim view", there now exists a new, brighter view of the Middle Ages. It is this newer, brighter way of judging the Middle Ages that forms the basis of the present account. A number of prerequisites of the industrial breakthrough of the 1700s and 1800s had been fulfilled by the end of the Middle Ages.

1. They went westward

The heading may sound like the title of a Western, dealing with immigrants crossing the American prairie. However, the subject is not North America 150 years ago, but Western Europe 1500 years ago.

The Roman Empire reached its greatest extent towards the northeast shortly after the beginning of the Christian era. "Limes" was the Latin name of this border area to the east of the Rhine and to the north of the Danube. It was constantly under pressure from the outside. However, thanks to their supreme military capacity, the Romans were able to resist this pressure for three to four hundred years. It was this capacity that failed in the 400s. Several reasons account for this failure.

Firstly, there may have been pressure from *external* factors. This does seem likely. Even small changes in the climate conditions can, in societies living just above hunger level, mean that this limit is passed. A fall in the grain harvest from fourfold to threefold will, after the storage of seed grain needed for next year's crop, mean a fall in the amount of available food of one third – down from three to two. This was the actual level. And, precisely in the period we are dealing with, such climatic changes did occur with the subsequent fall in harvest levels.

Secondly, the Roman Empire displayed increasing tendencies towards *internal* decay. During the 300s, the empire had been split up into eastern and western parts, of which the eastern part had the most economic resources. The western part experienced constant balance of payments deficits, which meant the loss of its precious metals. This was compensated for by a constant reduction of the level of precious metal in circulating currency. This debasement of the coinage eventually causing a breakdown of the monetary economy, which had hitherto functioned efficiently. The consequence of this was the growing isolation not only of the individual provinces but, also, of the great estates. An economy characterized by substantial division of labour was replaced by an economy based on self-supporting units, resulting in a weakening of the central regime and its defence system.

The actual reason for the fall of the West-Roman Empire seems to have been mass-migration; Burgundians coming in across the upper Rhine and Franks across the lower Rhine. This migration from the north and east took place mainly in the 400s. After a period of relative stability, the Moors pushed north from present-day Spain and were not stopped until 732 at Poitiers, 250 miles north of the Pyrenees. Vikings pushed forward to regions around the North Sea and further towards areas along the Atlantic. Magyars reached Central Europe from the east and Saracens attacked the coastal areas bordering the Mediterranean.

2. The European melting pot

As far as politics and culture are concerned, the period after the breakdown of the Roman Empire was one of instability. Correspondingly, it is generally held that the period was characterized by economic decay. As will be seen, however, it is doubtful whether this holds true. At least, this opinion ought to be modified.

The expression: "melting pot", has been used to characterize the United States. Down into the pot came migrants from Europe supplemented with slaves from Africa. Out of this process came an alloy called Americans. Of the original population – the Red Indians – little was heard; they were confined to special reservations and museums. In Western Europe, after the fall of the Roman Empire, the melting pot functioned quite differently. The process in this case, on the whole, took place in accordance with conditions stipulated by the resident population. Out of this came not barbarians, but inhabitants highly adjustable to the prevailing conditions.

The majority of the migrants to the Roman provinces to the west and north of the Alps came from the area close to the "limes". They were already acquainted with the Roman economy. Some had served as Roman legionaries, a few, even as officers. As part of their pension schemes they were offered farm estates upon retirement, which made them conversant with Roman farming methods and Roman style economy. Others had worked in commerce and administration and had, through this, experienced other sides of the existing society. So, when the great migrations got underway around the year 400, considerable groups of the migrants were already under the influence of Roman traditions and possessed Roman qualifications. For this reason, they were not necessarily inclined to break with the traditions of the prevailing Roman economy and culture. This continuity and feeling of unity was further strengthened by the supremacy of the Catholic Church in religious, moral and cultural affairs. All in all, the society receiving the migrants was well prepared for fulfilling its role as a functioning society after the mass invasion. That this was the case is proved by the simple fact that a Roman language survived that close to the Rhine, the old "limes".

The breach with the past naturally differed in the different areas of the previous empire. It seems, however, that it was felt most keenly on the Italian peninsula. This was, in part, due to an increasing ecological crisis, which comprised the destruction of soil and forests. To this can be added the end of the supply of new slaves as the expansion of the empire ceased. Finally, the gradual breakdown of the economy in the provinces meant an end to the net-import of capital from the provinces beyond the Alps. Traces of Roman society in the British Isles seem to have disappeared within a short time. After the arrival of Jutes and Saxons around the year 400, what few remaining Roman traces there were disappeared. The same seems to have been the case in the Iberian Peninsula after the arrival of the Moors in the 600s and 700s.

What all this came to mean was that the area covered by present-day Belgium and France had the best chances of surviving as a coherent state or kingdom. With Charlemagne (768-814), the extension of this country reached its culmination. Charlemagne declared himself to be king by the grace of God. On Christmas Day, in the year 800, the Pope added his part to the honour by proclaiming Charlemagne, Roman Emperor. Behind this, a growing conflict between the secular and the clerical powers can be detected. At the end of his reign, the territorial possessions of Charlemagne corresponded almost to those of the former Roman Empire in the West, with the exception of Britain and the southern parts of Spain. Towards the east, his possessions went as far as the Elbe, but he never managed to invade Denmark or other Scandinavian territory.

Some may have already noted that the area under the control of Charlemagne corresponded fairly closely to that covered by the original European Community of the Six[1] over a thousand years later. After Charlemagne's death, his realm was split up. It has, however, until the present day, remained a symbol of European unity and of a state of Franco-German peace. His main residence was in the town of Aachen on the present German-Belgian border. Since the Second World War, Aachen has been the place where the Charlemagne Prize is awarded. This prize is given to those who contribute to the promotion of European integration.[2]

3. Papacy versus royal power

The formation of a new power structure after the fall of the Roman Empire took place within two different spheres. There was a clerical/religious sphere, built up around the papacy. Then there was a secular sphere, built up around the emerging principalities. The relationship between these two spheres was, on the whole, tense.

The countryside was sparsely populated, with vast trackless areas separating the few populated areas. Those local communities must, generally speaking, have been self-supporting. Protection of life, har-

---

1. The Benelux countries, France, (West) Germany and Italy.
2. Among the recipients, the former prime ministers, Edward Heath of Great Britain and Jens Otto Krag of Denmark, can be mentioned. Both men made great efforts to bring their countries into the European Community.

vest and farm animals was, however, a task beyond the scope of the individual farm or village. The feudal society grew out of this situation. In its most advanced form, it can be characterized as a system consisting of different layers of agreements, reaching from the farmers cultivating the soil through knights, kings, emperor and the pope all the way up to the Almighty.

Starting from below, the peasants, as well as having soil at their disposal, were offered judicial and physical protection by their feudal lord, the local squire. In compensation, they had to deliver part of the harvest to the lord and, in addition, work at the demesne, which was soil reserved for the direct use of the lord of the manor. At a later point of time, those payments in kind in Western Europe were replaced by cash payments. The local lord for his part had to provide his overlord with military assistance by sending knights, horses, wagons with supplies, and so on. The system was designed for a society with a shortage of efficient lines of vertical communication, as well as a shortage of the means of payment. This system was threatened by systems with a more direct contact between top and bottom, especially systems where a central authority had the possibility of levying taxes in cash.

The Catholic Church possessed, as a political and economic entity, throughout the Middle Ages definite strengths including a clergy that could read and write and keep accounts. After the fall of Rome, those abilities had survived within the Church and monasteries. To this should be added the fact that the Church kept the key to perpetual blessedness, which resulted in a great, seemingly eternal, source of wealth through gifts. Finally, the Church was an international institution stretching across frontiers. The medieval, Catholic Church deserves to be called the first and, so far, the largest multinational economic body. Its need for international transactions provides part of the explanation of why modern international banking had its breakthrough in Italy. The influence of the Church in secular affairs as a leading owner of landed property should be added to its influence over souls.

Counter to this, kings and princes were eager to gain power at the expense of the local Church. One way of obtaining this was to reserve the right to appoint the leaders of the Church, the local archbishops and bishops. Seen from the point of view of the prince, those positions had the advantage that the servants of the Church had to remain unmarried, so, in principle, they would leave no heirs. This increased the princes' margin for political manoeuvring. This conflict between the

Church and the secular powers concerning the right to appoint Church leaders is known as the Investiture contest. It was resolved around the year 1200 to the advantage of the Church and the papacy. As a money economy gained a foothold and the economies of the towns were strengthened during the latter half of the Middle Ages, the balance of power switched back much to the benefit of the secular powers.

The Holy See can be said to have represented the idea of European Unity. It was the one and only economic and political institution stretching between the shores of the Mediterranean, the Atlantic, and the North and Baltic seas. Latin was its common language and represented a common culture and common human values. The latter points would turn out to be important in times to come. The economy of the Ancient World, in Athens and Rome, had been that of the elite, and made possible by the ownership of slaves. This factor was in contradiction to Christianity – at least as far as persons of your own colour and creed were concerned – and had far-reaching implications for the economy. This should actually be considered to be one of the major factors behind economic development in Western Europe in the centuries to come.

The refusal to use slaves had an impact on the economy on both the supply side and demand side. On the *supply side,* the use of hired labour meant a change in the relative factor prices, which made capital cheaper compared to labour. This, in turn, meant there was an incentive to use labour-saving production methods, which was exactly what took place in Western Europe as Christianity gained ground. On the *demand side,* the existence of a large fraction of the population having an effective demand for mass-produced consumer goods – as opposed to luxuries demanded by a small elite – was to form the basis for mass production. Through these mechanisms, the Church had a double effect on the development of the economy of Western Europe.[3]

4. Developments in agriculture

4.1 Important innovations
Differences in soil and climate caused differences then as now in farming between northern and southern Europe. A generally accepted bor-

---

3.   The analysis as it is presented here, is inspired by J.R.Hicks (1969).

derline is said to run east-west along the Loire river in central France, and from there along the Alps towards the east. North of this line, the soil generally contains more clay and is harder to cultivate. To this should be added a damper climate, which meant more advantageous conditions for farming. All in all it meant steadier production – with the proper crops and methods of cultivation.

A major aspect of the development of north-western Europe during the Middle Ages was precisely the adaptation of such new crops and methods of production. That the years after the fall of the Roman Empire until the Reformation saw a movement of political and economic power to the north is partly explained by this:[4]

a. The wheel plough came into use. It cut deeper into the soil. An entirely new feature was its ability to turn the upper part of the soil around. The soil increased its capacity to retain moisture and the use of nutrients was improved. The wheel plough is generally considered to have followed the expansion of German agriculture eastward in the 1100s and 1200s.

b. A change occurred from tilling the fields in two shifts to three shifts. Where, previously, it had only been possible to plant a crop on a given lot every second year, it was now possible to plant crops in two years out of three. This meant an increase from three times during a period of six years to four times in the same period, which corresponded to an increase of one third for the same extent of soil.

c. New crops were introduced. The traditionally dominant crops, spring barley and autumn wheat were now supplemented by rye and oats, the introduction of which made it possible to feed an increasing number of horses – and stronger ones at that.

d. Better utilization of the labour force throughout the year occurred because of a greater variety of products. This meant an increase in labour productivity and a decrease in the danger of crop failure.

e. Better harnesses for horses were introduced along with an increased use of horseshoes. This made the horse a better draught animal. In

---

4. B.H.Slichter van Bath (1963, Chapter 3).

relation to its strength, it consumes less than oxen and demands less care and labour. This meant the saving of energy – read calories – hereby released for human consumption. It also meant an increase in transport capacity over land and increased possibilities for widening the trade area.

f. The "ancillary trades" of agriculture grew as the use of water and windmills increased. This meant falling costs for grinding corn, for smelting and hammering iron, thereby lowering costs in the production of all sorts of iron tools and equipment.

It is now generally held that what happened was that already known methods of production were taken into general use. This leads us to two problems: Firstly, why were those possibilities not realized much earlier in the well-organized Roman Empire? And secondly, why did the new, efficient methods of production not spread much faster than they actually did? A probable answer to the first question, about the use of methods of production with low labour productivity in the Roman Empire, can be found by referring to the access to cheap labour through the supply of slaves from the barbarians living behind the "limes". As long as there was a steady supply of slaves, there was no need to economize on labour through the introduction of new methods of production. This can explain why a society able to build amphitheatres seating forty thousand spectators and aqueducts carrying water over long distances to towns with hundreds of thousands of inhabitants did not organize the use of water and windmills.

The second question, concerning the slow spread of new production methods, has usually been answered by referring to the conservatism of farmers. Another possibility could be that it was the result of rational calculations. Some of the above-mentioned reforms increased the productivity of the soil, the so-called area productivity. Others increased the productivity of the labour force. The increase from two to three phases in the crop cycle is an example of increased area productivity. Growing use of water-mills and windmills is an example of increased labour productivity. A spread of the use of windmills and water-mills should therefore be expected to occur when labour is scarce. The changes already mentioned, from a. to f., may not have taken place at the same time as an overall "reform package". The order of appearance – at least as far as England is concerned – fits into the above se-

Fig. 2: As long as there was a steady supply of slaves, there was no need to economize on labour. This may explain why a society able to build amphitheatres seating forty thousand spectators or more did not organize the use of water and windmills.

quence. About, and shortly after, the year 1000 when soil was the abundant factor and labour the scarce one, a substantial number of water-mills were taken into use.[5] The transfer from two to three phase farming is mainly supposed to have taken place after 1200 when conditions had changed and soil had become the scarce factor and labour the abundant one.

A further explanation of the transformation of agriculture at this time could be a positive change of the climate in the period around 1000. In the Northern Hemisphere, this seems to have been the case during the period from 900 to 1300. The existence of biological "threshold values" may have the consequence that even relatively small changes in average temperatures can be of substantial importance for the yield. This may have had special implications in Northern Europe and caused it to catch up with Southern Europe.

5. A similar movement may have taken place throughout greater parts of Europe after the mid-1300s as the result of the Black Death.

4.2   Consequences for society

The technological developments of the period had radical effects on the military and political structure of society. This applies to the development of feudal society as well as to the early growth of towns and commercial centres.

The heavy wheel plough can only be used in "large scale" agriculture. This meant a strong incentive towards cooperative farming among the farmers of the individual village and manor. This worked in favour of the feudal system. To this can be added that changes in the equipment of the horse, including the stirrup, is supposed to have favoured the horseman by comparison with the infantryman. However, an army of horsemen could not be permanently quartered in barracks – it had to be spread out where the forage was grown. It was not until the introduction of cannon in the late 1300s that a substantial change took place in this area.

The growth of feudal society meant a concentration of ownership within farming. The manor offered protection to its farmers and their families. As his part of the bargain, the farmer had to present a portion of his harvest to his feudal master. Another way to pay for the services of the manor could consist of the farmer working a specified number of days on the demesne of the manor, that is the arable land belonging to the owner of the manor and grown directly under his control. Note the difference between the two types of "payment" on the side of the tenants. This turned out to be important later on.

The first type of payment – in the form of grain, eggs and other products of the farm – is based on *decentralized, small-scale farming.* The current contributions to the proprietor of the manor were made as a predetermined part of the harvest, often a tenth, or tithe as it was called. To this should be added specified amounts of goods in case of special events such as marriage. The relationship in this scheme of things between the lord and the peasants cultivating the fields was of an indirect nature, at least for as long as the contributions were delivered on time. This gave a greater degree of freedom to the farmers in organizing their work and selecting their methods of farming within the framework set up by the villages themselves. Services in kind to the proprietors of the manors were, in due course, replaced by cash payments, so much more so as grain prices were reported at an early point in time. After 1200, contributions in Western Europe were to an increasing degree fixed as specific amounts of money at the time when the farmer took up his tenancy. In the years to come, this eased a process leading towards increased freehold. On the whole, this seems to have been the case in the western and southern parts of Germany, the Netherlands, France and England.

The other manorial system was called *demesne farming*, and organized the tilling of the soil and production under the direct control and supervision of the manor. The farmers placed their labour under the control of the proprietor of the manor or his superintendent. The personal relationship between the farmer and "his" soil that exists under traditional tenancy, and which might endure for generations, disappears. The work is performed under the control of inspectors on behalf of the proprietor, and the farmers are paid, mostly in kind, by the products grown on the demesne. In its milder form, the actual nature of the manorial system can be a mix of the two types described – the small-scale (collective) farming and the large-scale demesne farming. In its harsher form, demesne farming developed into direct serfdom, with loss of personal freedom. As opposed to the system of tenancy practised in Western Europe during the late Middle Ages, the system based on demesne farming, serfdom and contributions in kind practised in Eastern Europe was difficult to convert into a system based on cash payments. This factor, however, made it more difficult to end the system in a peaceful fashion – as was to be seen centuries later in Russia and Eastern Europe.

5. An Eastern frontier

In the centuries after 1000, north-western Europe seems to have benefitted from an improvement in the climate. Simultaneously, partly as a result of this, there was an increase in population size. This may, via two channels, have stimulated economic development. Firstly, this was by increasing the density of the population in certain areas, thereby opening possibilities of an increased division of labour at the local level. Secondly, it gave a surplus population incentives to take new land into cultivation, as well as cultivating new areas with a view to long-distance trade. The first phenomenon, increased demographic concentration, was seen in what corresponds to present-day Belgium and northern France. The other phenomenon, the spread of "westernized" cultivation into new areas, took place towards the east and the north spreading from areas between the Rhine and the Elbe.

After the millennium, the area around the Baltic must have experienced a *"frontier movement"* corresponding to what took place eight centuries later on the American prairie west of the Mississippi. In Eastern Europe, including the areas along the Baltic, the population so far had made their living by hunting, fishing and a primitive agriculture using the so-called slash-and-burn method, which limits the use of the same soil to a few years. This type of farming had now to give way to more intensive cultivation. In Southern Scandinavia, including Denmark, the local populations, assisted by newly-founded monasteries, seem to have been able to make those transformations on their own. To the south of the Baltic, the changes took place under the leadership of immigrants from the West. Within the framework of a feudal system, tax exemptions were granted to the settlers by the feudal lords. All in all, this meant the creation of a system dominated by great estates, as compared to the farms to the west of the Elbe. From this, Eastern Europe developed into an agricultural society dominated by great estates based on demesne farming.

From a wider perspective, this can be seen as part of the explanation why societies in Western and Eastern Europe, as far as politics and economics are concerned, developed along different lines. In Western Europe, the system of agriculture from late medieval times favoured development where the farmers themselves were responsible for their work and their farms as long as they paid their lords the dues and taxes they owed them. This points towards an economic system and society based on taxation in cash. In Eastern Europe, the development went in the opposite direction. Here the farmers spent their time working on the demesne under the guidance and instructions of a representative of the proprietor of the estate, from whom they received their pay in kind, typically as food and lodging. This points towards a society, where the majority of the population lives in serfdom, without personal rights, and forbidding them the right to leave the estate where they were born.

This difference between East and West deepened during the latter part of the Middle Ages when the feudal system in the West, more or less, fell apart. A major feature of these years was a strengthening of economic ties between Eastern and Western Europe and the inclusion of the countries around the Baltic in a common European economy. East-west trade in itself was not a novelty. It did, however, change its nature. Whereas, in the Viking Age, it was mainly concerned with expensive items like furs, amber, precious metals, jewellery, weapons and slaves, it now consisted of bulk goods from the East like grain, hides, lumber, tar, salted fish including herrings and from the West wine, salt and barrels.

A striking fact, though perhaps just sheer coincidence and one of the freaks of history, is that the borderline between Western and Eastern Germany during the second half of the 1900s, was pretty close to the medieval border line between the two agricultural systems; small scale tenant farming and large scale demesne farming. In this way the north-eastern borderline of the Roman Empire around the Elbe became the border of the area under the Treaty of Rome fifteen hundred years later.

6.   The brief Middle Ages of the Nordic countries

When viewed as a transitional period between the fall of Rome and the Renaissance, it is incorrect to speak of the Middle Ages as far as the Nordic countries are concerned. They were never directly connected to Roman political and cultural life. Considered on the basis of their written sources, they did not enter historic times until 1000. For those countries and the rest of the areas bordering the Baltic, the Middle Ages only cover a period of four to five hundred years from the introduction of Christianity after the millennium to the beginning of the 1500s. If the Middle Ages of the Nordic countries were short, the period was hectic as well. Processes of transformation and development, which in areas to the west of the Rhine had been underway for centuries, in the Nordic countries and the rest of the Baltic area took place within a much shorter period. This is true in the case of agriculture, its structure and ways of cultivating the soil, and also applies to the nature and size of trade. There is a widespread disposition to believe that dynamic and fast changes in economies are something new. This is not so. Around 1100, most of the territory of present-day Denmark was still covered by forest. But from then on things changed in a hurry. Recent research in the origin of the names of villages and local communities indicates that 1500 new villages were founded between 1050 and 1250 in the present-day area of Denmark. The size of the population seems to have accordingly increased from half-a-million to one million, a level which, after the Black Death in the 1300s, was not reached again until the second half of the 1700s.

Unfortunately, there were no economic historians in those years to undertake the writing of the history of their day and age. What was written deals mainly with the heroic behaviour of kings, knights and leading servants of the Church and monasteries. What a shame that was, because as a growth study it could have been of interest even eight hundred years later. To take Denmark as an example, it would have been the story of a society building two thousand stone churches within 150 years. That means an average of 12 – 14 churches a year, some with a tower, a few even with two. This must have been a society experiencing fast growth, where the grandchildren listened with astonishment when the elders of the family told about the "old days", meaning the times when there were no churches and no priests, the times when half of the old village left to found a new village out on the other side of the forest.

Chapter 2

The growth of trade
1200-1500

The industrial breakthrough in the second half of the 1700s and the early 1800s is traditionally considered the principal divide in recent European economic history. It was during those years, that some hitherto virtually stable economies entered a new stage of self-increasing growth. This view has lately been supplemented by a theory about a previous commercial revolution. The innovations of the eighteenth century within the field of *production* of goods had, as its prerequisite, a development within the field of *trade* in goods. Large-scale production requires, what the great British economist and philosopher, Adam Smith, had already called "the extent of the markets". Without markets of the necessary size, there could be no large-scale industries. So it is proper to ask what conditions should be fulfilled so as to ensure markets of the necessary size? This is a major theme of this and the next two chapters.

1.   The Plague and the Hundred Years War

Before 1800, our knowledge of the size of the population of Western Europe may at best be characterized as qualified guesses. That said, it is fair to say that the population of Christian Europe from 1000 to about 1300 is estimated to have increased from 18-20 million to 60-70 million. This corresponds to an annual growth of 0.4 per cent. At that time, there first occurred a halt in the growth of the population and later, from the middle of the century, a direct fall from which it took centuries to recover.

The lack of precise figures has given rise to doubts concerning the time for and the reasons behind the population decline in the late Mid-

Table 2.1: Estimated size and growth rates of population, c. 1000 to c. 1700.

mill.	c.1000	c.1300	c.1500	c.1600	c.1700
British Isles	2	5	5	7	9
France	5	15	16	18	19
Germany	3	12	13	16	15
Italy	5	10	11	13	13
Total	15	42	45	54	56
Growth rate Promille p.a.					
British Isles		3.1	0.0	3.4	2.5
France		3.1	0.3	1.2	0.5
Germany		4.6	0.4	2.1	-0.6
Italy		3.1	0.4	1.7	0.0
Total		3.4	0.3	1.8	0.4

Source: C.M. Cipolla (1993, 4)

dle Ages. One line of thinking favours an explanation corresponding to the theories on population of Thommas R. Malthus (1766-1834).[1] According to these the decrease in the size of population began around 1300 due to a shortage of food. According to another theory, the decrease set in with the coming of the Black Death. Since the first may have served to promote the second, both explanations may be true.

In terms of the distribution of wealth, development in the 1300s must have meant great changes. The growth of population – the workforce in farming – must have meant: 1) a relative increase in the price of food compared to that of other goods and 2) an increase in rent, that is to say the incomes of the owners of land rose compared to the incomes of the labour force. By far the majority of that labour force was to be found in agriculture.

At the time, this must have been felt as a decrease in the supply of food and prolonged working days. Expressed in present-day terms, the tendency led in the direction of increased rent in favour of the Church, of monasteries and other great landowners, all at the expense of tenants, labourers in agriculture and the then small urban populations. The sudden decrease in population from the middle of the century meant a reversal of this development. It is estimated that the first wave of the plague – or Black Death, as it has been called – caused the death

1.   See Chapter 5, section 3.

of a third of the population, although with substantial variations of extent between regions. New plagues followed, supplemented and promoted by the sufferings of the Hundred Years War between England and France (1338-1453). Parishes and churches without a congregation were widespread. Under such conditions, it must have been difficult to keep the farms populated by tenants. At the same time, the price of food fell compared to the price of products of the towns. All in all, the net-result was that the incomes of the landowners fell, which was to the advantage of the labour force in farming and the inhabitants of the towns. The period after 1350 is normally referred to as a period of crisis, a view that, however, does require a degree of qualification. For any dependent on their own labour who survived the plague and the wars, it meant an increase in their standard of living and improvement of their working conditions. Since history, however, was written by those who could write, and since they were to be found in cloisters and on the great estates, what was left in the written sources was a description of a prolonged crisis. In England the reaction was the passing of a law by Parliament in 1351, "the Statute of Labourers", which, under threat of imprisonment, made it illegal to demand or offer increased wages and to leave contracted jobs. This can be seen as what we nowadays would call an incomes policy. It should be added that, as with other examples of incomes policy, it did not work, at least not for long.

Very different and more far reaching were the effects in Eastern Europe, that is in the area of the great estates to the east of the Elbe. There, the farmers had fewer chances of escaping the great landowners – the further east, the worse the chances were. The conditions for the majority of the farming population changed for the worse, resulting in lifelong serfdom and a further concentration of farming around the great estates.

2. Prerequisites for the growth of trade

The period after 1000 saw a new type of trade appearing: long-distance trade in mass goods. Long-distance trade was not a novelty as this had taken place for over a thousand years. What was new was that it involved bulk commodities like grain, wood, tar, salt, salted fish, etc. A large part of this trade took place between the countries around the

Baltic and the North Sea. This leads us to the question as to which conditions should be fulfilled to make this new type of trade possible:

a. The cost of transportation of mass products should be sufficiently low to enable the products to bear the costs of transportation, including risks of all kinds[2]

b. There must be security of life and goods for the travelling trader

c. Market places must be established where sellers and buyers can meet and get an idea of market conditions

d. Business law must be established, rules and commercial habits must exist concerning stipulation and fulfilment of obligations, possibilities of bringing cases to courts, protection of the rights of foreign tradesmen, and so on

e. A generally accepted means of payment must exist

f. There must be possibilities of clearing (cancelling out) balances to reduce costly physical transfers of bullion over long distances

g. Rules must be established concerning the financing of activities transcending the capacity of individuals.

Some of the points mentioned above are partly of a technical nature, such as the costs of transportation. However, as soon as the risk factor is included, the institutions of society are involved. The same can be said about the existence of market places and systems of payment. The question of the existence of business law is not so "technical" either. In order to establish functioning commercial channels, it is necessary that the goods delivered are as agreed upon, that the coinage is genuine, that the buyer has money on his bank account, etc. To put it briefly, a wide set of norms, a business morality, must exist as a necessary basis if a monetary economy is to function well.

---

2.   The export of grain from North Africa to Ancient Rome was possible due to the fact that the Mediterranean on the whole is more calm than the North Sea and the Baltic.

3. A commercial revolution

The term "commercial revolution" was coined in the middle of the 1900s to counterbalance the strong interest in the English industrial revolution. It is not surprising that a leading book on the subject was written by an historian of Italian origin.[3] It is a widely acknowledged fact that a rich development within commerce and banking took place in Northern Italy during the Renaissance. The novelty is that manifestations of this process dated as far back as shortly after 1000.

Many of these commercial innovations from Italy and the Mediterranean were soon adopted in Northern Europe where a corresponding commercial area developed to such an extent that the author of the book speaks of a "Northern Mediterranean" consisting of the area around the Baltic and the North Sea. He even goes so far as to compare Jutland to Italy as a peninsula separating two seas, while comparing Lübeck and Hamburg, situated at the root of the peninsula, to Venice

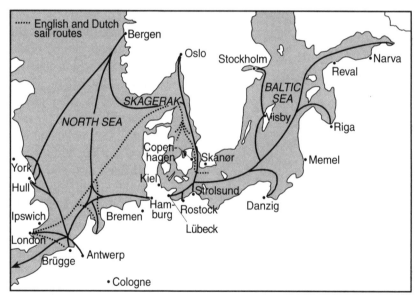

Fig. 3: The Italian economic historian, R.S.Lopez, speaks of a "Northern Mediterranean". He even goes so far as to compare Jutland to Italy while comparing Lübeck and Hamburg, at the root of the peninsula, to Venice and Genua.

3.   R. S. Lopez. The Commercial Revolution of the Middle Ages 950-1350 (1971).

and Genoa[4] As a long-time resident of this area, this may be a proper place for the author to remind readers of the differences in climate.

3.1 Transport

Facilities for transport over land did not change substantially until the end of the 1700s. The roads of the time were well below the standard of the great Roman roads. In practice, this made the use of heavy vehicles impossible over long distances. An innovation worthy of mention was the axle, which increased stability and lowered the friction of the wheels. An exception to the high cost of transportation over land was the transport of live cattle – they transported themselves, though they had to be able to feed again before they were brought to the slaughter-house. The trade of present-day Switzerland, Austria and southern Germany was much enhanced when the St. Gotthard Pass was opened up to commercial transport in the 1200s.

It was not until the introduction of railways in the 1800s that a means of cheap mass transportation over land was made available. In the meantime, the best possibilities were afforded by the rivers. Most of the early commercial centres were situated on riverbanks and at the mouths of rivers. It was not until the 1700s that canals gained major significance. All in all, it was transport on the open sea which contributed most to development in the late Middle Ages. This was the result of a combination of inventions. The light, fast ships of the Vikings and Normans were replaced by a heavier type, the cog, developed by sailors and merchants in the Netherlands.[5] It carried a bigger load and was manned by a smaller crew. The rig was changed and the rudder was moved from the starboard side to the stern and fixed to the keel. All this meant lower costs in transporting bulk goods on the open sea, bringing the countries around the Baltic and the North Sea closer to one another even though it was dangerous to sail round the northern point of Jutland.

Of equally great importance was the opening around 1300 of annual voyages from the Mediterranean through the Straits of Gibraltar to north-western Europe. The geographic position of the towns of the Netherlands, Bruges, Antwerp and, later on, Amsterdam at an interna-

---

4.   R. S. Lopez (1971, 113).
5.   It should be remembered that the Netherlands in those days included present-day Belgium.

tional crossroads was of fundamental importance for their development.

3.2 Security of life and goods

Another condition that had to be fulfilled was the security of the travelling trader and his goods. This applies to his travels as well as his stays in foreign places. As an example of the former, the first half of the 1200s saw the construction of a number of castles to protect the traffic in the Danish sounds and belts connecting the different parts of Denmark, and connecting the Baltic with the Kattegat, Skagerrak and the North Sea. Some of those castles still exist and can be seen as landmarks. Castles that are now and then considered to be the lairs of robber barons along European rivers might just as well have served for the protection of traffic, albeit for a decent fee paid as a toll to their owners. Among other examples of an endeavour to assist and protect the travelling merchant were the rules meant to protect his rights in case of shipwreck. Originally he lost the right to the cargo, even if it were saved. This was changed so that he kept at least part of it. Should he die in a foreign place, it had been the rule that the local community confiscated his property. This was modified as well.

The above can be summarized by observing that the travelling merchant was granted increased protection by the law and by the courts. This is not to say, however, that infringements and injustices did not take place. It should rather be seen as proof of the growing interest of those in power to ensure that trade was healthy and running smoothly.

3.3 Establishment of markets

A third necessary step was the establishment of markets, i.e. meeting places for wholesale traders. The medieval wholesale markets were restricted to special times of the year depending on the season such as the sheep shearing, fishing for herrings, etc. The market at the southern point of present-day Sweden, Skanör, can be taken as an example of this. The basis of it all was the so-called harvest herring, which appeared in the Sound in September and October. The major items that were dealt in were herring, salt and barrels. Along with these items, however, a variety of other goods were also traded. Those activities started around 1100 and flourished for three hundred years. This particular market was to benefit from the positive interest displayed by the Danish king who saw in it a source of income. Administered in the proper fashion, this would mean a net income not only for the fisher-men and tradesmen, but also for the royal tax collectors.

Among the famous European markets in those days were the great fairs in the area of Champagne in northern France. The area is situated on the route from northern Italy to the southern Netherlands from where the route proceeded to England, Norway (Bergen), Hamburg, Lübeck and places around the Baltic. The markets in Champagne de-veloped into an almost permanent institution moving between four towns of the area. The markets lost their importance, partly because of the new route via the Straits of Gibraltar and partly because the local prince, their "owner", overtaxed whatever remaining trade there was.

Originally, the goods being traded had to be present in order to en-sure that the quality was as expected. By introducing strict definitions of the qualities of the goods, such as grain, it became possible to make agreements without actually having the goods to hand. This served to reduce the costs of transportation, enlarge the number of buyers and sellers and improve the price formation.

This, in turn, meant further specialization of commerce to such a degree that some of the previously visiting tradesmen established themselves as permanent residents in foreign places. Part of the present-day major business-street in Copenhagen was, in the 1300s, called "Tyskmannegade" (the Germans' street), and in Bergen there still exists the remains of "Tyske Bryggen" (the Quay of the Germans).

3.4   Business law

After 1200, Italian business law reached the Netherlands via Barcelo-na. An important branch dealt with the situation where several persons were involved as buyers or sellers. A person might invest his money in another person's business journey. If the journey was a success, the de-positor gained a fixed amount of the surplus that had been agreed on beforehand. In case of loss, the investor was only responsible for the invested capital. This was the case for a so-called commenda. There were other types of arrangement where all the participants were per-sonally liable with all their assets for the common enterprise.

With the growth of individual business operations – the size of ships and their cargoes, the length and duration of the journeys – the need for such collective arrangements increased. The outcome was the cre-ation of the limited company at the end of the 1500s.

3.5 Monetary and fiscal institutions

The development of the monetary and financial institutions in the Middle Ages is normally attributed to Northern Italy. This seems fair enough as the development of banking techniques took place in this part of the world. Further development, however, along with extended use of the innovations, took place in Northern Europe, first in the Netherlands and then in England.

A distinction must be made between payments and credits (delayed payments). As far as *payments* are concerned, there must have been a shortage of means of payment. Barter trade was widespread at a local level in spite of its shortcomings. One problem with barter trade is for the two parties involved to find each another in the first place. The next problem is to reach agreement on "the terms of trade". All this is made easier through the existence of a developed monetary economy – they do not have to meet in person and the market will produce the relative prices.

The advantages of a monetary economy are obvious, as are its problems. Acceptance of the mint presupposes confidence in the weight and purity of the coins. Occasionally, kings, who took the chance to debase the mint, caused inflation. Compared to the levels of inflation in the twentieth century, this problem seems to have been modest. The physical transfer of the bullion – gold and silver – was risky as well. Piracy was occasionally accepted as a business and highway robbery could occur. This, along with the evaluation of the purity of the mints, promoted the use of transfers between banking accounts. In the 1200s, the centre of this activity was in Lyon which, eight hundred years later, is still a major financial centre in France. With the decline of the markets of Champagne, new centres appeared, first in Bruges and Antwerp, later in Amsterdam and London. Those centres handled both local and long-distance payments, including the exchange of currencies.

Organized *credits* posed a problem in that it was considered a sin to set and demand interest among Christians. The usual explanation is that such loans in those days would be consumer credit extended to people in trouble. So the prohibition could be said to protect people in distress.c.1700

The simplest type of credit is a loan granted by a *pawnbroker*. A more advanced form of loan was available at *deposit banks* and given to holders of accounts in the bank. Similar credit could be obtained by trusted customers from *currency dealers and goldsmith bankers.*[6] Through this activity, the banks developed the ability to handle wider functions in a flow-of-funds system and even acquired limited capacity to create means of payment. A fourth type of credit institutions were the international commercial houses of northern Italy and southern Germany, known as *merchant banks*. The House of Fugger of southern Germany is well known, as is its rôle in European politics around 1500.

The role of Italian banks in the Middle Ages is partly explained by the needs of the Catholic Church. As a large "multinational" economic organization, it had a need for international money transfers. The heyday of Italian banking is closely connected with that of the Catholic Church. In principle, the prohibition against paying interests was upheld. In practice, the internationalization of the economy opened up possibilities for hiding the payment. It could be done by fixing the loan in a foreign exchange and charging for the exchange into the local currency, and back again. Another possibility was the bill of exchange sold by the issuer below its nominal value.

Related to the development of the technique of payments and credit was the *technique of accounting*. Of particular importance was the development in Northern Italy of the double entry bookkeeping system. This was related to the rise of the merchant banks after 1200. The development of this system must be seen as the result of the need to keep an overall impression of complicated economic operations involving large assets and liabilities spread over a wide range of contractors and customers. To bring this about it was necessary to have skilled personnel that could read, write and calculate. The double entry bookkeeping system was only transferred, after a considerable delay, to Northern Europe. The Hanseatic League of the 1300s to the 1500s does not seem to have taken advantage of this system.

4. Forces behind the growth of the markets

In section 2, Prerequisites for the growth of trade, a number of innovations behind the growth of commerce were listed. Some of those were of a technical nature. The majority, however, were of an *institutional*

---

6.   The appearance of goldsmiths as bankers can be explained by their ability to monitor the purity of precious metals.

nature in the sense that they dealt with *rules and norms of society* in general, and those of business in particular. Which leads us to the question: why did those changes take place?

The sea captain, who replaced the oar-like rudder with a rudder fixed to the stern, gained a personal advantage from his innovation: a safer boat and a larger cargo. However, many of the novelties were of a different type as explained in sections 2 and 3. Security of life and goods, along with the existence of an accepted system of business law, comes close to what are known as social goods, that is to say, goods that cannot be bought on the market by an individual.

To take an example, why were the Danish kings prepared to use scarce resources to protect foreign merchants visiting the herring market at Skanör? It was because, as a political and economic measure, it paid to do so. Where the Viking kings, a hundred and fifty years previously, had made a living from plundering foreign countries, they now had new ideas concerning the use of the sword and the arm of the law. Now, the aim was to protect the seafarers, native or foreign, on their way to and from the great market and the ships on their way between the Baltic and the North Sea. One of the factors behind this development was what could be termed "economies of scale" as far as military matters were concerned. Where, previously, the local squire was responsible for protecting his tenants and the local population, the harvest and livestock, it was now the king's responsibility. Part of the economic gain from this could be retained by the king through a wide range of taxes and duties levied on trade.

An essential factor in deciding the type and level of taxes is the time horizon. In the short run, taxes may be raised further. This, however, incurs the risk that trade moves on to new channels. This was what happened to the markets in Champagne when trade in the early 1300s moved to Bruges. Another example of a short-sighted tax policy was the sale by kings and princes of grants and privileges to merchants and artisans, specifically the sale of the authority to collect taxes. In all those cases, the outcome was increased income in the short run at the cost of lower long-term tax revenue and a less dynamic economy in the long run.

If growth of trade was the top priority, then those enjoying political supremacy should be in its favour. A society, where merchants and townspeople held a relatively strong position, must have had a favourable attitude to trade, whereas societies dominated by producers' interests and a prince in fiscal trouble must have been reluctant towards allowing competition and innovation. It is striking that such different cities as Venice, Amsterdam or London were dominated by merchant interests and all had a strong navy when their economies peaked.

5. Regional developments

It seems proper to speak of a southern, a north-western and a northern region in describing the economic development of Western Europe from 1250 to 1500.

By the end of the period, around year 1500, *the southern region* had reached the highest level of economic development among the three. The southern region, first and foremost, means the city-states of Northern Italy. Spreading out from Florence, Pisa, Genoa and Venice, the Renaissance was at its highest. The basis for this was the importance of the cities procuring trade between the Orient and north-western and northern Europe. The Iberian Peninsula[7] might also be included as part of the southern region. As an economic and political entity, the area had reached a stage of transformation. After seven hundred years of Moorish rule, the Moors, by the end of the 1400s, had been forced back to Africa. From an economic point of view this did not necessarily mean a step forward as the previous society had been characterized by an efficient agriculture and an advanced system of horticulture. With a view to weakening the influence of the Moors, expeditions along the coast of Africa were organized. Spain and Portugal were, in the second half of the 1400s, preparing for a short, glorious period related to the great voyages of discovery.

The north-western region had its centre around the eastern part of the English Channel and the nearby North Sea coast. The core of this region was situated in present-day Belgium and Northern France. Here, as in Northern Italy, the centre served as a commercial crossroads. An east-west route stretched from the Baltic to the English Channel and further along the coast of the North Atlantic Ocean. There was a north-south route from the Rhône and the Rhine rivers to the British Isles and Norway as far as the town of Bergen, and even further north to the great fishing areas along the Norwegian coastline. Besides a

---

7.   Corresponding to the present Spain and Portugal.

great transit trade with bulk goods like wool, grain, fish, salt and wine, the area had a substantial production of cloth. Originally, the English had exported the wool for further processing in Flanders. From the

Fig. 4: From the early Middle Ages on, the town of Visby, situated on the island of Gotland, played a leading role in the Baltic trade. Here a recent picture of the walls of Visby.

1300s, the English had pursued a policy aimed at processing the wool in England. An export duty on wool was introduced while cloth was left duty-free. As a result, English producers obtained their raw materials at a lower price than their competitors on the Continent;[8] in reality, a piece of pre-mercantilist economic policy. As far as commercial activities were concerned, the centre remained in Bruges until the silting up of its harbour due to a storm in the early 1400s. From there, the centre of commerce moved to Ghent and Antwerp. It was not until the end of the 1500s that Amsterdam took on the leadership.

Finally, a *northern region* can be spoken of, closely related to trade with the Baltic area. Here it is harder to point to a specific centre. For a century or two after 1250, Lübeck played the part. By the end of this period the picture was less clear. The majority of the goods traded were agricultural products (grain) and those from the fisheries and the forests. Only the fisheries seemed to have a definite centre of activity: Skanör, then part of Denmark, now the southernmost part of Sweden. The products of agriculture and forestry were shipped from a vast number of new towns at the mouths of rivers, especially on the southern coast of the Baltic. Thanks to its situation south of Jutland at a narrow point between the Baltic Sea and the North Sea, Lübeck for centuries had played a central role in east-west trade. From the 1300s, the town, as other towns of present-day Northern Germany, had permanent representatives in the major trading cities of Northern Europe. The Hanseatic League can be said to have originally consisted in the informal cooperation between those representatives and their hometowns. In the middle of the 1300s, the merchants and their hometowns felt themselves under growing pressure from Dutch and English merchants. One reason for this was the development of new types of ships able to sail directly from the Baltic via the Skagerrak, north of Jutland, across the North Sea. Another threat to Lübeck and its merchants was the rise of a stronger Danish kingdom. After years of war between Denmark and Lübeck, backed by other German towns, a peace agreement was signed in 1370, which is considered by some to mark the birth of the Hanseatic League. However, due to changes in the pattern of trade involving the strengthening of the position of England and the Netherlands, the same period marked the beginning of the loss of power by the Hansa.

8.   E. Carus Wilson (1987, 674).

Chapter 3

Commercial capitalism I. 1500-1750 Policies and institutions

The period around 1500 marks an epoch in the economic history of Western Europe: one only has to mention the Renaissance, the voyages of discovery and the Reformation. These historical events and changes took place within a period of fifty years. The period around 1750 does not mark a break to the same degree, although it saw the beginning of something essentially new, a transformation in the production of material goods. The previous centuries had seen a transformation within *commerce. Now it was production's turn.*

The term commercial capitalism implies the fact that the growth of trade in material goods required increasing amounts of capital. Corresponding to this, a number of new institutions and instruments were created. Production itself, however, was still of a traditional character and the pattern of costs was still dominated by high variables and low fixed costs.

This chapter deals mainly with institutional development throughout the period, including the attitude towards economic policy known as mercantilism, which received its name as it gave way to liberalism and classical economics. The wider economic and political developments of the period are dealt with in the next chapter.

1. The growing power of the state

Feudal society had been characterized by a system of layers connecting bottom with top. The end of the Middle Ages saw a change in this, including a strengthening of the power of the state.

a. *The extension of the money economy.* The feudal economy, on the whole, had the characteristics of a barter economy and was based on self-sufficiency. At the "bottom" of the system, the need for, and access to, liquid means of payments must have been modest. But higher in the system changes were under way. By using cash as a means of payment, the king could pay mercenaries in order to become independent of his local vassals, hereby increasing the power of central government. The supply of precious metals was increased during the later part of Middle Ages and was further increased after the discovery of the Americas. This cleared the way for a so-called great monetary reform in the 1500s which improved the possibilities of collecting taxes in cash. In present-day language we would say that the great monetary reform paved the way for a gigantic tax reform, increasing the command of the central authority over the resources of society.

b. *The extension of markets.* Between the extension of markets and the strengthening of the state, a positive interaction took place. The prince had an interest in the growth of trade, especially long distance trade, in order to tax the resultant activities. Furthermore, the introduction of new, overseas commodities such as coffee, tea, sugar and tobacco opened new possibilities for taxing consumption.

c. *The development of weapons and weapons systems* favoured the State. The late 1300s saw the introduction of gunpowder used in primitive cannon. Along with knights and their lances, it also meant an end to the heavy cavalryman in his armour. Furthermore, fortifications were strengthened to resist cannon fire, which made them more costly. Finally, as mentioned above, the feudal army was replaced by mercenaries. Military activities were subject to economies of scale.

d. *The development of a bureaucracy outside the Church.* The functioning of an administrative system assumes the presence of an elementary capacity in reading, writing and arithmetic. Here, the Church and the monasteries had held an advantage for centuries. Diffusion of the necessary capabilities through the setting up of latin schools and universities meant a strengthening of the secular, central powers of society.

The development described above took place over centuries. It was, however, speeded up after 1500. As early as the 1200s, the feudal system in its original form was in decline in France and Italy, soon followed by England. But the tendency towards centralization in the meantime was stopped and put in reverse, as happened in the first half of the 1600s during the Thirty Years' War. Especially in Northern Germany this was strongly felt. In most of continental Western Europe, with France as a leading example, this was followed by a rapid strengthening of the central powers known as absolute monarchy.

In its efforts to secure its existence, the state and central powers had to overcome both external and internal resistance. External resistance came from neighbouring states in the form of quarrels over borders, hereditary rights, royal symbols on flags, etc. Internal resistance involved holders of all sorts of privileges such as tax-benefits, concessions and monopolies, etc. Between those two forces, the external and the internal, there was a close connection: The state and central powers had to overcome internal opposition in order to resist external enemies. External pressure served then, as now, to promote the unity of the state. From here, it is time to turn to the branch of economic policy called mercantilism, along with its aims and its means.

2. Mercantilism

It is possible to state with a high degree of agreement what is meant by concepts such as keynesianism and monetarism. The situation is quite different when it comes to mercantilism. As a branch of economic policy it is related to a period of three hundred years or more from the end of the Middle Ages around 1500 to the breakthrough of liberalism in the 1800s. The term itself was coined when it was confronted by its successors, first the Physiocrats and then the liberals. The term obtained widespread use through Adam Smith's "Wealth of Nations" first published in 1776. Mercantilism has since then been the subject of many misunderstandings and deserves to be mentioned and evaluated on its own merits.

In present day analyses of economic policy, one finds a distinction between *intermediate* goals and *final* goals. This distinction seems necessary to get a closer understanding of mercantilist policy. As a fre-

Fig. 5: The mercantilists' view of precious metals, was that they served only an intermediate goal behind which were found some final goals. Here an old money chest, situated at the stairway of the Danish Ministry of Finance. Over the years it has given rise to many jokes concerning its possible contents.

quently mentioned intermediate goal in present-day economic policy, the long-term interest rate can be mentioned. Its actual size is easy to control – it can be followed day-by-day in stock market lists to an accuracy of several decimal points. It is widely used in politics as an indicator of success – any increase is almost certain to cause criticism from the political opposition. But our deeper concern with the height of the interest rate is caused by its wider impacts on the economy and members of society. Here we meet the final goals, such as the size of investments, the growth rates of GDP, the development of employment, the costs of housing and the distribution of incomes and welfare. However, a more precise knowledge of all this demands access to statistical information – which for good reasons did not exist when we go back even a hundred years – not to mention three to four hundred years ago. Nor did a well-defined economic terminology exist in those days. But this does not mean that the mercantilists did not have final goals on their minds when they spoke of what we call intermediate goals.

2.1. Aims of mercantilism

Posterity has especially noted the mercantilists' concern for the position of the balance of payments (BoP) and the stock of precious metals. In many, not to say most, history books, this has developed into the postulate that they did not know the difference between monetary phenomena and tangibles – the difference between the nutritive value of a gold coin and a sack of corn. But this overlooks the fact that the two goals, a surplus on the BoP and a stock of precious metals, are only intermediate goals representing some very real goals. Secondly, and now it becomes directly embarrassing, it is not mentioned that modern economic policy had the two goals high on the list during the major part of the 1900s. Since the world crisis of the 1930s, the net-position of the BoP and the exchange reserves have been central themes of economic policy in most countries.

Furthermore, it should be kept in mind that decision-makers in those days had an entirely different view on what we call national wealth or national income. We relate the concept to the position of the entire population, that is, a broad measure of the material well-being. Such ideas were foreign to the writers and civil servants of those days. In an absolute monarchy the wealth of the state was synonymous with the resources available for the court and national defence. It is a fundamental misconception, when analyzing their thoughts, to look for a concept corresponding to the present-day national product or national income.

The main theme of economic policy during the period of mercantilism was, as stated above, to strengthen both the external and the internal position of the state. The *external* position was to be strengthened through the command of strong military forces, including the necessary international liquidity to hire an army at short notice. And the governments on the European continent desired the means necessary to construct and keep expensive fortifications. And, finally, the greatness of the state would be shown through the splendour of the prince and the extravagant expenditure of the court.

The *internal* coherence and the unity of the state were to be promoted, local duties and tolls abolished, internal means of transportation improved. Within the borders of the state, common weights, measures and business law should be established, just as there ought to be common standards for manufactured products like cloth, furniture, etc. As part of this, provincial laws were to be replaced by laws covering the entire state and a common monetary system introduced. Expressed in present-day language, the aim of mercantilism was to create an *internal market* within the single state. The French minister of finance during the reign of Louis XIV (1661-1715), Jean Baptiste Colbert (1619-83), recommended in a memo that the king ought to bring all of his country under one law and one system of weights and measures. All of this can be found as part of the agenda of the EC and EU more than three hundred years later. The joy of recognition would be great, if the statesmen of the late 1600s under the leadership of Louis XIV and Colbert, could have had the chance of attending a meeting between their successors in the European Council of the EU. But to their joy would be added a good deal of envy.

2.2. *Means of mercantilism*
To illustrate the means of mercantilism, some of its major intermediate goals and the corresponding measures are stated below.

As a leading intermediate goal, the state had to collect and hold international liquidity – a reserve of international exchange. To do so, it was necessary to have a surplus on the current accounts on the BoP or a production of gold or silver. To realize those goals, imports should be limited and exports expanded. This should be done through a system of prohibitions and taxes to reduce imports and a system of subsidies to promote the production of goods that could replace imported goods or sold on foreign markets. The loss of foreign exchange should be limited by prohibiting the export of precious metals. As an intermediate goal to strengthen the army, an agricultural policy should be conducted that ensured the recruitment of the necessary number of soldiers from among the agricultural population, while industrial policy should increase the resources at the disposal of the state. As a part of this, an effective internal use of the resources of the country was to be encouraged, an important part of which was the creation of an internal market within the borders of the state. To promote the division of labour within the framework of a monetary economy, a policy ought to be pursued that aimed at securing the necessary means of payments for transaction purposes. Finally, the tax system should enable the state to finance its expenditures on the court, the army and the navy.

The description of the policy of mercantilism given above is presented in present-day language far from the ridicule to which it has been subjected. Dozens of quotations can be found showing that the mercantilists did not distinguish between money and income. But such confusion can still exist. What does it mean when it is said that: "Uncle John has money"? That he has a well-filled wallet – is liquid – or has a high income? Probably both. The interest in precious metals was most strongly felt during the early stages of mercantilism. As part of this interest, the seafaring nations of Western Europe invaded the recently discovered overseas nations in their hunt for gold and silver. Another method was to attack the silver fleets of other nations on their way back across the Atlantic. This early type of mercantilism has been named "bullionism", after the word bullion.

Through the growth of towns and their economic importance, the focus of the policy changed towards the conditions of the urban trades. Corresponding to this, the emphasis on the BoP policy was supplemented with an interest in industrial policy. As a typical though early example, the Stock Exchange building in Copenhagen can be mentioned, which was constructed in the early 1600s. At the same time, social security was made part of mercantilist policy. In England this was seen in the famous Poor Law of Queen Elizabeth I (1558-1603) from 1601. The key word here was "indoor relief", where the said door is the door to the poor house. The poor of the community were to be placed in the poor house where they, so far as possible, should be made useful. Part of the programme was that women and children unable to provide for themselves should be taught a trade to become useful members of society.

A central theme in Adam Smith's and the liberals' confrontation with mercantilism was the postulate that it was a hindrance to an efficient division of labour. In this they were only partly correct. As far as the *internal* division of labour was concerned, that is within the borders of the state, the mercantilists endeavoured to overcome a number of hindrances created either by mankind or nature. At the same time, the mercantilists had to accept the existence of local monopolies, sold as part of a short-sighted policy by the government. Here was an open conflict between the fundamental position of the mercantilists and what could be obtained in practice. The confrontation with the liberals seems more appropriate as far as *the external* or international division of labour is concerned. However, Adam Smith and his contemporaries should be prepared to forgive their forerunners since it was not until after the Napoleonic Wars that David Ricardo (1772-1823) gave a general proof of the theory of comparative advantage as an argument for international free trade.

That it was Great Britain, the new, fast-growing industrial country, that took the lead in the clash with mercantilism is no surprise. The country had, from the middle of the 1700s, seen a fast growth in its foreign trade. British industry and trade, under those conditions, had more to win than to lose by a general liberalization of foreign trade. It deserves to be mentioned that Adam Smith was not blind to the advantages of mercantilist policy to Great Britain. One of the best-known mercantilist undertakings, the English Navigation Act of 1651,[1] had as one of its aims to secure the existence of a great merchant fleet that could be used as auxiliary ships by the navy in case of war. Referring to this, Adam Smith not only found the Navigation Act excusable, but outright praiseworthy.

2.3. English versus French mercantilism

English mercantilist policy distinguished itself from French mercantilism in several ways. To put it briefly, even if British mercantilism was protectionist, it was not *dirigiste* to the same degree as the French. Although the different British trades and crafts had their guilds and corporations seeking to restrict competition, the possibilities of having such regulation accepted and supported by the courts were limited. To this should be added that the British central authorities did not seek to regulate production by setting up rules and specifications concerning the qualities of goods, as the French did. This meant a wider range of possibilities in the methods of production and the character of the goods. The British textile industry, especially, was decentralized, part of it being organized as "putting-out industry". Normally

---

1.   The act granted English ships privileges in carrying goods to and from England and her colonies. It was at the beginning especially directed against Dutch shipping.

this was done by a merchant who bought the wool, distributed it among the spinners, had it back as yarn, sent this to the weavers and so on. As will be understood, production itself was decentralized, but the financing, the selling, and the entire organization were centralized. The putting-out industry can therefore be seen as an intermediate state between traditional handicraft and the industrial mode of production.

To this must be added a special feature of English law, the existence of *Common Law*. Besides the Statute Law given by the Parliament and the King, there existed law created by the courts, or rather a natural law existing in its own right and revealed in concrete cases by the King's courts. Should the King seek to limit the freedom of business by granting monopolies or other favours, time and again he met opposition from the courts referring to the Common Law. Normally, they had the support of the Parliament against the King's granting of monopolies. As early as 1623-24, this resulted in the Statute of Monopolies. The law confirmed the practice of the courts by stating the, few, exceptions where limitations in the conduct of business were allowed. The most important of those was in the case where a person had developed new products and new ways of production. Here, the inventor was granted a sole right to the invention for a period of fourteen years. Expressed in present-day language he was granted a patent for this period. Through the Statute of Monopolies, the liberty of business became both a part of Statute Law and a part of Common Law and enjoyed through this a high degree of judicial protection. From England, the basic view on monopolies – that they deserve to be prohibited – was transferred to the colonies in North America and formed part of the business law of the USA.

English and British mercantilist policy was described as protectionist without being *dirigiste*. The mercantilism of *France* was both. It has given the name to an extreme type of mercantilism: *Colbertism*. Jean-Baptiste Colbert (1619-83) was minister for more than twenty years – from the assumption of government by Louis XIV in 1661 – to his death. To secure the quality of products, be it furniture, cloth, etc., the government issued decrees stating their specifications in great detail. More than a thousand such directives were issued. The internal trade and exchange of goods was promoted by the construction of roads, canals and locks regulating rivers, etc. As an outstanding example can be mentioned the construction of a system of canals and locks connecting the Mediterranean with the Bay of Biscay. Where the canal reaches its peak rise, it is about two hundred meters above sea level; an impressive construction considered the tools and facilities of those days. Among the measures of Colbert was a tariff reform seeking to establish a common French tariff-area for the northern half of the country. To this should be added the strengthening of the guilds of towns, support for the establishment of firms, including some of those who supplied the royal court. Outside the borders of the country, an active colonial policy was pursued, which caused Anglo-French wars to be fought in such remote places as North America and India.

What has been described about English and French trades points to a significant difference. The products from the French manufactures were meant for a limited, exclusive circle of costumers at home and abroad, seeking to live up to the standards of the French court. The English putting-out industry was meant for a broad, anonymous group of buyers. Here, we can speak of a beginning of mass-production with a view to mass-distribution. Only some technical details were lacking for the introduction of a full-scale industrial production.

3. The breakdown of a research monopoly

An important step around year 1500 in creating modern society was the decay of the Church's position within the sciences.

Until then, the learned world had its main function in confirming the truths in the sacred books. This was done through a set of dogmas with due respect to the writings of the Fathers of the Church. It is this collection or construction of ideas that has been named Scholastisicm, and it is this way of thinking which the Renaissance criticized as introverted. According to the new ideas, independent observations should replace reading and interpreting the texts of the Church Fathers and classical literature.

As an example may be mentioned the study of human anatomy. For religious reasons, post-mortem examination of the human body had not been allowed. When possibilities for this were opened up, it turned out that it had been the anatomy of the dog that had formed the basis of the teaching at the medical schools for centuries!

The spiritual excitement of the Renaissance resulted in the foundation of new universities; for example in Sweden in 1477 (Upsala), Denmark in 1479 (Copenhagen). These universities kept their character as institutions for the education of priests, although they were gradually given wider frames of reference and took up new fields of research, including the natural sciences. An important contribution to the emancipation of the learned world was the invention of the art of printing – or rather, of interchangeable types. The invention itself may be seen as a precondition for the spread of Martin Luther's (1483-1546) critique of the Catholic Church and, through this, the spread of the Reformation in the 1520s and '30s.

Indeed, the Renaissance opened new possibilities for independent speculation and thinking, but this did not mean a transition to a state of general freedom of thought. This was what Galileo Galilei (1564-1642) faced when, in 1633, he was forced to repudiate his own ideas of the earth as a globe circling around the sun, and thus not the centre of the universe. Rather the period should be seen as the beginning of the dissolution of the previous concentration of spiritual and intellectual power. In short, a movement was on its way towards a more pluralist society where narrow, established interests lost their power to resist change.

The 1600s provided a number of ground-breaking works within the field of the natural sciences; suffice it to mention the Newtonian system, the introduction of differential calculus and the realization and measurement of the "hesitation", or rather the speed, of light. However, it would be a misconception to conclude that such cognition within the field of natural sciences from the outset found its way into practical use. The first impact on society of the new knowledge seems to have been in a more indirect manner through attempts to transfer the new freedom of reasoning within the natural sciences to the social sciences. It was as a result of this movement that the so-called *natural law* saw the light of day around 1700. From this time on it was tempting to start to reason about the relations between the individual and the state, including the rights given by nature to the newborn members of society (ref. chapter 5 section 1, The period of enlightenment).

To conclude from what has been said above that the scientists of the 1600s were without practical sense would be utterly wrong and unjust. Although their scientific work did not immediately find its way into practical use, they themselves were involved in all sorts of practical undertakings. Isaac Newton (1642-1727) held, among other positions, a job as a director of the newly established Bank of England. Ole Rømer

(1644-1710), the scientist who first measured the speed of light, assisted in the construction of the fountains of Versailles and later, besides being a director of the University of Copenhagen, as chief constable and chief of police he reorganized the Copenhagen fire brigade. He also measured the length of the main roads in the country and organized a register and evaluation of all the real estate in Denmark. All this can be seen as preparation for the changes in society that would take place later, but not as a direct contribution to a change in the traditional ways and means of production.

4. Political institutions

Around the middle of the 1600s it was a characteristic of the countries in Western Europe that they were in a state of political unrest. The core of the matter was the internal division of power. England saw an open civil war during the years 1642-49, concluding in the execution of the King. After this followed a period of political unrest lasting until the so-called Glorious Revolution in 1688 and a definite weakening of the power of the King. France, since the beginning of the 1600s, had seen endeavours to strengthen the position of the King. The 1640s saw a growing opposition to this, developing into an open revolt during the years 1648-53. In Denmark, repeated military defeats and the miserable financial situation of the crown paved the way for a *coup d'etat* in 1660. After one hundred years of political and religious unrest the time had come for clarification.

The three countries, England, France and Denmark, can be taken as examples of three different solutions to the conflicts over the division of powers. The English solution pointed in a direction where the civil population, the townspeople, gained a substantial influence over the ruling and development of the country. The French solution points towards the absolute monarchy as stated by Louis XIV on his ascent to the Throne in 1661 having reached the age of majority: "The State, that is me".[2] In Denmark, the absolute monarchy was based upon a written constitution given by the King himself. No restrictions were stated to limit his rule and behaviour, apart from the stipulation that

2. Whether he said this is uncertain. That he meant it, however, is certain. Through his 54 years as a reigning monarch, he did not appoint a prime minister, not even Colbert.

he (or she) should be a Lutheran according to the Augsburg Confession. Although his powers in a formal sense were unlimited, the Danish land-owning nobility in reality had substantial power, whereas the French nobility, considered as a social class, on the whole lost its power in politics.

Along with England might be mentioned the seven northern provinces of the Netherlands. Throughout the 1600s it had the character of a city-republic, though with the house of Orange as a potential dynasty.[3] Both England and Holland, the latter being the leading one of the Netherlands northern provinces around 1600, were characterized by their highly developed trade and shipping, a strong group of merchants and, for that time, a large population living in towns. No wonder that the towns won a major influence in those two countries. The trade and occupations of the towns, and especially foreign trade, never had the same importance in France as they had in England and the Netherlands. This enabled the French king to rule without the support of the towns and, in so far as they supported him, their aim was often to obtain favours such as subsidies and monopolies. Compared to England and the Netherlands, things were turned upside down: The tradesmen of the French towns were made dependent on the king, not the other way round.

The core of the conflicts between the kings and the rest of society was the right of taxation. In the history of parliaments, the power to tax and to authorize expenditure is a central question. It is in this regard that English political tradition deviates from that of the rest of Europe. The English Parliament arrogated this power to itself at an early point of time compared to the countries at the European continent.

All in all, English society of the 1600s and 1700s seems to have developed in a way that was characterized by a dispersal of the power within society. At the beginning, this development was only sketchily underpinned by theories. But in the years around 1700, the theory of the separation of powers, that is the splitting of functions and powers between a legislative, an executive and judicial branch, took a more firm form. This development in British political life was followed with

---

3. After the peace of Westphalia in 1648, where the Republic of the United Netherlands obtained recognition, Prince William II of Orange tried to obtain absolute power through a *coup d'état*. He failed, mainly due to the resistance of the citizens of Amsterdam.

keen interest on the other side of the English Channel. Francois Voltaire (1694-1778) and Charles Montesquieu (1689-1755) both stayed for longer periods in England, where they obtained a close impression of the habits and the political life of the country. However, the admiration of Voltaire seems to have had its limits as he is quoted as saying that: "the English had a hundred religions and only one sauce."[4]

5. Economic institutions

Recent research shows that a number of the economic institutions emerging during the growth of commercial capitalism from the 1500s can be traced back to the previous period. Rather than speaking of innovations, it seems more apt to talk of the spread of existing institutions.

From Italian banking, Northern Europe had the *giro-banks;* that is to say banks which assisted in making payments between holders of accounts in the bank. They did so originally – at least in principle – without lending money to their customers. As in the Middle Ages there still existed a substantial confusion as far as the supply of money was concerned. Different sorts of coins and exchange were circulating side by side, and their internal rates of exchange were unstable. To avoid the risks of those changes, a practice developed in Amsterdam, among other places, whereby contracts and payments were fixed in a special unit of account defined as the equivalent to a certain amount of precious metal. It did not circulate as a tangible means of payment. It was used in the setting up of contracts and in transfers between accounts. Should it form the basis for payments "in cash", the amount to be paid in cash would be calculated on the basis of the current exchange rate of the coins in question. Both for trade within the borders and across the borders of countries, this "artificial means of payments" had the advantage that different sorts of uncertainties and costs were reduced. The system reminds one of the present-day ECU and Euro, whose introduction was partly based on similar ideas.

The note issue of the *business banks* developed gradually, starting with the issue of negotiable claims. This, too, was under way before 1500. Note issue in itself is not equivalent to monetization and an in-

---

4.   G. M. Trevelyan (1967, 425).

crease in the amount of means of payment. If the reserve ratio between precious metal and the notes is one to one, the supply of money has changed its form, not its size. Monetization through the banks takes place when a less liquid asset (an IOU) through a loan in a bank is replaced by a more liquid asset (a drawing right on a bank account) at the disposal of the general public. On the whole, the banks at this early stage mainly served as giro-banks, that is, moving money between the accounts of its customers. Normally they did not participate in "making money".

The existence of *central banks* (national banks) with present-day functions belongs to a far later period.[5] It is only about 150 years ago since the monopoly of note issue became a general rule in Western Europe, and did not happen in the USA until the early 1900s.[6] The rise of the central bank as "the bank of the banks" and as "lender of last resort" to banks in temporary difficulties belongs to the 1800s as well. Until then, there were no central banks where business banks could ask for temporary assistance. This corresponds to the fact that economic crises did not have the wave-like character of the business cycles of later times, but rather of short, financial crises.

Another aspect of the economic and financial institutions of the 1600s was the development of *the corporate form*. Here the development of the joint-stock company, with its limited responsibility, deserves to be noted. As already mentioned it can be traced back to Northern Italy. The background to its spread was the new patterns of trade in the late 1500s following the voyages of discovery. Participation in this type of trade was accompanied by larger risks than the traditional trade in wool and cloth across the English Channel. As early as around 1600, companies with trading concessions were established in the Netherlands and in England. They were granted monopolies for trading in specified overseas areas. The companies were, at the same time, involved in trade and shipping. In the latter part of the 1600s, the corporate form was introduced in the spheres of finance and banking.

---

5. The Swedish Riksbank (the Bank of Sweden) is considered the first central bank. Opened as a private bank in 1656 it was taken over by the state in 1668, operating as a note issuing bank. At its 300 year jubilee in 1968 a fund was set aside to finance a Nobel prize in economics.
6. A central bank has through the major part of the 1900s been characterized by the following functions: the note issue, the exchange rate policy, the interest rate ("cost and availability of credit"). Besides this, it serves as the bank of the central government. The liberalization of the international money and capital markets has reduced these functions towards the end of the 1900s.

Two scandals, which occurred at almost the same time in England and France in the early 1700s meant that the joint-stock companies fell into discredit (Chapter 4, sections 4 and 6). Therefore, it was not until the 1800s, as a result of railway construction, that the joint-stock companies made their final break through. An additional way of financing early large-scale commerce was the issue of bonds with a fixed rate of interest and date of repayment.

The introduction of the new financial instruments led to a need to establish special *Stock Exchanges*. In the 1690s, as a result of a rapid increase in the number of limited companies, a regular edition of stock-lists was started in England.[7]

A major motive for establishing joint-stock companies was to spread the risk of the large financial engagements involved in overseas trade. The same motive gave rise to organized *insurance business*. A well-known example is Lloyds Coffee House. Here, a well-organized insurance system developed during the 1700s, first and foremost within the field of shipping. Originally, organized insurance was limited to loss and damage and it was not until the end of the 1700s that it expanded into life insurance after the introduction of a mortality statistics.

---

7.   G. Parker (1974, 556ff).

Chapter 4

Commercial capitalism II
1500-1750
Changes in the balance of power

Mainly due to the voyages of discovery, the patterns of international trade and economic activity underwent substantial changes during the period 1500-1750. At the beginning of the period, the centre of European commerce and finance was still in Northern Italy, supplemented by an area in present-day Belgium. The discoveries, for a while, moved the centre to Spain from where it shifted in less than a hundred years first to Flanders and Antwerp and then, by the end of the 1500s, to the northern provinces of the Netherlands and the city of Amsterdam. By the end of the 1600s, the centre moved once again, this time across the North Sea where England emerged as the leading nation in international commerce.

As far as the political development of the period is concerned, the Great Power system appeared, which was to dominate Europe for almost three hundred years until 1918. These powers were France, Austria (the Holy Roman Empire and the House of Habsburg) and, with growing strength in the 1700s, Great Britain, Russia and Prussia. That the political map of Western Europe was rather stable until the Napoleonic Wars does not mean that it was a period of permanent peace along the borders; quite the reverse. But the wars did not cause major movements of the borders. The largest changes were in the balance of power overseas. Here, Great Britain gained the position as the leading colonial power. In the Baltic, Sweden replaced Denmark as the leading nation by the middle of the 1600s. From an economic point of view, the long-run benefits to Sweden seem to have been modest.

To Denmark and Sweden, the growing power of the Netherlands and England had very direct consequences. The commercial interests of the Dutch and the English in the Baltic area were growing. From here they imported grain, wood, materials for shipbuilding and high quality steel for the production of cannon. In return, they supplied goods from overseas areas via English and Dutch ports. Both military and mercantile motives suggested that the passage of the Sound – the Øresund – should be kept free by dividing the possession of its coasts between Denmark and Sweden. Neither Danish nor Swedish rulers of the time seem to have understood this simple fact of foreign policy.

1. Forces behind the voyages of discovery

The voyages of discovery can be briefly characterized by stating that more was found than was sought. One voyage set out to find the passage to India and discovered two continents in the Western Hemisphere stretching from polar climes in the north to a sub-polar climate in the south. It should be said, at this early stage, that the story is told from the point of view of those who made the discoveries. Had it been told from the point of view of those who were "discovered", the story would have been quite another.

The background to the voyages of discovery should be sought for at two levels. Just as in the case of the space journeys after the Second World War it required first, the existence of the necessary technical abilities and second, the existence of the motivation to make use of the possibilities.

Increased knowledge of astronomy was among the *abilities*. Forgotten perceptions of the Earth as a globe were revived in the second half of the 1400s. To this should be added the construction of larger, more seaworthy ships and the introduction of better navigational instruments such as compasses and sextants. And, last but not least, the newly gained superiority of the Europeans with regard to weapons, primarily, their use of cannon, made it hard, not to say impossible, to resist their advance.

The *motives* for participating in the discoveries were common to a number of countries. Territorial expansion might reduce expenditures on imports. The establishment of a regular sea route to India that bypassed the Near East could save money for several reasons such as tolls, tariffs, profits to middlemen, etc. There might be the possibility for the re-exportation of goods and, finally, there were chances of getting hold of precious metals in one way or another.

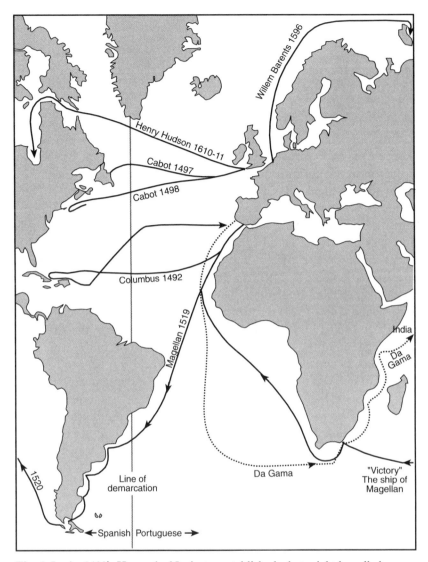

Fig. 6: In the 1400's Henry the Navigator established what might be called an oce-anographic institute. By the end of the century the activities culminated in a series of landmark achievements in the history of mankind.

Besides such economic motives, purely political motives manifested themselves as well. Both Portugal and Spain wanted to push the Muslims back from the coasts of North Africa. In the middle of the 1400s there were still Moors in both Portugal and Spain. Were the two countries to feel safe from threat, the Moors should not only be driven out, but also kept at a distance. For other countries, neglecting to undertake ventures across the oceans might, in itself, prove to be risky. So the mere fact that Portugal and Spain took the initiative was a sufficient motive for others to do the same.

The Portuguese prince, Henry the Navigator (1393-1460), established in the middle of the 1400s what may be called an oceanographic institute, organizing expeditions to not too distant groups of islands, Madeira and the Azores, and along the west coast of Africa. By the end of the century, it culminated in a number of landmark achievements in the history of mankind. In 1487, the Portuguese, Bartholomew Diaz made his way round the Cape of Good Hope. In 1492, the Italian, Christopher Columbus (1446(?) – 1506), in the service of the Spanish king, was the first to land in the West Indies, returning in 1493 with seventeen ships and fifteen hundred men to establish a permanent Spanish settlement. In 1497, the English/Italian, John Cabot (c.1450-c.1500), sailed from England to Newfoundland; while in 1497-98, Vasco da Gama (1469-1524) reached India by sea. Finally, Fernando Magellan's (c.1480-1521) expedition of 1519-22 completed the first circumnavigation of the globe. By then, the colonization of the Americas and India was already underway. The New World was later to become the goal of millions of emigrants from Europe. One might well wonder whether one of the motives behind the discoveries was to get rid of a surplus population. This is not likely. As a result of the Black Death, a substantial reduction of the population of Europe took place around 1350. This reduction in the size of population had not been fully replaced by the middle of the 1400s. It was not until the 1800s that population pressure seems to have become a major motive for mass emigration from Europe.

2.   Impacts of the voyages of discovery

Colonization and the accompanying plunder, especially in the Americas, caused a substantial increase in the supply of precious metals in Europe. At first, it went mainly to Portugal and Spain, but from there, however, it spread out over North-West Europe. The ample supply of money must have promoted its use and, through this, expanded the monetary economy and division of labour. Simultaneously, the overseas contacts brought a flow of new, mainly tropical, goods to Europe: spices and tea from Asia, coffee from Indonesia and America, from where Europe also got sugar, tobacco, cacao etc. From the temperate-zone in America, Europe got the potato which, in the long run, proved to be of substantial importance. The potato thrives on poor soil and gives a high and stable output of calories compared to other crops.[1] It has been argued that the introduction of the potato was part of the ex-planation behind the decrease in death rates from the end of the 1700s.

As a solution to a conflict between Portugal and Spain, and in accor-dance with a decision by the Pope, the two countries entered an agree-ment concerning the division of the Americas. According to this, what lay to the east of a certain degree of longitude should belong to Portu-gal and what was to the west, to Spain.[2] The agreement explains why the language spoken in Brazil is Portuguese and why that in the rest of South and Central America is Spanish.

There were distinct differences between the reactions of the Portu-guese and the Spanish to the discoveries. To the Portuguese, it was trade that mattered. To the Spanish it was the prospect of acquiring silver and gold. Portugal turned to the East, to present day India, In-donesia and even the Philippines, setting up trading posts. Spain turned to the West, concentrating on the chance of getting precious metals, especially silver. At first, it was done through outright plunder and later through mining organized along European lines, though it did include the use of forced labour. It was not until a hundred years afterwards that the Spanish took up farming in their overseas posses-sions.

The increased supply of precious metals in Europe in the 1500s caused what has been called a *price reform*. First, the increased supply of money caused a rise – about fourfold – in the general price level. Second, the increase in the money supply meant a widening of the money economy and, through this, a promotion of the division of la-bour. At the same time, wage increases were lower than the price in-creases for goods, especially foodstuffs. This meant that a redistribu-tion took place at the expense of townsmen and to the advantage of

1. The well-known Irish Famine in the 1840s was due to special circumstances; potato plants in other parts of Western Europe were also disease-stricken at the time.
2. It has been suggested that the Spanish had some idea of the existence of the Pacific Ocean lying to the west of the Americas. Later on, at least, they argued that the islands of the Pacific were covered by the agreement. The Portuguese, by then, had established themselves in the Philippines, and could not accept this argument.

landowners. This was exactly the opposite of what had happened two hundred years earlier after the Great Plague. On the other hand, the towns had the advantage of the growth in trade, especially those involved in the new, overseas trades.

3. The Mediterranean countries

3.1 Italy

Towards the close of the 1400s, the city-states of Northern Italy still flourished. However, at the beginning of the 1500s, changes came about.

The new trade routes round southern Africa meant from the very beginning increased competition for the towns at the foot of the Italian peninsula. The monopoly position that Northern Italy had, more or less, held in the trade with the Far and Middle East was brought to an end when Portugal and Spain opened the new sea routes at the end of the 1400s. With the loss of its position as a stepping stone between the Orient and Western and Northern Europe, the economy of Northern Italy seems to have fallen into decay. Examples include a sharp decline in the production of cloth and the stagnation of, or direct decline in, the population of towns. During the first forty years of the 1500s, the population of Florence fell from 72,000 to 60,000 and the population of Pavia was more than halved from 16,000 to 7,000.[3] During the second half of the century, the trade with the Near East grew again. But as a leading seafaring part of Europe – one could not speak of Italy as a nation at that time, only as a geographic area – it had lost its leading position, primarily to the Netherlands and England.

Around 1500, Italy held a position as a producer of highly sophisticated manufactured goods, exported to north-western Europe. A hundred years later, the situation had changed profoundly. Italy now imported highly manufactured goods and exported raw materials and semi-manufactured products like olive oil, grain, wine, wool and raw silk. It had, in addition, lost its position as a leading financial centre as this had moved, via Lyon, to the Netherlands. As a leading expert of

3.   C.M. Cipolla (1993, 241f).

the economic history of Italy has observed: "Italy had begun her career as an underdeveloped country".[4]

3.2 Spain, Portugal [5]

For centuries, the Iberian Peninsula had existed apart from the rest of Western Europe. This came to an end in the early 1500s. As far as the *economy* of the two countries is concerned, the discoveries meant a profound change. For Portugal, especially, it was the trade in tropical products that made the difference. For Spain, it was the access to precious metals. As far as *politics* are concerned, the rise of Spain was partly caused by the marriage of the heir to the Spanish crown, Joanna the Mad (1479-1555), to the heir to the empire of the Habsburgs, Philip the Handsome (1478-1506). Apart from present-day France – and even then only parts of it – the possessions of the enlarged Habsburg Empire covered most of continental Western Europe, as well as the overseas Spanish possessions. The heir to these gigantic possessions was their son, Charles V (1500-58) who, in 1519, was elected Holy Roman Emperor.[6]

The period of *Spanish* political grandeur was, however, brief. Although income from the Americas flowed in, the means flowed out again as payment for the wars necessary to keep the empire together. Conditions were, in some senses, favourable in that the country had inherited from the Moors highly developed agriculture and horticulture, including irrigation systems, along with the production of high quality Merino wool. To this, should be added the new possibilities based on the overseas possessions. All this was, however, squandered before the end of the 1500s, and the main explanation seems to be the absence of development in the internal economy of the country. The expenditure of the government was only partly covered by its income from the extraction and importation of gold and silver. So, the government looked for other sources of income such as the sale of economic concessions which, in turn, tended to freeze the economy. The rights granted to sheep farmers serve as an example; according to these they were allowed to let their flocks of sheep graze freely over wide areas, making more intensive agriculture impossible. Another hindrance to the devel-

4. C.M. Cipolla (1993, 249).
5. Although Portugal, in the narrow, geographical sense, is not a Mediterranean country, it is so closely related to Spain that the two countries are dealt with as a whole.
6. Charles V was the first prince to be able to say that: "The sun never sets on my possessions".

opment of the country was the persecution of Arabs and Jews – even of those Jews who had converted to Catholicism. The Inquisition, led by the Holy Church, became notorious for uniting the functions of both prosecutor and judge.

As part of the Habsburg Empire, the Netherlands was closely related to Spain. When the king from his base in Spain tried to introduce strict religious control over the Netherlands, this caused a revolt followed by a war of liberation in the 1580s. In 1588, the Spanish mounted a naval expedition, the Great Armada, for a counterattack. As a result of heavy storms, and defeat at the hands of the English navy, the Spaniards definitively lost their naval supremacy and their position as a leading sea power.

The area and population of *Portugal* was far smaller than that of Spain and it never tried to play a leading rôle in the politics of Western Europe. As far as its economy is concerned, its development did not differ much from that of Spain. Portugal, too, missed the chance of developing its internal economy. Compared to the size of the country, Portugal managed to assemble very large colonial possessions, keeping control over many of them until well after World War II. Taken as a whole, the fate of Spain and Portugal after their short period of wealth calls for reflection regarding the future of countries suddenly becoming rich on the basis of finite resources such as oil and natural gas.

4. The Netherlands

In the 1500s, the Netherlands covered an area corresponding to parts of present-day Northern France, Luxembourg, Belgium and The United Provinces.[7] From an economic point of view, it has been an area rich with possibilities. From a political point of view, it has been an area rich with conflicts, wars and suffering. The name itself, "the Low Countries", gives part of the explanation as it consists of areas situated at the lower part of the Scheldt, Maas and Rhine rivers. This location, close to the North Sea and the English Channel, opened up possibilities for high earnings from commerce and shipping, not only on the

---

7. The name Holland will not be used, although, throughout history, it constitutes a major part of the provinces of The United Netherlands.

high seas, but also on some of the largest navigable rivers of Western Europe. At the same time, the rivers offered the area rich soil and ample water – occasionally, too ample. From an agricultural point of view, it is reminiscent of similar areas in other continents grouped around the mouths of rivers and able to feed large populations within relatively small areas.

In the wake of the economic advantages and general attractiveness of the area, political problems inevitably followed. Three great powers throughout modern history had it as their sphere of interest; France, Germany, albeit under different names and forms, and, at some distance, England. The list, to be complete, should also include Spain in its heyday. Few other areas have been so exposed to the conflicts between the great powers of Europe as the Netherlands. This is mentioned in order to remind the reader of the historical and geopolitical reasons behind the active rôles of Belgium, Luxembourg and the Netherlands in the process of European integration after the second World War.

As part of the heritage of Charles V, the Netherlands in 1506 was included in his total German-Spanish possessions. The town of Bruges, situated close to the English Channel, had developed in the Middle Ages into a leading sea port and trade centre equal in importance to Venice and Genoa. In the early 1400s, the access to its harbour had closed and its position as a commercial crossroads between Western and Eastern Europe and Southern and Northern Europe had been taken over by Antwerp, situated on the banks of the Scheldt. To this should be added that Flanders in the 1500s envisaged a growth in its manufacture of cloth – partly at the expense of Northern Italy, as mentioned in the previous section – the basis of which was the import of high quality wool from England and Spain.

In 1566, the tensions between the population and the Spanish rulers led to open revolt. The motives were both of an economic and a religious nature. The Spanish wished to stop the spread of Protestantism and Calvinism, especially in the northern provinces (later to be called The United Netherlands) where the position of Catholicism was weak. The Spanish showed their willingness to use hard measures against dissenters, for instance, the introduction of the notorious Inquisition to the Netherlands. The conflict led, in 1566, to iconoclasm with the destruction of altars, paintings etc., in Catholic churches. This meant the beginning of an open uprising against Spanish rule.

In 1579, the seven northern provinces established themselves as an independent entity under the name "The Union of Utrecht", thereby laying the foundation for what we recognize today as the distinction between Belgium and the "Netherlands". During the following 70 years, they were under constant pressure until 1648 when the existence of "The United Republics of the Netherlands" was recognized as part of the Peace of Westphalia.

The latter part of the Middle Ages had seen flourishing economic life in Flanders, centred on Bruges, Gent and Antwerp. The middle of the 1500s saw Antwerp reach its peak as a trade centre, not only of trade within Europe, but of overseas trade as well. However, the religious and political conflicts that began in 1566 brought this to an end. The Inquisition and the persecution of non-Catholics drew a great number of persons otherwise active in business out of the southern provinces. The population of Antwerp fell from nearly 200,000 in 1550 to some 50,000 in 1590. Besides emigration, first of all to the northern provinces but also to England, the decline of Antwerp is explained by the fact, that the northern provinces closed the passage of the mouth the Scheldt, thereby cutting off access to the harbour of Antwerp.

The decline in trade of the southern provinces was matched by the rise in that of the northern provinces, especially, that of Amsterdam. Religious tolerance started an influx from Portugal, Spain, France and Flanders of Jews, Huguenots, Calvinists and Protestants plus Puritans from England. All in all, the Netherlands – in spite of external political problems – lived through a period when the sciences and the fine arts flourished. Dutch universities were considered the best in Protestant Europe, with the University of Leiden as the foremost. A number of foreign scientists sought refuge in the country, including René Descartes (1596-1650), John Locke (1632-1704) and Baruch Spinoza (1632-77), just to mention a few. The same years saw the peak of the Dutch school of painting represented by painters like Anthonius van Dyck (1559-1641), Frans Hals (1580-1666) and, the best known of them all, Rembrandt van Rijn (1606-69).

As a trading nation, the United Netherlands was, in principle, in favour of free trade. The expansion of England meant increasing competition on the Seven Seas from the middle of the 1600s. By the end of the century, the Netherlands had to divert part of its expenditure from its navy to its army to protect itself against France under Louis XIV. This meant a decline in the, hitherto, strong Dutch navy and a final shift in the balance of power in favour of England. A similar effect was, apparently, achieved by the protectionist English shipping policy under the Navigation Act.

5. England

A number of the economic advantages enjoyed by the Netherlands were found in England as well: a favourable climate for agriculture, proximity to the sea and access to the oceans, navigable rivers, and so on. To the above list should be added that, unlike the seven provinces of the Netherlands, England enjoyed rich sources of coal and iron ore and, whereas the Netherlands was situated in the middle of an area of tension, England was situated at its fringe across the English Channel, and was able to gain the status of a great power on its own.

The 1500s are remembered for Renaissance rulers with despotic inclinations. Best known, perhaps, is Henry VIII of England (*1509-47*). As part of his confrontation with the pope and the Catholic Church, he confiscated the vast possessions of the Church. To strengthen his position, he relied on good relations with Parliament, a policy continued under Elizabeth I (*1558-1603*). During the succeeding Stuart period, the royal house sought to move the system of government towards absolutism. In 1688, this was brought to a halt through the "Glorious Revolution", which meant that the English king from then on played a more modest role than his colleagues on the continent.[8]

As a colonial power, England had a rather late start; the party of Puritans who left Plymouth aboard the "Mayflower" in 1620 is the best remembered. They left for Virginia, named after the "Virgin Queen", Elizabeth, but did not get any further than Cape Cod, south of present-day Boston. The reason that those emigrants became so famous is that they went out to make a permanent settlement making their living through farming, and not just to set up a trading post. Later, others were to follow, founding settlements in Rhode Island, Connecticut, New Hampshire and Maine, now known as New England.

---

8.   In her speech at the celebration in 1989 of the two hundredth anniversary of the French Revolution, the British prime minister, Margaret Thatcher, reminded the hosts of the fact that Great Britain had just passed the three hundredth anniversary of a similar revolution – one that took place without bloodshed.

Major exports from this area were fish and lumber. The southern English colonies exported as their main items, tobacco, rice and cotton. It is worth noting, that from the beginning there was a high degree of complementarity between the home country, the colonies in America, in Africa and in Asia. An idea of the development in the north American colonies can be seen from the rise in the size of the population of European origin: 1630: 4,000; 1660: 75,000; 1700: 250,000; 1740: 905,000. In 1770, shortly before independence was declared, the number was 2,150,000. As will be seen, the thirteen colonies were already a very important trading partner for Britain before the industrial breakthrough in the home country.

A special feature of the English colonies was that they comprised vast areas with temperate climates, both in the Northern and the Southern Hemispheres (North America, New Zealand, Australia and the Cape Colony in South Africa). This factor made those possessions more suited for permanent emigration from the home country and this, again, meant a high degree of solidarity between the home country and the rest of the empire, tied together by a common language.

With the discoveries and the new pattern of trade, there followed, as mentioned above, an increased demand for capital. English business seems at this point to have enjoyed the advantage of a low rate of interest. Part of the explanation for this is the control by Parliament of the expenditures of the Crown and the reluctance of the Bank of England (founded in 1694, only six years after the Glorious Revolution) to finance the expenses of the king. Independence of the banks from the political authorities is considered part of the explanation why Britain, along with the Netherlands, developed an efficient financial system so early on.[9] In the early 1700s, the interest rate in England fell from 10 per cent to 3 per cent per annum.

The Treaty of Utrecht in 1713 marked the end of a period of war between England and France. It was followed by a period of hectic economic activity, which finished with a scandal known as "The South Sea Bubble". The South Sea Company had been set up as a limited company to conduct trade and colonization in the South Seas. The price of the shares was boosted by speculation until, in 1720, the bubble finally burst. The story had wider implications, through the "Bub-

9.   C.P. Kindleberger (1993, 56). A Financial History of Western Europe. Sec.Ed. NY. Oxford.

ble Act", according to which limited companies could be set up only by special Act of Parliament. This law reduced the number of limited companies for a substantial period and was not abolished until 1825. As will be related in the following section, France underwent a similar scandal in the very same year.

6. France

From a geo-economic point of view, France holds an exceptional position among European countries. It is the only country that borders on both the North Sea and the Mediterranean. Due to its size and its geographical position, France has a more varied background to its economy than the rest of Western Europe. To this, should be added that, until the unification of Germany in 1871, France was, measured in terms of both area and population, the largest country in Western Europe.

Among the countries of Western Europe, France is known for its centralized style of government, which may seem surprising considering the variations from north to south, and from east to west. Those differences, however, may have caused – at least when viewed from Paris – a need for a high degree of centralization in order to make a coherent entity of the country. The special geo-economic features of the country should also be taken into consideration in order to understand the French tradition of a protectionist trade policy, which is still influencing the policy of the European Community (EC/EU). Within the borders of France, to the north you find agriculture based on crops of grain and roots and, to the south, a Mediterranean agriculture based on olives, citrus fruits, wine and silk worms. In addition to this, the country possesses a wide variety of raw materials. Finally, at that time France had a large population by comparison with other countries of Western Europe. All this makes it easier to understand why the economic policy of the country developed a tradition of being more inward-oriented than, for example, Great Britain, the Netherlands and the Scandinavian countries.

Towards the end of the 1500s, Henry IV (*1589-1610*) brought religious persecution to a halt by the Edict of Nantes of 1598. In 1685, this was revoked by Louis XIV and persecution resumed. It is surmised that about half a million well-qualified craftsmen, merchants, bankers, etc., left the country as a result of this and settled mainly in the Northern Netherlands and England. This outflow was a setback for the French economy and, correspondingly, a boost for the receiving countries. It should also be said that the French economy during the reign of Louis XIV, in spite of the efforts of Colbert, experienced a growing financial crisis caused by high expenditure on the army and the court in Versailles, combined with an inexpedient system of taxation.

Just like England, France was hit by a financial scandal in 1720. At his death in 1715, Louis XIV left a large public debt. A Scottish banker, John Law (1671-1729), offered his assistance to administer and reduce the debt. The offer was accepted and in 1716 John Law obtained permission to start a bank, which was granted the right to issue notes against bullion deposits. After a short while, the bank set up the Mississippi-Company to start plantations and trading posts along the Mississippi River. From then on, the bank behind the project started to issue bank notes based on the assets of the Mississippi-Company. In practice, it meant that the French government, for a short time, financed its expenses by issuing paper money. In 1720, it all came to an abrupt end. Confidence was lost; and the owners of the shares and those who placed their savings in John Law's Bank lost their money. Two things were left for posterity: the name of the city of Nouvelle Orléans (New Orleans), since it was founded during the regency of the Prince of Orléans, and a deep distrust of banks, bank notes and bank accounts. This, along with the collapse of the French currency during the French Revolution some seventy years later, meant that for long periods, ordinary French investors preferred to keep their assets in government bonds, railway stocks or – even better – hard cash.

From the early 1700s, an ecological crisis was underway in some parts of Western Europe. One aspect of this was a growing shortage of wood, which seems to have been felt less in France than in England. This meant that the French did not have the same incentive to find alternative sources of energy or to replace wood by coal when smelting iron. Another difference between the two countries worthy of mention is the relative size of the urban populations. Shipping and foreign trade formed a basis for a rather large urban population in Britain, representing a substantial demand for mass products. The French economy had, to a higher degree, the character of a dual economy where by far the main part of the population lived in the countryside in an almost self-sufficient economy. Even though the French population was three times as big as the English, it did not form the basis of a corresponding home market. Seen from the demand side, Great Britain had by far the best prospects for starting mass production.

7. Germany

From 962 to 1806, there existed in a formal sense a "German Holy Roman Empire" of which, in its later stages, it was said that it was neither Holy, German nor Roman. It stretched originally from Sicily in the south to the Baltic and the North Sea in the north and, in a historical atlas, it may seem impressive. The truth is, however, that its unity was limited and that for long periods, it did not really exist.

A coherent economic and political entity covering a substantial part of German speaking Europe, did not exist until 1871 when the Prussian king, after his victory over France, was crowned German Emperor. It may seem odd, that this part of the world – as opposed to France – remained divided into so many minor and major dukedoms, principalities and kingdoms for so long, not least when one considers the fact that it represented a vast, common language area. Part of the explanation may be that the European great powers, from the time of the peace of Westphalia in 1648, pursued a policy that kept the area divided. This was, in part, made possible because of the competition between the Habsburgs on the Austrian throne, and the Hohenzollerns on the Prussian throne.[10] It was not until the defeats suffered during the Napoleonic Wars that widespread public feeling arose in favour of a united Germany.

As already mentioned, the area between the Rhine, the Danube and the Elbe had formed the border of the Roman Empire to the northeast. What was to the east of the Elbe was colonized in the 1100s and 1200s. Apart from the Hanseatic towns on the coast, the economy of the area was dominated by agriculture. Some mining did take place: salt in Lüneburg, silver and copper further to the south. As mentioned in Chapter 2, the area south of the Baltic in the Middle Ages had trade relations with Flanders and the Netherlands, supplying grain. By the

---

10. Richelieu (1585-1642), a cardinal of the Catholic Church and a leading French statesman at the time of the Thirty Years' War (1618-48), let catholic France intervene on the Protestant side in the war to weaken the Habsburgs and in order to avoid the creation of a strong, united Germany.

end of the Middle Ages, the southern parts of the German area flourished. Substantial silver mining took place in Bavaria and centres of trade between Southern and Northern Europe developed, among the best-known developments was that of the House of Fugger.

However, the area lost its position in ensuing years. The Fuggers went bankrupt, mainly due to losses on loans to Spanish kings; the silver mines met growing competition from silver coming in from the Americas, transit trade diminished due to the new trade routes and growing competition from Antwerp and Amsterdam. The gloomy situation was compounded by the devastation of the Thirty Years' War. All in all, it seems fair to conclude, that the area, which now constitutes the German Federal Republic and Austria, from an economic point of view, fell back to a position of relative anonymity for two to three centuries. It may seem strange that this description also goes on to explain why they played a major role in European politics at the same time. Part of the explanation for this is that they both had great rural populations, which enabled them to raise great conscript armies. A further factor is that they, due to their geographical position, were used by Britain as part of its policy of maintaining a balance of power on the continent.

Trade, between the more than three hundred separate customs entities of the present German area, was hampered by all sorts of tariffs and tolls. The development of manufactures was held back by gild monopolies and state supervision. Agriculture, especially to the east, was dominated by large estates where the peasants lived under conditions close to serfdom. Germany still had a long way to go, to find its "proper place" in the European economy and politics.

8. The Scandinavian countries

About 1500, the Scandinavian countries held a favourable position in the economy of the countries grouped around the North Sea and the Baltic. In the overall economy of this area, they served as suppliers of staple goods like timber, fish and grain. In the case of Denmark, cattle may be added. Catches of herring in Danish waters were declining, however. At the same time, Norwegian fisheries, all the way up to Lofoten, north of the Polar Circle, were increasing. From a political point of view, Denmark-Norway, united under the same king since

1380, could be characterized as a "middle sized" European power. This can be seen from the marriage of the Danish king, Christian II (1513-23), to the sister of the later Holy Roman emperor, Charles V. The next 150-200 years saw substantial changes in this situation. The position of Sweden was strengthened in relation to that of Denmark, as a result of which in 1658, Denmark, lost the southern provinces of the Scandinavian peninsula to Sweden. Furthermore, the voyages of discovery and subsequent new trade routes meant a change in the patterns of trade.

Contrary to what took place in other parts of Northern Europe, the Reformation did not cause great disturbances in the Scandinavian countries. It took place without major violations and with a clear and lasting result. The Scandinavian countries were thereby spared the internal conflicts and even civil wars that tormented other European countries. On the contrary, the Scandinavian countries took advantage of the religious conflicts by receiving refugees from France and the Southern Netherlands.

Three soldier kings dominated Swedish and Scandinavian politics within less than a century; Gustavus II Adolphus (*1611-32*), Carl X Gustav (*1654-60*) and Charles XII (*1697-1718*). For a short period, Sweden played a major rôle in the politics of Central and Eastern Europe. However, Dutch and British interests in keeping the Baltic open to trade proved to be so strong that they did not allow either Sweden or Denmark to play a decisive rôle in the Baltic.

The geo-economic conditions meant, then as now, that there were substantial differences in the economies of the three countries. Denmark and southern Scandinavia had by far the best potential for farming. However, the Danish economy was more one-sided than the Norwegian and Swedish economies where, in both countries, farming could normally be combined with forestry. The peasantry could in this way enjoy additional sources of income, partly based on work at times of the year when there was little work to be done in the fields. This was especially true in Norway where the possibilities of shipping lumber to the markets of the Netherlands and England were good. All in all, the possibility of additional income from fishing and forestry must have been better in Norway than in Sweden. Since the Middle Ages, fishing as far north as Lofoten was important to the Western European supply of salted and dried fish – especially for consumption during Lent. The mining of iron, silver and copper was of importance both to Norway and Sweden. Both countries had the advantage of easy access to charcoal. Swedish iron was known for its high degree of fineness. Sweden held a leading position as a supplier of high-quality iron to Britain in the 1700s, especially when the supply of British charcoal dwindled. Compared to Norway, the conditions for agriculture were better in Sweden, which on the whole was self-sufficient in terms of foodstuffs.

The Norwegian economy was characterized by a substantial deficit of agricultural products balanced by a surplus from fishing and forestry. Such an economy requires a relatively large foreign trade, which was organized as triangular trade: Norway supplying England with timber, England supplying Denmark with iron and Denmark supplying Norway with grain. There was, furthermore, the Norwegian export of dried fish to Catholic areas. As it held the upper hand, Denmark granted itself a monopoly of the Norwegian grain market, which made it possible for a long time to sell low-quality grain at high prices. Viewed from Denmark, this ensured favourable terms of trade. Viewed from Norway, it must have been seen as exploitation by the mother country of her colony.

The existence of alternative employment to agriculture in Norway and most parts of Sweden had implications for the social structure of the two countries compared to Denmark, where such possibilities were few. Among Danish peasants, freeholders were the exception, by far the majority of the farmers were tenants. In Norway, it was the other way round; most of the farmers were freeholders. Sweden held a position in between the other two. To the south and in the centre of Sweden there were great estates, while other areas, mainly with poor soil, were dominated by smallholdings. On the whole, there were more smallholders in Norway and Sweden than in Denmark where the typical farm had more arable land at its disposal.

Although farming conditions were better in Denmark than in her two sister countries, the social situation of Danish peasants seems to have been less favourable. On the whole, the Danish peasantry, as tenants, enjoyed less personal freedom. The amount of work to be done at the manors increased through the 1700s, and regulations arose, restricting the freedom to leave the farms. The higher productivity of farming in Denmark, however, must have been accompanied by material benefits. The standard of living must, on average, have been highest in Denmark, followed by Norway where it was, again, higher than in Sweden.

Part II
The growth of industrial society

The previous chapters described how an extension of the markets secured the necessary conditions for mass-*distribution*. The next development is the start of mass-*production*, which took place with the industrial breakthrough and is the topic of the following three chapters. The period begins with the use of the very first, primitive steam engines and ends when Henry Ford (1863-1947) drove the first model T off the assembly line.

Chapter 5, Early Industrialization, deals with the period from 1750 to 1830. The three keywords of the period are cotton, coal and iron. So far, the new production methods were concentrated on a few products and posterity, without being sure of the answer, asked itself what was essentially new about what took place. Posterity may, furthermore, have discussed when the "breakthrough" – called a "revolution" by some – took place. Even here, the uncertainty is great. The answers range from the middle of the 1700s to the first quarter of the 1800s, depending on what is meant by "industrial breakthrough". On the political scene, the major European event was the French Revolution, followed by a strengthening of the position of Great Britain. For history in the long term, the creation of a new nation outside of Europe, the USA, deserves mention.

Chapter 6, Industry begins to spread, covers the period from 1830 to 1875. The title of the chapter refers to a spread both as far as the variety of products is concerned and as far as the geographical area involved. Two innovations left an unmistakable mark on development: railways and the chemical industry, soon to be followed by the electrical industry. It was in this period that applied physics and chemistry made their way into industry. Assisted by railways, industry established itself over the European continent as Germany prepared to take up a position as a leading industrial, military and political power.

Chapter 7, Approaching the Great Showdown, deals with the years 1875 to 1914, the First World War. Britain had, by then, consolidated its position as the leading naval and colonial power. The British economy was characterized by its vast overseas engagements; as much as a third of its national assets were placed overseas. However, in Europe, the balance of power developed in favour of Germany. Falling transport costs meant stiff competition in Western Europe from American and Russian grain, causing a widespread agricultural crisis and the introduction of protectionist policies in most countries. Just as the beginning of the 20th century was characterized by fast growth, it was also a period of increased tension.

The dates of genuine revolutions are usually celebrated as national days, whether it is 17th May in Norway, 4th July in the USA or 14th July in France. The so-called industrial revolution comes off poorly in this respect. It is not possible to indicate even an approximate date by stating a given year – or even a decade. Depending on the criteria used, different results will be reached. Three such criteria are

1. changes in production processes,
2. changes in output of production, its size and composition,
3. changes in the structure of society.

If the starting point is an interest in the history of technology and technological change, then the first criterion is valid. If economic growth is the main theme, then the second point is valid. And, finally, if it is the social and political balance of society which matters most, then the third point is the decisive one. As the "industrial revolution" can be seen through different glasses, its emergence can be dated differently. Technological changes appeared first, their subsequent impact on size and nature of production somewhat later, and the impact on the structure of society, such as the degree of urbanization, the growth of a political labour movement, etc., appeared last. The time which elapsed between, at the one end, the first fundamental changes in production processes within mining and iron manufacturing and, at the other, changes in social structure through the appearance of industrial towns inhabited by thousands of factory workers, almost spans the century from the second quarter of the 1700s, to the first quarter of the 1800s. Taking this background into account, what matters is not the exact timing of the industrial breakthrough, but awareness of the criteria.

As far as change in the production processes are concerned – normally taken to be the leading criterion – three changes merit special attention: a change in the sources and use of energy, the introduction of new materials and, finally, the substitution of mechanical devices for human labour.[1]

a. The leading source of energy had so far been wood, and, in terms of mobile energy sources, human or animal strength. To these, the sources of wind and water-power were added. The growing consumption of wood had, as stated above, caused an increasing energy crisis, resulting in attempts to use coal in the form of furnace coke. At a later stage, gas was used as a source of both heat and light.

b. Production took advantage of new raw materials. An important aspect of this was the introduction of synthetic materials to replace natural products. An early, leading example of this are the bleaches and dyes used by the textile industry. The needs of the expanding textile industry reached such a size that demand could not be met with traditional raw materials. This can be seen as the introduction of natural science into industrial production.

c. Mechanical accuracy, speed and tirelessness thanks to the new engineering industry supplemented the traditional skills and qualities of the labour force. This made it possible to repeat the same process of production, over and over again, with an accuracy that even the most highly-skilled workers could not live up to, and formed the background to the development of an industry based on interchangeable parts.

If it is doubtful *when* the industrial breakthrough took place, there is, however, no doubt as to *where* it took place: in England. It was especially

1.   David Landes (1969, 1).

in the Midlands and in Northern England. The cotton textile industry was concentrated around Manchester and the iron industry around Birmingham. Scotland was also home to early industry. It was, however, in England that the first great industrial centres developed. It was also from here that fundamental changes in the economic and social life of Great Britain spread after the Napoleonic Wars.

Chapter 5

Early industrialization 1750-1830

The epoch-making economic event of the 1700s was the growth of the iron and cotton industries in Great Britain.[1] From a political point of view, the first part of the period was characterized by a softening of restrictions on political and economic life carried forward by the Age of Enlightenment. This was followed by the French Revolution and the Napoleonic Wars, after which a period of reaction followed. The period covered by this chapter finishes with the July Revolution of 1830 in France. The end of the period marks the beginning of a new wave of innovation and investment, initiated and driven forward by the steam locomotive.

1. The Age of Enlightenment

As well as matters of religion, the Reformation had involved the question of the power structure between the Church and the State. After the conflict was settled, on the whole, to the advantage of the State, a new problem arose: the relationship between state and individual. This was a leading theme of the social scientists of the Age of Enlightenment. It had its centre in France and England, from where it spread over Europe and across the North Atlantic. Scandinavia, Central and Eastern Europe experienced the movement, which came, via Germany, under the designation of the Age of Reason.

---

1. So far the name England has been used. Formally, a union with Scotland was formed in 1707. If Wales is added, the area corresponds to Great Britain. If the Isle of Man and Ireland (nowadays Northern Ireland) are included, it corresponds to the United Kingdom. In the following, the name Great Britain will be used in relation to events taking place after the establishment of the union with Scotland.

The background for the Age of Enlightenment is to be found in the progress of the natural sciences in the previous century, with the works of Isaac Newton (1642-1727) as a leading contribution (main work published in 1687). Another major factor was the contemporary political development in England, where the power of the king was reduced by the Glorious Revolution of 1688. An early literary expression of this was in the exposition by John Locke (1632-1704), "Two Treatises of Government" published in 1691. According to Locke, all human beings are born equal, free and independent. They have, however, to live within the framework of a social structure. The function of the government – and this would, in those days, mean the king – is then to secure the balance between the interests of the general public and those of the individual. If the king failed to do this, it was not only the right of the citizens, but also their duty, to replace him by a new head of state.

Within the social sciences, the successful attempts by Newton and his contemporaries to bring order to the physical world were followed by attempts to bring order to social life by proving the existence of a system of Natural law. These laws, just as those of physics, were formulated beyond the will and power of human beings. This entire way of thinking was, of course, inconvenient to absolutist rulers. They ran the risk that something new and inconvenient would be uncovered as a result of these studies. According to the new ideas, a ruling prince did not get his power directly from God. Instead, it originated from an agreement – a social contract – between the prince and the people, which both parts had a duty to observe. Society should be organized in a way that corresponded to the internal qualifications of human beings for living together. The leading exponents of those ideas were the French philosophers, Voltaire and Montesquieu, who were both much impressed by their stays in Great Britain; in Voltaire's case, his exile lasted three years.

Montesquieu's work, "The Spirit of the Law" (1746) had the most direct consequences. Inspired by his observations in Great Britain, he describes an ideal society where there are sharp distinctions between the legislative branch, the executive or administrative branch and the judicial branch of the total system of government. British public life could hardly be said to have lived up to those standards, but this way of looking upon government had profound consequences later on in the 1770s for the constitution of the newborn United States of America.

A culmination point in the collection and presentation of knowledge was marked in France with the "Great Encyclopedia", the writing of which was left to the most outstanding scholars in France. The work was published in seventeen volumes between 1751-65. At times, it received royal financial support. At others, it was stricken by censorship and prohibitions. Similar initiatives saw the light of day in other countries. In Great Britain, the writing of an English dictionary was assigned to Samuel Johnson (1709-84), who undertook this task pretty much on his own. He completed it within eight years, partly overlapping the period of the writing of the French encyclopedia.

2. Economic Liberalism

The idea of society as a system given by Nature does not accord with the ideas behind the interventions of mercantilist policy in the economy. If such a "natural" situation exists in the economy, it is hard to explain the need for the restrictions and regulations of mercantilist policy. The philosophy that led to the existence of a Natural Law, also led to the question: Is there a "Natural Economy" as well – and if so, what is this economy like?

This was the question preoccupying two partly related lines of thought in the third quarter of the 1700s: the French Physiocrats and British social scientists such as David Hume (1711-76), and his fellow Scotsman, Adam Smith (1723-90).

As mentioned in section 1, the Age of Enlightenment, the middle of the 1700s was characterized by substantial intellectual commotion. The centre of this in the middle of the century seems to have been France, though with close connections abroad. There was in those circles, a clear understanding that France needed economic and political reform. This was expressed by a group, adherents of "Government by Nature", known as the "Physiocrats". The leading representative of the idea was the court-physician, Francois Quesnay (1694-1774). He was followed by a group recruited from the French upper class. Among its members were persons with direct access to the highest circles in French political life. Quesnay himself was the personal doctor of Madame Pompadour (1721-64), the mistress of Louis XV for a number of years. The works of the Physiocrats are confined to a relatively short period, normally placed between the years 1750 and 1780. In spite of their close relations and access to governing circles, their thoughts concerning the functioning of the economy and corresponding economic reforms had little impact on contemporary French society. And, in spite of their good will, they were unable to prevent the developments that led to the French Revolution in 1789.

The theoretical starting point of the Physiocrats was that all consumption in society had its foundation in agricultural production. It is agriculture that opens access to the riches of Nature. Only in so far as agriculture is able to produce a surplus can there be economic activity beyond agriculture. This surplus corresponds to its production after the deduction of the necessary seed corn, foodstuffs and the consumption of the peasant population. It was called *the net product*. Urban trades were spoken of as sterile, which meant that they consumed part of the net product and did not add anything to it. This actually meant that the ideas behind mercantilism were turned upside down. According to the new way of reasoning it was not the urban trades that deserved interest and support, but agriculture, which had to be made more effective in order to offer the rest of society a larger net product. Whereas mercantilists had focused their interest on urban trades – both commerce and manufacturing – the Physiocrats concluded that agriculture deserved the lion's share of attention.

To contemporary, knowledgeable observers it was evident that French agriculture was inefficient, dominated as it was by smallholdings, and still farmed in a medieval fashion. Since farming occupied, by far, the majority of the population, the waste of resources was equally large. Against this backdrop, it is easy to understand that the Physiocrats made themselves advocates of reforms inspired by British and Dutch agriculture. To further their aims, the plethora of subsidies and monopolies granted to the urban trades was to be abolished. Their ideas of "good economic policy" were expressed in a sentence, later attributed to extreme liberalism: "Laissez faire, laissez passer". As will be appreciated, it was hardly possible to dissociate oneself further from mercantilist ideas.

The positive attitude of the Physiocrats towards agriculture might tempt one into believing that this was accompanied by an interest in the well-being of the peasantry, but this was not so. Their attitude to the peasantry could be seen from the position of agriculture in the model they made of the economy. Quesnay, who named it the "Tableau Économique", set it up. It comes close to present-day input-output tables, showing the flows between different sectors of the economy and the output delivered for final use as consumption or investments. The more efficient agriculture becomes, the more it is able to deliver for final consumption *outside* the agricultural sector. This, however, means that the net product of the Physiocrats does not correspond to our National Product. The consumption of the peasants is not included. Their consumption is treated as the use of raw materials corresponding to the use of foodstuffs by their livestock. This is inherent in the way they defined the net product.

The ideas of the Physiocrats, nevertheless, marked an important step forward in the perception of the economy. Mercantilists had mainly considered "wealth" as a stock; the total assets at any given point in time. The net product of the Physiocrats was a flow to be measured over a period, and behind this was a change in the field of interest from the building of stocks to the size of current income. At the practical level, the writings of the Physiocrats meant an increased interest in agricultural policy and reform, as well as support for the idea of more liberal conditions within business. It seems fair to consider the Physiocrats as forerunners of liberalism, which can be seen from the fact that Adam Smith did not hesitate to recognize their ideas which undoubtedly inspired him during his stay in France in the 1760s.

The growing acceptance of the freedom of the individual led to the question of how to find a balance between, on the one hand, the wish of the individual to pursue his self-interest and, on the other, the interests of the rest of society? In the case of individuals drawing the borderlines for themselves, how can society, including the economy, be prevented from ending up in chaos? How can self-interest and the common good be harmonized? The liberals had some surprising answers to these essential questions.

A possible solution to the contradiction could be that human consciousness assisted everyone in finding the proper balance between the two opposing forces. According to this idea, finding the balance took place "inside" the individual. An advocate of this line of thought was the philosopher and economist, David Hume (1711-76). A pupil and junior colleague of Hume, Adam Smith (1723-90), who was also Scottish, took up the question. At first, he supported the explanation based on inner balance. In a work written in 1759, "The Theory of Moral Sentiments" – note the title – Smith replaced the intangible consciousness with a reluctance to be criticised and the fear of loss of reputation in the eyes of others. After this came Smith's travels in France (1764-66), as tutor to the son of an English nobleman, and his meeting with the Physiocrats and the persons behind the Great Encyclopedia. Upon his return, he finished the work he had started during his stay in France, "An Inquiry Into the Nature and Causes of the Wealth of Nations", later known under the shorter title, "The Wealth of Nations", published in 1776.

It is beyond the scope of this account to go into the details of this great work by Adam Smith. The essential elements are the considerations forming the core of Smith's liberalism. As in his earlier book, the "Moral Sentiments", he deals with the question of the relation between self-interest and the interests of the rest of society. The solution to the dilemma, however, has now changed. The balancing does not take place within the individual, but outside in the economic system. In pursuing his personal goals, the individual will pursue the goals of other individuals and, thereby, those of society. This will occur if the economy is organized in the right way, that is to say, if the existence of sufficient competition is ensured.[2] Thus the conflict between selfishness and social considerations disappeared and the philosophical foundation of economic liberalism had been laid with the assistance of Adam Smith's well-known "economic man".

Smith's ideas seem to have attracted wide interest at the time of the book's appearance, not least, in the thirteen British colonies in North America. Here a war of liberation started at the time the book was published, in part as a reaction to British mercantilist trade policy towards her colonies. Then came the French Revolution, the Napoleonic Wars and the post-war reaction which meant a backlash against the spread of liberal ideas. It was not until the 1830s and '40s, that the message of liberalism had a wider impact on the economy of Western Europe.

---

2. A few famous lines from the "Wealth of Nations" deserve to be quoted here: "It is not from the benevolence of the butcher, the brewer, or the baker that we expect our dinner, but from their regard to their own interest. We address ourselves, not to their humanity but to their self-love, and never talk to them of our own necessities, but of their own interests." Adam Smith (1776, 13).

3. Early ecological crisis

During the 1700s, parts of Western Europe experienced a growing ecological crisis. Opinions differ as to the severity of the crisis which was felt in densely populated areas as an increasing shortage of wood and pressure on the food supply. The shortage of food was partly neutralized by new methods of production, the introduction of new crops such as clover and roots, and the cultivation of new land through draining or irrigation. All in all, this meant an increase in area-productivity. It is, however, more doubtful what happened to the labour-productivity (yield per worker per unit of time) of the peasantry. If it was decreasing, this must have been felt as a pressure on their income. A similar development may have been felt by parts of the urban population in the case where rising food prices were not offset by an increase in their productivity. It was no doubt felt differently in different areas. Where agriculture was undergoing rapid reforms, with a corresponding increase in labour productivity, the impact on real incomes and standards of living may not have been felt at all, whereas in other areas, it may have been felt with considerable strength. Such a difference seems to have existed between Great Britain and France in the second half of the 1700s.

That contemporaries were aware of the possibility of a food-shortage can be seen from the "Essay on the Principle of Population" by Thomas Robert Malthus, first published in 1798. The book was written as a spontaneous reaction to another work expressing a very optimistic view on the future of the British economy. The central theme of his theory is an expectation that the production of food cannot keep up with the growth of the population. Rather arbitrarily, it is postulated that where the size of the population develops according to a geometric progression (1-2-4-8-16...), doubling every 25 years, the production of food within the same time frame develops according to an arithmetical progression (1-2-3-4-5...) due to the limits of the productivity of the soil. In present-day language, this means a severe fall in the marginal product of labour to almost zero and a corresponding fall in the average wage of labour.

To the general tendencies of this sort, the case of France during the 1780s had some additional special circumstances. In 1774, France had started a liberalization of her economy, including foreign trade in grain. Since, at the same time, Great Britain switched from exporting to importing grain, the new export-market for French grain caused an increase in its price in France. In 1786, a new trade agreement between the two countries was signed, prolonging the arrangement. Then followed a failed harvest, causing a severe shortage of grain and correspondingly high prices of bread. Malthus tells us, on the basis of information, collected during a visit to France in 1802:

> "Now it is generally agreed that the condition of the lower classes of the people in France before the Revolution was very wretched. The wages of labour were about 20 sous, or tenpence a day, at a time when the wages of labour in England were nearly seventeen pence, and the price of wheat of the same quality in the two countries was not very different".[3]

It can be no surprise then, that discontent boiled over in Paris, one of the few towns in Europe with a population of as much as half a million. It was, also, the capital of a misgoverned society.

The ecological crisis of Great Britain seems to have taken a somewhat different direction. There, the crisis seems primarily to have been felt as a shortage of wood in the form of both timber and fuel. Of special importance to the industrial breakthrough was the shortage of charcoal for the production of iron. Would it be possible to find other means of smelting iron ore such as using ordinary coal? If that were to be the case, then Britain would have the advantage of disposing of ample supplies of coal and iron ore, each to be found near to the other. An important contribution to the change in the British iron industry was thus an increasing crisis in the supply of traditional fuel – an energy crisis, as we would say after the experiences of the 1970s. To put it another way: whereas the ecological crisis of the 1700s in France led to the Bastille Day and a political revolution; the result on the other side of the Channel was a so-called "industrial revolution".

4. A self-sustaining growth process

Certainly, substantial changes had previously taken place in the ways and means of production. This had been the case within agriculture in

---

3. T.R. Malthus (1958, vol. I, 230). 7th ed. as reprinted in Everyman's Library. London, 1958.

north-western Europe, about, and shortly after 1000, and again in the mid-1600s. Those changes took place, however, without starting a self-sustaining dynamic process of growth. The tendency had been, hitherto, that any increase in production was followed by a corresponding increase in population. Against this background, it is tempting to ask what was the difference between the previous changes and the changes that took place from the mid-1700s? *What was crucially new about what took place during the industrial breakthrough?*

Rocket programmes and research in outer space have caused the appearance of a new word: *spin-off,* meaning that inventions, meant for use in one way, turn out to be useful in other, unforeseeable ways. What happened around the mid-1700s was the beginning of exactly such a dynamic process of spin-offs. As long as consumption consisted almost entirely of the most elementary food, clothes, accommodation and heating, and as long as the most important means of production were spades and ploughs, saws and scythes, there were few chances of starting up a chain-reaction of "spin-offs". From the mid-1700s, however, things were different; with due regard to the eternal truth that all short answers to economic questions are wrong, it can be said that from then on there was continuous interaction between innovations. Where inventions, previously appeared in isolation from each other, so to speak, there was from then on *a constant interaction between process-innovations and product-innovations.* This, to make a long story short, was what was crucially new about it all.

Process-innovation means the production of already known products in a new way – through a new process. Among the best known examples from the 1700s, is the spinning of yarn by means of machinery, one spinster handling several spindles instead of the traditional, single spinning wheel. Or, the melting of iron ore, using mineral fuel instead of charcoal. *Product*-innovation means the appearance of new, hitherto unknown products. Examples include high-speed transport by railway, electric light, communication by telegraph or telephone and, at a later date, antibiotics. It is characteristic of the early stages of industrialization that process-innovation was initially predominant and brought about in its wake increasing product-innovation. The steam engine was meant as a process-innovation – a new and cheaper way of pumping water out of mines – a new way of performing an old task! It was, however, developed to such a degree over the ensuing century that it could be used for drawing railway wagons. From this, new ways and means of transportation developed, which deserve to be called new products.

Looked upon in that way, what was crucially new about what saw the light of day in the 1700s were not the process-innovations within the textile industry. It was rather an entirely new source of energy, mineral coal, which replaced charcoal and saw use as a new energy source instead of animal or human strength. And it also meant new materials like iron replacing wood in the construction of tools and machines. The process of interaction is illustrated by the chemical industry, which grew after 1800, and through process-innovation, the costs of materials for bleaching and dyeing textiles were brought down. Synthetic products replaced natural materials like urine; the new processes giving rise to new by-products, which turned out to be useful. The search for new processes gave rise to new products that, again, gave rise to the search for new processes, etc., etc. An example of this interaction is provided by the attempts of Graham Bell (1847-1922), in the late 1800s, to develop a technique that allowed several signals to be sent simultaneously along the same telegraph line. To his great surprise he unexpectedly invented a new product, the telephone, while he was searching for a new process, a way of transmitting signals!

It is often said that "things are developing at an ever faster rate". The expression, in itself, is not very precise and may obscure the fact that fast and radical changes have taken place in previous times as well. If the expression is to be given a more precise meaning, it could be said that the more known products and processes there are, the more there are possibilities for interaction between process-innovation and product-innovation. Development then acquires the nature of an exponential function – and as such, it does go "at an ever faster rate".

5. Technical development

5.1. *The textile industry*

The textile industry is traditionally considered to be the starting point of modern industrialization. This view is correct insofar as it was here that modern mass production, based on the use of mechanical equipment under a factory roof, gained a foothold and got underway. The two major processes in textile production are spinning and weaving, accompanied by a number of other processes such as the cleaning and combing of wool or cotton, bleaching, dyeing, and so on.[4] Of the two processes mentioned first, spinning was traditionally by far the most labour intensive. It took five spinsters – it was normally a woman's job – to keep one weaver supplied with the necessary yarn.

The first step in the modernization of the industry was the introduction in the 1740s of "the flying shuttle", which doubled the productivity of the weavers. It now took ten spinsters to supply one weaver. The 1760s and '70s saw the introduction of two inventions that turned this situation upside down. The first was the "spinning-jenny", which made it possible for one person to control a number of spindles. However, the "spinning-jenny" was still not driven by mechanical power. Then came the second invention, "the water-frame" where the spindles were driven, first by water-power, and later on by steam. It was the introduction of this machine that gave the production units the character of a factory. The quality of the yarn was poor, however, as it could not serve as the warp, i.e., the threads going lengthwise in the material. This state of affairs changed with the introduction of the "spinning-mule", which combined the high quality of the spinning-jenny with the high productivity of the water-frame. The outcome was yarn of a higher quality than that of the best spinsters in Britain, or even India, renowned for its fine cotton fabrics.

Those early steps in the modernization of the textile industry only concerned the production of the yarn, not the actual weaving of the material. It was not until the 1820s, that a reliable mechanical loom was introduced. Then the technique was transferred from cotton to wool. Spinning productivity grew so fast that one person by 1815 was able to produce as much yarn as 200 people had been able to around 1750. It should also be noted that the quality of the yarn was higher in 1815 than in 1750.

This was, in itself, an impressive development within sixty-five years. Nevertheless, the question may be put as to whether this truly represented the breakthrough of industrialization. There is something missing. If the progress in textile production had been an isolated phenomenon, industrialization might well have stopped at this stage. At this point, we still cannot speak of an interaction between new process-

---

4. A concentrated description of the technical development in the production of textiles, especially spinning and weaving, can be found in D. S. Landes (1969, 80-88).

es and new products. This is where the mining and iron industries, the steam engine and tool industry come into the picture.

5.2. The iron industry

Iron production was the other main area where fast and radical changes took place in the 1700s. Here, as well, it was a question of process innovation causing a sharp fall in costs and an increase in quality. Speaking of iron production, one has to distinguish between pig iron, or raw iron, cast iron and malleable iron, or wrought iron, ranked according to increasing purity, which means according to a lowering of the carbon and mineral impurity content. Cast iron has the drawback of being more sensitive to pressure and impact than wrought iron. The production of wrought iron, according to traditional methods, was based on the use of charcoal. When attempts were made to produce iron on the basis of fossil fuel, coal, it turned out that it was only possible to produce cast iron. Furnace coke had to be used in order to reach higher temperatures than could be attained by using ordinary coal. Part of the iron was used for the production of the huge cylinders of early steam engines (section 5.3) used to operate the bellows of the iron furnaces and pump the water up from the ever deeper coal mines.

Further steps forward in the production of iron were made in the 1780s, when increased heating of cast iron made it possible to produce wrought iron. The foundation was hereby laid for the development of the British iron industry. Two raw materials, coal and iron ore, found close to each other, could be used in the production of wrought iron – lots of wrought iron.

5.3. The steam engine

The development of the steam engine is a long story, stretching a hundred years or more from 1712 when the first example was taken into use to operate a water pump in a mine, until the time it was available in a form which allowed its use in ships and locomotives. By comparison, there were only twenty-five years between the invention of the internal combustion engine and the construction of the first automobile in 1886, and, from there, only seventeen years before an internal combustion engine helped prove that heavier-than-air flight was indeed possible.

The development of the steam engine during its first hundred years can be divided into three stages. The start is related to the name of an Englishman, Thomas Newcomen (1663-1729), and his engine. First, steam was led into a cylinder and then cold water sprayed into the cylinder, whereupon the steam condensed and a vacuum developed in the cylinder. As will be understood, it was atmospheric pressure that moved the piston of the engine. The small difference in pressure on either side of the piston meant that the volume of the cylinder had to be very large to produce even a minimum of energy. This again, meant that the diameter of the cylinder had to be large, with the result that it was wellnigh impossible to get the piston and cylinder to fit exactly. The entire construction and way of functioning meant a colossal consumption of coal and a corresponding waste of energy.

The next major contributor was the Scotsman, James Watt (1736-1819). When he was a young man, he held a position as a toolmaker at the University of Glasgow. Whilst repairing a model of a Newcomen engine, his interest in its construction was aroused and he reached the conclusion that the condensation of the steam should take place, not in the cylinder itself, but outside it. In this way, it would be possible to avoid constantly having to heat the heavy cylinder with steam first and then cool it down again in order to condense the steam. A patent based on the idea of a special condenser was granted in 1769 and, from then on, Watt's talents gave rise to a number of patents. One of his inventions made it possible to transform the longitudinal motion of the piston into a rotating motion, which allowed much wider use of the steam engine than had hitherto been possible.

The third decisive step was the introduction of the high-pressure engine. Watt was fully aware that a high-pressure engine could generate more energy, but believed that such machines would be far too dangerous in service, due to the risk of the cylinder exploding. He tried, via his patents, to prevent the production of high-pressure engines. After the expiry of the patents in 1800, it was possible for others to take up production of the high-pressure engine. Where the previous engines operated with an atmospheric pressure of 1.5, it was now increased to 2.0. It might sound not much of a difference, but it was sufficient for the construction of engines that could be used in ships and locomotives.

The life and work of James Watt includes the strange coincidence that he and Adam Smith met in Glasgow. The local authorities in Glasgow forbade Watt to set up his own workshop in the city, on the grounds that he was not a member of the local guild of blacksmiths. In his capacity of Professor at the University of Glasgow, Smith arranged things so that Watt could establish himself within the framework of the University, beyond the reach of the city authorities. So, as will be seen, two major forces behind the development of modern industrial society, met at an early date: liberalism and the steam engine!

5.4. *The tool industry*

The appearance of the tool industry formed the background to widening the industrial breakthrough. One example can illustrate this. Until about 1800, a bolt, along with its corresponding nut, was tailor-made by hand to fit. If a machine was dismantled, nuts and bolts had to be kept together in pairs. In case a nut, or its corresponding bolt, should be changed, a new one had to be made to measure.

This in itself restricted the use of machines in the growing textile industry, as elsewhere. To overcome this problem, a special lathe was invented. A lathe has a substantial advantage over even the most skilled metal worker. It works rapidly, accurately and never gets tired. Most importantly; it is able to repeat the same operation, again and again in exactly the same way. So, from then on, nuts and bolts were no longer produced as inseparable pairs, but in their hundreds and thousands in series where they were all made to fit.

The new tools gave rise to something basic in industrial society: the machine industry. This new industry produced cylinders and pistons with a higher degree of precision than had been previously possible, which made steam engines more efficient and reduced the waste of energy. The next great step forward was just around the corner: production based on interchangeable parts. From there, the assembly line and Henry Ford could be seen on the horizon. This stage belongs to the next chapters and the story of a young, industrial climber: the USA.

6. The French Revolution – short and long-term effects

The French Revolution and the following twenty-five years of uprisings and wars left Europe under the sway of two different forces. On the one hand, those in power in 1815 wanted to restore the political situation to what it was before the revolution, the "ancien régime"; and on the other were political forces that, once set free, could hardly be stopped, or developments once underway be held back.

After the naval battles of Aboukir Bay (1798) and Trafalgar (1805), the French navy lost its importance, leaving Great Britain as undisputed ruler of the waves. Britain saw in this a chance to blockade France effectively, cutting her off from supplies of raw materials of all sorts from overseas. The Royal Navy took upon itself to capture any ships – even from neutral countries – suspected of carrying goods to France or to areas dominated by France. This was the direct cause for the French declaration in 1805 of a *Continental Blockade* against Great Britain. This meant that the two countries each tried to stop the trade and supplies of its opponent. France wanted to prevent Britain obtaining her normal supplies of food, timber and so on, from the Baltic area. Britain wanted to cut off the supplies to France of cotton from America and metals from Sweden.

As part of the Peace of Tilsit signed in July 1807 between France and Russia, the latter joined the Continental Blockade, and Denmark was forced to follow suit at the same time. According to French plans, the Danish navy – the only remaining fleet apart from the Royal Navy – would control the traffic in the Baltic. It was for this reason that a British expeditionary corps arrived at the gates of Copenhagen a couple of months later. After bombarding the city for four nights – the first time a capital had been subjected to such a massive attack – Denmark had to surrender most of its fleet to the British. This meant that the possibilities of controlling trade in the Baltic as part of the Continental Blockade were severely diminished.[5]

The French policy is perhaps better known as the *Continental System,* which meant, according to the French, that the blockade was part of a wider policy. By means of the Continental System, Napoleon endeavoured to create an economic and political entity on the continent under French leadership and dominance, thus pushing Britain out into the periphery of Europe.

The *external* part of this policy consisted in cutting off the well-established and efficient British iron and cotton industries from their markets in order to enable corresponding European, that is to say,

5. Russia was not a very keen participant in the blockade of Britain. The fact that Russia did not live up to its obligations seems to have been a major reason behind Napoleon's decision to launch his fatal campaign against her in 1812.

French/Belgian[6] industries to grow up. The *internal* part of the system consisted in the promotion of trade within French-dominated areas through cuts in tolls and duties, improved transport facilities etc. Furthermore, French business and family laws were introduced in adjoining territories.

The French plan might well remind one of similar ideas presented some hundred and thirty years later.

Chapter Eight will give an account of German plans in the Nazi period to create a European economic system built up around Germany as the centre with the most advanced sectors of the economy. The surrounding countries would fulfil the rôle of suppliers of food and raw materials to Germany. Finally, the system and ideas of Napoleon I could remind one of French opposition during the years of President de Gaulle to British membership of the European Community.

If the question were to be asked as to what were the *economic effects* of the French Revolution and the Napoleonic Wars in the years 1815-30, the answer would be that the trends towards liberalization, which were felt before and during the first years of the Revolution, were effectively stopped. Two examples of this will be given below, and they apply to most of Europe.

Financing the wars had caused a sharp increase in the money supply and corresponding inflation on both sides of the English Channel and the North Sea. The consequent uncertainty concerning banks and monetary matters had long-term effects, which cast a shadow for years to come.

To start with, for the first ten years or so after the war, a *deflationary policy* was pursued in order to bring down price levels. Such a policy in itself meant a slowing down in activity and economic growth. The consequence of all this was the rise of a restrictive view on monetary policy. In practice, this resulted in the observation of a strict connection between the amount of deposited bullion and the number and value of notes in circulation.

---

6. The area covered by present-day Belgium and Luxembourg was incorporated into France. at the time of the Napoleonic Wars

Another general trend of the postwar years was a *protectionist trade policy*. The exceptional conditions, during the years of revolution and war, had meant the establishment of trade and production that could not be expected to survive under normal peacetime conditions. In France, this was the case for parts of her textile and iron industry. In Britain, bringing marginal land into use had expanded farming and food production, and this was production that under normal conditions could not compete with grain from abroad. All in all, the prewar tendencies towards the liberalization of foreign trade suffered a severe setback. It was not until the mid-1800s that an easing of the conditions of foreign trade occurred again.

The *political effects* of the war years may be characterized as a reaction against the liberal and democratic movements of the revolution. However, this period did leave a damaged absolutism behind it on the European continent. So-called constitutional monarchies were on their way forward. Absolute monarchies set no formal limits to the freedom of action enjoyed by the monarch, whereas the term "constitutional monarchy" implied the existence of written limitations to the freedom of the monarch, though the wording, however, did not clearly indicate where the limit was. Typically, it became a question of gaining the consent of the public – or parts of it – for the income and expenditure of government. Such a development began in several countries after 1815.

Examples of this tendency are provided by the German states of Bavaria, Baden Württemberg, Hesse and Saxony, all of which between 1818-20 obtained written constitutions, limiting the power of their princes. Norway was transformed into a constitutional monarchy in 1814 at the close of the Napoleonic Wars. This constitution was upheld during the subsequent union of Norway and Sweden over the next ninety years. Sweden too, introduced formal limitations to the power of the King. It was not until after 1830, or rather 1848, that a similar development took place in Denmark.

From the beginning, government under a constitutional monarch was understood to mean that any powers, not explicitly handed over to other authorities, still rested with the King. His functions could be characterized as residual, whose core was the "relations with foreign powers". The sphere, where absolutism for many reasons had its most long lasting effects has no doubt been foreign policy.

7. National developments

7.1. Great Britain

Early industrialization in Great Britain was a coincidence of natural and institutional prerequisites.

Among the favourable *natural* prerequisites were the ample deposits of coal and iron ore. To these may be added, favourable transport conditions on navigable rivers, a long coastline with many natural harbours and, from the 1700s, a growing network of canals. A relatively large part of the population lived in towns, representing a substantial market for mass-produced products such as textiles. As for favourable *institutional* prerequisites, it should be mentioned that the production of textiles already in the early 1700s, was organised as a so-called putting-out industry. This meant that finance and distribution were organized in, more or less, the same way as for large-scale industrial production. Finally, there was the absence of well-organized resistance to reforms. The guilds had traditionally played a smaller role in Britain than on the Continent. At the same time, the merchants of London, Bristol, Liverpool and other centres of commerce and shipping were in a strong position. All in all, the conditions were much more favourable for the decentralized development of a trade like the textile industry than across the Channel.

Great Britain already had inaugurated a process of softening its traditional mercantilist policy at the time of the French Revolution. This was, however, brought to a halt by the Napoleonic Wars. During the years of war, the country had been forced to rely on an increased degree of self-sufficiency, partly as the result of the Continental Blockade. This resulted in an increase in the price of food and political unrest in the growing urban areas. After the war, the price of food might have been expected to fall. However, the political influence of the landowners was so strong that a policy of protection against competition from cheap, foreign grain was initiated by Parliament. According to the Corn Law, importation of grain was only allowed when the price in Britain was above a certain limit. The law was hard to administer and gave rise to great fluctuations in the price of grain. To stabilize prices, and the incomes of the landowners, a system based on the so-called "sliding scale" was introduced in 1828. This was originally a French idea, and worthy of mention because for forty years it has formed the basis of the EC's Common Agricultural Policy (CAP) known as the system of variable import levies. The latter three words explain how it works. The starting point is a threshold price per unit of grain. If the price of foreign grain is above this, it can be imported free of duty. If it is below the set threshold, a (variable) levy has to be paid corresponding to the difference between the threshold price and the lower price of the foreign grain. The system guarantees that imported grain can never appear inside the home market at a price below the fixed threshold price, regardless of how much cheaper it actually is than grain produced by the farmers of the home country. The protectionist policy gave rise to criticism on social as well as wider economic grounds from the end of the war onwards. The critique by David Ricardo (1772-1823), in which he formulated his theory on economic rent, was to become famous.

One may wonder why the landowners still held the upper hand in the formulation of economic policy as late as the end of the 1820s when, already about 1800, half of the British population lived in towns. However, elections to Parliament were based on an outdated division of constituencies. Some of the new, industrial centres had no representation at all, while small villages with few inhabitants, so called Rotten Borrows, still sent representatives.[7] It was not until 1832, after the July Revolution of 1830 in France and the accompanying upheaval, that parliamentary reform took place and growing British industry strengthened its political position. This, however, belongs to the next Chapter.

7.2. Belgium and France

As far as early industrialization is concerned, there are several similarities between Belgium and Northern France. In the border areas between Belgium, France, Luxembourg and Germany, nature has left substantial deposits of coal and iron ore. The first to take advantage of this, on a large scale, did so in what is now called Belgium.

From a political point of view, the period 1750-1830 was a very changeable period for *the Southern Netherlands*. First, it was a part of the Habsburg Empire (Austria). Then as a result of the French revolutionary wars, it formed part of France and, from 1815 to 1830, an invo-

---

7. Rapidly growing industrial towns like Birmingham did not send representatives to Westminster, while non-existent towns like Dunwich, submerged beneath the North Sea, still sent one!

luntary part of a new kingdom born as result of the Congress of Vienna, the United Netherlands. Finally from 1830, after an uprising and a civil war, it was established as an independent kingdom. Within forty years, the population comprised peoples from four different nations, all living within the same space, which must be close to a world record.

Since the late 1500s, the economic centre of the Netherlands had been situated in the northern part centred on Amsterdam. The beginning of modern industrialization meant a change in all that. The Austrian Netherlands – as opposed to their neighbours to the north – had access to deposits of coal and iron ore and, therefore, the chances of starting an iron industry. Furthermore, in Flanders there was a traditional, highly developed textile industry, ready to copy the latest innovations of British industry. Consequently, the area had every chance of accelerating its economic development by closely following the example from across the Channel. The decision taken at the Congress of Vienna to unite the southern and the northern provinces of the Netherlands came exactly at the time when the development of the southern part of the new, united nation was gaining speed.

Even before the French Revolution, the reform of the textile industry in Flanders and Northern France was underway. As in Britain, wool had to give way to cotton, and growth mainly took the form of a rapid increase in the production of cotton goods. In spite of French attempts to speed this up, as part of the Continental System, this development was in fact slowed down due to a shortage of raw cotton; a result of the British blockade. The years of war and blockade, however, gave rise to a growing demand for home produced goods. This was especially felt by the textile and iron industries as suppliers to the French army.

All in all, the period up to 1815 seems to have had positive effects on the development of the economy of what was to become Belgium. An iron industry based on equipment and know-how smuggled out of Great Britain arose with astonishing speed. In the 1820s, this was followed by a radical transition introducing the use of coke, puddling and new blast furnaces in the production of iron. At the time of independence, Belgium was, by far, the leading continental iron producer.

For *France*, the period from 1750 to 1830 was characterized to an outstanding degree by war, unrest and a corresponding strain on the economy. The Seven Years' War (1756-63) and the Revolutionary and

Napoleonic Wars (1792-1815) had, in total, covered thirty-one years, or two fifths, of this period. To this can be added the involvement of France in the American War of Independence (1775-83). In spite of the latter's outcome, the overall result was a reinforcement of the British position as a colonial power and "ruler of the waves" and, from 1815, a leading player in the balance-of-power politics on the European continent.[8]

Section 2 described how influential circles, the Physiocrats, from the 1750s onwards, tried to carry out reforms of the French economy, especially, its agriculture. One has to ask how could it be that, despite the prominence of their advocates, these initiatives did not lead to the desired results, and why they did not stop developments leading to the Revolution of 1789? The usual answer is that the financial position of the state was beyond repair, partly due to the expenses related to the support of the North American colonies during their war of liberation. This, combined with centuries old tax privileges, made it impossible to carry through the necessary reforms. When the National Assembly was finally called in 1789, it was simply too late to carry through the required reforms within the existing social structure.

The Revolution did have a permanent effect on the French economy through the abolition of a number of internal trade restrictions. Since the late 1600s, initiatives had been taken to create a common French tariff area, but so far without the desired results. In this respect, the Revolution meant substantial change; already in 1790, the National Assembly abolished all such internal levies and tolls and contributed towards strengthening the unity of the French economy.[9] Furthermore, the dirigiste system of Colbert was confirmed and strengthened by the regime of Napoleon.

The years of war and blockade had offered the French iron and textiles industries favourable sales conditions that could not last in time of peace. When, after the war, iron exports from Britain and Sweden started up, this soon gave rise to requests for protection. The demand for protection spread to other trades and within a few years France had established a system of protection shielding the textile and iron industries as well as agriculture. A general principle of French customs pol-

---

8. As result of the Seven Years' War, France had to give up its possessions in Canada and India. Napoleon sold the remaining French possessions in North America to the USA in the Missouri deal and, at the Congress of Vienna, Britain obtained the southern tip of Africa, including the Cape of Good Hope, from the Dutch.
9. P. Ashley (1920, 269).

icy explicitly stated that protection of one part of the economy was not to be at the expense of the other parts. This all sounds fine, but does not really withstand close examination. An important aspect of customs policy is to influence the allocation of resources in society, normally to promote or maintain the use of labour and capital in trades subjected to increasing competition from abroad. The "no influence" principle, mentioned above, was put forward in a report in 1828, and since then has been part of the explanation for the high French tariffs.

The Revolution meant extensive confiscations of the property of the Church and of the nobility. The rules of inheritance already before the Revolution had aimed at leaving equal shares to the heirs. This idea of equality was further emphasized, resulting in a steady reduction in the average size of French farms. The impact of this on the structure of the French economy was twofold: it kept a relatively large part of the population occupied in small-scale farming and delayed the process of industrialization by keeping a relatively large part of the new generations in the countryside.

7.3. Germany

The change in the trade routes during the 1500s, followed by the Thirty Years' War (1618-48), left most of the area of present-day Germany in a state of economic isolation. The years from 1750 to 1830 did not see substantial changes. Two obstacles barring Germany from playing an active part in the economic life of Western Europe still existed. There existed a division of the area into a great number of economic entities, separated by taxes, tolls and duties, and, on top of this, the absence of a coherent, internal transport system.

The French Revolution and the Napoleonic Wars aroused national feeling which, in the long run, resulted in the creation of the German nation. However, the result of the Congress of Vienna and the peace agreement in 1815, conspired to keep the German area divided in such a way that the Germans would serve as a counterbalance to France, but could not be a menace to the European balance of power.[10] In 1806, the Habsburgs had given up the title of Emperors of the Holy Roman Empire. Part of the explanation of why they did not resume the title after the war was that it was impossible to reach agreement on whether the

---

10. H. Kissinger (1994, 80f)

Fig. 7: The Congress of Vienna, 1815. The ministers of foreign affairs and representatives of the eight signatories to the Peace of Paris. The print corresponds to present-day "family photos" at the EU summits. A central figure seated in the middle of the picture looking to the left is lord Castlereagh, British Foreign Secretary. Standing in front of him in elegant white knee-breeches is Prince Metternich of Austria. Seated two places from the right is the French chief negotiator, Prince Talleyrand. The Swedish representative, Count von Löwenhielm stands fourth from the left. Denmark is not present in the picture – being one of the countries that had to pay the bill for being on the loosing side by ceding Norway to a Swedish-Norwegian union.

title and the crown should go to Vienna or Berlin, to the dual monarchy of Austria-Hungary or to the kingdom of Prussia.

As will be imagined, early industrialization left the German area unaffected. German iron production was still based on small and scattered iron works using charcoal, of which there was an ample supply. However, steps were taken already in the late 1700s that pointed towards a modernization of society. The personal rights of the peasantry were improved by law and educational reforms were carried out aimed at improving the education level of the general public.

Not least in Prussia, with its military tradition of the 1700s, the defeats in the Napoleonic Wars gave rise to reflection. Since the Middle Ages, great estates had dominated agriculture in the eastern parts of the kingdom. Here, the conditions of the farmers had developed in ways that came close to serfdom. With a view to changing this, reforms were enacted that granted increased personal freedom, including the right of peasants to leave the estates. However, these reforms were not accompanied by economic reforms enabling the peasants to establish themselves on their own farms, so the impact on the agricultural structure was limited. Later in the 1800s, when German industrialization got under way, the freedom of movement meant an increased supply of labour for the towns and growing industrial areas.

Another set of reforms concerned the level of education of the general public. Here too, Prussia holds a position as a pioneer among the German states. This tradition dates back to the second half of the 1700s, and was initially motivated by the wish that future soldiers and non-commissioned officers should be able to read and write. This was backed by the institution of a primary school system, supervised by the government. Another part of the programme was the establishment of technical universities. So, both at a basic and more advanced level, steps were taken that would soon serve to assist Germany in developing into a modern industrial society.

There were, however, still some essential difficulties to overcome. Here the 1830s saw some important steps forward.

7.4. The Scandinavian countries.
The wars, the political upheavals and the changing climate of the international economy, all had their clear impact on the economy of the Scandinavian countries throughout the years 1750-1830. However, early industrialization only had a minor direct influence on the three countries. As to internal relations between the three countries, the Napoleonic Wars and the ensuing peace meant the fulfilment of an old Swedish wish: the dissolution of the Danish-Norwegian union and its replacement by a Swedish-Norwegian union.[11]

The period from 1750 to the early 1800s – more precisely, to 1807, and the strengthening of the Continental Blockade – have gone down in the economic history of the neutral, seafaring countries as a time of flourishing overseas trade. Among the countries making the most of this situation were Denmark and Norway; which meant that these two

---

11. Sweden in 1809 was forced to give up Finland to Russia. At the Congress of Vienna it was confirmed that Russia could keep Finland and Sweden had Norway as compensation.

countries were among those most affected by the end of the favourable conditions for their overseas trade (section 6). The political reaction, after the years of revolution and wars seems to have been stronger in Denmark than in the rest of Scandinavia. Both Norway and Sweden saw the beginning of a constitutional monarchy through public representation in the government of the country, including public finances. Similar developments did not take place in Denmark until the 1830s, and then only with great wariness. Finland entered a period of a hundred years of Russian absolutism.

The effects of an economic slump in the first half of the 1700s had, in all three countries, led to a reinforcement of the mercantilist aspects of economic policy. Colbert and Colbertism had found keen pupils in the Scandinavian countries. Then, in the second half of the 1700s came a period of growth in trade of which Denmark and Norway took particular advantage.

The economies of Denmark and Norway already had in those days some of the characteristics of what are now called "small, open economies".[12] This explains that, first, the ideas of the Physiocrats, and then, the ideas of the liberal thinkers were received with positive interest at an early point in time. Examples of this include the publication of Danish-Norwegian Economic Magazine (1755-64) advocating reforms, especially in agriculture. A translation of Adam Smith's "Wealth of Nations" into Danish/Norwegian[13] was published as early as 1779 and a start made to liberalizing Danish foreign trade from the 1780s, culminating in a liberal Danish-Norwegian tariff reform of 1797.

A major event in Denmark in the 1750-1830 period was the far-reaching structural reforms of agriculture. Danish agriculture was, traditionally, a mix of Western and Eastern European style agriculture. This meant that part of cultivation took place on the "demesne" of the big estates, i.e., the ground and fields under the direct control of the manor, and the other part took place on the soil of tenant farms, which were normally cultivated on a cooperative basis by the farmers of the village. This meant that most peasants lived in villages. At the personal

12. At the peak of the trade boom, about 1800, it is estimated that Norway had an export quota (total exports of goods and services expressed as a percentage of total production) as high as 30 per cent. Ståle Dyrvik et al. (1979, 248).
13. The translation was made by two young Norwegians, the sons of a merchant, while staying in London. In its written form, the Norwegian language in those days was very close to Danish.

level there were substantial restrictions placed on individuals. Within wide age brackets, they were not allowed to leave the estates where they were born without the consent of the landowner.

During the second half of the 1700s in Denmark, as elsewhere, a deepening ecological crisis occurred. One of the signs of this was that tenant farmers had to work for an increasing number of days on the demesne. In the 1780s, serious steps were taken to "modernize" Danish agriculture as stated above. For many years it was held that this took place due to the "good will" of leading estate owners supported by the Prince Regent (Frederik VI).[14] Modern research has concluded that the reforms corresponded with the interests of the landowners. As the workforce grew, labour was getting more abundant. All in all, a cheaper way of having the demesne cultivated was to make use of hired labour and it was more profitable to have the tenants pay cash for the land at their disposition. Anyway, a number of reforms took place in the late 1700s. The number of days worked by the tenants on the demesne was fixed and a future reduction in that number was foreseen. The practice of collective farming was superseded by the splitting up and redistribution of the common fields of the villages so each farm, in principle, now had its fields grouped together. Shortly after the reforms were decided on, many farmers moved out of the villages to be closer to their fields. As will be seen, the reforms were based on the idea that the individual farmer should be given more responsibility in order to increase the overall efficiency of agriculture. So, in this respect, it corresponded to the ideas of liberalism as well. At the personal level, the farmers were given the freedom to leave their farms.

The reforms were to take place over a period of time. It should be added that the reforms continued a tradition in Danish agricultural policies, which favoured medium-sized farms, that is, farms of 20 to 40 hectares or 70 to 100 acres. Until the end of the 1960s, most Danish arable land was still cultivated by farms of this size. That the reforms concentrated on this type of farm meant that smallholders were not affected by the reforms. There were still a substantial number of people occupied in farming, who lived in houses, or rather, shacks, with no, or very little, ground attached. This group was, more or less, forgotten by the reformers and it was not until the end of 1800s that legislation was

14. King Christian VII (*1766-1807*) was insane for almost forty years and totally unable to participate in ruling the country.

passed in order to assist them. All this has been explained in some detail, since it is widely held that the efficiency of Danish farming, in the 1900s is due to the openness which dates back to the reforms of the 1700s.

The Danish-Norwegian tariff reform of 1797 was a break with more than two centuries of mercantilism. The reform meant the abolition of a vast number of quantitative restrictions, mainly in the form of import prohibitions. Furthermore, it meant the reduction of some, almost prohibitive, customs duties that had been circumvented by smuggling.

The peace of Kiel in 1814 between Denmark and Sweden, followed by the Congress of Vienna, fulfilled, as mentioned earlier, the old Swedish wish to create a Swedish-Norwegian union. It was against the wishes of the Norwegians who, for a short time in 1814, hoped and fought for their political freedom. This meant the end of their existing tariff union with Denmark and the beginning of a tariff union with Sweden. For Norwegian industry, this must have meant a change for the worse; it was, undoubtedly, more difficult to build up Norwegian industry in direct competition with that of Sweden. A problem for the trades and industries of Norway was the fact that they ran the risk of clashing with the interests of Swedish business where the Swedes would hold the upper hand. It was actually problems of this sort, plus wider national interests, that caused the final break between the two countries shortly after 1900.

For the three Scandinavian countries, the years after 1815 meant a period of deflation. In this, they did not differ from other countries in Western Europe. It is, however, likely that the setback was more felt; in Denmark and Norway because of the loss of income in international shipping and commerce, in Sweden due to falling income from the export of timber and iron.

7.5. The USA

The economy of the USA had still not reached such levels of strength and size that would allow it to exert a major influence on the economy of Western Europe. The shipping of bulk cargo was still too expensive to make American grain a threat to European farmers. The opening in the years 1817-25 of a system of canals, via the Hudson River to the Great Lakes, meant a drop in transport costs. But the freight rates across the Atlantic were still too high. Important American exports were tobacco and cotton from the South, timber and salted fish from the North. These goods could sustain the costs of freight, and to this must be added substantial shipping activity. As will be remembered, part of the explanation behind the war of liberation from Great Britain, was a wish to escape British mercantilist policy in order to enable American merchants to trade wherever and with whomsoever they wished.

As with the shipping of other neutral countries, American shipping had the opportunity to generate high incomes during periods of war. The situation of the USA during the Franco-British blockades was reminiscent, in this respect, of that of Denmark and Norway. Britain reserved the right to search American ships for contraband, and tensions were further increased and American resistance galvanized, by the British contention that sailors born in the former colonies before 1784, the year of the end of the War of Independence, were British subjects. As such, they could be obliged to serve in the Royal Navy.[15] The crisis culminated in 1814 when a British expeditionary corps occupied Washington DC and burned down the official buildings of the town, including Capitol Hill and the White House.

The political life of the young, independent federation of former colonies in those years was preoccupied by problems similar to those of the member countries of the European Communities two hundred years later. The American constitution was rather vague on the distribution of powers between the federal authorities in Washington DC and local authorities in the member states. There were spokesmen for strong, centralized power, mainly found among the merchants in the coastal towns to the north, as well as spokesmen for leaving power at the level of the individual state, mainly found among the farmers and the greater landowners to the west and to the south. One problem, dividing the two wings, was whether there should be a national or central bank. The Federalists, on the whole, were in favour, the Confederalists against. The result was that a First National Bank (1791-1811) was followed by a Second National Bank (1816-36), after which more than 75 years elapsed before the present Federal Reserve System was created in 1913, partly as a reaction to repeated financial crises at the turn of the century.

---

15. When American ships were stopped and searched, adult American crew-members were forced to leave their ship and enrol in the Royal Navy.

Chapter 6

Industry begins to spread
1830-75

The above heading takes two factors into account: first, that industrial methods of production were applied to new product areas and, second, that they spread in geographical extent on the European continent and in North America. Economic growth was especially strong in Germany and the USA in the latter part of this period.

In terms of *technology*, both the opening and the close of this period were characterized by *transport revolutions*. The first of these took place on land in the form of railway construction; the second, at sea with the transition from ships built of wood to those built of iron or steel. This allowed the construction of merchant ships of far greater carrying capacity, which improved the economics of carrying bulk cargoes. Technologically, the close of the period also witnessed the beginning of the electrical industry.

Politically speaking, the period opened with the revolutionary currents of the July Revolution of 1830 in France and ended with the newly established German Empire. This, after a series of rapid and victorious wars against Denmark, Austria and France, assumed its position as the leading continental power as well as that of the coming challenger to British supremacy. At the same time, the 1871 Communard uprising in Paris was a dramatic indicator of the arrival of the labour movement on the Western European political stage.

Economically speaking, the period was marked by the breakthrough and ever-increasing strength of liberal economic opinions. In 1834, the German Zollverein was set up with Prussia as its main driving force. In 1839, the Anti-Corn-Law League was founded in England whose aim was to bring about free trade. By the close of this period, most European countries had adopted the gold standard and the free movement of capital. At the same time, however, falling farm prices were threatening the established system of tariff agreements. The period after the middle of the nineteenth century may best be characterized as that of Laissez-Faire.

1. Technical development

Section 4 of Chapter 5 discussed the nature of the dynamic process, which was initiated with early industrialization. What was new in terms of development was the increased interplay between *process*-innovations on the one hand and *product*-innovations on the other. It goes without saying that the enigmatic and unpredictable interaction between process and product innovation has a greater opportunity to unfold, the more products there are in existence. The growth of the chemical industry, in particular, speeded up this development.

1.1. Transport and communications

The significance of transport in general, particularly that of railways, on the economy is well expressed by the statement that they produced both a forward and backward effect. What was meant by the *forward* effect was that the reduction of transport costs had widespread consequences in broadening markets. Large-scale operations could thus be embarked upon in many more areas and on a much greater scale than previously. The *backward* effect meant that the production of the railway rolling stock and railway construction, in itself, led to the development of new products, as well as playing a part in the development of a machine tool industry that would subsequently be available for other spheres of industrial endeavour. Another derivative effect was that the large scale of the construction work created a need for new methods of finance. The solution was a rapid spread of the share issuing, limited company.

Two inventions were necessary before commercially run *railways* could be established. One was a reliable high-pressure steam engine where the weight and size of the locomotive could be kept down relative to the power produced. The other was for rails that could take the weight of a locomotive and its train of heavily laden trucks. The first steam train came into service in 1825, in a coal mining area of North-eastern England, using the already existing rail track linking Stockton and Darlington, while the first line to be specifically built for steam locomotion was opened in 1830 between Liverpool and Manchester.

The opening of the Liverpool and Manchester Railway was accompanied by a remarkable and tragic event, namely, the first railway fatality. William Huskisson (1770-1830), the President of the Board of Trade and a fervent advocate of British industrial development, was knocked down and killed by a locomotive.

The need to provide a coherent service, without having to constantly load and unload goods trains, meant the introduction of a standard track gauge and rolling stock dimensions. As British railway contractors pioneered the building of railways on the Continent - as well as further afield, in the USA, for instance - the development of railways was influenced by British standards. Common brake and coupling systems made it possible from very early on for rolling stock to cross Western European borders. This was a major reason for the increase in transnational trade from the mid-nineteenth century onwards.

After the July Revolution of 1830, Belgium was separated from the Netherlands and became an independent nation. A complete plan for a Belgian railway system was ready that very same year. One of the reasons for Belgium being the first country with a coherent railway network was its great similarity to Britain: a high population density along with natural advantages, which favoured rapid industrial development, to which could be added the country's modest geographical extent.

France already by the 1840s, with its tradition of centralized government, had a railway plan whereby Paris constituted the hub from which spokes radiated all over the country. It took, however, about twenty years for it to become reality. Its effects can still be felt to this day in that it is still hard to travel across the system of spokes - it is usually simpler to travel via Paris. Although there was extensive railway building on the continent during the 1840s, it was only in the 1850s that railways could be deemed to have had their full effect in a more comprehensive transport transformation.

As the Zollverein served to unify the economy of Germany, so did the railways, partly due to competition between individual German states. All in all the railway meant a leading step forward in the development of "a German economy". As an example of a "late starter" can be mentioned Sweden, starting building railways in the mid-1850s. Although attempts had been made in the 1840s to attract foreign capital for a "Swedish railway company", these had been fruitless. It was only when the state took an active interest in the creation of a railway network that things begin to happen. In the 25 years after 1855, almost 6,000 kilometres of railway were built.

While the first railways were being built, there was also extension and improvement of transport along the *waterways* of Europe. The new element here was the steamship, which could now sail up and down rivers and canals with barges in tow. This was to be the main use of the steamship for freight for many years to come. On the high seas, only the transport of passengers and mail could sustain the high cost of steamship operation. Only when the price of manufacturing iron plate fell, was it possible to build larger, ocean-going vessels suitable for the freight of bulk cargoes across the oceans.

Navigation on the waterways of Europe had traditionally been subject to tolls and dues. The background for this was that rivers and straits were considered to be the property of the local rulers and their use, a legitimate object of taxation. Tolls for passage had thus been collected on the Danish Sound since the 1420s. By the mid-nineteenth century, the pressure to abolish these obstacles to free navigation was rising, and in the early 1850s, the USA took the lead in attempts to abolish the Sound tolls. This eventually came about as a result of an international agreement in 1857, where Denmark obtained substantial compensation in the form of a lump sum. Another contemporary example of this trend towards free navigation is provided by the Dutch removal of restrictions on the Scheldt, which had hindered navigation to Antwerp. The new possibilities in transportation soon had a significant impact on the way *postal services* were organized. Closer economic links increased the need for communication. At the same time, the new means of transport ensured faster and safer delivery of letters. Payment, however, remained a problem, because the payment systems were confusing and the division of the cost between sender and receiver was complicated. This difficulty was eventually resolved with the appearance in 1840, of the young Queen Victoria (*1837-1901*) in profile on a standardized, printed receipt for prepaid postage, the "penny black". Other countries rapidly followed suit in introducing the use of stamps.

In 1820, Hans Christian Ørsted (1778-1860) "discovered" electromagnetism. From then on the invention of the electric *telegraph* was only a matter of time. It was the American, Samuel Morse (1791-

1872), who was to translate the idea into practical reality. Initially he had trouble raising the necessary funds from private finance sources to bring his idea to fruition. However, in 1843, Congress decided to support him to the tune of 30,000 dollars for a telegraph link between Washington DC., and Baltimore, a distance of about 50 kilometres. Barely ten years later, telegraph wires in the USA alone stretched over a total distance of 20,000 kilometres. As early as 1851, a telegraph cable had been laid across the English Channel and, as an indicator of the strong contemporary faith in technical progress, attempts were made in the mid-1850s to lay a cable across the Atlantic. The technical problems were, however, considerable and a reliable connection was achieved only in 1866. As part of the attempts to reduce the high installation costs of telegraph connections, work was carried out to find out how to transmit several signals simultaneously through the same cable connections. A young American, Graham Bell (1847-1922) decided to tackle the problem and in 1875, by chance, he discovered that it was possible to convey sound by electric cable. Thus the telephone was born, a patent applied for the next year and the inventor demonstrated his telephone at one of the world exhibitions of the day.

1.2. The iron and machine industry

Progress in the mid-nineteenth century led to a rapid rise in the demand for iron and steel products. Besides rails, there was a call for all kinds of pipes and tubes for plumbing, water and gas supply, drainage and sewers for the rapidly growing urban populations. On the one hand, this gave rise to a need for greater productive capacity while, on the other, high and remunerative prices kept those alive who were using older production methods. This double effect is assumed to have been one of the reasons why the German iron industry, a late starter, but with all the latest technology, achieved efficiency levels well beyond those of the original producer nations.

An important innovation was the development of a new, cheaper way of producing steel. Steel had, hitherto, been five times as expensive as wrought iron, but in 1856, an Englishman, Henry Bessemer (1813-98), motivated by the sharp rise in the demand for steel during the Crimean War, introduced a new method for the purification of molten steel. The consequences of this were, again, great and unpredictable and included the new types of ship mentioned earlier as well as the construction of steel frames for skyscrapers, though they had to wait for the lift to really get off the ground.

The German, Werner Siemens, (1816-92) built a dynamo in 1856 to replace the heavy batteries that were otherwise necessary for operating a telegraph. The Prussian wars of the 1860s gave rise to a strong demand for telegraphic equipment. In order to meet this demand, Siemens built an improved version of his dynamo in 1866. This, in effect, cleared the way for the construction of both the electric generator and electric motor, and is yet another example of the interaction between new processes and new products where "the new leads to the new".

The USA took the lead in the mid-nineteenth century in the production of light industrial products such as watches, clocks, locks, sewing machines and handguns. This group of items and their like were to be subsequently called consumer durables. The American Civil War (1861-65) was to accelerate this process, especially in the North. To start with, there was a great demand for equipment such as weapons, boots, uniforms and so on for the conscripts. The modern-day clothing and footwear industry can trace their origins back to these events. A consequence of the Civil War, with its mass recruitment to the armies, was the manufacture of agricultural machinery. So as to ease the workload at harvest time in the cereal-growing northern states, much use was made of the mechanical reaper equipped with a rotating canvas sail. Shortly after the end of the Civil War, the reaper and binder was developed. New machines were also produced for ploughing and sowing, among the first of which was the mechanical seed drill. The demand for agricultural machinery was so great that it formed the basis of the strong and independent expansion of the American machine industry.

Another effect of rapid agricultural expansion was the growth of the meat industry, which was accompanied by a corresponding development of refrigerators. The inspiration for the mass-production techniques, yet to come, can be traced back to the large abattoirs. The cattle walked up ramps to the top floor of the slaughterhouse where the slaughter proper took place. The carcasses were then hung up on hooks that by means of ropes, pulleys and the force of gravity conveyed them down through the abattoir where they were cut up and the meat was finally packed. Subsequently, Henry Ford was to reverse this "disassembly line", starting with the component parts and ending with the whole.

1.3. The chemical industry

The chemical industry came into existence as a result of process innovation. Naturally occurring substances became the subject of such widespread demand that attempts were made to produce them synthetically.

The growing production of cotton cloth increased the demand for bleaching agents and dyes. Bleaching had hitherto taken place by soaking in buttermilk, or, by washing in bleaching ponds with subsequent drying in the sun. This process was not only time consuming and labour intensive but also required plenty of space. It was possible to accelerate it by using soda lye and chlorine. To meet this growing demand, a method of producing soda was invented at the end of the eighteenth century. Although the invention was French, the demand for it was in England and it was there that production methods were developed during the first half of the nineteenth century.

The manufacture of synthetic dyes was also a result of cross-border cooperation. A German chemist, employed in England in the 1850s, was responsible for the development of production methods for the synthetic manufacture of dyes. The basic ingredient was tar oil, a by-product of gas production, and the result was aniline dyes. These products were the outcome of systematic laboratory experimentation and they thus represent the direct application of natural science and research to applied technology. One might have reasonably expected Great Britain to become the leading producer of synthetic dyes, but this was not to be. Instead it was Germany where chemists were trained in a systematic fashion and the necessary connection between scientific research and business communities was forged. The Bayer Company was founded in 1861 with a view to the production of aniline dyes. BASF (Badische Anilin & Soda Fabrik) started up production that very same year and Hoechst followed suit the year after. Within the space of a few years, Germany had thus gained a solid lead in the development of a chemical industry.

German research efforts were also to play a decisive role in the manufacture of artificial fertilizers. The starting point here was the analysis of plants' consumption of nutrients, and fundamental knowledge was generated by the self-same circles, which had occupied themselves with the synthesis of plant dyes. On the one hand, an awareness arose that plant growth could be promoted by other types than animal fertilizers, while on the other, it was realized that such fertilizers could be produced by synthetic means; among others as a by-product of metal production.

In this way two new areas of industrial production, chemical dyes and chemical fertilizers, saw the light of day and whose development potential was very considerable. The fledgling chemical industry had great problems getting rid of its waste products so the German chemical industry was, in the main, sited along the banks of the Rhine. The factories could take all the water they needed from the river and they could pour back into it the waste water after use, at no cost whatsoever. Another way of getting rid of waste products was by further refining, and this area was to afford entirely new avenues of cooperation between scientific and commercial production. If waste products could be turned into a further source of income, instead of being simply a burden due to their disposal costs, they could significantly enhance the profitability and development potential of companies. The German chemical industry displayed its great superiority through its proficiency in such organized developmental work.

1.4. *The organized transmission of skills and technology*

Training to become an engineer was originally an activity with a military purpose, usually, the construction of fortifications. Those trained in such arts could, however, also apply their knowledge and skills for civilian purposes such as the construction of roads or canals. Keeping pace with a growing demand, a new type of engineer appeared alongside the military engineer, namely, the civil engineer whose training was aimed at practical applications, but rested on a knowledge of natural science at a high level.

The "École des Ponts et Chaussées", founded in Paris in 1747, was the first polytechnic institute of learning and was supplemented by the École Polytechnique in 1794. The training of engineers continued within a military framework, but at the beginning of the nineteenth century many civilian polytechnic institutes were established. As part of a wider Prussian industrial policy, a German training course in civil engineering was set up in 1821.[1] Hans Christian Ørsted was the first head of the Copenhagen Polytechnic Institute when it was established in 1829.

There still was, however, an institutional divide between research and application, and it was in precisely this area, that the emerging

---

1.   S. Pollard (1974, 110).

German chemical industry was to make substantial contributions. In early nineteenth century Germany, chemistry as a school subject had been extended to comprise independent laboratory experiments carried out by the students themselves. This led - as something entirely new - to the training of undergraduates at German universities and polytechnics who were used to carrying out chemical experiments and analyses on their own. The way was thus clear for them to transfer this method of working to business life. To sum up, it can be said that the training of engineers served a dual purpose; the development of knowledge and the transmission and application of that knowledge. The same can be said of other specialist courses of training that evolved in the nineteenth century, in agronomy and pharmacy, for instance.

The frequent international exhibitions or *"world exhibitions"* of the time provided another form of education in skills.

The first of these was the Great Exhibition of 1851 in London's Hy-

Fig. 8: The Great Exhibition, London 1851. The building, designed by a former gardener Joseph Paxton (1801-65), who had designed the hot houses of some great estates, was innovatory in its own right. Its use of steel and glass pointed towards new construction methods. The lavish use of flowers, palms and other ornamentation was subsequently known as the Victorian style.

de Park where the actual exhibition building was a sensation in its own right. In the 1840s, a new type of greenhouse of cast iron and glass was built for some country mansions. It was decided to erect the exhibition building - the Crystal Palace - according to the same principles and so the civil engineer entered into the hitherto reserved domain of the architect with this radically new construction method. The Great Exhibition was a success where all the latest technical achievements could be seen and admired, and where production and exploitation licenses could be acquired after paying the appropriate fee. Other world exhibitions followed at a brisk pace: New York in 1853, Paris in 1855, London again in 1862 and so on. And it was not only contemporary "hi-tech" that enjoyed success: at the 1862 exhibition, a sack made of jute was on display, and though this commodity had been unknown in Europe before then, in no time at all it became the basis of a rapidly growing jute sack industry.

The frequent international exhibitions of the latter half of the nineteenth century should be seen as an expression of internationalization. With the growth in the number of industrial products, a basis was laid for increased international specialization and thus for new areas of international economic relations. In other words, there was a sharp rise in international professional contacts throughout this period. However, the majority of the population did not directly participate in this internationalization. They did not receive more visitors from abroad nor did they travel abroad more often themselves. The exception was those young people who emigrated to the far corners of the earth or went off on shorter or longer journeys as migrant workers. The encounter with the outside world was, for most people, restricted to the realization that an ever-larger part of their income depended on sales abroad and that they used more and more of their income to buy foreign goods.

2. Monetary and financial affairs

2.1. Improvement of the monetary system
The modern economic system is often described as a circular flow consisting of a flow of goods and services travelling in one direction while a flow of payments or money travels in the opposite direction constituting the monetary flow.

The transport revolutions of the nineteenth century affected the circulation of goods, which thanks to falling costs became far more widespread as restrictions either disappeared or were much reduced in effect. In the meantime, there were, however, practical problems affecting the functioning of monetary circulation. Due to modern-day communication systems and rapid access to information, we tend to overlook some of the problems that could arise under less technically advanced circumstances. Three preconditions for easing transactions are listed as follows:

a. the use of a commonly acceptable means of payment;

b. a high degree of centralization in the transfer of payments, which would increase the possibility for clearing convergent flows of payment and limit the need for the actual physical transfer of means of payment;

c. security concerning the capacity of the parties to an agreement to honour their obligations, i.e., to deliver the goods on the one hand, and to be able to effect payment as agreed, on the other.

These preconditions apply to trade within a given country's borders as well as to international trade. They do not specifically apply to the trade of industrial society. The trade centres of the Middle Ages had also had to find solutions to these problems, though the expansion of trade as a result of industrialization must have made the need for appropriate solutions more pressing and acutely felt. In this instance, not only did economies of scale make Great Britain the leading industrial nation, they also made her the world's premier banking nation.

The English currency unit, the pound sterling, was already linked despite its name to a specific gold value from 1815 onwards. The English emphasized the importance of a policy that strengthened belief in the stability of the pound.

As early as 1717, Sir Isaac Newton in his capacity as director of the Bank of England had fixed the price of gold at £3 17s 10d per ounce. That price remained the same until September 1931,[2] except for suspension during the Napoleonic Wars and World War I. When the pre-

2.   C. P. Kindleberger (1990, 261).

cious metal content of English coinage is taken into account, it has to be said that the pound sterling enjoyed a unique degree of stability over very long periods of time. A vital precondition was thus met which ensured that foreign banks, stockbrokers, etc., would carry out their transactions through British banks.

To this could be added that British overseas trade underwent relatively fast growth during the first half of the nineteenth century so that Great Britain's own overseas trade prompted the establishment of close banking ties with those countries with whom she was engaged in trade. Two advantages accrued from this situation for British banks, both of which were marked by economies of scale. The first was the greater possibility of settling accounts by means of clearing, while the other was use of information about the financial solidity and the business practices of companies and foreign banks.

Slow transport and poor communications, in the first half of the nineteenth century, meant that there was great uncertainty about whether transactions were feasible or not. Routines had to be established which assured producers that they would get their due payment once they had sent the goods. Conversely, the purchasers had to be sure of the receipt of said goods once they had paid. However, with transport times, sometimes of several months for goods and mail, and all dependent on winds and weather, there was, of necessity, a long period while both payment and goods were on their way. Part of the solution to this problem lay in the introduction of documentary credit whereby both the seller's and customer's local banks agreed to put up a caution for their respective clients, and so effectively guaranteeing payment. This is an instance of transfer of risk where banks, for a suitable sum, place their ability to evaluate creditworthiness at the disposal of their customers. In addition to this, a bank might extend credit by means of a discount on bills of exchange or other means. The evaluation of risk pertaining to banking requires an especially dense information network and paves the way for large-scale operations in the banking world. With the invention of the steamship and the electric telegraph, some of these costs and problems of information were reduced. The upshot was that the English banking system not only became the financial centre for the handling of domestic international payments, but also for those of other countries. Furthermore, as trade over great distances involved risks in transportation, it was logical that a tradition of brokering international insurance should arise in London. Thus a business complex appeared in Great Britain whose services not only catered for British overseas trade requirements, but for those of other countries as well.

The international predominance of British banking has been explained by economic factors, among them economies of scale. However, to this a political explanation can be added which is the nation's position as the world's leading military and naval power. Whatever could be labelled as a "political liability" in connection with overseas ventures was invariably reduced in risk by British political and military strength. The American economist, C.P. Kindleberger, has pointed out, along with other observations of this kind, that Venice's period as a centre of banking coincided with Venetian naval supremacy. Afterwards, in accordance with political events, both roles devolved to the Netherlands who, in turn, relinquished them to the British. Whereupon, after much hesitation the rôles were assumed by the USA; as Kindleberger puts it, under an atomic umbrella.[3]

2.2. The money supply

A problem of an altogether different nature is posed by the question of the adequacy of the means of payment, or, the total sum of available money. Couched in modern terms, the aim must be to ensure that there is a flexible supply of money and, at the same time, stable financial institutions.

It has to be made clear from the outset that the policy being pursued was not a monetary policy in the modern sense, nor was there interaction between monetary and fiscal policies. What policy there was consisted mainly in avoiding the repetition of past mistakes, which included the rapid expansion of public expenditure and its financing by printing money. In 1797, Britain had suspended Sterling's gold convertibility and did not wish to have to repeat the experience. Consequently, after the Napoleonic Wars ended, Great Britain pursued deflationary policies.

There were, during this period, three schools of thought on the question of money supply, which meant, in this context, the extent of the issue of banknotes. The differences concerned the degree of elasticity in the creation of money, including the significance of foreign trade for the money supply. As mentioned above, the background to this was

3.   C. P. Kindleberger (1990, 260).

the frightening experience associated with the expansion of the money supply during the Napoleonic Wars. The three schools of thought, listed below in order of increasing the recommended flexibility of money creation, were as follows:

a. the State sets an absolute ceiling on the circulation of notes. This ceiling is not affected by fluctuations in the level of bullion reserves. This system was operated by France and must be regarded as centralistic in that it presupposes that the state designates a fixed upper limit for notes in circulation. This system does not prepare the way towards the same degree of depoliticization of monetary policy as the other two which, in part at least, allow the amount of notes in circulation to vary according to the level of precious metal reserves;

b. the amount of notes issued corresponds to the precious metal reserves plus a set figure known as "the quota". Because of this, the system is known as the quota system. The theory behind this system has been called the "currency theory". Its adherents point out that it dampens fluctuations in the amount of money, thus lessening the risk of price fluctuation. The relatively high level of stability in the circulation of banknotes serves to limit speculative movements in the money and capital markets;

c. notes may be issued at a given ratio or quotient to the reserves of precious metal: accordingly this system is known as the quotient system. The theory behind this has been labelled the "banking theory". Adherents argue that this system affords a desirable degree of flexibility in the money supply, which should, therefore, be better able to adapt to fluctuating levels of economic activity.

Couched in more modern terms, this dispute seems to have touched on the question of the "money"-multiplier. Under system a. the multiplier would, in principle, be zero. Under system b. it would be one once the quota had been used, and under system c., possibly over one, depending on the setting of the quotient.

Formally, the quota system prevailed when the Bank of England underwent reform in 1844. However, it was really the quotient system with its elastic money supply that held sway during the latter half of the nineteenth century as a new and growing source of means of payment appeared over and above the circulation of banknotes. This new source was the deposits paid into merchant banks (demand deposits), which could then be used as money on account. This is how a relatively uniform system evolved among Western nations throughout the nineteenth century where the creation of money took place in three layers. The bottom layer consisted of precious metals. Above this, there lay a middle layer of banknotes, and above this, at the top, was a third layer of deposits in merchant banks.

A more advanced version of this set-up would appear for the first time during the period in question, characterized by a clear distinction between the central or national bank and the merchant banks. The modern central bank holds the monopoly of banknote issue; it does not, however, conduct ordinary banking business. Instead, it has become the bank for the state and the commercial banks. In this latter capacity, it has acquired, over time, the rôle of "lender of last resort", which means that a merchant bank can turn to the central bank with the hope of obtaining a loan in order to overcome temporary liquidity problems.

Considering that the English banking system is generally considered to have been the most advanced prior to the World War I, it should be noted that the Bank of England only acquired the role described above at a later stage. From an ultra-liberal standpoint, any banks wanting to set themselves up as note-issuing establishments should be allowed to do so as long as they could fulfil certain requirements concerning liquidity and solidity. During the first half of the nineteenth century, there was thus no monopoly on the issue of banknotes in Britain and the Bank of England conducted ordinary banking business by means of several branches.

The Bank Charter Act of 1844, however, forbade the setting up of any more note-issuing banks. In the USA, the prevailing political dogma, which held sway for over a century, was that no central bank should be established at all,. The upshot was a plethora of banks issuing their own banknotes. It was only in 1913, with the setting up of the Federal Reserve System, that the USA finally acquired what could be considered to be a central bank although, formally, it is still a union of banks – and members of its own staff.

Conditions on the European continent were closer to the later central bank scenario. In Denmark, for instance, the Danish National Bank had a monopoly on note issue from the moment it was established in 1818. It withdrew from ordinary banking in the mid-nineteenth century, that is by ceasing to have any customers other than banks and the State.

As mentioned earlier, the advantage of a monetary system based on precious metal reserves is that it ensures discipline in matters of monetary policy. Two precious metals, gold and silver, have been used, and as the availability of these two metals has fluctuated in relation to each other, so too have their relative market values. Advocates of a less stringent monetary policy have wanted the more abundant metal as the monetary base. Many countries have experienced bimetallism, which is when the values of both gold and silver are reflected in the issue of banknotes at the same time. As is well known, bad coin drives out good, which tends to go out of circulation. Other countries again have changed their currency base at some midway point, with the tendency being towards gold and away from silver in the period around 1870. As mentioned above, Great Britain adopted the gold standard for its currency issue in 1815.

A precious metal monetary standard presupposes in its pure form that: 1) the currency unit is defined as a specific amount of the said precious metal, 2) that the central bank is duty bound to buy and sell the said precious metal at the set price, 3) that it is freely possible to melt down coin and, 4) that the said precious metal can be freely imported into or exported from the country.

Should these conditions be observed, and the individual set prices for each currency upheld, then the system assumes the nature of a regime of fixed exchange rates. In the 1860s, France took the lead in creating a currency union comprising Belgium and Switzerland as well as Italy and Greece for a short period. Because of the make-up of its members, it was known as the "Latin Currency Union". The participants in the German Zollverein had already created a currency union in 1838. After victory over France in 1871, when France agreed to pay Germany a large "indemnity" of five billion francs in gold (and surrender Alsace and most of Lorraine), Germany adopted the gold standard for its currency in 1873. In that same year, Congress resolved that the USA should convert to gold from 1879 onwards. During the 1870s, Denmark, Norway and Sweden established a currency union based on gold, the Scandinavian Currency Union, which lasted for forty years until August 1914.

*Table 6.1: Structure of money supply (USA, UK and France together),
1815, 1872 and 1913.*

Percentage	1815	1872	1913
Total Money Supply	100	100	100
Gold	33	28	10
Silver	34	13	3
Currency and coin	26	32	19
Demand deposits	6	27	68

Source: Robert Triffen reproduced from Fontana 5(2) p.606.

A common characteristic in the development of monetary policy in the late nineteenth century was the further change represented by central banks switching from quantitative regulation of loan options - the rationing of credit through the refusal to offer discounts on bills of exchange for instance - to regulation by means of changes to the interest rates for loans from central banks, corresponding to "the English model". The latter came about through central banks introducing changes to bank rates as a primary tool of monetary policy. This made the money market subject to a higher degree to price adjustments rather than quantitative control, which was well in tune with the ideological currents of the day. The evolution of the composition of the money supply is shown in table 6.1. The growing significance of the deposit account or the cheque at the expense of ready cash is clearly shown by the evolution evident in the "Demand deposits"-entry.

2.3. *Monetary and financial institutions*
It might be useful to start with a reminder of the distinction between circulating capital and fixed capital. Circulating capital consists of assets tied up in raw materials, work-in-progress and stock and credit extended to customers, while fixed capital is tied up in property, plant, transport equipment and so on. When viewed from a financial point of view, the new aspect accompanying industrialization was the increase of the capital share represented by fixed capital, and that it was other capital than land that increased. As fixed capital is tied up over longer periods of time than circulating capital, then, in principle, a new type of financial need had arisen. The question then became within which institutional framework was the new need to be dealt with? In this in-

stance too, the answer - as in the case of the issue of banknotes - was different on each side of the English Channel. On the English side, the merchant banks would, in the main, keep to financing circulating capital, which implied short-term commitment. On the continent, however, banks would participate more directly in the raising of fixed capital and the German Gründerbanks, or investment banks provided a leading example of this tendency.

Because of the bad experiences around 1720 mentioned earlier, the British had displayed a reluctance to allow the establishment of share-issuing companies for almost a century, though when the building of canals gathered pace towards the end of the eighteenth century there was an upturn in the rate of company formation. This was due to the fact that canals were long-term investments with correspondingly modest current return on capital. However, as most of the investments did eventually turn out to be profitable, share-issuing companies greatly increased in number and reputation. When the construction of railways began to get under way after 1830, it seemed logical to use the same form of financing, and after this, the pace of company formation rose dramatically. Although British banks tended to steer clear of long-term projects, they did, however, develop a useful feature for the financing of circulating capital. This was the overdraft, which was appropriate for customers with a fluctuating need for such capital availability.

The pattern of finance comprising the role of banks developed differently on the continent. Some of the explanation may lie in the later industrialization of Europe, in particular in the case of Germany. Starting 50 to 100 years after Great Britain, technological development meant that plants were larger and had become more capital intensive. The technological leap demanded must have been greater in this instance than in the early industrialization of England. Another aspect was that the possibility for self-financing from current profits must have been correspondingly smaller. Briefly put, there was a need for broader absorption of the surplus from savings in order to meet the financing requirements.

During the 1820s and 30s, two investment banks were established in Belgium, which actively promoted the setting up of new industrial enterprises. It was first in the 1830s that their activities became widely significant. Part of the reason for this was the execution of the 1830 plan to build the Belgian railway network. In France, an investment bank, the Crédit Mobilier, was established in 1850, partly inspired by its Belgian predecessor. An important sphere of activity for the bank was participation in railway construction both inside and outside France. Whereas the input of Crédit Mobilier was confined to the actual establishment of a given company, from which it would subsequently withdraw by selling its part of the shares, the German banks went further. They would hold on to their part of the shares in order to participate in the running of the company. Through the membership of the bank directors on several boards of firms, a basis was laid for cooperation and the correspondingly easy road to the formation of cartels in industrial life. If German industry has attained a high degree of concentration, this in no small part is due to the close connection with the banking world.

The leading creditor nations of the day were Great Britain followed by France. Initially, British savings were mainly placed in Western Europe, partly as a result of the British export of railway material and accompanying know-how. The middle of the century saw a change in investment strategy as investment went further overseas including the colonial empire. This wave of investment was more active with a greater degree of subsequent direct involvement in the running of the enterprises in question. The European share of British overseas investment fell from 2/3 to 1/4 in the period between 1830 and 1870. Conversely, the share in the Dominions and India rose from only 2% to about one third of British overseas investment. The size of French foreign assets is considered to have been half that of Great Britain's. More than half of these were placed passively in the form of state loans to Eastern European countries, including Russia.

3. Trade policy

In order to appreciate fully the great significance of customs policy in the nineteenth and early twentieth centuries, it is important to bear in mind that the arsenal of politico-economic instruments was small indeed. Public finances in peacetime were modest and, correspondingly, the notion of a fiscal policy as part of a wider policy of economic adjustment was unknown. Monetary policy as part of a wider policy of stabilization was, at best, only used with great hesitation and, at worst, it directly reinforced the market fluctuations it was supposed to curtail.

It must be added that the fixed-rate system of the gold standard for lengthy periods of time prevented countries from pursuing an active exchange rate policy or an independent monetary policy. Consequently, much came to rest on customs and trade policy.

Four partially contradictory considerations were current:

a. promotion of domestic industries, i.e., securing the home market;

b. promotion of export industries, i.e., ensuring access to the trading partner's market;

c. ensuring state revenues, i.e., fiscal concerns;

d. general political considerations, including those of foreign policy.

Examples of the latter concern include the strengthening of the unity of Germany through the creation of a common tariff area, the Zollverein, as well as the efforts in Great Britain in the 1900s to establish an imperial preference system in order to bolster the cohesion of the British Empire. A more up-to-date example of this is provided by the EC's common tariff in the first years of the community.

After the end of the Napoleonic Wars, *Great Britain* sought to protect its corn producers by means of a Corn Law. Opponents of the Corn Law were mainly from the circles involved with the burgeoning industry of the day. The corn duty impinged upon wages by increasing the workers' cost of living and thus affected production cost levels. The corn duty also increased the share of income represented by rent from land at the expense of that represented by profit. There was also the wider issue of trade policy interests where British industry had a massive competitive advantage and wanted to spread the gospel of free trade to potential markets. In 1832, there was a parliamentary reform of constituency boundaries, which increased the representation of the rapidly growing industrial areas in Parliament. This was, however, insufficient at first to bring about a change in tariff policy.

So, in 1839, the reform movement was organized in the Anti-Corn-Law League whose leader was Richard Cobden (1804-65), a calico printer from Manchester. The League used all the means of mass agitation to increase pressure on the Tory administration. The League was to give rise to the term "Manchester liberalism", which is regarded as a radical form of liberalism. That the notion of free trade should gain so much currency in Manchester is not surprising. The city was the heart of the new textile industry, which had an interest both in the workers being able to buy cheap food and in the free access to export markets.

The 1840s saw some years with bad harvests and, in the winter of 1845/46, there was the prospect of famine in Ireland. The result was that the Tory Prime Minister, Robert Peel (1788-1850), whose party had pledged to maintain the Corn Law, had a change of heart in January 1846 and, more or less, suggested their complete abolition. This split the party and, shortly afterwards, Peel was forced out of office and lost the leadership of his party. It would be mistaken to think that the abolition of the Corn Law was solely due to the triumph of free trade ideas. The Bill was also part of a tax reform, which introduced direct income tax. Primarily, there seem to have been reasons of tax policy and short-term food-supply worries behind this reform rather than a widely held belief in the blessings of free trade. Another point is that, shortly after duties were lowered on corn, they were also lowered for other categories of goods and any remaining duties were fiscal in nature. In 1849, the Navigation Acts were repealed which greatly benefitted Norwegian shipping among others. That Great Britain should be the first country to institute free trade on a broad scale should come as no surprise in view of British superiority in terms of its industrial production and its merchant navy.

After the Napoleonic Wars, *France* had adopted increasingly protectionist policies, a trend which was confirmed after the 1830 July Revolution during the reign of the "Citizen King", Louis Philippe (*1830-48*). There was, however, also a French free trade movement led by the economist Frédéric Bastiat (1801-50) which was, in part, inspired by Britain. The blend of interests though, free trade and protectionism, was altogether different in France where export industry played a far smaller role in the economy.

After the proclamation of Emperor Napoleon III in 1852 (*1852-70*), there was a prospect for change. One of his chief concerns was to create good relations with England. His policy of expansion in Northern Italy and elsewhere required compensatory action and in 1859-60 a Commercial Treaty was negotiated with the British about tariff reduction. The chief British negotiator was Richard Cobden who lent his name to the treaty. The Cobden Treaty was the prototype for later treaties and has gone down in trade history as the central pillar for an interim network of European bilateral trade agreements. These treaties contained as a standard feature a *most favoured nation clause* (MFN) which meant that a tariff reduction granted to one country, from then on, is automatically extended to countries with whom an agreement on most favoured nation status is concluded.

As originally drafted, the Cobden Treaty was to last for ten years though either party could revoke it before expiry. During those first ten years, it was hotly debated in France and contributed to the decline of the Emperor's popularity amongst the bourgeoisie. It was nonetheless extended. However, it was cancelled by the mid-1870s, in the midst of an economic depression with a fall in farming prices. A shift in French policy back towards protectionism took place. The particular protectionist policy that was subsequently developed in France, especially in the agricultural sector, has since had an influence which stretches all the way forward to the EU Common Agricultural Policy, the CAP of today.

Germany's trade policy in the nineteenth century was largely determined by the purely nationalistic efforts to assemble the Germany under Prussian leadership. After the Napoleonic Wars, Germany consisted of about forty tariff and duty areas, some of which were quite small. Under Prussian leadership, cooperation in trade policy was gradually established between these areas by means of a customs union with freedom from duties on the inside and a common tariff towards the outside world. It is hard to indicate the precise date of the establishment of the German customs union - the "Zollverein". Most would say that it started around 1834, at the time when Bavaria, among others, joined. In order to keep protectionist Austria out, Prussia, the dominant partner in this cooperation, sought to steer a free trade course.

In the mid-1840s, however, there was a brief, protectionist intermezzo. In 1841, the German economist, Friedrich List (1789-1846), strongly impelled by nationalist sentiments, propounded his theory which justified a tariff barrier for new fledgling industries (the infant-industry-argument) as an exception to free trade. Great Britain's transition to free trade at the end of the decade, along with free trade signals from France in 1852, turned policy firmly back in a liberal direction. Thus it can be said of Germany that it maintained an economic

course which favoured free trade until the time following the proclamation of the German Empire in 1871.

Free trade policy, at the time, corresponded with the interests of
the influential Prussian landowners. As mentioned earlier, German
agriculture in the regions east of the Elbe was characterized by large
estates. As long as these were dependent on a net export of grain,
care had to be taken about access to their export markets. The
growth of German industry meant, however, that the importance of
the home market for farm products grew as well. After the Empire
was created, another factor manifested itself, namely, that the
shared expenses - mainly military - were to be met out of the common customs revenue. This was counterbalanced by the fact that the
growing German industry proved itself to be strongly export-oriented. So Germany ended up, in trade and tariff policy terms, between
Britain and France, in that Germany applied protectionist policies
to its agriculture, but pursued free trade policies to a greater degree
for industrial products.

The USA, notwithstanding much high-flown rhetoric about liberalism, has to be characterized as predominantly protectionist. Liberalism was mainly advocated and represented by the farmers and planta-
tion owners connected to the Democrat Party. Protectionism was es-
poused by urban enterprises linked politically to the Republicans. In
the USA - as in Germany later - the customs constituted the central
governments largest common source of revenue. Traditionally, the
forces behind the Republican Party supported the federal authorities,
while the Democrats wanted power to be decentralized, which was also
reflected in their trade and tariff policies.

It may seem odd that the USA in the latter half of the nineteenth
century pursued such a protectionist customs policy since it was at this
time that American industry laid the foundation for its world-wide
predominance. High labour productivity and a high level of earnings
in American agriculture provide an explanation. In order to attract labour, American industry needed to maintain a higher cost level than
European industry. For that reason, a tradition for tariff protection of
basic industries arose, especially against the British iron industry. As
an independent processing industry subsequently developed in America, the protectionist rationale was extended to include it. Furthermore, American industry, in the course of time, reached such a size

that a high degree of competition would prevail within the nation's own customs area. In America's case, any interest in promoting competition and the free play of market forces would manifest itself to a greater extent in the question of anti-trust legislation rather than in any concern about the conditions for foreign trade.

The high level of protection and the growth of competition meant an increased interest in the trading possibilities outside Western Europe. An area which attracted particular attention was the Far East. A particularly nasty instance of this was provided by the Opium wars in China.

   The reactions of China and Japan to Western expansion, however, were radically different. Around 1860, both countries had trade agreements forced upon them, which set a ceiling of five per cent on their import duties. Whereas the Chinese reaction can be categorized as passive to the extent that there was no attempt at independent industrialization, the Japanese reaction was most definitely active. From the start of the Meiji Period in 1868, reforms along Western lines got under way of both the civilian and military sides of Japanese society.

Tabel 6.2: Annual growth rates of GDP. Total and per capita. 1820-1913. Fixed Prices.

Per cent.	Total		Per Capita	
	1820-70	1870-1913	1820-70	1870-1913
Great Britain	2.0	1.9	1.2	1.0
France	1.3	1.6	0.8	1.5
Germany	2.0	2.8	1.1	1.6
Italy	1.2	1.9	0.6	1.3
Austria	1.4	2.4	0.7	1.5
Belgium	2.2	2.0	1.4	1.0
Netherlands	1.9	2.2	1.1	0.9
Switzerland	n.a.	2.4	n.a.	1.5
Denmark	1.9	2.7	0.9	1.6
Finland	1.6	2.7	0.8	1.4
Norway	1.7	2.1	0.5	1.3
Sweden	1.6	2.2	0.7	1.5
USA	4.2	3.9	1.3	1.8

Source: A. Maddison (1995, table C-a and 3-2).

4. National developments

Table 6.2 shows the average annual growth rates (GDP, at fixed prices) during the periods 1820-70 and 1870-1913. These figures are to be treated with great caution. This is because the primary source material was generated when there was no such thing as the compilation of industrial production figures or statistics, and that what agricultural statistics there were may have been woefully incomplete. To this can be added index problems related to calculations over such long periods of time.

An indicator of where the respective countries stood in relation to the industrial breakthrough is to be found in the growth rates for the periods 1820 to 1870 and 1870 to 1913. Two countries, Great Britain and Belgium, have stagnant growth rates; both overall and per capita. From being the countries with the highest rates of growth in the first period, with the exception of the USA, they had slipped down by the second period to a position among those countries with the lowest per capita rates of growth. The spread in national levels of income inaugurated by the start of British industrialization seems to have continued until the middle of the century, then being replaced by a narrowing of national income differences towards the end of the century. The above can also be put in the following fashion, Great Britain's economic predominance peaked around 1870, after which time Germany, in particular, experienced rapid growth.

4.1. Great Britain

1830 saw the start of railway construction in Britain, which was to grow so rapidly that, at the close of the 1830s, almost 4,000 kilometres of track had been laid and by the end of the `40s about 15,000 kilometres of track were in use. As mentioned earlier, such intense investment worked both "forwards" and "backwards" - backwards in the sense of the knock-on effect on the economy through the derived demand, forwards because of the opportunities the newly constructed railways provided for cost savings and the proliferation of economic activity. The three leading growth industries in the British economy at the time were still textiles, coalmining and iron. In the textile industry, the spinning mills of the 1820s were soon supplemented by weaving mills. This superiority in production methods was reflected in the balance of trade, which showed a large surplus, and which became the basis for major overseas investments. At the outset of this period, most of the investment capital went to Western Europe, among other things into railway construction, though later on, the share represented by purely overseas investment would increase considerably.

4.2. France

Two mutually divergent pictures of economic growth in France can be drawn from Table 6.2. The divergence is due to the relatively modest growth of the French population compared to demographic developments in the other countries. The first two columns would indicate that France had the lowest rate of growth in both periods. The picture changes, however, if allowances are made for the differences in population growth because, in per capita terms, France is suddenly on a par with most of the other countries. In fact, from 1870 to 1914, French rates of growth exceed Britain's and are not far behind those of Germany. These circumstances can also be expressed in the following manner. The basis of the French difference, during the period in question, was in the development in population size rather than in that of productivity. The figures may also be used to expose myths concerning the development of German productivity vis-á-vis that of the French. During the first period, per capita growth rate figures were at the same level; during the second, German annual growth was only 0.1 percent point higher than that of the French. However, it should be remembered that Germany started from a considerably lower point of departure and was thus able to reap the benefits of being a late starter. Finally, the German position was strengthened around 1870 as a result of border changes in its favour at the expense of France and Denmark.

4.3. Germany

Germany's economic development in the period 1830-70 is affected by three decisive factors, all three of which had to do with the unification of the hitherto divided nation. The first was the creation of a common, single market free of obstacles in the form of customs duties. This development took place under the aegis, and within the framework, of the German customs union, the Zollverein. The second factor was the physical connection of points within the area by means of improving the canal system and building a coherent railway network. The latter, as far as Prussia was concerned, was built partly for military purposes, whose inspiration was provided by the clear significance of railways in the American Civil War. The third factor was the political and military linking up of the separate states in a new German Empire by the end of the period.

The isolation in relation to the Western European economy, which had marked the majority of German states for centuries, was thus brought to an end. By 1871, Germany was economically and politically prepared to step forward as a global power on a par with Great Britain and France. In just seven years, Prussia had won three wars, each in a short space of time. Denmark was defeated in 1864, Austria in 1866 and, finally, France in 1870-71. In addition to military organization and political calculation, there was also industrial development behind this achievement, especially the growth of the German steel industry. However, intensive German industrialization only dates from the period after 1870 when Germany, among other things, benefitted from the annexation of the provinces of Alsace and Lorraine, together with their rich iron ore deposits.

4.4. Belgium and the Netherlands
In terms of industrial development, *Belgium* was at the same level as Britain in the mid-nineteenth century. In 1830, the country was separated from the Netherlands as an independent state and a constitutional monarchy was established. Its sensitive location between France and Germany, given the lessons of history, did not bode well for the future. Belgian security was, therefore, guaranteed by the neighbouring states, including Great Britain. It was this treaty obligation that in 1914 provided the formal basis for Britain's entry into World War I alongside France and Belgium against Germany.

As part of the creation of the new state, a decision was taken to establish a coherent railway network as soon as possible and this is why, unlike most other countries, the Belgian railway system was developed from the outset as part of an overall plan. This early and rapid creation of its railways gave the country a disproportionate position for its size in the European iron industry. As mentioned in Section 1.1, Transport and Communications, Belgium was among the pioneers in developing a railway industry producing rolling stock and equipment; a branch of industry which, towards the end of the century, moved on into the production of material for electric tramways.

While over the previous couple of centuries, the centre of economic gravity had moved away northwards from the area that would become

Belgium to *the Netherlands*, by the mid-eighteenth century the process had reversed and continued that way throughout most of the nineteenth century. There are several reasons for this shift.

The Netherlands had experienced a weakening of its maritime power throughout the eighteenth century. This became apparent in the latter half of the century when, during the Seven Years war (1756-63) and the War of American Independence (1776-84), the Royal Navy imposed blockades which seriously hampered Dutch sea-going trade and commerce. Another reason lay in the fact that the Netherlands, unlike Belgium, lacked the natural pre-conditions to take part in the early stages of industrialization. A third reason is that the Guilder, for long periods of time, was overvalued. In order to maintain its position as an international financial centre, it was important that the Dutch currency could inspire confidence abroad.[4] To achieve this, the stability of the currency rates had to be ensured and, if necessary, a deflationary policy was pursued. In the long-term, this acted as a damper on the development of industry. Then there were the fruitless attempts in 1830 to quell the Belgian uprising, which had been costly and had seriously weakened Dutch State finances.

4.5. The Scandinavian countries

The Scandinavian countries saw a late start to industrialization. In the case of Sweden, the steep growth in British mining and iron production was directly harmful. The linkage of the three countries, Denmark, Sweden and Norway, to industrialization in its infancy was principally that of suppliers of raw materials such as grain, timber and salted fish, a long- established role. Their advantage lay in geographical proximity to the areas of growth, chiefly, Britain. The figures for the per capita rise in GDP for the period 1820-70 for the three countries were below the equivalent figures for Great Britain, Belgium, the Netherlands and Germany, though on a par with those for France.

In the case of *Denmark*, the period from 1830 to 1870 corresponded, more or less, with the so-called corn-sales period. What marked this epoch was that agriculture was still the mainstay of the economy and that, by far, the chief export was grain. Access to the most important market in Europe, the British, was freed from restrictions in 1846 at a time when neither Russian nor American grain had reached Western

---

4.   A. Maddison (1991, 35).

Europe in significant quantities. Under these circumstances, Danish farming experienced some prosperous years in the period around 1850, which helped to prepare the way for the structural changes later on in the century. Industrial style production in the towns was limited to the tobacco, sugar and soap industries, steam-powered milling, brewing and the production of consumer items, chiefly in the area of food and household goods. As long as grain remained the staple export, there was no particular need for ancillary industries to promote exports. In the final quarter of the century, changes brought about by structural adjustments in agriculture gave rise to the growth of a modest Danish machine industry.

Norway's economy, just like the Danish, can be characterized as being one-sided in this period, only in this instance it was the products of forestry and fishing which characterized Norwegian exports. As far as forestry is concerned, most exports were in the unprocessed form of whole logs. The processing of timber into cellulose or paper was yet to come. British industrial growth gave rise to an increasing demand for timber for building and for pit props for the shoring up of mine shafts. This great Norwegian timber export trade had already laid the foundations of an extensive merchant fleet. Thus, the mid-nineteenth century was marked, in Norway's case, by growth in the shipping sector. This led to Norwegian industry suffering from the side-effect of Norwegian ships loading cheap British iron as return freight in British ports. Norwegian ironworks, scattered as they were, were consequently subject to stiff competition. On the contrary, however, Norwegian shipbuilders were able to take advantage of the upturn in the shipping business. Because of the difficulties in establishing an internal transport system, Norway, as the century progressed, acquired the characteristics of a dual economy with large income and lifestyle differences between the coastal cities and the more remote areas of the country. In terms of GDP growth per capita, Norway was one of the countries at the bottom of the scale in this period. One of the reasons for this was a relatively high rate of population growth, about 1.2 per cent per annum which led to the massive emigration towards the end of the century when about ten per cent of the population left each decade.

Sweden's mining and iron industry had for centuries enjoyed the advantages of good quality iron ore and easy access to charcoal. However, technical progress in metallurgic production methods had reduced the scope of these advantages. The industrial revolution meant, in the short-term, increased competition for the Swedish iron-ore extractors and the iron industry. However, like Norway, Sweden experienced an upturn in the export of timber. At the same time, Swedish agricultural production grew so rapidly that, from being a net importer of grain in the mid-nineteenth century, the situation was reversed and Sweden became a grain exporter. For a time, at least, the expansion of Swedish agriculture provided work for the growing population, though this trend was to turn down sharply a few decades later. By comparison with Denmark and Norway, Sweden was, at the mid-century, much closer to an industrial breakthrough. The country had an early start in the iron industry with its access to all the necessary raw materials. A proportionately larger number of people were employed in industrial style enterprises, including those which used mechanical power. For all that, however, there was no development of a Swedish machine industry until the very end of the century.

4.6. The USA

Throughout this period, economic links between Europe and the USA were restricted by the great expense of bulk freight. So economic interchange was restricted to those goods that could pay their way across the Atlantic. The USA exported sub-tropical agricultural products such as tobacco and cotton as well as timber for shipbuilding from the northern states. Imports tended to consist in the main of machinery and luxury consumer goods. America was an important trading partner to Western Europe, but still far from having a decisive influence on overall economic activity.

The years between 1830 and 1870 were the years when the North American continent was opened up. This process started with the expansion of navigation in the Mississippi Delta and on the Missouri River with the stern-wheel paddle-steamers later made famous on the cinema screen. Then there was the construction of railways from the port cities on the East Coast which, by the mid-century, stretched west beyond the Mississippi and were to reach California at the end of the 1860s. The period starting in the mid-nineteenth century was marked by the tension between the southern slave-owning states and the so-called free states in the north. Among other things, the economic consequences of the showdown, the American Civil War of 1861-65, meant the speeding-up of technical progress in agriculture and a shift in the political centre of gravity to the north-eastern cities and the mid-western farming belt. At the same time, impetus had been given to the development of American industry for the manufacture of a range of consumer durables.

However, in the mid-nineteenth century, America's greatest significance for Europe was as a destination for the swelling stream of emigrants. At the time, most of them still came from the British Isles or Germany. Well known are the many Irish emigrants who left because of famine and religious persecution from the mid-1840s onwards. Between 1847 and 1852, the number of emigrants from Ireland totalled 1.2 million people, which represented a seventh of the total Irish population. What is not so well known is that a similar number of people left Germany as a result of the revolutionary upheavals of 1848. In the years 1850 to 1859, the total number of immigrants to the USA was 2.6 million, about a tenth of the American population of 23.6 million in 1850. The USA served as a social lightning conductor for Western Europe at a time of tense, fundamental change.[5]

5. Laissez-Faire

The period from the mid-nineteenth century to the start of the twentieth century has been retrospectively labelled as the period of "laissez-faire". Among the countries surveyed here, two stand out by being at the opposite ends of the spectrum. At one end, the USA, which maintained liberal measures even after the First World War and, at the other, Germany that preserved certain craft-based traits, retaining them in an industrial setting. In terms of the balance of political power in society, the increasing urban population acquired more significance, although the growing proletariat did not yet obtain any meaningful direct political influence.

The word "liberalism" is not used here in its narrow sense connected with foreign trade as opposed to protectionism. The laissez-faire period was marked by much protectionist tariff policy, so in that sense there was not much liberalism in operation. The word is used in its sense of the "absence of public regulation". It may be characterized as a condition of freedom to contract and free consumer choice - in other

---

5. Concerning the migration from the Scandinavian countries from 1870-1914 see chapter 7, section 7.4.

words, the freedom of individuals to dispose of their resources as they saw fit. The expression "Laissez-faire, laissez-passer" has been inherited by the langauge of economics from the Physiocrats of the eighteenth century, and a suitable rough translation might be that things should be left to their own devices, without any intervention from the state.

There were still clear indications of mercantilist thinking in the economic policies of 1830. There were guild rules still in effect, which limited the right of craftsmen to establish themselves and regulated where shopkeepers could open a business. There were definite rules governing the relationship between masters and apprentices. Import and export bans were used as part of economic policy. There were strict rules governing sea-borne carriage in order to protect national maritime interests. It was this thicket of rules that needed pruning.

As an example of the thinking of the time, the Danish Constitution of 1849 established that: "All hindrances to the free and equal access to trades which are not founded in the public good are to be rescinded by law." This promise was kept and enacted with the new Act on Trades of 1857. The next paragraph of the Constitution reads as follows: "Any person unable to support himself or his dependants shall, where no other person is responsible for his or their maintenance, be entitled to receive public assistance, provided that he comply with the obligations imposed by statute in such respect." There was not much hurry to enact at least the first part of this paragraph. In terms of social policy, in Denmark and elsewhere, there was a tendency during those years to abandon traditional forms of social provision without replacing them with new ones.

The economists had provided the theoretical basis for a revision of the inherited economic system as well as for the substitution of state control by free competition. In 1859, the English zoologist, Charles Darwin, (1809-82) published his book, "The Origin of Species", which pointed out that humans themselves were the product of a process of natural competitive selection. As J.M. Keynes writes in his essay, "The End of Laissez-Faire": "The economists were teaching that wealth, commerce and machinery were the children of free competition - that free competition built London. But the Darwinians could go one better than that - free competition had built man." In other words, competition had replaced the Creator himself.

Chapter 7

Approaching the Great Showdown
1875-1914

The years between the Franco-Prussian war 1870-71 and the outbreak of World War One in 1914, formed a period of peace in Western Europe. The area of unrest was, then as now, the Balkans. But a constant state of tension existed between France and Germany due to the fate of Alsace-Lorraine, lost by France in 1871.

The period began with political fears as result of the socialist uprising in Paris during the war. Especially in Germany this gave rise to restrictions on the development of a democratic governmental system. Thus, the growing economic and military potential of Germany was not accompanied by any democratic means of control. On the contrary, under a regime of officers and great estate owners – the Junkers – the opinion was held that democracy was an inconvenience that ought to be avoided.

Another trend was the spread of industry. Apart from Great Britain, Belgium and Northern France, only a few and scattered industrial areas existed in 1875. Farming was still the occupation of most people. However, in addition to Germany, industry was now spreading to the Netherlands, Scandinavia, parts of Austria-Hungary, Switzerland and Northern Italy. In Eastern Europe, Russia too saw the beginnings of modern industry, in part related to the development of a Russian railway system financed through loans from Western Europe.

More than forty years of peace ended in 1914 with the outbreak of "the Great War", later demoted to simply the "First World War". Just as Europe had been through thirty-year period of wars, destruction and political upheavals in the 1600s, the continent once again entered upon such a time in the summer of 1914.

1. Technical development

Technical development in the forty years after 1875 had a more direct effect on consumption and living conditions than that of the previous forty years. In homes, open fires were replaced by kitchen-ranges of wrought iron, making it easier to prepare hot meals and supply the household with hot water. First, the new paraffin lamp and, later, the electric light meant more light hours – and more working hours. The risk of cholera and other epidemic diseases was reduced as a result of better sanitary conditions, including better toilets, towards the end of the period. The electric tram and the bicycle came into use – the former was to change the pattern of great cities. Industrialization from now on had an impact on most aspects of everyday life.

The invention of the *electric generator* and the *electric motor* opened new possibilities of the use of mechanical power. Belts, hanging from the roof, and leading to the machines performed the transmission of power from steam engines to different machines. This system, besides being dangerous, had a tendency to demand large-scale production. The electric motor served to counterbalance this trend. This was the case in the textile and wood industries. It must be added, however, that the electric industry itself was dominated by large-scale production and big business, with the Siemens Corporation – named after its founder and the inventor of the generator – as a leading example.

The generator also opened new possibilities for the use of water-power. In 1873, a factory owner in south-eastern France constructed a *turbine* driven by water. The turbine had the advantage, compared to traditional water-mills, that it could be driven by powerful streams of water, falling from great heights. Used together with the generator and the electric motor, it had the advantage that the energy could be transported over great distances. This made it not only possible to use new sources of energy, but to do so in places where it was difficult or impossible to use traditional fossil fuels such as coal.

Through this, entirely new areas were brought within the reach of industrialization. Outstanding examples are Norway and Switzerland, but others deserve to be mentioned such as Austria, Northern Italy, parts of Sweden and Finland, etc. For Norway, cheap electricity meant the beginning of an entirely new branch of production: nitrogen fertilizer or Norwegian saltpetre. For Switzerland – as for Norway – it meant the beginning of the production of aluminium. For both countries, access to cheap electricity has been an important factor in the shaping of the structure of their economic life.

Another new source of energy was the *combustion engine*. At first, it was driven by gas. In 1886, however, two Germans, Wilhelm Maybach (1846-1929) and Gottlieb Daimler (1834-1929), succeeded in constructing a motor driven by petrol. It had better fuel economy than the steam engine and could be more lightly built. This structural lightness, with its consequent mobility, opened up entirely new avenues, soon to be explored in automobiles, ships and aeroplanes.

Another important contribution about the same time was the invention by the German engineer, Rudolf Diesel (1858-1913), of the compression-ignition engine. In 1897, he succeeded in constructing a workable motor using oil as fuel. Compared to a petrol engine, it could be constructed in bigger units and convert more energy, which made it a substitute for the steam engine. Besides superior fuel economy by comparison with the steam engine, it had an advantage in the way that the fuel was fed directly into the engine. Both labour and fuel storage space could be saved, two qualities that were very important in shipping. Burmeister&Wain, a Danish shipyard, in 1912 pioneered the use of the diesel engine at sea by being the first to install one in a ship, a merchant vessel, the MS Selandia. At that time Rudolf Diesel was working on a smaller version of his engine for installation in lorries and locomotives. He was never to see the successful results of his efforts because he disappeared on the journey by sea from Antwerp to Harwich in England, where he had planned to start up the production of the new engines.

About 1880, electricity gained widespread use as a source of energy. So, naturally enough, the question arose of whether it could be used for lighting. Around the middle of the century, gas had come into use for this purpose. However, its distribution costs were high so it was mainly used for street lighting and similar uses. The demand for domestic lighting was modest, though the invention around 1880 of a reliable *incandescent lamp* meant a breakthrough in the use of electric light in the home. The American, Thomas Edison (1847-1931) made this invention.

Finally, in 1875, Graham Bell invented the *telephone,* which added new dimensions to communication. As with other inventions within the field of communication, it spread very fast: In 1887, the number of telephone subscribers in the United States was about 150,000, in Great Britain 26,000, in Germany 22,000, in Sweden 12,000 and Denmark, 4,000.

The *electric tramway* is considered to have promoted both the growth and the present structure of the great cities by allowing long distances between residential and industrial areas and the concentration of special shopping areas. Department stores can be seen as one result of the electric tramway.

Whereas the tramway soon came to form an important part of the transport system, for a number of years two other novelties within the field, the automobile and the bicycle, were reserved for sportsmen of a certain financial standing. A necessary prerequisite was the invention by John Dunlop (1840-1921), an Irish vet, of the pneumatic tyre. About 1900, the bicycle was equipped with a freewheeling hub and hub brake, whereby the technical conditions were fulfilled for the popularity of the bicycle. The cost of a bicycle in those days, however, still corresponded to a female teacher's salary for three months, and road surfaces were seldom fit for cycling.

In 1869, the opening of the Suez-Canal was celebrated, at high cost and in the presence of the French Imperial couple. At the outset, the canal was far from an economic success and in 1875, Great Britain, as part of a rapidly concluded bargain with Egypt, won control. The aim was to facilitate and secure British commercial interests "east of Suez", at a time when British industry met growing competition on the European markets. The Kiel Canal, or Emperor Wilhelm Canal, to give it its correct name, was built in the 1890s on the basis of an existing canal. The aim of the project was both commercial and military. It made it possible to move the German fleet from the North Sea to the Baltic without having to sail around Jutland.

Already in the 1880s, plans were presented for a canal from the Gulf of Mexico to the Pacific. It turned out to be a very complicated task, partly due to the unfavourable climate. However, the project was carried out and the Canal-Zone brought under the control of the USA. In 1914, the Panama Canal was opened to traffic.

An important step forward in the development of carriage by sea was the construction of riveted steel ships. The background for this was a fall in the price of steel plate. This made steamships competitive with sailing ships in the transport of bulk cargoes like grain and coal, the breakthrough taking place around 1870. Another innovation, within the field of ship propulsion, was placing a propeller at the stern instead of paddle wheels on either side of the ship. Those developments led to a dramatic drop in the freight rates across the Atlantic, thus contributing to the agricultural crisis in Western Europe during the 1880s and '90s.

In 1882, railway traffic was opened between Switzerland and Italy through the St. Gotthard tunnel and the Simplon tunnel was completed in 1906. The two lines supplemented the line crossing the Alps through the Brenner Pass leading from Austria to Italy. This had been already completed in 1867 to connect Austria with its provinces situated south of the Alps. The introduction of the electric locomotive around 1900 meant that the tunnels could be made longer, which explains why the early lines had to climb higher up in the mountains and offer, from a tourist's point of view, the most exciting routes.

As mentioned earlier, the essential element in the dynamics of industrial society was the speeding up of process and product innovation. This characterized the years up to the First World War. A special feature of this period was, as already emphasized, the increasing importance of the new electrical industry as well as that of the chemical industry. Furthermore, it was characteristic that many innovations were now directly aimed at the household: as consumer goods.

Table 7.1 Sterling and Mark-exchange rates vis-a-vis Danish Kroner. Middle of the year. 1875-1913.

D.Kr. per	£	Mark		£	Mark		£	Mark
1875	18.25	88.70	1888	18.15	89.00	1901	18.14	89.00
1876	18.15	88.65	1889	18.17	88.95	1902	18.19	89.00
1877	18.20	88.90	1890	18.17	89.15	1903	18.15	89.05
1878	18.15	89.10	1891	18.15	89.15	1904	18.16	89.05
1879	18.13	88.70	1892	18.14	89.00	1905	18.18	88.90
1880	18.13	88.60	1893	18.15	89.00	1906	18.20	88.95
1881	18.18	88.80	1894	18.12	88.90	1907	18.21	89.05
1882	18.18	88.95	1895	18.15	88.90	1908	18.16	89.15
1883	18.19	88.80	1896	18.14	89.00	1909	18.19	89.05
1884	18.13	88.75	1897	18.11	88.95	1910	18.18	88.95
1885	18.11	89.00	1898	18.14	89.05	1911	18.18	88.95
1886	18.07	88.75	1899	18.18	89.00	1912	18.22	89.00
1887	18.09	88.95	1900	18.19	89.15	1913	18.26	89.25

Source: Danish Statistics, the library.
Note: The exchange rates stated as Danish crowns per pound sterling and per 100 marks.

2.   Monetary and financial affairs

In the mid-1870s, most countries in Western Europe were "on the gold standard". They remained on it until the outbreak of war in 1914. Those forty years have gone down in the history of international economics as *the gold standard period*. Table 7.1 shows the exchange rates of the Danish crown (D.Kr.) vis-à-vis the pound sterling and the German mark through the years 1875 to 1913.[1] The difference between the lowest and the highest sterling-rate is 0.19 crowns. Compared to the average exchange rate for the thirty-nine years (18.165 crowns) the deviation corresponds to 5.2 thousandths, or just half of one per cent. To call this stability would be no exaggeration. Throughout the entire period, the price of gold was fixed in most currencies and the free movement of capital prevailed. As will be made clear, it is a misconception that a scenario with frozen exchange rates and a common capital market is some new invention, which has never been tried before. The new aspect of the EMU[2] is that this must now be realized under entirely different conditions, with a far greater public sector and a much wider spectrum of political goals concerning employment, economic growth and the distribution of income. Such goals were no part of the aims of leading politicians and economists in those days dominated by liberal economic ideas.

As long as the countries lived up to the conditions of the gold standard system, the exchange rates would be linked to one another within strict limits,[3] as was the case even without specific agreements between the central banks. However, the countries could choose to go one step further and establish a real currency union. This was what the Scandinavian countries did around 1875 within the framework of *the Scandinavian Currency Union*. Here closer cooperation between the three participating central banks was agreed upon and, what was more obvious to the general public, branches of the governments of the three countries such as the postal services, had to accept payments in all three currencies. The outbreak of the First World War meant an end to the union as the three countries had to leave the gold standard. In the mid-

1.   Those were the exhange rates available to the author from the Danish Statistics. Cross exchange rates between the pound and the mark can be calculated on the basis of the table and will confirm the conclusions of the text.
2.   The Economic and Monetary Union of the European Communities.
3.   The cost of transporting the gold opens a narrow band, within the so-called gold points, for such changes.

dle of the 1920s, the cooperation was reestablished only to suffer a final breakdown in 1931 as the result of the economic and financial world crises after 1929.

1865 saw the setting up of what was later known as *the Latin Currency Union*. There were more members than in the Scandinavian union, but it was, however, less stable. The participants included, for shorter or longer periods, France, Belgium, Switzerland, Italy, Greece and Austria.

A monetary system based on the gold standard is, on the surface, governed by a few simple and automatic rules according to which the amount of bullion in the coffers of the central bank and the rules concerning note issue mark the limits of liquidity. The exchange rate is fixed through the price of gold and the interest rate follows pretty closely the international interest rate, thanks to the free movement of capital. There does not seem to be much room for a monetary policy under such conditions. In practice, however, the system functioned somewhat differently.

Firstly, under normal conditions, the central banks did not go to the limit of their note issuing capacity. Secondly, when under pressure, they might have waivers going beyond the limits. On the whole, the system seems to have been characterized by a considerable degree of elasticity in the supply of liquidity. One aspect of this was the use of a variable discount rate by the central banks, instead of quantitative restrictions on credit. The price mechanism thereby, in accordance with the general tendencies of the period, took over the rôle of credit rationing in the distribution of capital. Furthermore, governments had certain possibilities to manipulate the internal interest rates by selling government bonds abroad and buying privately issued bonds on the home market.

The pattern of development of commercial banks up to 1875 was continued on one side of the Channel according to British traditions where the commercial banks supplied short-term capital. On the other side it was according to German traditions where the banks get involved in the long-term financing and management of their customers. Due to the size of their engagements, the German banks went even further than that, assisting in organizing cooperation to avoid unfavourable competition and to promote rationalization.

The gold standard period saw an expansion of the international capital market and a change in its pattern. As for British investments, a growing portion was placed overseas in the form of direct investments, especially in the colonies and dominions. The pattern of foreign investment of other European countries was somewhat different. There, investments in bonds, typically government bonds, formed a larger part. And a greater part of the loans was granted to other European countries, mainly in Eastern Europe.

The size of British investments outside the British Isles can be appreciated by the fact that Great Britain's National Income in 1913 is estimated to have been almost ten per cent higher than the National Product. This means that the net income from interest and dividends from abroad corresponded to about one-ninth of the national product of the home country. In the case of current savings, about half were placed outside the country[4] and about one-third of total national wealth was placed outside the borders of the country.[5]

The wisdom of this can be questioned seen in the light of what was to come, (Section 6, below). Would it have been better if a greater part of savings had been placed at home in the British Isles as investments in capital equipment? For Britain and London as a financial centre, the overseas assets were no doubt an advantage. In spite of the rather modest gold reserves of the Bank of England, the international assets of Britain and the invisible incomes of the Balance of Payments[6] were so large that her liquidity could not be doubted. The great foreign investments were important to the British "financial and commercial complex" of the City of London. The wish to return to this state of affairs after the First World War turned out to the bane of the British economy.

3. Trade policy

As far as geography was concerned, the years around 1875 were busy with the tearing down of walls and barriers. The construction of railways in Eastern Europe and in the Americas, along with new, larger ocean-going ships, meant a dramatic drop in transport costs. Humans showed that they were able to overcome natural barriers; and then, as a result of this, governments got busy erecting new barriers in the shape

---

4.   C.P.Kindleberger (1990, 260).
5.   A. Maddison (1991, 39).
6.   Foreign net-incomes on interests and profits.

of restrictive trade policies. This brings us to the question: how can it be explained that while engineers were drilling tunnels through the mountains to facilitate trade, customs officers were placed at the end of the tunnels in order to collect new and higher customs tariffs which then reduced trade?

The following simple points may serve as an answer:

a. economies were getting more sensitive to international business cycles, and one way of preventing this was to preserve internal demand for internal production,

b. a new pattern of production costs meant high fixed costs and low variable costs, and this gave rise to more flexible prices caused by dumping, wildcat competition and so on,

c. the agriculture of Western Europe, and thereby its farmers, faced sharply falling grain prices from the end of the 1870s,[7]

d. the wish for security of supply in case of war and extraordinary conditions of trade,

e. fiscal needs caused by growing public expenditure, especially on military programmes,

f. a lack of economic policy instruments, such as adjustment of taxes and public expenditure,

g. a corresponding absence of international bodies to promote economic cooperation and a comprehensive picture of international economic matters.

The following description of the trade policy of Western European countries will leave the impression that it was a period of extreme protectionism. It should be underlined from the outset that, compared to the 1930s, it was a period of liberal conditions for international economics and division of labour. It was not until the 1960s that foreign

---

7.   From the mid-70s to the mid-80s, the prices fell about 25 per cent and to the mid-90s, about 35 per cent. Sv.Aa.Hansen (1972, 212).

trade regained the relative importance of the years just before the First World War.

In 1846, *Great Britain* had made a dramatic cut in the duty on grain, followed by further tariff cuts. By 1860, with very few exceptions, only the import of consumer goods of which there was no production in Britain was liable to duties. Or, to put in another way, the remaining duties were so-called fiscal duties meant to give an income to the government and not to offer protection to British industries. Three other North Sea countries, the Netherlands, Denmark and Norway, having close economic ties to Britain, followed her example in pursuing a liberal trade policy. This was particularly the case for the Netherlands and Denmark, which, for a number of years, based their economies on serving the British their traditional breakfast.

Even the British stronghold of liberalism had to go through a discussion of renewed tariff protection, firstly because the economic backlash of the 1870s and '80s was felt rather strongly in Britain. Secondly, it was because competition from the growing industry of Western Europe was felt to an increasing degree, as was the competition from overseas grain. And thirdly, and this might be the most important reason, the idea spread that an area of imperial preference involving Britain and her dominions, Canada, Australia, New Zealand and South Africa, should be set up. A prerequisite for this, however, was that Britain should have something to offer which meant that she had to increase her general level of tariffs. The policy, however, was not carried through at this point of time, so that for the time being Britain stuck to liberalism.

France returned in the 1880s and '90s to her original policy of protectionism. This return to traditional French policy began shortly after the fall of Napoleon III in 1870. When the price of grain kept falling in later years, this was met by steadily growing pressure for increased agricultural protection. This, in turn, meant that protectionist groups in manufacturing industry saw a chance to unite with farmers'representatives in realizing a protectionist policy which, in principle, granted farming and industry the same high level of protection. In 1892, a tariff offering high protection – the Méline tariff – was passed which, on the whole, formed the basis of French customs duties until the realization of the external customs tariff of the European Economic Community in the 1960s.

Germany took a position between the British and the French. The Zollverein had followed a modest line which was not changed with the establishment of the German Empire in 1871. The great Prussian estates were net-exporters of grain and had, so far, an interest in free trade. The rapid economic growth of Germany, including the rapid growth of the urban population, meant that this was to change. By the end of the 1870s, agriculture and industry united in promoting a protectionist policy. During the following years, the protectionist line was strengthened further and, at the outbreak of the First World War, Germany's policy had to be characterized as protectionist. It should be noted, however, that the German chemical and electrical industries did develop as export industries. Balancing the respective interests of German agriculture and manufacturing industry would leave Germany placed somewhere between Britain and France – as was actually to be the case later on. As part of its protectionist agricultural policy, Germany imposed import prohibitions as well. This was the case from the late 1880s with regard to live pigs. For Denmark, as for the Netherlands, it meant that the export of pigs had to be switched to the British market, from then on mainly in the form of bacon.

In the *USA*, the Civil War (1861-65), for financial reasons, had caused substantial increases in tariffs. Protectionist forces, on the whole, dominated the years until 1914. The Republicans were still the most protectionist party. However, the difference between the two parties was diminishing. At the turn of the century, the average tariff level was as high as fifty per cent, which made the USA one of the most protectionist countries of the industrialized world. It is normally thought, that those high tariffs could not be explained by a corresponding need for protection: rather, they were the result of odd political deals in Congress.

Denmark, Norway and Sweden through the 1800s had developed a tradition of a rather liberal trade policy, giving them a common character of "small, open economies". After the establishment in the early 1800s of the Swedish-Norwegian union, the two countries offered one another special treatment. In 1873, they set up a genuine customs union, shortly before the creation of the Scandinavian Currency Union. During the 1880s, debates on extending the customs cooperation to include Denmark took place. However, the plans failed, partly due to the growing agricultural crisis. Denmark continued its free trade line, whereas in 1883 Sweden changed its line in favour of a more protectionist policy. Norway retained its customs preferences vis-à-vis Sweden and its duties from the earlier customs union with Sweden. This meant that for some goods it was cheaper to import them into Sweden via Norway, the so-called draught. In 1897, Norway left the customs union. This meant that the three Scandinavian countries were separated for a number of years, and it was not until the creation of the European Free Trade Association (EFTA) in the 1960s that effective initiatives to create free trade between the three countries were taken.

4. Colonial policy

After the three Prussian wars during the 1860s, more than forty years of peace ensued between the great powers of Western Europe. More to the point, their aggressiveness was temporarily channelled overseas to faraway places.

The more lucrative areas seem to have been taken up at an earlier point of time by the British. These were areas in the temperate-zone with a climate similar to that of Western Europe, and suitable for immigration from Europe. There might have been some possibilities still in South America, but the Monroe doctrine – America's backyard for the Americans – put forward by the USA in 1823, along with growing American strength put a lid on any ideas in this direction. To this, may be added that Great Britain early on had taken possession of the most valuable tropical areas such as India. Napoleon I had attempted, unsuccessfully, to compete with the British by invading Egypt and the Near East in 1798-99. This was later followed up by expansion on the south-western coast of the Mediterranean in Algeria and Tunisia. The Netherlands at an early point in time had established itself in Indonesia.

The area between India and China – Indochina – was colonized by the British from the west who took Burma and Malaya, followed in the 1850s from the east by the French who invaded what was to be called French Indochina. All in all, there was not very much left for Italy, united and established in 1861, or Germany, united in 1871. What was left for Germany were some areas with an unhealthy climate in Africa and – perhaps – some possibilities in China. There, the Germans would have to compete with Russia, Great Britain, the USA and Japan. Although there was not much left to take over, the few remaining scraps from the end of the 1800s were, now and then, to cause diplomatic crises, which led to the period being known as that of "gun boat diplomacy". Under those conditions, it was understandable that Austria, backed by Germany, turned to the Balkans. This area might provide chances of securing special arrangements and economic favours, although this would have to be at the expense of Turkey and Russia. Germany also showed its interest from a geopolitical point of view through trade agreements; an interest which was easily explained. In case of a blockade during a war with Russia, France and Great Britain, the main external suppliers of food would be Denmark, the Netherlands and the Balkans. It can be no wonder then, that the Balkans were the direct reason for the outbreak of the First World War.

The Scandinavian countries have, on the whole, stayed away from colonialism. As a trading nation, Denmark attempted to obtain colonies in the 1600s in the Caribbean, in West Africa and on the coast of India. Only the colonies in the Caribbean – the Virgin Islands – were kept until this century. The USA made several offers to buy the islands, but the sale was not realized until 1916. In the 1600s Sweden sought to establish colonies between present-day New York and Washington DC. They had, however, to give way to the English. Finally, it should be mentioned that Denmark and Norway have for centuries had special relations with Greenland and Iceland, of which the relations with Iceland may have given Denmark a modest surplus.

It is an open question whether the colonies "paid" their way. That private persons and businesses made great fortunes in the colonies is obvious, and from the point of view of private economic interests, they undoubtedly paid their way. However, when seen from the wider point of view of the colonizers, it becomes doubtful. It was costly for the taxpayers of the colonizing countries to maintain the necessary lines of communication, which included naval expenses, armies of occupation, a large colonial administration and so forth. Seen from such an overall consideration, the net-advantage to the home country shrinks, and perhaps even disappears. The best argument for participating was probably that others were doing this, so it was necessary to do the same for reasons of foreign policy.

Finally there is quite another question left out of the reckoning here: the consequences for the peoples who were colonised.

5. The beginnings of modern social security

In 1830 and 1848 revolutionary currents had swept across Europe. They could be characterized as the uprising of the middle classes directed against outdated regimes such as "l'ancien régime", reestablished in France after the Napoleonic Wars and backed by the Holy Alliance established in 1814-15. The economic result of this was a movement toward liberalism, granting free right of establishment in many trades and abolishing a number of public regulations dating back to mercantilist traditions. In 1871, after its defeat by Germany, France experienced the Communard uprising, based on an ideology far more dangerous to the Establishment than the two previous revolutions. Contrary to those, it did not spread to other countries – although indirectly it had its consequences.

In 1867, after the war between Prussia and Austria, a general franchise for men was introduced in *Germany* (by then the Confederation of Northern Germany). Within a short time, a well-organized Social Democratic movement sprang up, gaining representation in the Reichstag. The government realized that this might pose a threat to the entire political system. The outcome was "socialist legislation" carried through in 1878 and the following years under the leadership of the German chancellor, Otto von Bismarck (1815-98). Firstly, it consisted of a number of anti-subversive measures meant to make the future work of the Socialists difficult. Secondly, and this is more relevant to the history of social security, initiatives were taken to silence critical voices by introducing a number of social security measures.

Germany was the country in Western Europe where the traditional organizations of the trades had survived the best. For this reason it was natural to build a new system of social security upon the remains of the old system, the guilds. The result was the introduction of a system of social security having some of the characteristics of insurance. According to rules laid down by law, participation was compulsory for persons and businesses, and these were mainly larger firms in manufacturing industries and their labour-forces. It was financed by compulsory insurance premiums paid by both sides. A sickness-insurance scheme based upon these principles was established in 1883, one for accident insurance in 1884 and old-age pension and invalidity-insurance in 1889. With the German social security legislation of the 1880s, the design of the future social security systems of the continental parts of Western Europe was established. Austria followed already in 1887 and 1888, introducing accident insurance and sickness- insurance respectively. In France, unlike Germany, the guilds and organizations on which to build the system did not exist. However, in 1910 a pension scheme like the German was established based on obligatory participation and the payment of premiums. The principles of those schemes have been carried on and have formed the basis of the social security schemes of the original six Common Market countries.

The schemes adopted in *Denmark, Sweden and Britain*, whose salient points will now be described, were based on somewhat different principles.

In *Denmark*, the Old Age Security Scheme of 1891 marked a dividing line. According to the law, payments to the aged were separated from traditional payments to the "poor" as a special group of benefits. Furthermore, it was decided that the expenses related to the scheme should be covered out of the general budget of the central government. This meant that the scheme from the very beginning was paid for out of taxes,[8] and not by premiums as the German schemes. A sickness insurance scheme was introduced in 1892. Participation was voluntarily. It was based on independent health insurance societies being heavily subsidised by the government in order to bring down the premiums of the members. In practice, the societies were closely related to the trade unions and the labour movement. The members were accepted in public hospitals at special, very low prices, and the true cost was paid by the municipalities. This was the beginning of a tradition of free treatment in Danish hospitals and a tradition of "no money between patient and doctor". Later schemes concerning unemployment insurance and disability followed. The unique points in the Danish schemes were 1) the high degree of financing through public means and, 2) the low costs of the health services to the members of the insurance schemes.

In *Sweden* the modernization of social security started somewhat later. In 1913, a law was passed establishing old-age pensions, organised as an insurance scheme based on premiums. It differed from the German scheme in that the entire population was covered by the system, not only "the workers" or "the employed". In practice, since everybody had to participate, the way it was financed came close to being funded by the central government. If we merge the special features of

8. In practice, it was done by introducing a new, still existent tax on beer.

the Danish and the Swedish schemes, we have a system overwhelmingly paid for through taxes as opposed to premiums, thus covering the entire population and not just "the insured". It is these two features taken together that form what has come to be known as "*the Scandinavian model*" of social security.

In *Great Britain*, social security was based on voluntary insurance schemes, which accorded with the dominance of liberal ideas in the country's politics during the second half of the 1800s. On the whole it was based on putting those in need into the poorhouse. However, in 1908, a law was passed which introduced payments to the elderly. The higher their income, the lower was the payment, and all of it at a very modest level. The scheme was one hundred per cent tax-financed and in this it resembled the Danish old-age pension scheme.[9] In 1911 came insurance schemes covering need arising from sickness, accidents at work and unemployment. Participation was obligatory for workers and other employed people. The schemes were financed from three sources; the premiums paid by the insured, their employers' contributions and, finally, subsidies from the government; that is, through ordinary taxes. The British social security system did not have the character of a general scheme, covering the entire population and paid for through taxes, until after the Second World War. This was done on the basis of a report named after the British economist, William Beveridge (1879-1963).[10] This system and the principles behind it have since been known as "the Beveridge system". Although the greatness of Lord Beveridge is not in doubt, a Scandinavian may be allowed to mention that these principles can be traced back to previous Scandinavian social security legislation.

From the description given here, it might be tempting to think that a fully-fledged social security system in Western Europe was already in existence before 1914. This was not the case. Firstly, many needy people were simply outside the system – for instance, the self-employed and their dependents, the unemployed, married women and widows, children of single mothers, etc. Secondly, the amounts offered were so small that they would normally have to be supplemented by loans and private charitable gifts, if such could be obtained. On the whole, char-

---

9. The Danish law of 1891 is said to have been among its sources of inspiration. F. A. Ogg and W. R. Sharp (1949, 582).
10. William Beveridge was Director of the London School of Economics from 1919 to 1937. For his further contributions to British politics see Chapter 13 section 1.

ity played a much larger role in those days than later. To understand how small were the reserves of ordinary labouring families, it is worth noting that a Danish industrial worker, in full-time employment around 1900, spent 90 per cent of his income on daily needs; food, lodging and clothes. There was only a little left to build up any sort of reserve for unforeseen events in the economies of such families. Finally, it must be mentioned that those who received social assistance ran the risk of losing their civil rights, which they could only regain after the assistance had been repaid.

Another social aspect of the development of industrial society was the problem of *labour protection* or *industrial safety*. This covers the rules concerning the conditions of working life. Descriptions of child labour in British coal mines and textile factories in the early 1800s are well known. Those dark sides of the industrial society were dealt with at an earlier point of time than the matters of general social security described above. In the mid-1800s legislation existed in Great Britain protecting children and women against the worst sorts of abuse. That these two groups were protected by legislation before the adult male population can be seen as the outcome of the idea that men were able to take care of themselves and enjoyed the liberty of making agreements. However, many problems remained unsolved and risks unrevealed. One was the risk of industrial accidents. Many lines of production involved the transfer of energy from steam engines via shafts and driving belts, which caused accidents. A need was felt to limit these risks, and one way of doing this was to establish public factory inspections. It started in Germany in the 1870s from where it spread, reaching Scandinavia in the 1880s. In the Anglo-Saxon part of the world, the system developed differently, most of all in the USA. Here, insurance companies took over the rôle of inspection to a higher degree. The higher the risk, the higher the premium that the employers responsible would have to pay, which can be said to be the liberal way of dealing with the problem.

6. The Long Depression?

As explained in relation to table 6.2, a general increase in comparative growth rates took place from the years 1820-70 to the years 1870-1914. This was the case whether measured in absolute figures or per capita.

The two exemptions were Great Britain and Belgium, where both experienced declining growth rates, while for Western Europe as a whole, growth rates were increasing. This in itself does not fit in with the fact that the period from the mid-1870s to the mid-90s has become known among economic historians as "the Long Depression". The expression is still used and deserves comment:

Firstly, the growing importance of the urban trades meant that unemployment became easier to observe. Seasonal unemployment in agriculture means shorter and easier working days, whereas in construction and manufacturing industries it means pure unemployment. The relations between employee and employer in urban trades are such that the employer is quicker to free himself of his obligations towards those he employs.

Table 7.2. Percentage annual change of GDP (fixed prices) and consumer prices. 1870-74, 1874-94, and 1894-1913.

Pct. p.a.	Change of GDP			Change of consumer prices		
	1870-74	1874-94	1894-1913	1870-74	1874-94	1894-1913
Great Britain	2.4	1.8	1.8	1.1	-1.5	1.0
France	3.3	1.2	1.7	1.0	-0.2	0.4
Germany	4.5	2.1	3.3	4.2	-0.8	1.4
Italy	0.7	2.1	3.3	5.3	-1.0	1.2
Austria	2.5	2.4	2.4	n.a.	-1.2	1.4
Belgium	2.5	1.9	2.0	2.1	-1.5	1.1
Netherlands	1.6	2.3	2.2	4.4	-1.3	0.6
Denmark	2.0	2.2	3.3	1.2	-1.2	0.5
Finland	3.1	2.2	3.2	6.7	-1.6	1.7
Norway	3.3	1.4	2.6	5.2	-1.3	1.7
Sweden	4.8	1.2	2.7	4.5	-1.2	1.5
USA	3.3	3.6	4.4	-2.7	-1.3	0.7

Source: A. Maddison (1995 table c-16a and 1991 table E2).

Secondly, the main indicators of business cycles were the price series and the explanation for this is simple. Nothing better existed in the form of industrial production statistics or in national accounting. Prices had a general tendency to fall during those years, with consumers' prices going down on average by one per cent per year (table 7.2). For debtors, such a development must have caused trouble.

To this general development may also be added a particular drop in the prices of agricultural products caused by the growing import of grain from the USA and Eastern Europe. Among all occupations, agriculture was still the one that employed the most people, and this may explain the use of the term – the Great Depression. The use of the term by British historians can also be explained by the fact that in those years British industry experienced growing competition from foreign industry, not least from the expanding German industry.

A simple year by year average of the growth rates of 16 countries during 1873 to 1893 shows that only two years come out with negative figures, 1876 and 1893. For the rest of the years the average growth rates are positive. To characterize the period as a time of constant crises seems misleading. Rather it should be underlined that it was followed by a period from the middle of the 1890s with exceptionally high growth rates.

7. National developments

In sections 2 and 3, a description is given of monetary matters and trade policy, including the development of individual countries. To avoid repetition, this section will concentrate on structural matters of the individual countries.

7.1. *Great Britain*
If a place had ever existed since the fall of ancient Rome that deserved to be called the "Capital of the World" it must have been London around 1900. The position of London as the capital of the leading colonial power confirmed this, as did its position as the world's major financial and commercial centre. To this may be added that Great Britain was a country without serious internal political tensions. The problems felt during the first half of the century over the question of political representation had lessened after the greater part of the male population obtained the right to vote. Both from an external and an internal point of view, it was a country of great strength and self-confidence.

Fig. 9: If ever a place existed since the fall of Rome which deserved to be called the "capital of the world", it must have been London around 1900. Ludgate Hill seen from Fleet Street as some will recall it from their school textbooks.

Of course, if asked whether this is really a correct description, posterity may have both some doubts as well as comments to make. Change was under way. Other countries were catching up, which can be no surprise. Problems also existed on a deeper level. Was Great Britain about to lose some of its economic dynamism? Three reasons will be suggested why such a development might have been on its way.

Firstly, there seem to have been problems with the level of education at both the primary and more advanced levels It was not until 1870, that a law was passed instituting a system of public education and making school attendance both a right and an obligation. So far the only schools open to children of ordinary people were the Sunday schools organised by religious and charitable societies.[11] In Prussia, a system of elementary schools had already been established – at least in principle – before the Napoleonic Wars, and such a system soon spread to neighbouring countries. In the area of higher education, the British were lagging behind as well. This was especially so within the field of applied natural science. A British study group visiting Germany in the 1890s observed that a single German engineering school produced more graduate engineers than all the similar British institutions put together.

Table 7.3. Net-savings and net-investments in Great Britain and Germany as a percentage of the net national product/income (NNP/NNI).

Pct. of NNP/NNI	Net-savings	Net-investments*
Great Britain:		
1860-79	10.9	7.7
1880-99	11.0	6.9
1900-14	13.2	7.5
Germany:		
1851-70	9.2	8.5
1871-90	13.8	11.4
1891-1913	16.1	15.0

Source: B.R. Mitchell (1976,813 after S. Kuznets).
Note: The difference in the separation of the periods is due to the source.
* Exclusive of changes in stocks.

Secondly, the net investments in British trades and industries were relatively modest. Table 7.3 contains figures concerning the net-savings and net-investments of Great Britain and Germany through the years up to the First World War. As will be seen, the differences in the

11. M. Bruce (1979, 147).

saving rates were modest; two to three percentage-points higher for Germany than for Britain. However, the situation was quite different with regard to net-investments. Here the figures for Germany after 1880 were twice the figures for Britain. While Germany placed just about all of its savings *in the home country*, Great Britain placed almost half of its savings *outside the home country*. Seen from the investors' side, this may have been a wise thing to do in so far as investments in overseas railways, telegraph lines, plantations, etc., yielded the highest interests and profits. But for the rest of the population of the British Isles, faster growth in the available capital to finance more and better machines etc., would undoubtedly have been to their advantage. To this should be added the risk of losing some of these overseas investments through wars and political upheavals.

Thirdly, it has been argued that there was only a low level of internal demand. British industry was export-orientated and concentrated around a few goods such as textiles, coal, iron and products from the metal industry. Access to foreign export markets had been an important part of the expansion of those industries. Now, however, increasing customs duties protected the expanding European markets and the market in USA, and the remaining overseas markets did not offer much in the way of compensation. This left the home market as the target for new and expanding branches of British industry, and this is a rôle it failed to fulfil. Related to this, a fourth reason for the lack of dynamism may be cited. This was an outdated system of management where the owners even of large firms still tried to manage the companies themselves instead of leaving this to the new figure in business, the professional manager. This seems to have made a difference to the contemporary developments in the USA, and probably in Germany too.

Still, even when all this has been said, it is nevertheless worth mentioning that British goods were renowned for their high quality. While steel production of Germany grew faster than in Britain, the quality was inferior. The expression "Nuremberg goods" used in those days was not very complimentary, and the relationship between British and German industry recalls the comparisons made between European and Japanese industry in the 1950s. Finally, it should be remembered that Britain still had by far the highest per capita income among the European countries. Looked upon that way, her position seemed unchallenged – so far at least.

7.2. France

The peace treaty signed with Germany in 1871 forced France to give up two of her richest industrial areas, Alsace and Lorraine. In the Ruhr district Germany had ample sources of coal, and iron ore was plentiful on the French side of the former border. Through the surrender of the iron mines, German iron and steel production was boosted at the expense of France.[12] For this, and for deeper political reasons, the peace clearly represented a national catastrophe.

Taking this background into consideration, the French economy developed remarkably favourably in the years that followed. The annual growth per capita during the period 1870-1913 (table 6.2) amounted to 1.5 per cent, well above that of Britain (1.0 per cent) and close to that of Germany's (1.6 per cent). Thus, it would be misleading to describe the economy of France as stationary, all the more so considering the losses in 1871 and losses in the production of wine and silk caused by diseases which attacked vines and silkworms. On top of this must be added the general agricultural crises of Western Europe which was felt especially by the grain producing agriculture of Northern France.

Of all countries, France is the only one that borders both the Mediterranean and the North Sea. Consequently, two very different pictures can be presented of the French economy in the early 1900s. One portrays a country dominated by efficient, grain growing farms in the north-eastern part of the country, a young and fast- growing automobile industry, pioneering work in an infant aeroplane industry, the establishment of water-driven power stations and a growing aluminium industry, etc. Another picture will show an economy dominated by small farms growing olive trees on terraces as had been done for centuries, and small family businesses serving local villages and local farmers. Such striking differences can always be found in economies at an early stage of their transition. However, in France they were very marked, giving the country the character of a dual economy that lasted for many years; according to some, even until after the Second World War and her accession to the European Economic Community. In the same way as Great Britain, France had surpluses on her Balance of Payments, but the pattern of her foreign investments was different.

12. In the 1880s a new process for melting the French phosforous iron ore was invented. This in itself increased the value of the mines, while the waste products became the basis for the production of fertilizers. D. S. Landes (1991, 258f).

Firstly, a major part was invested in Europe, mainly in Russia and other areas in Eastern Europe. Secondly, it was mostly placed in government bonds. What was meant as a safe type of investment would turn out to be very risky in view of the results of the First World War and the Russian Revolution.

7.3. Germany

Under the political leadership of the chancellor, Otto von Bismarck, the year 1871 saw the realization of the desire to create a united German nation. Many years of competition between Prussia and Austria ended when the King of Prussia took the title, Emperor of Germany, in the Hall of Mirrors at Versailles.

Even before this took place, Prussia had prepared for this future event by creating what might be called an industrial infrastructure. This meant the creation of a transport system based on waterways, a tightly-knit system of railways, an advanced system of higher education institutions and technical universities, supplemented by laboratories and research centres in the manufacturing industries.

An important part of the institutional set-up was the financial sector represented by the commercial banks. As already mentioned, the German banks served as investment banks, participating in financing the fixed investments of its business customers. This was not only done through loans, but also through the ownership of shares in the firms and through representatives on the boards of the firms. Furthermore, there existed in Germany a tradition of cooperation in business within the framework of guilds. All in all, this meant that there was a widespread wish to promote cooperation in big business to avoid "harmful competition" and promote cooperation in the form of market-sharing deals, price agreements, etc. Where the British (and American) attitude was that such agreements in principle were illegal, the German attitude was more pragmatic. What mattered was whether the agreement, from an overall point of view, resulted in substantial cost reductions, served defence purposes or in other ways aided society. The German legislation concerning monopolies was formulated so as to make a distinction between what may be called "good" and "bad" monopolies. Where the traditional Anglo-Saxon position can be said to be based on principle of *prohibition,* the German can be said to be based on a principle of *control or inspection. Here* the function of the authorities is to see whether firms keep within the limits of the "good" monopolies. This, combined with the growth of military expenditure, is part of the explanation of the dominance of big business in Germany from the end of the 1800s and the existence of a military-industrial complex.

7.4. Belgium and the Netherlands

Development in *Belgium* in the period after 1870 is similar to development in Great Britain. As the pioneer industrial country on the Continent, it now met growing competition in her key industries; mining, iron and the textile industry. As in Great Britain, Belgium had already experienced a decrease in her growth rates. The high degree of specialization and the limited home market meant a strong dependence on foreign trade. More than half of the produce of industry was exported, mainly to France. Besides coal and steel, railway equipment was among the major items, from the end of the century supplemented by electric tramways. From 1863 onwards, the conditions for navigation on the Scheldt had been eased once again when the Netherlands stopped demanding tolls and customs duties for passage. The upturn Antwerp had experienced, when river traffic was opened earlier in the century, was further promoted and it soon regained its position as one of the foremost harbours of Europe.

Another significant element in the economic and political history of Belgium during this period was the acquisition of the Congo. As a result of private expeditions, partly financed by the Belgian King, it was declared to be a privately owned colony with the Belgium King as head of state! The colony was run in a cruel manner, using slave labour recruited among the natives. After strong foreign criticism, the area was granted the status of a Belgian colony after compensation was paid to the royal family. Until then, the Congo, as opposed to the Dutch colonies, had only played a minor role in the Belgian economy. This was to change with the First World War.

While Belgium was among the earliest industrialized countries, the *Netherlands* is among the group of countries whose industrialization came rather late, despite its geographical position close to the growth areas. Dutch historians have much discussed when an industrial break through took place.[13] The result seems so far to be that it should be placed in the 1890s. As an explanation for this "delay", the lack of raw

---

13. Their discussions are similar to those among Danish historians.

materials like coal is mentioned and a relatively high level of costs, including wages.

The reason why the development, according to Dutch historians, since the Napoleonic Wars seems unsatisfactory, is perhaps caused by comparing the Netherlands first to Belgium and then, from the middle of the century, to Germany. If comparisons had been made instead to areas with similar characteristics, a development parallel to that of their own would have been seen. A comparison with the Scandinavian countries shows (table 6.2) that Dutch growth rates during the years 1870-1913 were at the same level as those of Norway and Sweden, and a bit below those of Denmark. Although the geo-economic conditions of those two countries were similar, including the nearness of the English market for food exports, the Netherlands had big problems and high costs in increasing its agricultural production through drainage. It took time and costly investments, which can serve to explain why Denmark was able to expand her agricultural production faster and cheaper than the Netherlands. In a wider context it seems that it was less that the Netherlands was not up to par, but that its great neighbour, Germany, took an unusual step forward, whereby the Dutch lost some of their traditional feeling of economic superiority.

7.5. The Scandinavian countries

The years 1875 to 1914 saw the involvement of the Scandinavian countries in the industrial breakthrough. The details were different in the three countries corresponding to differences in their natural basis. What they had in common was an acceleration in their growth rates from the 1890s, and that foreign demand played a substantial role in the process.

Judged from the growth rates, *Denmark* took the greatest advantage of the favourable international economic climate in the years before First World War (ref. tables 6.2 and 7.2). The latter indicate that the start was a bit more modest in Norway and Sweden. This may have been partly compensated for by the fact that Denmark in the 1870s and early 1880s underwent a deterioration in her terms of trade due to the fall of the price of grain while she was still a net-exporter. The transfer of Danish agriculture from vegetable to animal production was symbolized by the start of the first cooperative dairy (1882) and first cooperative slaughterhouse (1887). The Danish reaction to the falling agricultural prices differed from that of most other countries in Western

Europe, where the reaction was to protect agriculture through increased customs duties. The Danish reaction can partly be explained by the fact that Danish agriculture was a net-exporter of grain, which meant that protectionism could never be a satisfactory solution – not even for agriculture. For the rest of the Danish economy, the change of agriculture meant the start of the specialised production of milking machines, and of equipment for diaries and slaughter houses such as refrigerating plants, etc.

Fig. 10: Tyskebryggen – Quay of the Germans – in the town of Bergen in the late 1800's. Note the gabled houses, some of which date back to the Middle Ages.

Norway experienced in the years after 1870 a stagnation in her exports of timber. However, growing world trade meant good years for Norwegian shipping. As a by-product this caused a growth of Norwegian shipbuilding. The use of water-power for the production of electricity opened up possibilities here, as in Switzerland, for quite new industries such as the production of nitrogenous fertilizer (Norwegian saltpetre) and aluminium. A common characteristic of these industries was that the costs of the necessary investments were high and had to be financed through the import of capital, mainly from Great Britain and Sweden. The capital was, to a large extent, supplied as direct investments, which meant a high degree of foreign ownership in the expanding parts of Norwegian economy. As a consequence of this, the Norwegian parliament, Stortinget, in 1907 passed a law limiting the possibilities of foreigners to own Norwegian industries. This has to be seen against the background of Norway's unilateral decision in 1905 to leave the union with Sweden only two years before. The direct background to this was the so-called consular divergence. Norway wanted to have consulates of its own to take care of Norwegian foreign trade and shipping. The Swedes could not accept this, being in favour of joint consulates for the two countries. This quarrel was, of course, only a symptom of deeper conflicts. For Norway, separation from Sweden meant the end of a period which first saw a union with Denmark lasting for four hundred years and then a union with Sweden for almost a hundred; a period spoken of by Norwegians as "the night of five hundred years"!

In *Sweden*, for centuries, there had been a tradition of mining (iron, copper, and silver). On the basis of this, she had developed a small, highly specialised metal industry such as the production of cannons and guns. The new methods of production where smelting was based on ordinary coal instead of charcoal, reduced any native advantage for Swedish iron industry. On the other hand, Sweden was rather fast in taking up the new methods of production and from the 1870s an expansion of the iron industry began. At first, it was mainly pig iron and raw materials for the iron industry that were exported. But the 1890s saw the beginning of a machine industry producing dairy machines, turbines, electro motors, and even combustion engines. However, it could still only be said to form the basis of a metal industry that was yet to come. Parallel to this, the production of matches and fertilizers formed the basis of a coming chemical and pharmaceutical industry – just think of Alfred Nobel (1832-96), the inventor of dynamite. More important at this stage was the development of a woodworking industry with wood pulp and paper as its leading products. At the outbreak of the First World War, primary products (including agricultural products) still made up 55 per cent of total exports and semi-manufactured products another 25-30 per cent.

An important feature of Swedish economy during those years was the construction first of a railway system and then of power stations.

Industrial production had so far been limited to areas with easy access to sea transport and the traditional use of water-power. Those restrictions were eased and entirely new possibilities opened up for the spread of industry. Finally, economic growth gained such a momentum that internal demand for investment and consumer goods became an important addition to the demand of the export markets.

The difference between the stage reached by the Danish economy and those of Norway and Sweden may be best illustrated by the difference in the relative number of emigrants. In the years between 1840-1914, the total number going to overseas areas from the three countries amounted to 2,168,000, out of which 2,050,000 left after 1865. An idea of the relative size of emigration can be had from the frequencies of emigration, i.e the annual number of emigrants per 100,000 inhabitants. Calculated in that way, Norway was among the countries in Europe with the highest rates of emigration. During the period 1881-90, the average, annual figure was 963, or just below one per cent.[14] This means that almost ten per cent of the Norwegian population left their home country within ten years. The similar Swedish figure was seven per cent and the Danish as low as four per cent. In so far as emigration was a result of push effects, this seems to indicate a substantial difference in living conditions and prospects in the three countries at that time.

7.6. *Italy, Spain and Portugal*

Turning from the group of Western European countries which, taken together with Austria and Switzerland at the close of the 1800s had began a period of rapid economic growth, we come to the southern border area, *Italy, Spain, and Portugal*. Although scattered islands of industrial production and organization could be found here, they existed almost in isolation from the surrounding society. A common feature of the three countries was a low level of education with an illiteracy rate of 60 per cent in Italy and as high as 70-80 per cent in Spain and Portugal. Another hindrance to economic development was internal political unrest and lack of leadership. In Italy, this was the case to such a degree that it was not until 1861 that the Italian peninsular became a political unit – but without becoming an economic unit.

---

14. K. Hvidt (1971, 24ff and 186ff).

The city-states of Northern *Italy* experienced after the Renaissance a set-back succeeded by stagnation, which kept the area outside the development of Western Europe for more than three hundred years. Part of the explanation was the separation of the area into a great number of small entities. The area suffered a further setback when it was decided at the Congress of Vienna that the Habsburg Empire, as compensation for the loss of the Austrian Netherlands (present-day Belgium and Luxembourg), should have the most advanced areas of Northern Italy. Under the leadership of the Kingdom of Sardinia, whose political centre was in Northern Italy despite its name, and with French support, the area was united as the Kingdom of Italy between 1859-61.

During the first years of her existence, Italy kept close ties to France resulting in a mutual free trade policy and, from 1865, Italian membership of the Latin Currency Union. Participation in this union, with its fixed exchange rates and the free movement of capital, was hampered by deficits on the public budgets and recalls the problems of Italy in the 1990s in relation to the Economic and Monetary Union of the EC.

As time passed, dependence on France was felt to be a hindrance to the development of the country and in 1887 it came to an outright customs war between the two. After this, Italy turned to Germany for capital imports and German participation in the development of the industries of Northern Italy. The growth of this area was facilitated by the nearness of the Alps and the new possibilities of producing electricity on the basis of water-power. This was very important since Italy has few coal-mines. Part of the background to the growth of a mining and iron industry was the demand due to the construction of railways and an ambitious naval programme.

By far the major part of the urban trades were, even more so than in France, what may be called small business such as clothes manufacturers, producers of shoes and leather goods and other goods demanding high degrees of skill such as musical instruments – goods, where Italy still holds a leading position. After ten years of relative stagnation, a period of high growth followed from 1897 until the outbreak of the First World War with an average growth rate well above 3 per cent. The number of industrial workers now showed a marked increase even in more advanced branches of production. As an example, the production of typewriters established in 1911 by Camillo Olivetti may be mentioned.

However, this is only one side of the story. Quite another could be told by referring to the emigration figures over the same years. During the five year period, when emigration peaked, the total number of Italian emigrants was 400.000 out of a population of 35 millions. This corresponds to more than one per cent a year, and even more than the Norwegian rate in the 1880s. This may be taken as proof that the industry of Italy was unable to absorb its population surplus, which was done instead in Chicago and the other new industrial cities in the north-eastern part of the USA.

Differences in geographical position have meant that *Spain and Portugal* have been more concerned with trans-oceanic affairs than Italy. Especially in the case of Portugal this has been supplemented by close ties to Great Britain. It was indeed more than a coincidence that David Ricardo, to illustrate the importance of international trade, chose in addition to English cloth, Portuguese wine! Their position on the Atlantic also allowed both Spain and Portugal to establish fishing industries.

For *Spain*, her possessions in South and Central America gave rise to considerable troubles in the 1800s when the USA started to practice the Monroe doctrine – "America for Americans". It meant involvement in costly wars, causing deficits on the Spanish public budgets and the neglect of the infrastructure in the home country.

As well as mining in the colonies, Spain traditionally had a substantial mining industry in the home country. As far back as the Moors, silver had been mined, and additionally lead, mercury, zinc, and iron ore were extracted, as was coal. In spite of the bounty of Nature, a manufacturing industry on the basis of these raw materials was not established. Because of the lack of Spanish capital, the mining industry was left to foreign owners who exported the products as raw materials. The size of this production can be illustrated by the fact that Spanish mines at the outbreak of the First World War produced one-fifth of world production of lead. Catalonia had the best possibilities for industrialization as it bordered on France and in Barcelona had a major centre. Around the town of Bilbao, situated on the Bay of the Biscay, a steel industry grew up from the turn of the century, which had the government as its customer and was protected by high customs duties. However, modern industry was still an exception, and by far the major part of the population was still employed in agriculture.

Portugal had traditionally close relations to Great Britain, with vintage port for the libraries of English country houses as its speciality. After the Congress of Vienna, her enormous colony, Brazil, started out on the road to independence, first through a personal union with the Kingdom of Portugal, then as an independent Empire, and finally as a republic after 1889. Unlike Spain, Portugal retained substantial colonies in other continents and in the Pacific. The loss of Brazil meant a setback to the commercial life of Portugal and especially Lisbon,.

The overall impression of the stage of economic development of Spain and Portugal at the outbreak of World War One is that an industrialization was hardly initiated, apart from the position of Spain as supplier of raw materials to the fast growing industries of nearby countries.

7.7. The USA
The period between the American Civil War (1861-65) and the outbreak of the First World War covered the time when the USA took its place among the leading countries of the world economy.

The thirty to forty years after the Civil War saw a tremendous growth both in American agriculture and American industry. It was the period when "the frontier was closed"; that is, the period where the vast area between the Mississippi River and the Great Lakes to the east and the Rocky Mountains to the west, was made an integral part of the American economy. And it was the period that saw the growth of the great industrial cities on the East Coast like New York, Philadelphia, Baltimore, Chicago and the great industrial centres situated around the Great Lakes.

American farming was characterized by an exceptional high labour productivity compared to European agriculture. But American industries experienced high growth rates as well. One of the characteristics of American manufacturing industry, the mass production of standardised products of high and uniform quality, had developed during the Civil War through the production of farm machinery and equipment, especially for the troops of the Northern States. The new ways of production were now transferred to civilian ends. A related part of this was the introduction of "Taylorism", so named after Frederic W. Taylor (1856-1915). The central theme of Taylorism is the division of a given production into separate processes and a study of these processes to include how much time they take. Taylorism meant the introduction of the stop-watch in the workplace. A peak was reached with the introduction of the assembly line by Henry Ford in 1913-14.

Capital concentration and new methods of management spread, beginning in the great railway companies.[15] To operate a railway system, with lines running over several thousands of kilometres, meant a challenge to the management of these companies. The complexity surpassed what had been seen in any other branches: Technical aspects such as keeping the tracks in order, operating security systems and the rolling-stock, maintaining station buildings, administering the staff, setting prices, financing investment, etc., all needed to be handled at the same time. All this had to be done to cope with activities spread out over a wide area. To handle those problems a new theory of management was developed that opened the doors to a new person in business: the professional manager, whose introduction meant the separation of management from ownership.

Another aspect of the development of big business was an increasing concentration of capital and growing monopolization. The USA, from its past as a British colony, had inherited the "Common Law" and with it the general rule that limitations on the freedom of enterprise were invalid. As such, they were not protected by the courts, which meant that it was difficult to enforce them. The story of American monopoly policy is to a high degree the story of American business seeking to avoid this rule, and the endeavours of Congress to have such a rule enforced. An early example of the first is the establishment in 1882 by John D. Rockefeller (1839-1937) of the Standard Oil Company as a trust. In principle, the participating firms still existed as independent entities, but they left the decisions concerning prices, market sharing, etc., to a group of "trusted" persons, which actually meant that they gave up their independence. In 1890, Congress passed what came to be known as the Sherman Anti-trust Act. This meant the beginning of a year-long fight between Congress and big business, part of the problem being that it turned out to be difficult to make the judicial system enforce the legislation against manufacturing firms. Apart from the anti-trust policy, a major theme in the economic policy of the USA at the close of the 1800s was monetary policy or rather, gold or silver or both? As part of the financing of the Civil War, the amount of circulating notes had been increased dramatically, prices had gone up and the redeemability of the bank notes was suspended. After the war, a law was passed aiming at a reduction of prices and a return to the gold standard

15. Alfred D. Chandler, Jr. 1995.

at the former price of gold. This was realized at the beginning of 1879. The background to this was a tight deflationary policy at the expense of settlers and other debtors. Since silver was more abundant than gold, this caused pressure from those groups to accept also silver as a basis for the monetary system. The quarrel ended in 1896. A leading senator sought the presidency from outside the two main parties on a silver programme. For the first, and so far the only, time, a candidate from outside the usual parties threatened to win. However, the Republicans won on a traditional monetary programme, and the banks remained on the gold standard.

The 1890s proved to be a shaky period in the economic history of the USA. This can be seen from the year-to-year changes in the growth rates of the GDP. On average, they amounted to 8.5 percentage points in the 1890s.[16] The largest difference, however, was reached in 1908-09 when a drop in the GDP of 8.2 per cent was followed by an upturn of 12.2 per cent. After this, it was realized that the entire American banking system should be put under more strict control in order to regulate credit expansion and the money issue. This was done through the Federal Reserve Act of 1913. After 125 years, the USA finally had a central bank that survived and still exists as the present-day Federal Reserve System.[17]

For Europe, the growth of the American economy meant an increasing sensitivity to its existence. As already mentioned, the construction of steel ships meant a sharp drop in freight rates and an opening of the European grain market to the efficient American farmers. At the same time, the importance of the American market to European producers increased. Mass-emigration continued, but from the turn of the century it came especially from Southern and Eastern Europe. As to its Balance of Payments, the USA had so far been a net-importer of capital in order to finance investments in its infrastructure. Now this changed. At the close of the century, the current account of its BoP switched from deficit to surplus. The USA had started its career as a net-lender on the international capital market.

---

16. To illustrate, the following growth rates (percent, fixed prices) shall be quoted: 1894 – 2.9; 1895 +12.1; 1896 –2.1; 1897 +9.5. Here the year-to-year differences amount to 11-15 percentage points. Source: As table 18.4, to which is refered.
17. As a curiosity it should be mentioned that each dollar bill has, in barely legible lettering, an indication of whether they were issued in Boston, Chicago, St Louis and so on. This may be seen as a tribute to the traditional scepticism towards a centralized banking system.

Part III
The Great Showdown

The period between 1914 and 1945 represents a watershed in terms of both the economic and political history of Europe. It would be hard to find a correspondingly brief period of history that marked such a definite break with the past and with such deep and far-reaching changes in economics and politics. Not even the French Revolution of 1789, along with the subsequent Napoleonic Wars, constituted as great a change. In 1815, restoration of the conditions which prevailed before the French Revolution and the ensuing wars was the order of the day. In 1945, there was no wish to turn the economic or political clock back to 1939, let alone 1914. On the contrary, there was a desire to draw lessons from the bad experiences of the period in order to bring about a new and different world.

To those who lived through it, the period from 1914 to 1945 must have seemed full of sharp contrasts as it lurched between war and peace, boom and depression, liberalism and central planning. Seen from a distance, however, the period comes across as a coherent whole, and as a period of fundamental change. This applies to the two wars, which were, generally speaking, fought between the same countries. In the ideological sphere, on both occasions, democratically governed countries were challenged by those with autocratic governments. In politico-economic terms, the inter-war period was marked by great instability and failing economic growth. Although the economic train of events of the 1920s contrasted sharply with that of the 1930s, both decades did have the following feature in common: they revealed the fundamental shortcomings and weaknesses of economic policy. This was particularly true concerning the significance of the role played by the public sector in the economy, and also applied to the inadequate appreciation of the parameters governing international economy.

In 1914, the countries of Western Europe were clearly dominant in global political terms. The great showdown, however, left them in a less dominant position between the two new superpowers, the USA and the Soviet Union. Whereas, previously, the main concern of the European great powers had been how to place themselves vis-à-vis each other, their main headache was finding a position between the two superpowers where the main challenge was the containment of Soviet expansion in the wake of the Second World War.

The great showdown thus left the Western European nations with a two-sided problem. At home, they had to organize themselves in a new way so as to avoid the repetition of exhausting economic, political and military struggles. Abroad, they had to ensure that they were in a position to safeguard their own freedom and future, situated as they were between the two superpowers.

The 1914-45 period may safely be characterized as that of bad experiences. Politically, this meant a total of ten years of devastating military conflict; economically, it was the story of about two decades of economic unrest, disintegration and stunted growth. The three following chapters are about the bad experiences: ten years of war in 1914-18 and 1939-45, eleven years of bungling between 1918 and 1929 and a decade of depression from 1929 to 1939. Chronology has been ignored in the treatment of the two wars so as to deal with them as one. The reason for this is that for the generations that lived through them, the wars represented an overall, common European catastrophe. Equally, the reason why the three periods are treated as a distinct area, and which together cover only thirty years, is that the sum of all the political and economic experiences was to have a deep impact on, and considerable influence over, the ensuing post-war period.

The best thing to be said about bad experiences is that lessons are subsequently drawn from them. A discussion of the efforts to turn the experience to good use follows in Part IV: Reconstruction and High Growth.

Chapter 8

Ten Years of War
1914-18 and 1939-45

1. Growing ideological clefts

Politico-philosophical resistance to the concentration of power in the hands of the state had arisen in France and England during the eighteenth century. This criticism was based on a new view of the relationship between the individual and the state, with greater emphasis being placed on the freedom of the individual vis-à-vis the state. As far as decision-making powers over the state apparatus were concerned, there was a trend towards a democratic mode of government with free and universal suffrage as its ultimate consequence. The trend within economic thinking was towards economic liberalism, which meant a considerable reduction of the role and power of the state in economic affairs, along with extensive freedom of economic action for the private citizen. In the case of the right to political representation and influence, the question of with whom arose. Democratic thinking brought in its wake a new, broader, popular understanding of what it meant to belong to a nation; in other words the emergence of national consciousness. Absolute monarchy had caused much grandiose rhetoric to be uttered in homage to the absolute ruler. The new trends, which first made themselves felt to any significant extent during the French Revolution, replaced homage to the absolute ruler with that of homage offered to the general public itself.

The flow of eighteenth century thinking had consequently settled into three distinct lines of political thought, which were to give rise to new types of conflict. First, there was the question of the introduction of democratic governance. Second, there was the question posed by choice of national allegiance. And, third, came the question of the degree of economic liberalism.

Democratization of government, along with rising national consciousness seem to be particularly dangerous processes. To start with, more democratic rule could lead to the emergence of conflicts between sections of the population; conflicts which would otherwise have been suppressed. Apparent calm, if freer conditions were to prevail, could be shown to be a deceptive cloak over tensions and conflicts within the structure of a given nation state. Another aspect is that chauvinism and provoking conflict abroad may be used by the state as a lightning conductor for domestic social and political conflicts. A historical period with growing democratization and increasing national consciousness posed many serious threats to international order and tranquillity. It was not so strange that the long period of peace in Western Europe after the Congress of Vienna in 1815, seemed ever more fragile towards the beginning of the twentieth century.

The Russian Revolution added a fourth problem in 1918 to the three already in existence, which was that there now was a choice between a property-based, capitalist society and a socialist/communist society. This question had already been raised at an earlier date by Karl Marx (1818-83), who was the leading theorist and advocate of socialism. It was only with the Russian Revolution of 1917-18, however, that the problem made its entry on to the European political stage as a question of common concern. Initially, the Revolution gave rise to the support by Western countries of counter-revolutionary movements and direct involvement in Russian politics through military intervention. At that time, the fledgling Soviet society was still propagating the idea of imminent international revolution. This, along with the prospect of huge economic losses on earlier investments in Russia, led to great scepticism in the West towards the Soviet Union. Thus, the basis was laid for a new ideological dividing line, which was to leave a deep imprint on both the latter part of the great showdown and the period that followed.

With the death of Vladimir Ilyich Lenin (1870-1924) and the growing power of Joseph Stalin (1879-1953) in the mid-1920s, Soviet policy underwent many changes. First the system was liberalized for a while under the New Economic Policy, NEP, which, among other things, allowed foreign economic activity in the country. Then, significantly, the Soviets announced that they would concentrate on their own economy and leave the world revolution to fend for itself. In reality, the result was that the Soviet Union became economically and, in part, politically isolated from the rest of the world. Even in the years of crisis in the 1930s, the Communist parties in Western Europe only played a limited role.

The exception to this, which was to have a decisive effect on future events, was Germany where democracy had been introduced at the time of the Peace of Versailles. The German Communist Party gained considerable support due to the massive unemployment around 1930. This was largely at the expense of the Social Democratic Party and was accompanied by unrest in the labour market, all of which paved the way for the hitherto politically insignificant National Socialist Workers Party to set themselves up as the largest single party. Although their voter support was inferior to that of the Communists and Social Democrats combined, the Nazi Party was able to take over the reins of government in January 1933. After this, the Nazis soon put an end to democracy.

The Soviet Union was to play a double role vis-à-vis Germany in the great showdown. Firstly, the very presence of Communism served as a pretext for Nazism to pass itself off as a defender of western values. Resistance to the Soviet Union and Communism thus served as a figleaf for the Nazi regime based on dictatorship and violence. Secondly, the existence of the Communist Soviet Union meant that Germany was eventually caught in an exhausting war on two fronts in the Second World War. The Soviet Union, therefore, on two occasions, exercised a decisive influence on the fate of Nazism, first, as part of the background to the Nazi movement's initial growth and, later on, as a signal factor in its annihilation.

Nazism may be said to have constituted the most developed and malignant version of the anti-democratic social model known in the interwar period as Fascism. The movement manifested itself for the first time in Italy in the early 1920s under the leadership of a former Socialist newspaper editor, Benito Mussolini (1883-1945). The movement favoured the creation of the corporate state (note the distinction between "corporate" and "cooperative") where the government and the business organizations run the country without the participation of parliament. Political life was organized around a single party system and the government was thus anti-democratic and anti-parliamentarian. Chauvinism and a wish to return to the greatness of the past marked the Fascist movement. In the case of Italian Fascism, the long-vanished Roman Empire was the chosen example. In accordance with this, the Italian Fascist Party projected pictures of a new Italy as the dominant Mediterranean power with new possessions around the Mediterranean. The Fascists acceded to power in Italy in the mid-1920s. In 1932, a Fascist dictatorship was set up in Portugal under Antonio de Salazar (1889-1970). In Spain, three years of civil war between Fascists and various Socialist movements came to an end in 1939 with victory for the Fascists and the establishment of a dictatorship under the leadership of Francisco Franco (1892-1975). This regime came to power with the help of Germany and Italy which recognized Franco's government from the outset of the civil war. Unlike Italy, Spain and Portugal did not get directly involved with the Germans during the Second World War, but remained formally neutral. In both countries, dictator and dictatorship weathered the post-war showdown and democratization only got under way after the deaths of the dictators.

2. The expansion of Germany and Japan

As mentioned in earlier chapters, economic development in the main, had bypassed Germany for centuries. With the exception of areas close to large river ports connected to the Baltic and the North Sea, the German economy had not enjoyed the upturn of the seventeenth and eighteenth centuries as had the economies of England, the Netherlands or, for that matter, Denmark. During this period, the Kingdom of Prussia emerged from the Principality of Brandenburg to form the core of German unification in the nineteenth century and the creation of the German Empire in 1871. At this time, there was a decisive shift of real power away from the Austro-Hungarian Empire towards the new German Empire. The German speaking area must have been the most populous in Western Europe at the time. However, the dynastically determined borders of Germany corresponded poorly with the national lines of division. This was a universal problem. Within the German Empire, there were also problems with minorities. However, the fact that there were large German-speaking minorities outside the borders of the Empire was to prove equally problematic, especially when they started to appeal for help from the fatherland.

By the year 1900, the situation arose where Germany was no longer just a threat to its continental neighbours. Great Britain began to feel that its interests were threatened. The British had stayed out of the Prussian wars of 1848-51 and 1864 against Denmark, the war of 1866 against Austria as well as that of 1870-71 against France. The interests of Great Britain lay overseas and, at the turn of the century, it became obvious that German maritime ambitions extended beyond the mouth of the Elbe and the shores of the North Sea. Extensive German naval construction programmes could not be solely for purposes involving Germany's continental neighbours. British vigilance was entirely justified.

This is how the situation arose that was to influence the outcome of the two wars of the great showdown. German wars of expansion on the European continent led to the involvement of the Anglo-Saxon world; first Great Britain and then the USA. Germany had become the second largest industrial power by the turn of the century, exceeded only by the USA. It was natural for Germany to seek territorial expansion, particularly towards the East, in order to ensure both the supply of raw materials and food as well as a sphere of economic influence. After all, that was only what the French and British had successfully done overseas, and even smaller neighbouring states such as the Netherlands and Belgium were doing it.

While the new German Empire was seeking to define its global position, the old Habsburg Empire sought to strengthen its position to the south-east in the Balkans. Seen from a wider perspective, this development posed a two-sided problem. There were movements agitating for the union of the hitherto much divided German areas and Austria into a "Greater Germany" across existing borders, while, at the same time, an expansive foreign policy was being pursued which disregarded borders drawn according to national criteria. The former, i.e., the desire for German union, led to the annexation of Austria and parts of Czechoslovakia by Nazi Germany in 1938. The latter, expansion into foreign areas, provided the direct cause of both wars; Austria obliged in 1914 and Nazi Germany did the same in 1939.

The idea, as it was expressed at the time, was to provide "Lebensraum". The significance of this was underlined by events in the latter half of the First World War. The Allied blockade, with the consequent shortage of food, was a major reason for the collapse of the German home front. Subsequently, the vulnerability to blockades increased as the armed forces became increasingly dependent on the supply of industrial raw materials, not least that of oil.

As a part of their expansionism, the Germans built up the notion of a map of the geography of European resources with Germany at the hub as the country where the most advanced industrial production took place. The areas to the north, west, and to a certain extent, the south would be allotted the task of supplying manufactured and semi-manufactured goods. Such a role was probably what the Germans had in mind for the Scandinavian countries, the Netherlands, Belgium, Northern and Eastern France, and the non-German parts of Czecho-slovakia. The larger net-suppliers of farm produce and basic raw mate-rials, including oil, lay to the east. The Germans developed in this way a geo-political outlook whereby the neighbouring countries were to ar-range their economies in such a way that they catered first and fore-most for purely German interests. This deserves mention in order to shed some light on the reasoning of the victors of both world wars. Then they thought it reasonable that Germany should not only be re-quired to pay large war reparations, but even that German industrial development should be held back and the country permanently re-duced to the level of a predominantly agricultural economy. The fact that the borders of German speaking areas were unclear, and that some of these areas were outside German territorial boundaries, only in-creased the risk of Germany engaging in cross-border disputes. To this could be added that, in the border areas with France, Czechoslovakia (formerly known as Bohemia) and Poland, there were raw materials in-cluding iron ore which Germany badly needed. So, national-political and economic reasons were potential causes of conflict with all of Ger-many's neighbours.

Furthermore, although 20 to 30 years later, conditions in the Far East developed in such a fashion that Japan eventually posed a similar threat to the USA as Germany did to Britain. The Japanese supply problem was similar to that of the Germans, if somewhat more pro-nounced. Japan had undergone rapid industrialization, but lacked raw materials. This was the background, among other things, for ex-pansion into Manchuria in the 1930s. The closest major supplier of crude oil was the Netherlands East Indies, although the USA was al-so a major supplier. Japanese armaments programmes took the sup-ply problem into account by planning the construction of a large na-vy, which would protect Japanese supply routes; a development gave rise to much American concern. In autumn, 1941, the USA consid-ered imposing an oil embargo on Japan. It was precisely such a move that the Japanese sought to pre-empt, and with temporary success, by the surprise attack on the US Navy at Pearl Harbor on 7th December 1941.

To sum up, it can be said that from the outset of the twentieth century, rising tensions were making themselves felt throughout Europe, With the rise of Japan as an industrialized nation, this field of tension widened to include the situation in the Far East and relations with the USA. This was how the basis came about for the eventual globalization of military conflicts, which was one of the hallmarks of the Second World War.

For the ensuing period, the globalization of conflict meant that the possibilities of maintaining neutrality were curtailed, particularly after the Second World War. During the First World War, of Germany's neighbours, only Denmark, the Netherlands and Switzerland remained outside the conflict. In the Second World War, only Switzerland and Sweden plus Ireland, as well as Spain and Portugal with their tainted regimes, remained aloof. The great showdown was also the day of reckoning for the idea that a country could live in an area of tension caused by power politics without running the ever-present risk of itself suffering possible military involvement. Realizations of this nature were, without doubt, strong contributory factors in making possible the political and economic groupings that arose in the wake of the great showdown resulting in a development towards economic and political integration.

3. The strategy that failed

On 18th June 1815, the Napoleonic Wars came to an end at the battle of Waterloo. On 1st August 1914, the First World War broke out. The 99 intervening years represented a uniquely long period of peace in the history of North-West Europe by comparison with previous centuries. Despite extensive armaments programmes, including naval armaments, the thought of prolonged military conflicts between European nations must have seemed alien and far-fetched to the general public in 1914.

In the 1914-18 and 1939-45 wars, German/Austrian aggression was their direct cause and both ended up on the losing side. In order to understand the course the wars took, the focus will now be placed on some of geographical and military factors that influenced the German choice of strategy.

The geographic factor, essentially Germany's position in the middle of Europe, meant that there was always the risk that in case of war the country would have to fight on several fronts at any given time. The most likely prospect was that of fighting on a western and an eastern front at the same time. After Russia, Germany was the nation with the largest population in Europe although Great Britain, France and Italy were not far behind. In total terms, however, the balance of population advantage lay with Germany's potential opponents. Demographic and geographic reasons thus dictated German interest in avoiding a war fought simultaneously on western and eastern fronts, as well as in prosecuting the war in such a fashion that the outcome was not dependent on the nominal strength of the armies. In other words, war had to be fought as a *blitz krieg* where potential enemies did not have the time to bring their collective, nominal advantage to bear on the course of events. There was, furthermore, the relative isolation of Germany from the sea, which implied the risk of being cut off from vital strategic raw materials such as high-grade iron ore and petroleum based fuel. This, in turn, demanded rapid conquest and the economic exploitation of conquered areas. As far as the latter aspect is concerned, the crude Nazi view of the populations of occupied countries was a real obstacle to carrying out the required exploitation effectively.

In the latter half of the nineteenth century, military technology had developed in such a manner as to favour defensive rather than offensive warfare. Inventions and innovations such as the machine gun and the use of barbed wire, in conjunction with trenches and fortified positions, typified this trend. The hitherto fashionable massed infantry attacks in open country were, therefore, rendered extremely difficult, if not impossible. This development had escaped the attention of all the general staffs, a fact that was to cost the lives of millions of soldiers in the 1914-18 war. These were the features that indicated that the First World War would, in fact, be static.

In the twenty years between the wars, warfare was motorized with the introduction of armoured fighting vehicles and the use of aircraft, which meant, among other things, fighter-bombers and airborne troops. Such technological development indicated that the Second World War would be mobile. This was most clearly appreciated by the Germans.

With the construction of main railway lines in the latter half of the nineteenth century, and motorways in the 1930s, it became possible for the Germans to transfer troops and equipment rapidly from the Western to the Eastern Front or, vice versa. The same troops could then be used on several fronts at brief intervals. This presupposed, however, that the war could be prosecuted as a blitz krieg. The German General Staff was preoccupied by the question of whether to strike first to the

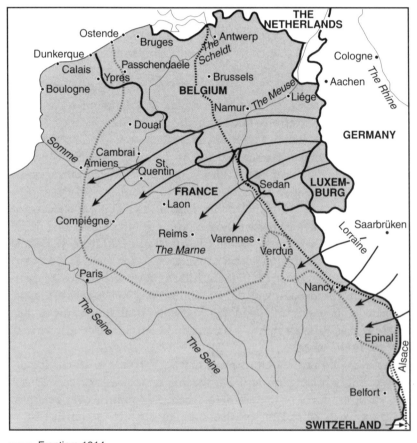

■■■ Frontiers 1914
∷∷∷ Situation of the front, August-September 1914
▮▮▮ Situation of the front, November 11th 1918

Fig. 11: The idea of the Schlieffen plan was to avoid a head-on confrontation on the Franco-German border. Odd as it may seem, the second attempt, in 1940, was the most successful.

west or to the east. Until the end of the nineteenth century, the prevailing view was that Russia was to be struck down first, after which the war could be directed westwards, principally towards France. However, as Russian mobilization was thought to be a much lengthier process than would be the case in France, this point of view changed. It was intended that the French army should not be given the time to seize the initiative on the Western Front. The result of this new thinking was the Schlieffen plan, named after the Chief of the German General Staff at the turn of the century, Alfred von Schlieffen (1833-1913). This plan was attempted on two occasions, first at the outbreak of the First World War and second during the campaign against France in May and June, 1940. Odd as it may seem, the second attempt was the most successful.

According to this plan, the principal German offensive was to be directed through the southern Netherlands and Belgium in order to avoid a head-on confrontation with the main French force on the Franco-German border. The French left flank was to be turned from the north by a scythe-like movement. At the same time, the Germans would be racing towards the English Channel. The plan presupposed the violation of Belgian neutrality, although Germany was bound by treaty to respect it. Dutch neutrality was also to be violated according to von Schlieffen's original version in order for the blow to be delivered with sufficient force. If the plan was successfully executed, it could then be rapidly concluded as German forces were moved eastward in order to take up the fight at full strength against the Russians before they could complete their mobilization. Experience from the Russian-Japanese war of 1904-05 played a part in all this, as it was then apparent that Russian military organization left an adversary with all the time in the world.

Germany did not march through the Netherlands in 1914. The offensive through Belgium and Northern France was not carried out with sufficient force or the required speed. After a little over a month, the offensive came to halt less than 50 kilometres to the north-east of Paris. The German forces in the central sector of the front were then pushed about 100 kilometres back. The rest of the war on the Western Front turned into static trench warfare after the armies dug in.

As mentioned above, the plan was used again in 1940 and, this time, it worked. The period of the war on the Western Front from September 1939 to May 1940 has gone over in history as the "Phoney War",

"La drôle de guerre" and "Die Sitzkrieg" respectively, all of which meaning that military operations were very limited indeed. It may seem odd that the Allies left the Germans undisturbed on the Western Front for eight months after the outbreak of war in September 1939. This lull allowed the Germans to stabilize their Eastern Front and secure their Northern flank by occupying Denmark and Norway. They thus gained access to the North Atlantic, setting up U-boat bases and ensuring the supply of Swedish iron ore. On 10th May 1940, the offensive in the West started with the invasion of Belgium and the Netherlands, the initial and decisive thrust going through the town of Maastricht. Events unfolded rapidly after that. By 4th June, the last British troops were evacuated from Dunkirk and on 22nd June, France and Germany concluded an armistice. Yet again, a German army had produced a victory in six to seven weeks. At that stage, the war was barely ten months old. The actual fighting, however, had only lasted about 14 weeks[1] and German casualties had been light.

The war against the Soviet Union was started a year after the victory in the West. By December 1941, the campaign on the Eastern Front faltered on the outskirts of Moscow. At the same time, the USA came into the war because of the Japanese surprise attack on Pearl Harbor. Hitler's declaration of war on the USA appears strange because this got President Roosevelt off the hook in terms of having to persuade the isolationists in Congress to agree to American participation in another European war.

German strategy seems to have been a hairsbreadth away from success during the Second World War. German war aims under Nazi rule, however, were so vague, or unlimited, that it was almost inevitable that Germany would end up in a global conflict. There was no strategy for such a contingency, only the hope afforded by the possible development of new weapons, including nuclear weapons.

During both world wars, each side sought to implement a blockade policy against the other. The German variant was in the form of submarine warfare against British maritime supply routes. The Allied variant consisted in cutting Germany off from the outside world. The

---

1. The Polish campaign had taken four weeks, the Norwegian campaign seven, including three that overlapped with the offensive in the West. Finally the campaign against the Netherlands, Belgium and France lasted for approximately six weeks.

German variant did not succeed; maritime transport could not be brought to a complete halt with the technology of the day, especially after the convoy system was introduced at the end of the First World War. The Allied blockade of Germany seems to have been instrumental in bringing about the collapse of the German Home Front in 1918. During the Second World War, levels of private consumption seem to have been reasonable in Britain and Germany. This, however, was most definitely not the case for the populations in German-occupied areas who were made to suffer, though Denmark was the clear exception to this pattern. Outright starvation with increased mortality rates occurred in Western Europe in France, Belgium and the Netherlands, although it must be pointed out that conditions were far worse in Eastern Europe. In Germany, the food supply tended to plummet once the war was over, just as it had been at its worst after the First World War.

The factors outlined above go beyond the scope of traditional economic history. They have nevertheless been mentioned at length because it was inevitable that the two wars would leave a deep impression on the generations that lived through them. The leading politicians of Western Europe in 1945 must, as children or youngsters in the First World War and mature adults in the Second, have been deeply affected by the course of events.

In Western Europe, the strongest feelings must have been felt in those countries which were directly affected by the German offensive planning as envisaged by the Schlieffen plan. The operating premise towards these nations was precisely the violation of international treaties of non-aggression or neutrality. It was no wonder then that it was Belgium, the Netherlands and Luxembourg, which, along with France, took the initiative in proposing entirely new models of European integration in the wake of the great showdown.

Table 8.1. Military casualties, 1914-18.

millions	France	GB	Russia	Italy	USA	Germ	Aust-Hun
Military personal	8,0	8,3	14,0	3,8	5,0	13,0	9,0
Dead and missing	1,4	0,8	1,5	0,5	0,1	2,0	0,9
Wounded	2,5	2,0	5,0	1,0	0,2	3,6	3,2
Prisoners	0,5	0,2	2,5	0,5	0,0	0,6	1,0

Source: Salmonsens Konversationsleksikon. 1928. Vol. XXIV page 837.

4. Casualties and costs

Casualties include fatalities and other direct losses in terms of the wounded, increased morbidity and so on. Costs cover material losses.

During the First World War, the loss of life as a direct result of military action was far higher among members of the armed forces than among civilians. During the Second World War, the civilian casualty rate was the highest, although the military casualty rates on the Eastern Front were enormous. Civilian casualties, however, in connection with the First World War were greater after the cessation of hostilities. This was due to the continued blockade against the vanquished which, along with the bad supply situation in general, led to actual starvation. This, in turn, led to increased morbidity and higher mortality rates. The deadly and ravaging epidemic of Spanish influenza has to be seen as a consequence of the war. The casualty figures are not reliable, especially those recording indirect losses due to increased morbidity and crippling wounds.

With the exception of the USA, the share of enlisted men dead and missing was ten per cent or more for the listed countries. For France, it was seventeen per cent while for Germany, the rate was about fifteen per cent. As we may assume that many soldiers did not serve in the front line, the casualty rates for soldiers in action are even higher. When evaluating the figures, it must be borne in mind that they are derived from limited sections of the male population eligible for conscription. Casualty figures for Poland and the Balkans may be added to those quoted above thus bringing the overall figure for military casualties to approximately 8.5 million. The high rate of civilian casualties mentioned earlier came about at the end of the war and in its aftermath. The global civilian casualty figure is set at about 15 million, of which 10 million were in Russia alone. As the post-war supply situation was particularly bad in Germany, Austria and Hungary, it was these countries which bore the brunt of the remaining civilian casualty figures. The total number of dead, military and civilian all told, as a direct or indirect consequence of the First World War is in the region of 25 million.

The equivalent figure for the Second World War was about 42 million, with 16 million of these being military casualties, and the remaining 26 million, civilian. The difference in the levels of military casualties becomes obvious in the case of Great Britain whose overall losses in Europe amounted to 198,000 casualties. Casualty rates on the Eastern Front were of an altogether different order of magnitude where the Soviet figure alone is 10 million. The total figure for German military casualties is 3.8 million, the great majority of whom were killed on the Eastern Front. By comparison, German civilian casualties were of the order of 3.1 million. Casualty figures show that the Nazi bombing of Great Britain, first in the form of the Blitz in 1940 and later on the V I and V II rockets, had a comparatively limited effect. The final figure for British civilian casualties is about 100,000. As mentioned earlier, the German population did not feel the effects of the war in terms of supply until the end. It is assumed, however, that rates of consumption took a nosedive in the occupied countries of Western Europe, particularly in France and the Netherlands. These countries also experienced mass forced conscription of labour for German industry. The civilian experience of the Second World War was far more direct than that of the First. The civilian population in the occupied areas of Eastern Europe undoubtedly experienced the worst plight and distress. There, the general supply problem brought on by the war was compounded by direct persecution by the occupying power which sought to annihilate the population as it was deemed to be racially inferior.

It is difficult to express economic and material losses in figures, although they can be divided into two categories. Direct loss was experienced after the war in the shape of a depleted national wealth as a consequence of war. Then, there is the deprivation suffered by the populations during the war in the shape of reduced civilian consumption.

To start with there is the loss of wealth in the form of damaged production equipment, something that both wars left in their wake. The fact that the First World War consisted mainly of static trench warfare, on the Western Front at least, meant that battle-related damage was limited, though the affected areas in Belgium and north-eastern France were subjected to extensive destruction. The damage, however, was restricted to a narrow band, generally less than 100 kilometres in width. Direct material destruction was undoubtedly on a much greater scale in the Second World War. This, on the one hand, was due to the advent of aerial bombardment and to the more fluid and mobile fronts on the other. As the Allies possessed bombers with greater range and payload capacity than those of the Germans, Germany suffered greater air raid damage than any other Western European country including Britain. Contemporary bombing techniques did not allow for intensive precision bombing of industrial targets, so city centres and residential areas were also hit. It is estimated that around three million British homes were either totally destroyed or heavily damaged; the equivalent figure for Germany is approximately ten million. Widespread destruction came in the wake of retreating armies applying a"scorched earth" policy. The fact that this war was mobile meant that this problem affected large areas. Fixed installations such as railways, roads, bridges, mines and public utilities were particularly vulnerable. This factor was a large part of the reason for the sharp drop in production at the war's end and in the immediate post-war period.

Besides the direct damage, there was also the general wear and tear on productive plant due to inadequate maintenance. The Second World War placed demands requiring a far greater industrial production capacity than in the First World War. New industries had emerged or had grown rapidly in the inter-war period. Examples of this were the car and aircraft production, along with the electromechanical and radio industries. The products of these large and new industries saw widespread and prominent use in the waging of war. The problem of inadequate maintenance seems to have reached its peak in Germany in that the lack of new investment and poor maintenance probably did more harm than enemy action.

To the above-mentioned types of material damage can be added other categories of damage. Besides the direct loss of wealth, there was also what might be termed wealth dispersal in the guise of the sale of overseas assets, or taking foreign loans in order to finance the war effort. Great Britain and France experienced a reduction of their net assets overseas during the First World War. In France's case, as well as the loans taken to finance the war effort, there was also the loss of the investments in former Tsarist Russia as a consequence of the Soviet Revolution. The problems involved in foreign loans were undoubtedly at their height after the First World War and the worst affected were Britain and France. The main creditor was the USA. Most of the debt was renounced by means of a moratorium when the post-1929 depression was at its worst. Although a considerable portion of the debt remained unpaid, its very existence exerted an influence on the international capital market throughout the twenties.

Additional to the loss of wealth, there was also contemporary impoverishment in the form of lowered standards of living during the two wars. In some countries living standards dropped to such a level that they constituted a direct threat to existence. The belligerent nations experienced a drop in GDP during WW I that varied between barely a fifth in Germany's case and a third in that of France in 1918. The food supply situation in Germany had been good at the beginning of hostilities and the reserves plentiful. As a result of the blockade, rationing was introduced in 1916. Rations were gradually reduced so that, by the last year of the war, they had reached the level of 1500 calories per adult per day. This was considerably below the average daily intake at the beginning of the war. Rationing was not introduced in Britain during the first years of the war as it conflicted with the prevailing liberal outlook. However, in the summer of 1917, after months of unrestricted submarine warfare, opinions changed and rationing was introduced for some product categories, though not bread.

During the Second World War there were far greater contrasts in developments in various countries in terms of production and consumption. In some of the occupied countries, production was largely unchanged, as in Denmark, or fell slightly, as in Belgium and Norway. France and the Netherlands, however, experienced a halving of their GDP from 1938 to 1944, while the war made itself felt in both countries through a drastic drop in levels of consumption. In fact, France is regarded as the occupied nation that made the largest contribution to the German economy during the war in terms of both manufactured goods and agricultural produce. When these deliveries stopped in 1944 the situation worsened sharply in Germany. It is reckoned that the German GDP was still rising in 1944, and the industrial production index was still rising up to and including the third quarter, even after the Normandy landings. A major factor in explaining this state of affairs was the increased exploitation of the occupied nations, including the forced conscription of labour. At this time, about twenty per cent of the civilian labour force in Germany consisted of foreigners, the vast majority of whom were there as a result of forced conscription.

A wartime economy would, in any case, have a tendency to trigger and release tensions arising from policies of distribution. The high levels of industrial activity would give rise to inflation with its accompanying losses and gains just as an extensive black market would arise. There is no doubt that these problems manifested themselves to a far greater extent during the First than during the Second World War. In the case of Germany, the problems with the distribution of goods and food undoubtedly played a part in fostering the revolutionary conditions that prevailed at the end of the war in the autumn of 1918.

In accordance with the title of this section – Casualties and Costs – this account has focused on the negative aspects of the wars. When seen in a larger context, it is noteworthy that the wars had positive long-term effects on production and economic growth in the post-war period. A war economy is marked by concentrated aims, pursued with a large consumption of resources. Using peacetime terminology, it could be said that it was a massive industrial effort in narrow sectors of the economy. This could give rise to some unpredictable spin-offs, which could be exploited in a civilian context in the post-war period. It is beyond doubt that these derivative effects manifested themselves to a far greater extent after the Second than after the First World War. The area where the First World War had the greatest post-war impact was that of aviation. In the case of the Second World War, the examples are more numerous and the technical breakthroughs more significant.

It is the case that, for most of these innovations, the basic invention with its underlying discoveries was made before the war. The war, however, led to rapid use on a large scale. Before the outbreak of war in 1939, the British had already taken steps to set up radar chains in Southern England in order to be able to detect incoming hostile aircraft. With the spur provided by wartime conditions, the system was rapidly developed and used on ships, among other things. Another example is the development of antibiotics. The existence of penicillin had been known since the early 1930s. Commercial exploitation was, however, out of the question because of the then prohibitive cost. Before the landings in France, the Americans decided that the risk of illness run by their advancing troops should be reduced to the greatest possible extent. In order to promote this aim, Anglo-American cooperation led to the development of mass-production methods for antibiotics. The jet propulsion engine provides a third example. There was parallel development of jet engines in Britain and Germany during the war. As Allied industrial production capacity was in better shape than its German counterpart towards the end of the war, it was that side which started producing jet aircraft first.

It was, however, the development of the atom bomb, which had the most far-reaching significance, along with the accompanying potential civilian use of nuclear energy. It has to be said that the main effect was in the military sphere. The existence of nuclear weapons has subsequently influenced foreign policy and so the process of European integration as well. These problems will be discussed, among other things, in connection with French resistance to Britain joining the Common Market in the 1960s.

5. Victors and vanquished

A more thorough discussion of the conditions at the end of both wars follows in later chapters. The subject dealt with here concerns some of the substantial differences between 1918 and 1945 in terms of the relationship between victor and vanquished.

In February 1918, the Germans had already concluded a peace treaty with the new Bolshevik government of Russia. On the Eastern Front, the Germans were clearly victorious. On the Western Front, however, although collapse was not imminent in the autumn, the long-term prospects must have seemed hopeless for the Germans. Austria-Hungary was in a somewhat different situation; the Rumanian Front had collapsed and the Austro-Hungarian forces were under pressure in Northern Italy. So, by the autumn of 1918, it was clear that Austria-Hungary had been militarily defeated. The same could not be said of the Germans since, in November 1918, there were no enemy troops on German soil. However, although the German High Command realized that defeat was imminent, the German civilian population was unaware that military collapse was just around the corner. This state of affairs laid the ground for the legend of the "stab in the back" so beloved by the Nazis. According to this legend, the German army was not defeated by the enemy in battle, but betrayed by Socialists, the Jews and suchlike.

In 1945, the situation was completely different. Germany was then under pressure from both East and West. In addition to the war being brought home to Germany by means of aerial bombardment, the enemy armies crossed the German borders. When the fighting came to an end, the country was occupied and divided into four Zones of Occupation. The victors of 1945 were, therefore, far more visible as occupying powers than those of 1918. On this second occasion, no German could afterwards deny that the country had suffered a total military defeat, leaving no soil in which a new "stab in the back" legend could take root. At the end of both wars, there was strong support for the idea of putting Germany for ever out of the reckoning as an industrial power. This point of view carried more weight in 1919 than in 1945. Then there were two factors that dampened the wish to de-industrialize Germany. The first was the bad experience in connection with the peace settlement of the previous war when the peace terms gave rise to so much economic and political unrest. The second factor was that the victorious powers of the Second World War were themselves on a collision course. The onset of the Cold War between East and West meant that Germany was eventually seen as an ally rather than an opponent.

If one considers the entire course of the two world wars, it becomes difficult to point out any definite victors on the continent of Western Europe. All had experienced the bitterness of defeat and all had suffered losses. Victory in the wake of the great showdown did not devolve to any single nation or specific group of nations in the usual sense. Victory was at an altogether different level. Democracy had triumphed. The corollary to this was a new view of the relationships between European countries. The most costly and painful experiences of the 1914-45 period in Western Europe were those undergone by France, Germany, Belgium, the Netherlands, Luxembourg and Italy. They had all been directly affected by the wars. Due to their geographical position and historical experience, they had been the most deeply affected by the great showdown. The three Scandinavian nations had remained neutral during the First World War, but only Sweden managed to repeat this in the Second. In keeping with their position on the periphery of the European field of tension and their connections to Great Britain, they displayed a more hesitant approach to European integration as it gathered pace after 1945.

When seen in a global context, an objective view of Western Europe after 1945 would lead to the conclusion that this part of the world had been reduced to a more humble station than that of 1914. In terms of foreign policy, Western Europe would have to find its place between the two new superpowers, the Soviet Union and the USA.

Chapter 9

Eleven years of bungling
1919-29

The heading of this chapter contains a judgement that requires an explanation. The latter can be found in the economic development of the period in question and in the development during the years that followed.

From the end of the war to the crises of the late 1920s, eleven years elapsed. It was a period of economic unrest for Western Europe, oscillating between inflation and deflation, between stagnation and short periods of expansion. However, the overall outcome was a period of modest economic growth. Seen in retrospect, economies were in a stage of transition where ideas dating back from before the war failed, although without being replaced by new ones.

1. Growth and business cycles

The effects of the war complicate any appraisal of economic development or comparison between countries during the decade after 1918. Direct damage from the war on the Western Front was greatest in Belgium and France where the burden of reconstruction was the most exacting. There were, furthermore, problems at the end of the war when Germany and Austria had to face the consequences of a policy that prolonged the blockade.

A comparison of growth rates in neutral and belligerent countries in the period leading up to 1929 reveals a clear distinction to the advantage of the neutral countries – the Netherlands, Denmark, Norway, Sweden and Switzerland. With GDP = 100 in 1913, a simple average of the indexes of the five for 1929 was 156. For the belligerent countries of Western Europe – Italy, France, Belgium, Great Britain, Germany and Austria – the comparable figure was as low as 122. For the sixteen years from 1913 to 1929, the average, annual growth rate of the neutrals was 2.8 per cent and that of the former belligerent, 1.25 per cent. By comparison, the figures for the same period for the USA were 3.1 per cent and for Japan, 3.7 per cent.[1]

The differences in the growth rates of the countries of Western Europe cannot be entirely explained by war damage or by consequent supply problems, and the best example of this is the case of Great Britain. During the period 1919-29, the average growth rate was as low as 1.1 per cent, and the explanation for this must be sought in an unsuccessful economic policy. It is noteworthy that it was not until 1925, seven years after the end of the war, that production in the two largest economies of Western Europe, Great Britain and Germany, reached pre-war levels; after which the British economy suffered another setback!

Table 9.1: GDP in fixed prices (1913 = 100). 1919-29.

	19	20	21	22	23	24	25	26	27	28	29
UK	100.9	94.8	87.1	91.6	94.5	98.4	103.2	99.4	107.4	108.7	111.9
Germany	72.3	78.6	87.5	95.2	79.1	92.6	103.0	105.9	116.5	121.6	121.1
France	75.3	87.1	83.5	98.5	103.6	116.6	117.1	120.2	117.7	125.9	134.4
Italy	111.0	101.3	99.8	104.9	111.3	112.4	119.8	121.1	118.4	126.9	131.1
Austria	61.8	66.4	73.5	80.1	79.3	88.5	94.5	96.1	99.0	103.6	105.1
Belgium	79.9	92.5	94.1	103.3	107.0	110.5	112.2	116.0	120.3	126.6	125.5
Netherlands	112.4	115.8	122.9	129.6	132.8	142.5	148.5	160.4	167.1	176.0	177.4
Switzerland	95.3	101.5	99.0	108.5	114.8	119.1	127.8	134.2	141.4	149.3	154.5
Denmark	105.9	110.9	107.7	118.6	131.1	131.5	128.5	136.0	138.7	143.4	153.0
Finland	80.9	90.5	93.5	103.4	111.0	113.9	120.4	125.0	134.8	143.9	145.6
Norway	112.6	119.7	109.8	122.6	125.3	124.7	132.4	135.3	140.5	145.1	158.6
Sweden	89.4	94.6	91.1	99.7	105.0	108.3	112.3	118.6	122.3	128.1	135.9
USA	115.8	114.7	112.1	118.3	133.9	138.0	141.2	150.4	151.9	153.6	163.0

Source: A.Maddison (1991, Table A7)

The most obvious feature of the development is the lack of stability – lack of stable growth and lack of stable price development. This was particularly true during the first five or six years of the decade.

1.   Source as for table 9.1.

The countries that managed the best during the war experienced a short boom immediately after the war, caused partly by the rebuilding of stocks. This post-war boom only lasted until 1920, while 1920 and 1921 were, on the whole, characterized by a slump. Next, for some countries including the Netherlands, Denmark, Norway and France, there followed a short but hectic boom. From the middle of the 1920s a period of more widespread, though modest, growth followed.

Abolition of wartime restrictions took place within a very short period compared to what was to be the case after the Second World War. This seems, in part, to explain the unstable price development. At the end of the war, there was a high, unsatisfied demand due to a shortage of goods, supplemented by an unusually large supply of money; a combination that led to a sharp increase in prices as price controls were rescinded. From then on, policy lines split. Some countries, grouped around Great Britain, pursued a deflationary line as part of their exchange rate policies, while others allowed inflation to accelerate as in Germany and Austria. A few countries followed a middle course, as did France which allowed the Franc to depreciate without letting it lose its value entirely. Italy also stabilized its prices as a result of the Fascist takeover in 1922 and a strict policy towards the trade unions.

The cluster of deflationary countries grouped around Great Britain included the Netherlands, Denmark, Norway, and Sweden. Considered on the basis of the consumer price index, the policy was, on the whole, carried out by the end of 1923. The index by then had been stabilized at around 170 (1913 = 100), and this was followed by a few years of virtually stable prices. In 1925 the index for Sweden was 177, Great Britain 176, Switzerland 168 and the USA 168.[2] The special case of Germany and its galloping inflation is dealt with in section 6.3.

Part of the picture of the unstable development of the 1920s is the generally high and fluctuating rates of unemployment. Due to differences in the calculation of rates of unemployment, the figures must be read with caution. The figures refer to the number of unemployed as a percentage of the total labour force. In Germany, unemployment fluctuated from 0.7 to 8.0 per cent, in Great Britain from 1.9 to 11, being near the upper end after 1923. In the Scandinavian countries the figures were on the whole somewhat lower: for Sweden, around 3 per

2. A. Maddison (1991, table E3).

cent, somewhat higher for Norway, and for Denmark, on average al-most 10 per cent.[3]

2. The Versailles Peace Treaty

The war ended on 11th November 1918 with the armistice on the Western Front. Already on 18th January 1919, peace negotiations be-gan at Versailles outside Paris. This location was selected in part be-cause it was there that the Prussian king, forty-eight years earlier, was proclaimed German emperor. The term peace negotiations is some-what misleading as it soon transpired that it was rather the victors who negotiated amongst themselves than with the vanquished.

2.1. *A new map of Europe*

In drawing up the peace treaty of 1919, the enforcement of the princi-ple of national self-determination was aimed at. The American presi-dent, Woodrow Wilson (1856-1924), during the war had proclaimed these principles as part of his "fourteen points", announced in 1917. Other participants in the conference like France and Italy were less in-terested in this particular point. Instead, they had territorial interests to take care of. Furthermore, as part of its policy of containment vis-à-vis Germany, and in order to secure allies in future conflicts, France sought to give Germany "bleeding borders". That meant, letting the borders be drawn in such ways that German minorities were left under foreign control.[4] Barely twenty years later this turned out to be a source of trouble because it was from such minorities left in Czecho-slovakia and Poland that trouble-makers were given footholds that Na-zi-Germany exploited in the late 1930s.

It is said of the peace that three empires disappeared – the Habs-burg Empire (Austria-Hungary), the German Empire, and the Rus-sian Empire – and that eight new, self-governing countries were born – Czechoslovakia, Hungary, Yugoslavia, Poland, Estonia, Latvia, Lithuania and Finland. In order to give Poland access to the Baltic, it was necessary to establish a special corridor to Danzig, separating Eastern Prussia from the rest of Germany. Eleven thousand kilome-

---

3.   A. Maddison (1991, table C 6).
4.   Ole Lange (1988, 142).

tres of new borders were created, some of which cut right through existing economic structures and lines of communication. From an economic point of view, this splitting up of Europe into an increasing number of units seems to have been a backwards step giving rise to new customs barriers.

2.2. New and old debt

France participated in the peace conference with two leading goals in mind. Firstly, there was a new and an old score to settle with Germany; a new one from the war just over and an old one from the war of 1870-71 and the conditions of the peace treaty that France had then had to accept. Secondly, due to the recent war, there was an account with the USA that had to be settled.

During the war, the USA had given France – and Great Britain – substantial loans to finance the procurement of war materials. In 1917, the USA joined the Western allies, and from the beginning of 1918 it sent hundreds of thousands of troops to France. However, it was the general opinion of the French that France, as opposed to the USA, had shouldered greater burdens through the loss of human life. In compensation for this, they felt that it would be just if the Americans paid their part of the material costs of the war. Or, to be more precise, that France should be released from its war debt. The American reaction was firm and unlikely to be misunderstood: "You borrowed the money – didn't you?"

Since no solution to this dispute was likely, France decided that Germany would have to pay a corresponding extra sum in addition to war reparations covering direct damage from the fighting and the material costs of the French war effort. Compensation payments to invalids and dependants of war victims were also added. In 1921 the total amount of compensation Germany was expected to pay was fixed at an amount corresponding to its national product for well over two years, to be paid in gold dollars to prevent depreciation through inflation. Contemporary German inflation cannot, consequently, be seen as a way of evading the war debt, though the way this debt had an influence on inflation is another story.

It has been argued that the French did not expect Germany to pay the full amount. The real aim was not to get the compensation, but to reduce German savings and investments in order to thwart the development of Germany as an industrial nation. This was thought to be the only way to reduce the military threat from Germany and allow France to obtain the position as the leading European industrial nation.

The wisdom of the French position has been widely discussed. The contribution by the then young British civil servant and economist, John Maynard Keynes (1883-1946), is well known. His background was membership of the British delegation to the peace conference as a representative of the Treasury, the British Ministry of Finance. He predicted that the conditions of peace were such that they would be a hindrance to the development of democracy in Germany, perhaps even resulting in a communist takeover. For this reason, he left the British delegation and wrote what turned out to be a bestseller, a book with the title: "The Economic Consequences of the Peace". Apart from its economic analyses, the book presents a "close-up" of the leading personalities of the conference.[5]

In 1871, France had ceded Alsace-Lorraine to Germany. It was now handed back and the German region of the Saarland was internationalized – that is, put under French control for a period of fifteen years after which a referendum concerning its future would take place.[6]

As explained earlier, any rational use of the natural resources in this area implied cooperation across borders, so this meant that it was impossible to unite economic and national goals within a traditional framework.

3. Increased economic instability

3.1. New sources of instability

The capitalist economy at this stage seemed to contain a built-in tendency towards increased instability. Two reasons for this may be mentioned: the growing relative size of investments compared to total demand and the increased rigidity of prices in the goods and labour markets. The capitalist economy is – as the name indicates – characterized by its use of long-term capital such as machinery, buildings, all sorts of infrastructure, etc. This means that reinvestment may be postponed in

5.   Woodrow Wilson (1856-1924) of the USA, David Lloyd George (1863-1945) of Great Britain, George Clemenceau (1841-1929) of France and Vittorio Orlando (1860-1952) of Italy.
6.   This took place in 1935 shortly after the Nazi takeover in Germany. More than 90 per cent of the votes cast were in favour of a return to Germany.

case of a temporary slowdown of the economy without great distur-
bance to the current business performance of any individual firm.
Seen, however, in a broader context it means that some major components of demand may be unstable. Pre-industrial society had known financial and bank crises such as the British and French ones around
1720. Those crises, however, were of a different nature as they tended
to be short and abrupt. From the mid-1800s onwards, a new type of
crisis was making itself felt. This took the form of the repercussions of
the business cycle where especially sensitive sectors like the building
industry and industries producing new, durable consumer goods were
hard hit. All in all, there were clear tendencies towards an increasingly
turbulent economy.

Another trend that made the economy more vulnerable was increasing price rigidity in both the goods and the labour markets. In the
goods markets, this was due to a new structure of costs – high fixed
costs and low variable costs – that caused an increasing degree of monopolization, price agreements, market sharing, etc., bringing forth the
phenomenon of sticky prices. Movements of prices in the two types of
markets were partly replaced by movements of quantities that in the
labour market meant changes in the level of employment. A central
theme of the debate between economists following the recession after
1929 was whether the solution to the problem of the business cycle was
to increase the flexibility of prices and wages, or if other, more efficient, measures could be found such as demand management. This was
the debate that actually ended with the acceptance of the theories of
Keynes, which were to dominate political and economic thinking for a
period of thirty years after the Second World War.

Besides these general trends, there were some specific problems relating to the years around the First World War, which had a substantial impact on political and economic development in the 1920s.

3.2. Economic nostalgia

The war and the war economy meant a breach of the prevailing liberal
economic doctrines. The war was expected to be short, but instead it
was protracted with its outcome depending to a high degree on the industrial capacity of the belligerent powers. To mobilize their capacity,
they had to turn to strict regulation of the economies, which meant
that the price system as an allocating mechanism was partly replaced
by a command economy.

However, in spite of regulation, prices increased. As part of the regulations and the atypical conditions, the gold standard, along with its free export and import of gold and the obligation of central banks to sell gold, was suspended. In practice, this meant that the countries, even the allied nations, existed independently of each other in terms of monetary policy and the development of price levels. The price increases in the USA were the least dramatic or, to put it the other way around, the dollar had managed best in retaining its purchasing power. The situation of sterling was somewhat worse and, worse still, that of the French Franc. In short, the exchange rates of 1914 were no longer applicable. Exchange rates had to be adjusted in case of a re-establishment of the free movement of goods and foreign exchange.

There are clear indications that the liberalization of the economies, including the foreign trade of 1919-20, took place too fast, causing a short boom followed by a collapse in 1920. The background to this was a widely felt wish after years of regulation and controls to return to "business as usual". This was particularly true of financial circles in Great Britain who wanted to resume their pre-war position with London as the financial and commercial centre of the world which meant, among other things, re-establishing the pound sterling as the leading means of payment in international trade. To do so, it was argued, sterling would have to revert to the old gold price. That achieving this goal was going to be costly, as measured in terms of the lack of competitiveness, strikes, lock-outs, unemployment, and political turmoil, was only realized afterwards.

4. Monetary and financial matters

The new pattern of production and trade caused by the exceptional conditions during the war was in itself a problem. New overseas producers had appeared, causing dangers of over-capacity. Nevertheless, the changed conditions behind the monetary system turned out to be the most important in the long run. As previously explained (Chapter 7, section 2), London's position as a financial centre was based mainly on British foreign assets and only partly on the gold deposits of the Bank of England. However, financing the war had caused losses of foreign assets and an increase in loans from abroad. The result was a substantial reduction of the net income in interest and profits in the balance of payments. The position of the Bank of England as a financial intermediary had been weakened.

This was only part of a greater problem of a general weakening of the European economy in a global context, which would be felt even more strongly in the 1930s as a general problem of international liquidity. The other side of all this was an increase in the net assets and liquidity of the USA which gave rise to a need for the USA to step in alongside Great Britain as a supplier of international liquidity. The USA and the American banking system, however, were not yet prepared to let the dollar fill the rôle of a key currency. Put briefly, the UK was no longer able to be solely responsible for international monetary affairs and, as yet, the USA was not willing to take over. The global monetary system found itself in an interregnum.

The acquisition of liquid claims on any given country may take place in two ways. Firstly, the country may have a deficit on the current account of its balance of payments. Secondly, and more important, it may offer long-term loans whereby foreigners acquire short-term demands in the form of demand deposits (liquidity) on the lender. The USA only met these requirements to a limited extent during the 1920s when it followed a protectionist trade policy, repeatedly increasing its customs tariffs. It would supply no liquidity via the current account of its balance of payments. Furthermore, the loans it granted were mainly short-term and were liable be called back at short notice. This was what actually happened after 1929.

A return to "normality" meant, as far as monetary matters were concerned, a return to the gold standard, but the problem was at which gold price? As mentioned, Great Britain wanted to return to the prewar gold price – to take sterling back to par as it was argued this would strengthen confidence in sterling, but such a policy would mean that price levels should be brought down through a deflationary policy. A reduction in the gold content of sterling might mean a loss to sterling, the explanation being that a certain amount of gold could be changed back into a larger amount of sterling after the adjustment of the gold price.

For many countries, the prospects of obtaining the necessary gold reserves were small. Instead of the previous gold standard, these countries had to settle for the "gold exchange standard". Instead of having its own gold reserves in its vaults, the central bank would hold its reserves not as gold, but as demands on a central bank directly on the gold standard. The Bank of England typically performed this function for foreign central banks as their reserves in sterling replaced gold reserves under this system. However, this meant that the gold reserves of Great Britain not only served as its own reserves, but as those of other countries as well at a time when the British reserves were reduced by comparison with what they had been before the war.[7] All in all, this was an unstable situation, with Great Britain and the Bank of England having a substantial amount of short-term liabilities whereas British international assets were mainly long-term. Were sterling to come under pressure, this would lead directly to an international monetary crisis – which is what happened in 1931.

To sum up: the distribution of gold reserves had changed. The portion belonging to the USA had increased and that belonging to Great Britain had decreased. The USA, however, did not want to let the dollar fill the rôle of a key currency, so too much rested on sterling as no international institutions existed which could intervene in case of an international financial crisis.

5. Trade policy

As normal trade relations had been suspended during the four years of war, replacement industries had appeared to make up for what could no longer be imported from abroad. Great Britain had seen the birth of new firms in the chemical and electrical industries, which produced replacements for the supplies normally imported from Germany. In overseas countries, industries were set up to replace products from Europe. Some of those new industries – the so called "war babies" – were capable of surviving in an open market, whereas others were not, and here there was felt a need for protection. For Great Britain, this meant the introduction of exceptions to the principle of free trade. Soon afterwards, tariff protection for these new industries was agreed upon[8] where the level of customs duties was as high as 30 per cent.

Another tendency towards decreasing competition resulted from the adjustments to national frontiers in Europe. All in all, eleven thousand kilometres of borders were created, often interrupting well-established

7.   J. Foreman-Peck. (1995, 215).
8.   The Key Industries Act of 1919, followed in 1929 by The Safeguarding of Industries Act. C.Kindleberger (1990, 127).

commercial relations. An outstanding example of this was the splitting up of the former dual monarchy of Austria-Hungary into several separate customs units. The level of mutual suspicion was so high that for a time Austria and Hungary would not allow railway wagons to cross their mutual border for fear that the wagons would not return. Not only did duties have to be paid, but the goods had to be reloaded as well.

It seems fair to conclude that intra-European trade was damaged both because of the increased number of economic units and because of the general tendency to increase customs tariffs. In Eastern Europe, the new Soviet Union more or less isolated itself from the rest of the world from the middle of the 1920s. And across the Atlantic, the USA increased its customs duties even further.

To balance the picture it must be mentioned that several international conferences were called in order to handle the problem of increased protectionism. This was the case in 1927 when the League of Nations in Geneva held an Economic World Conference. As a result of the conference, two resolutions were agreed upon: one calling for a reduction of customs tariffs, and another calling for a limitation of quantitative import restrictions. The first lost its meaning when the USA passed a law to raise its customs duties immediately after the conference. The second was nullified when Germany – the foremost practitioner of quantitative restrictions – announced that it did not want to join the convention. Instead of marking a breakthrough in international cooperation, the conference marked a breakdown. As for trade policy, Western Europe and the rest of the industrialized countries entered the 1930s without having the necessary institutions to prevent a "beggar thy neighbour" policy in case of a depression.

6. National developments

6.1. Great Britain
In 1929, the British GDP (fixed prices) was 12 per cent above GDP in 1913 (Table 9.1). This corresponds to an annual growth rate as low as 0.7 per cent. Loss of tonnage apart, Britain had not suffered great material damage during the war, so this is not the explanation for the low growth rate. Three related points will be mentioned: low competitiveness, a low level of internal demand and structural problems.

The low level of competitiveness was due in part to an exchange rate policy that resulted in sterling being overvalued. In 1924-25, a major theme in British politics was the wish to bring sterling back to par. In 1925 Keynes was back in centre of the argument when he wrote three articles addressed to the Conservative Chancellor of the Exchequer under the title: "The Economic Consequences of Winston Churchill". In these articles he argued that the outcomes of the policy of the government would be unemployment and political tension. Instead of the announced policy, Britain would be better off conducting a more realistic one aiming at a less pretentious exchange rate. The consequence of the policy of the government would be a lower level of both foreign and domestic demand.

To these problems, the structural problems of British export industries may be added. In brief, the problem was that British industries used outdated techniques, produced the wrong goods and tried to sell them in the wrong markets. The outdated means of production can be explained in part by the early beginning of British industry. However, part of the explanation may be found in the low level of investment at home in the British Isles and the high level of capital export. The problem concerning the "wrong" or no longer suitable goods could partly be explained by the early start as well. Expressed in terms of the concept of "product cycles", the problem was that too few British industries were found at the front of the new product cycles and too many were found towards the rear of the old cycles.[9] Finally, there was the problem of the distribution of exports between markets. In comparison with other European countries, a relatively large proportion of British exports went to overseas markets. Those markets, however, suffered from low incomes due to low prices for their own export goods.[10]

In a situation like that, it would have been better if the British industries had a home market with a higher level of demand. Domestic demand was deliberately held down as part of the deflationary policy. In simple terms there was a growing need for a fundamental change in economic policy.

9.   A product cycle describes the total production of a product (often a durable consumer product) as a function of time. After a modest beginning, a sharp rise takes place. Then, after saturation of demand, production falls back to a stable level based on demand for replacement goods. At this stage, a major part of production is likely to have moved overseas to countries with lower wage levels.

10. In present day language, exports suffered from poor goods and country effects.

6.2. France

The war in the West had been fought on French and Belgian soil. In France, the battleground had covered about 60,000 square kilometres where important parts of the French mining, steel and textile industries were located. Great damage had been caused to housing, to transport facilities, to agriculture and the country had lost 1.4 million men or almost 10 per cent of the adult male population.

While Britain planned to return to the old exchange rate, France did not set up such a goal for itself and so the franc depreciated against the dollar and sterling. This went on until 1926 when the exchange rate was stabilized at a level corresponding to a devaluation of the franc. In 1928, the gold standard was reintroduced, though at a level which gave the franc a competitive edge. It is no wonder that France experienced in those years an expansion in tourism and that Paris flourished as an international centre for all sorts of artists; just think of "An American in Paris".

As far as the development of its GDP is concerned, the 1920s turned out to be a good period. Of all the belligerent countries of Western Europe,[11] France in 1929 was the one (1913 = 100) that had the highest GDP, 134,[12] compared to an average for a belligerent of 122.

The characteristic dual nature of the French economy was no doubt strengthened during those years as the tradition of small family farms, small shops and family trades continued. Meanwhile, in addition, France gained the position as the leading automobile producing country in Europe with the factories of Citroën, Peugeot and Renault. Even before the war, France had been ahead in the production of aeroplanes compared to the other countries of Western Europe and it seemed that France was well placed to enter the 1930s. Things, however, were to turn out differently.

6.3. Germany

Direct German material losses due to the war were limited, so in this respect the situation in Germany was similar to that of Britain. After the war, the German merchant navy was confiscated, but in this respect Britain too had suffered losses. Another type of loss was caused by border revisions leading to a loss of territory, mainly to France, but

---

11. Belgium, France, Italy, Great Britain, Austria and Germany.
12. Calculations adjusted to border changes.

also to Poland. Those losses covered as much as a third of former German coal deposits and as much as three-fourths of pre-1914 German iron ore deposits, the latter going mainly to France.

As in Great Britain, Germany's economy in the 1920s was unstable. While the explanation in Britain's case was a deflationary policy, for Germany it was a period of galloping inflation followed, from 1924 onwards, by a period of stabilisation. In the years between 1923 and 1928, the German economy seems to have developed favourably by comparison with that of Britain.

For posterity, the inflation of the early 1920s stands out as the most striking aspect of the German economy, and the resultant fear of inflation has been offered as one explanation of Hitler's success in the early 1930s, the stable German price level during the 1950s and 1960s, and even for the priority of price stability in the European Economic and Monetary Union of the 1990s. The basis for the German inflation was laid during the war. Whereas most other countries experienced a drop in prices from 1920, price increases continued in Germany. For a couple of years, this was combined with a substantial increase in production. In the summer of 1922 price increases had reached a level as high as 70 per cent a month. From January 1923, the rate of inflation rose further, and the background to this was a Franco-Belgian military occupation of the Ruhr, triggered by a delay in German reparations payments. The mines were held in mortgage by the occupiers, so to speak, while the reaction to this was that work in the mines and at the steelworks stopped. The workers received compensation in cash from the German government who financed this by printing more money. Inflation, once again, accelerated and, by the autumn the monetary economy suffered a total breakdown. The existing Mark was temporarily replaced by a Rentemark at an exchange rate of 10^{12} to 1, that is: 1.000.000.000.000:1.

From 1923 to 1928, the German GDP increased by more than 50 per cent, corresponding to 9 per cent a year – an exceptionally high growth rate even considering that 1923 was an abnormal year. The background to this was an extensive import of capital and know-how through the establishment of branches of great American corporations like Ford and General Motors, along with foreign loans to the German government. All in all, this meant that the German reparations decided upon at the end of the war were paid for by foreign means, so that Germany had a net import of capital in those years – a fact the Nazi regime of course later tried to hide. Foreign loans, however, made the German economy sensitive to changes in the international capital market. When the international money market in 1928-29 began to tighten, German banks were hit at an early point in time, and relatively hard. In 1929, even before the Wall Street Crash, German monetary policy was tightened and an economic recession had begun.

6.4. *Belgium and The Netherlands*

The fates of the two countries during the war years were widely divergent. German troops entered Belgium right at the beginning of the war as part of the Schlieffen Plan. From the very first day, Belgium was part of the theatre of war, which explains why Belgium joined France at the end of the war in demanding large war indemnities. The position of the Netherlands was quite different. The German army did not invade the country. Before the German submarine blockade of Britain, the Netherlands, like other neutral countries, took direct economic advantage of the war through high prices on export goods such as food. Then, at the end of the war, the Netherlands received the former German emperor as a refugee, which aroused hostility from the Belgians and other former German enemies. As for the twenty years between the First and Second World Wars, it can be said that the development of Belgium is reminiscent of that of France and the development of the Netherlands is similar to that of the Scandinavian countries (tables 9.1 and 10.1).

Compared to other belligerent countries in Western Europe, the economy of *Belgium* returned to pre-war levels rather rapidly. This happened in 1921-22, and from then on until 1928 Belgium reached growth rates of 3 to 4 per cent. As for France, the exchange rate policy is part of the explanation. Belgium chose, like France, to allow its currency to depreciate, which made it possible to prolong the growth from the years of reconstruction into the second half of the 1920s.

As mentioned earlier, Belgium previously had only limited economic relations with its one large African colony, the Belgian Congo. In 1913, trade with the Congo made up as little as 1 per cent of Belgium's total external trade. The war, however, brought a substantial change to this state of affairs. The colony's wealth of raw materials such as copper, tin, palm oil and copra now gave rise to substantial exports and income. As in Britain, Belgian industry, in the years up to the war had suffered from a lack of dynamism. Change began to be felt in the 1920s as new industries requiring refineries and factories producing synthetic yarn and textiles were established.

In 1922, closer economic cooperation began between Luxembourg and Belgium. Luxembourg had traditionally been closely connected with Germany, including membership of the German Zollverein as far back as the mid-1800s, until the war marked a shift in this policy. A currency and customs union with Belgium – Belux – was set up and by this means Luxembourg oriented herself towards France as well.

In the period from 1913 to 1929, the *Netherlands* stands out as the country with the highest growth rate of all the countries of Western Europe, indeed, even higher than that of the USA. The Netherlands did so much better than Belgium not solely because she stayed out of the war and had better chances of exploiting the upturn just after the war: her growth rates were higher all the way through the 1920s.

In some respects, the geo-economic conditions of the Netherlands are reminiscent of those of the Scandinavian countries. Like the latter, the Netherlands are part of a North Sea economy having close ties with Great Britain and a great tradition of shipping, international trading and finance. Like Denmark, it had a substantial export of high quality food to Britain in the 1920s, which made up more than 40 per cent of her total exports. So, like the Scandinavian countries, the Netherlands decided to follow Great Britain back on to the gold standard at the pre-war gold price.

A striking feature of the Dutch economy during those years was the establishment of some great multinational corporations under Dutch leadership such as Royal Dutch Shell and Unilever, both in cooperation with British firms. The Philips Company is another example. From producing electric bulbs, it expanded into new fields like radio receivers and household equipment. Besides a tradition of advanced agriculture, the Netherlands, in the 1920s, laid the foundation of a modern export-oriented industry.

6.5. *The Scandinavian countries*

The Scandinavian countries can, like the Netherlands, be considered part of a North Sea economy. Their economic growth around the turn of the century was closely related to their economic relations with Great Britain. For Denmark, Great Britain was by far the main market for its agricultural exports, which made up 80 per cent of total Danish exports. For Norway and Sweden, it was their leading market for timber, paper, pulp, iron ore and metals. Calculations seem to indicate that the relative size of GDP per capita of the Scandinavian countries at the outbreak of the First World War was for Denmark = 100, Sweden = 80 and Norway = 70.[13]

The three countries followed the example of Great Britain in their exchange rate policy, which meant that they had to conduct a strict deflationary policy. Sweden seems to have been hit the hardest during the early 1920s, as will be seen (table 9.1), and it was not until 1923 that the Swedish GDP regained its pre-war level. In 1924 the Swedish crown reached parity; in Denmark, this was achieved in 1925-26 and in Norway in 1926, though formally from 1928. Looking back, it seems strange that the countries should have made the effort to conduct such a tight deflationary policy. In Sweden, the reaction to this was seen at the beginning of the 1930s in what has been called a pre-Keynesian economic policy.

To *Denmark* the sharp drop in food prices after the war was felt as a fall in the value of exports, and was followed by concerns about the loss of exchange reserves. The representatives of the smallholders argued for a permanent cut in the international value of the Danish crown, while manufacturing industry was in favour of increased customs duties and the trade unions in favour of import restrictions. The outcome was, as mentioned above, a prestigious exchange rate policy taking the crown back to pre-war parity, combined with a high level of unemployment of up to 20 per cent of insured workers.

In the years before the war, *Norway* had begun the establishment of hydroelectric power stations. This was carried on in the following years supplying electricity to plants for the production of aluminium and nitrogenous fertilizer. All in all, capital-intensive branches of production partly financed through direct foreign investments and, at the same time, high capital investments in transport facilities in the country's interior helped to open up new regions to economic development outside agriculture.

Sweden had developed a metal industry at an earlier point in time than Norway based on her mining industries. Compared with the Norwegian metal industry, Swedish products were on the whole characterized by a

13. Angus Maddison (1991, table 1.1)

higher degree of processing. Compared with Denmark, the Swedish exports were scattered over a far wider range of products and countries.

For *Finland*, separation – or rather liberation – from the former Russian Empire meant a thorough redistribution of her foreign trade in favour of Western Europe, including Great Britain. This was the case for the important paper industry and also for the export of agricultural products sold in competition with Danish products in the British and then German markets.

6.6. *Italy, Spain and Portugal*

In 1915, *Italy* was led to believe by Britain and France that it might obtain favourable adjustments to its borders around the Trieste peninsula, and even obtain some former German colonies, if it entered the war on their side. However, at the peace conference, the USA under the leadership of President Woodrow Wilson (1856-1924) refused this, causing nationalist excitement in Italy and clashes with its former allies. The internal politics of Italy in those years were dominated by conflicts between left-wing organisations led by Communists and right-wing groups dominated by the Fascists. After the March on Rome, these clashes resulted in a Fascist takeover in 1922. Part of the programme was to re-establish an Italian/Roman empire with great possessions in North Africa. As for economic policy, Fascism meant an increase in military expenditure and the implementation of prestige construction projects. At the time, it may have looked impressive, but the general opinion is that the period left little of positive value for the development of the Italian economy after the Second World War.

If Italy in the 1920s was situated on the periphery of the Western European economy, this was even truer in the case of *Spain* and *Portugal*. There, too, the trend towards the establishment of Fascist regimes was underway. As for their economic development after the Second World War, see Chapter 15, section 7.

6.7. *The USA*

Besides Japan, the USA was the sole major industrial country that had a substantially larger GDP in 1919 than in 1913 (table 9.1). In 1919-20 it only suffered a minor setback, and in the following years it saw substantial economic growth.

In 1921, the Republicans returned to the White House after eight years of Democratic government under Woodrow Wilson. It was time to return to "business as usual". During the eight years from 1921 to 1929, the average growth rate was 4.8 per cent. So the idea spread that crises belonged to the past. "Prosperity forever" was the key slogan in the election campaign of the Republicans when for the second time they were re-elected to the presidency in 1928.

The steady growth of the American economy during the first part of the 1920s may be seen as the background to the euphoric atmosphere that was to dominate the stock market during the latter half of the 1920s. Share prices started a development that put them out of touch with the underlying real economy and the firms' actual earnings. When commercial banks participated in this by financing its customers' speculations, it developed into a national pastime – for a while anyway. So the prolonged period of speculation may be seen as the result of a lax monetary policy. A share market characterized by more realism might have been able to register the need for a slowdown at an earlier point of time.

The technology gap between the USA and Europe no doubt increased during the 1920s. Not only was competition from American

Fig. 12: The 1936 movie, Modern Times, by Charlie Chaplin, can be seen as a protest against the assembly line, the stop watch and Taylorism.

agriculture now felt, but so was competition from an expanding American manufacturing industry. Seen from Europe, the USA, in those years, gained a position in the world economy that it so far did not managed to live up to.

Chapter 10

Ten years of crisis 1929-39

1. Origin of the crisis

For analytical purposes it would be convenient to distinguish between those factors that *caused* the economic recession and those factors that *transformed* it to the rest of the economy. In practice, however, it is hard to make the distinction. As for the origin of the crisis, a large part of the responsibility must be placed with the USA, whereas for the subsequent spread of the crisis there seems to be collective responsibility for a reluctance to cooperate internationally. In fact each country pursued a policy that, from an overall point of view, worsened the crisis. In the language of economists, this lack of international solidarity resulted in the term "beggar-thy-neighbour" policies.

A widely held explanation at the time of these events was that *wages were too high.* According to this line of thought, business faced a profit squeeze that took away the incentive to invest. Therefore, the proper way of fighting the crisis was to reduce wages. It was this explanation and attitude that Keynes argued against in his "General Theory", published in 1936.

Another type of explanation, promoted by the Keynesian breakthrough, argued that the main problem was that *demand was too low.* Several possibilities existed to explain this:

a. *investments had been too large* in the 1920s causing downward accelerator-multiplier processes.[1] The high level of investments in the

---

1. An economics term describing an interaction between the demand for investment goods and consumer goods. At a certain time, the growth of investments will tend to slow down, and then the two start a spiral glide. The theory was formulated in the 1930s influenced by the development around 1929.

1920s meant that there was significant spare capacity in business causing a low level of investment in later years,

b. *monetary policy was too tight* at the time of the recession after having been too lax in the mid-twenties. For this reason the amount of investment actually undertaken was further reduced,

c. *the price of primary products fell,* causing a decrease in income for the countries exporting primary products due to a worsening of their terms of trade. As importing countries did not increase their demand correspondingly the result was a drop in demand at a global level. Furthermore, the balance of payments deficits of the producers of primary products compounded the problems of international monetary affairs,

d. *a shortage of international liquidity* made it necessary for each country to seek to balance the current account of its balance of payments, even in the very short run. Budding booms were stopped at an early point of time in order to protect exchange reserves. It was especially significant that the USA did not wish to step in and grant the necessary international liquidity,[2]

e. while the recession was at its height *competitive devaluations* took place, adding to economic instability and further reducing willingness to invest,

f. the result of all this was a sharp reduction in international trade and therefore in the international division of labour, causing foreign trade compared to GDPs to fall by as much as one third.[3] *Restrictions aiming at a bilateral balance of foreign trade and international payments* were particularly harmful even when in some cases the restrictions may have had a positive effect on employment levels, but a negative effect on the overall productivity of the factors of production.

Responsibility for the recession is, as stated above, normally placed with the USA. It was here that the stock exchange crash took place in

2.   Kindleberger (1986 and 1990, 151).
3.   In the case of a small country like Denmark, from about 30 per cent (1913) to about 20 per cent (mid-30s). Calculated as exports or imports as a percentage of GDP.

October 1929, and it was also here that the decline in production was greatest and lasted for longest. The USA, as the largest importing nation, meant the most to the global economy. Finally, not only did the USA fail to take steps to soften the crisis, but even went so far as to obstruct those initiatives which were taken when an Economic World Conference was finally called in London in 1933.

2. Growth and business cycles

How persistent the recession proved to be can be seen clearly from table 10.1, which shows that the return to 1929 production levels took six years for Great Britain and Germany, and ten years for France, Austria and the USA. Some countries, however, managed to get through somewhat more favourably. In Denmark, production levels never fell below what they were in 1929 and only one year, 1932, witnessed negative growth;[4] for Norway and Sweden, the picture was almost the same.

As for the time profile of the business cycle, Western Europe reached the depths of the trough sooner than the USA. Throughout

Table 10.1: GDP in fixed prices (1929 = 100). 1929-39.

	29*	29	30	31	32	33	34	35	36	37	38	39
UK	111.9	100.0	99.3	94.2	94.9	97.7	104.1	108.1	113.0	117.0	118.4	119.6
Germany	121.1	100.0	98.6	91.1	84.2	89.5	97.7	105.0	114.3	126.7	139.6	150.9
France	134.4	100.0	97.1	91.3	85.3	91.4	90.6	88.2	91.6	96.9	96.5	103.4
Italy	131.1	100.0	95.0	94.5	97.6	96.9	97.3	106.7	106.9	114.2	115.0	123.4
Austria	105.1	100.0	97.2	89.4	80.2	77.5	78.2	79.7	82.1	86.5	97.5	110.6
Belgium	125.5	100.0	99.0	97.3	92.9	94.9	94.1	99.9	100.6	102.0	99.7	106.5
Netherlands	177.4	100.0	99.8	93.7	92.4	92.2	90.5	93.9	99.8	105.5	103.0	110.0
Switzerland	154.5	100.0	99.4	95.2	92.0	96.6	96.8	96.4	96.7	101.3	105.2	105.0
Denmark	15.30	100.0	105.9	107.1	104.3	107.6	110.9	113.4	116.2	119.0	121.9	127.7
Finland	145.6	100.0	98.8	96.4	96.0	102.4	114.0	118.9	126.9	134.1	141.1	135.0
Norway	158.6	100.0	107.4	99.1	105.7	108.2	111.7	116.5	123.6	128.0	131.2	137.5
Sweden	135.9	100.0	102.1	98.4	95.7	97.6	105.0	111.7	118.2	123.8	125.8	134.5
USA	163.0	100.0	90.5	82.9	71.8	70.4	75.9	82.0	93.7	98.3	93.8	101.2

* Index for 1929 calculated as 1913=100.
Source: A. Maddison (1991, Table A7)

4. However, the growth during the early thirties mainly took place in agriculture and was accompanied by a sharp drop in the export prices of those products.

the period the USA differed in that it experienced another recession in 1937-38. Although its effects were also felt in Western Europe it was not as marked as in the USA, partly due to increasing armaments production in Europe as a reaction to the German military build-up. It is also noteworthy that France, Belgium and the Netherlands had great difficulties in starting an upward movement. This was partly due to an overvalued currency after British devaluation in 1931. It was not until 1939 that the French GDP reached the level it had been at in 1929.

As can be seen, the USA experienced a fall of its GDP of almost 30 per cent and Germany a fall of 16 per cent. It is no surprise that those countries suffered the greatest setback since they had both experienced a boom in the second half of the 1920s.

The losses caused by the crisis can be categorised into two types: firstly, current losses suffered during the 1930s caused by under-utilization of resources and secondly, the losses suffered by posterity, caused by reduced investments and delayed technical progress. A related loss was due to a decrease in the international division of labour, which took years to overcome after the Second World War. These two aspects of the crisis of the 1930s – an increasing technology gap vis-à-vis the USA and the reshaping of intra-European trade – were to become central themes in the post-war European economy.

At the end of the 1930s, Germany was the country that was the closest to the limits of its production capacity. Actual German production of a vast number of strategic goods exceeded that of France and Great Britain combined, but total German production capacity was far smaller than that of Britain, France, the Soviet Union and the USA taken together. A war, whose outcome would depend on industrial capacity, would have to be concluded within a short time and in a way that would not involve the USA. Until December 1941 and the Japanese attack on Pearl Harbor, it seemed likely that the German plans would succeed.

3. Economic nationalism

The international money market had, as previously mentioned, been under pressure in the late 1920s. In 1931, a chain reaction started involving the bankruptcy of Austrian and German banks, and causing great drains on the gold reserves of the Bank of England during the summer months. In September, the British government decided to abandon the gold standard and thereby the obligation of the Bank of England to sell gold. At the same time, it was decided to let sterling float, thus further relieving the Bank of England of its obligation to buy and sell sterling at a fixed exchange rate. The result was the depreciation of sterling of roughly 30 per cent and a strongly needed improvement in the competitiveness of the British economy after years of an overvalued currency.

Just as 24th October 1929 – the day of the Wall Street crash – is seen as a dividing line in the history of business cycles, so 20th September 1931 – the day when "Britain went off Gold" – is considered to be a dividing line in the history of international monetary affairs. It was accompanied by a change in British trade policy that meant an end to the free trade tradition of Great Britain and marked the beginning of a period of exceptional protectionism at the global level. Major components of the system of restrictions built up during the ensuing period were still in existence at the end of the 1940s. Restrictions in the international capital markets were exceptionally long-lived, where regulations on the movement of long-term capital survived until the 1980s, even within the European Communities.

3.1. *Motives behind the restrictions* [5]

The following motives behind the restrictions in international trade and finance can be identified:

a. protection of national foreign exchange reserves, related in principle to a system of fixed exchange rates,

b. reduction of the demand for foreign goods, thereby manipulating domestic demand in order to increase employment without the loss of foreign currency reserves,

c. securing an allocation of foreign exchange in accordance with social goals. The importation of raw materials and investment goods is given priority over the import of luxury consumer goods,

---

5.   The rectrictions described here include those in the international economy and those in the national economies caused as a result of the former.

d. prevention of the flight of capital, which would typically take place in periods when a reduction of the international value of the national currency was expected. This sort of capital flight would normally be of a short-term nature; permanent capital flight was more the result of political unrest and menace,

e. improving national bargaining strength vis-à-vis other countries practising an active trade policy; in this respect, the situation of the 1930s was reminiscent of the situation within the area of customs policy in the late 1800s.

3.2. Means of the restrictions policy

Traditional means and instruments in international economic policy such as customs duties and exchange rate adjustments are, so to speak, in keeping with the rules of a market economy. This is true in the sense that producers and consumers still respond to conditions in the market – that is, they make decisions and act on the basis of prices in the markets. The interventions mentioned here are of a different nature because in these instances the consent of public authorities is necessary for the transactions; it is not just a question of willingness to pay.

The restrictions may be directed towards the *flow of payments* or towards *the flow of goods* respectively; in the first case *exchange controls* and in the second, *quantitative restrictions*, QRs. In practice, however, the difference between the two may turn out to be small.

To ensure government control of international transactions it is normally necessary to impose an obligation on exporting firms to sell their foreign exchange to the central bank or a registered exchange dealer. This is because it is an inherent part of the system that public authorities must be able to monitor the sale of foreign exchange. The system works in such a way that it is only possible to carry through international transactions with the acceptance of an official administrative body, usually a branch of the Ministry of Trade or the Central Bank. In practise, it is necessary to have a licence indicating a specific amount of a specific item in order to have the goods released from customs.

A special case is the tariff quota, according to which a specific amount of a product is allowed to be imported at a lower rate than the ordinary duty. To administer the system, it is necessary to practise import control as well. So, in that respect, a customs quota is similar to an ordinary QR.

All those restrictions in foreign trade will have a built-in tendency to cause the system to affect national economies as well. In the case of import controls causing a shortage of certain goods, which is very likely, the importers who hold the import licences will then have the chance to charge above the normal prices. For that reason, a system of import controls will normally be accompanied by a system of price controls. In the case of exports being limited due to foreign import controls, exporting firms will tend to compete among themselves to obtain their share of exports. To prevent this, exporting countries will start to introduce export controls and regulate the prices of their export goods. So, as will be seen, the system soon leads to the widespread control of quantity and price both in the international and in the national economies.

3.3. Application of the restrictions policy
After Great Britain went off the gold standard in September 1931, and after the Nazi take-over in January 1933, four distinct groups of countries could be identified, each practising different systems of foreign trade control.

Firstly, there was a group linked to *Great Britain.* Apart from Britain and Ireland its European members included the Scandinavian countries. For Britain, however, the most important members were those belonging to the British Commonwealth. From 1932 onwards, as far as customs policy was concerned, they were parties to the Ottawa agreements, described at the end of this chapter, which offered one another tariff preferences. As for exchange-rate policy, after 1933 the countries floated as a group – that is, practising fixed exchange rates among themselves and floating against the rest of the world.[6] In terms of protectionist measures practised by members of the group, tariffs prevailed. Great Britain normally had substantial deficits in her trade with the rest of Europe, consequently, customs policy was used as a means of improving her trade balance. The Scandinavian countries, having substantial trade with Germany as well as their trade with

---

6. A more recent example of such a block float is the cooperation that took place within the European Monetary System, the EMS, where the participants let their currencies float, grouped around the DM.

Great Britain, had to adjust to the German system of restrictions in this part of their dealings.

A second group of countries was located in central and Eastern Europe, gathered around *Germany*. Apart from Austria and Czechoslovakia, their exports consisted mainly of agricultural goods. Due to low prices for primary products, these countries suffered severely from the crisis. Even before the Nazi takeover, Germany practised strict restrictions on imports, partly within a system of customs quotas which, from 1933 onwards, was supplemented by a strict system of quantitative restrictions aimed at creating a bilateral balance between Germany and each of its trade partners. Payments were organised on a bilateral clearing basis according to which, in principle, trade could take place without payments being made between Germany and its trade partners. As already mentioned, German trade with Scandinavia was organised in the same way. In 1936, when German rearmament was intensified and persecution of the Jews increased, the violation of exchange controls was made a capital offence; the principal aim being to prevent the flight of capital.

A third group of countries, less well defined, was associated with *France*. Its members were – besides France – Belgium, the Netherlands, and Switzerland. In principle, they tried to live up to the demands of the gold standard, including maintaining a fixed price for gold in their currencies. At a time, when other countries[7] allowed their currencies to depreciate, this meant in reality an appreciation of the franc and its followers. While France in the 1920s had enjoyed the advantage of an undervalued currency, it now had to suffer from an overvalued one. To protect its gold reserves in this situation, France had to introduce a system of quantitative import restrictions. One may well wonder at the Netherlands joining the group considering its own close trade relations to Great Britain. Compared to the members of the sterling block, the members of the franc group did not do too well in the 1930s, as can be seen from Table 10.1. In 1935, Belgium left the group and devalued, followed by the rest in 1936. After a sliding devaluation, the French franc was stabilized in 1937.

Finally, a fourth group centred on the *USA* was founded across the Atlantic. It consisted of countries in the Americas, including Canada. As far as its customs policy was concerned, Canada followed Britain as

---

7. Such as members of the sterling block and of the dollar block (see below).

a member of the Commonwealth. However, as far as its exchange rate policy was involved, the proximity of the USA made itself felt. In 1933, after the inauguration of President Roosevelt, the USA went off the gold standard and let the dollar float for a time. In 1934, the gold standard was re-established, but at a higher gold price.[8] The net outcome of this was a substantial depreciation of the dollar throughout the years 1933-34.

In 1936, an informal tripartite agreement was reached between Great Britain, France and the USA, aiming at the stabilization of their exchange rates, or, to put it another way, to prevent competitive devaluations. This agreement has been seen as a forerunner of the ideas behind the International Monetary Fund. It was hoped that the agreement would have resulted in a softening of the policy on restrictions, but in this respect it seems to have been a disappointment.[9]

4. National developments

4.1. Great Britain

For Great Britain, the thirties meant a break with the earlier essential doctrines of its economic policy. Externally, this was felt in the exchange rate and trade policies; domestically in agriculture and industry.

In September 1931, the British government and the Bank of England had to stop defending sterling and the gold standard. Sterling was floated which, in the short term, meant a depreciation against the dollar of 30 per cent. After the devaluation of the dollar in 1933, this fall against the dollar was reduced to 15 per cent. September 1931 meant the end of the exchange policy conducted since the conclusion of the Napoleonic Wars. The relation between sterling and gold was defined from now on by the exchange rate of the dollar and the price of gold in dollars. In spite of this, sterling retained its role as a key currency used by members of the sterling block in their internal trade. So even if conditions did change, the City of London still played a major part in the international financial and monetary system.

8. The value of the dollar measured in gold was reduced to 60 per cent.
9. F. Foreman-Peck (1995, 231f).

As far as the trade policy was concerned, the tradition of free trade originated in the repeal of the Corn Laws in 1846. As related earlier, at the close of the 1800s it had been suggested that customs tariffs should be introduced as part of a system of imperial preference, but nothing came of it. After the First World War, special tariffs were introduced to protect the so-called war babies and, in 1931, Parliament passed the Safeguarding Industries Act, enabling the government to introduce customs tariffs. The outcome of a conference held in Ottawa in 1932 had more direct consequences for the Commonwealth countries. Here it was agreed to establish a system of imperial preferences and, as part of this, Britain introduced a general customs duty of 10 per cent.[10]

It was this that marked the final British break with its free trade tradition. Agricultural products were covered by the Act, although most of the imports from Commonwealth countries were exempt from duty, while there were duty free quotas for third countries like the Netherlands and Denmark. In this way, British consumers still had the possibility of buying cheap food at world market prices. To assist British farmers, a support program offering direct price subsidies was introduced to keep producer prices above the consumer prices. The entire system of Commonwealth preference and British agricultural policy were later to become a central theme when Britain applied for membership of the Common Market.

British domestic economic policy saw a shift in industrial politics as subsidies were introduced with a view to the modernisation of key industries. These included mining, the iron and steel industry, shipyards and shipping. The modernisation and growth of those industries was further promoted by growing defence expenditure in reaction to the rearmament of Nazi Germany. During the years 1919-29, the British economy grew annually by 1.0 per cent. During the next ten years, the corresponding figure was 1.8 per cent. In spite of a weaker international economy, the British economy did better during this latter period.

4.2. France
In brief, the development of the French economy between the two wars can be characterized as the opposite of that of Great Britain with growth in the 1920s and direct stagnation in the 1930s.

---

10. Great Britain reserved for itself the right to offer non-member countries customs quotas under which imports were duty free. Those quotas were used in trade negotiations with third countries. Great Britain thereby contributed to the creation of a bilateral trade pattern in Europe.

After the USA, France was the country with the largest gold reserves in the early 1930s, and this was part of the reason why France did not devalue the Franc against gold, but remained at the old gold price. The need for an adjustment was not felt as keenly as it was in Great Britain. However, this meant that during the years 1931-33, France had its currency revalued upwards vis-à-vis members of the sterling and the dollar blocs. The result was an overvalued currency, accompanying problems in the balance of payments and ultimately the introduction of restrictions on foreign trade.

In spite of a deep and prolonged recession, the registered unemployment figures were not as high in France as they were in Great Britain and Germany. This is partly due to the fact that a substantial number of migrant workers, who had come to France from Spain, Portugal and Italy in the 1920s to compensate for the loss of men during the war, now had to leave. Furthermore, the tradition of "family shops" opened up possibilities to those who lost their jobs of being employed at least on a part-time basis.

In 1936, a coalition government was formed consisting of Socialist parties including the Communist Party. By including the Communist party in this Popular Front Government, France chose a different stance than the rest of the democratic countries of Western Europe where the Communists were marginalized. The Popular Front managed to introduce far-reaching reforms within social security, partly aimed at a reduction in the labour supply. This included a forty-hour week and two weeks' paid holiday. The right of collective bargaining was recognized and current strikes were brought to an end by wage increases.

The result was a deterioration in the balance of payments and pressure on the gold reserves. To stop this, the franc was floated and it fell by 40 per cent against the dollar and sterling. Even this was insufficient to secure an upturn, which did not take place until 1939 as a result of the beginning to rearm. Only a year later, the country was defeated and occupied by Germany.

4.3. Germany

In Germany, the recession was felt already from 1929 onwards due to the tight German monetary policy. In fixed prices, GDP fell by 16 per cent from a peak (1928) to a trough (1932), together with Austria the largest setback in Western Europe. Within manufacturing industries and urban trades the drop was far larger, and by 1932, 24 per cent of the labour force was unemployed.

With the memory still fresh of the harm caused by inflation in the early 1920s, great efforts were taken to protect the gold value of the Reichmark, even after Britain went off the gold standard in 1931. German competitiveness was therefore weakened, causing increased unemployment throughout 1932. Nazi support reached a peak of 37 per cent of the total votes cast at a general election in the summer of 1932. The party was at that time the largest in the Reichstag, although not as large as the Social Democrats and the Communists put together.

In January 1933, Adolf Hitler was appointed chancellor, Reichkanzler. The take-over was quite unexpected and in reality the new government took office without having what might be called a coherent economic programme. The Führer personally is said to have felt the deepest distrust for any sort of economist and was opposed to detailed arguments from that quarter. Nazism does not deserve the label of an ideology in the ordinary meaning of the word, which implies a coherent way of looking at society. An important part of their economic programme was a reduction of the burden of interest, which appealed to farmers and house owners feeling the pressure of a tight monetary policy, falling prices and growing unemployment.

The German economy after the Nazi take-over and before the attack on Poland in September 1939 can be split into two periods with 1936 as the dividing line. The first period was characterised by an expansion of public expenditure for civil purposes such as railways and a system of motorways, the autobahns. In addition, a growth in private consumption took place during this period as well as an increase in employment. Posterity has since questioned the size of this increase. The greatest rises took place in farming and construction; both sectors with a level of productivity below that of manufacturing industry. Part of the fall in unemployment – four hundred thousand – can be explained by "forced labour service".[11] The Nazis had promised the population bread and work. Even if the fall of unemployment was not based on a specified programme, the first years after the take-over left a feeling that the party had fulfilled some of its promises.

1936 saw a fundamental change in policy under a new Four-Year Plan when the emphasis was shifted from the civil to the military use of

11. R. J. Overy (1996, 41).

resources. From then on the German economy, in the light of the experience of the First World War, was based on a higher degree of self-sufficiency, examples of which include the production of synthetic petrol, rubber, textiles and an increased production of fertilizers. The German economy now had many of the characteristics of a command economy where wages and prices were under central control, which meant that Germany was capable of a substantial increase in its production without experiencing rising prices. Expressed in present day terms, we could say that it was due to a very strict "incomes policy", if necessary assisted by the SA-corps, the special Security Force of the Nazi Party, and by imprisoning leading trade union figures in concentration camps.

German economic policy in the years following the take-over in 1933 has now and then been labelled "pre-Keynesian", though this is based on a misunderstanding of Keynesian policy. According to this, the public sector may step in to supplement private demand during a period when this is too low, the so-called pump priming. As private demand increases, public demand is reduced to make room for the expansion. This, however, does not describe German economic policy in the thirties. On the contrary, public demand was still expanded as the German economy approached full employment due to growing military expenditure, which meant that private demand, including demand for private consumption, had to be held back. So what took place was, upon closer examination, just the opposite of Keynesian policies.

4.4. Belgium and the Netherlands

For *Belgium*, the years 1929 to 1939 were a frustrating period, for not until the late 1930s was the GDP level of 1929 regained.

In her exchange rate policy throughout the 1920s, Belgium had chosen to follow France, resulting in an increased competitiveness compared to Britain and a number of other European countries. Now, she followed France once again, not devaluing when Britain "went off the gold" in 1931. The result was diminished competitiveness and a severe economic setback. This policy was sustained until 1935 when the Belgian franc was devalued by approximately 30 per cent.

Both in its external and domestic policy, Belgium had hitherto pursued a liberal policy. In both these respects, the 1930s saw substantial changes as trade policy shifted towards protectionism in favour of the mining industries and agriculture. Another aspect of this was a substantial increase in trade with the Belgian Congo, which from being close to zero in 1913 now increased to ten per cent of external trade. This took place within a preferential area reminiscent of the British Commonwealth arrangements.

Throughout the 1920s, the *Netherlands* had experienced growth rates not only above the level of other European countries, but also higher even than those of the USA. This positive trend was interrupted in the 1930s and it was not until 1936-37 that production returned to the 1929 level. Compared with the Scandinavian countries, the Netherlands was hit substantially harder. By comparison with Belgium, however, she fared better by the end of the decenium.

As for Belgium, exchange rate policy must assume part of the responsibility for the prolonged economic recession. In the 1920s the Netherlands was among the countries that followed Britain in bringing its currency back to its pre-war parity. In 1931, she followed the example of France and Belgium in not devaluing its currency and, just as for those countries, this move meant a loss of competitiveness. This went on until 1936 when the Dutch guilder was devalued by 20 per cent, following the Belgian devaluation the previous year. One might ask why a country with an economy such as that of the Netherlands, including its close economic relations with Britain, chose an exchange rate policy that opposed the interests of its major export trades? Part of the answer is probably that this was due to the traditional interests of an influential financial sector. It was important for the government to prevent the flight of capital and, in order to avoid this, confidence in the Dutch guilder had to be maintained. This could only be done through a strict deflationary policy, and then only for a time.

Until the 1930s both Belgium and the Netherlands had traditionally pursued liberal trade policies. As small, open economies, they might have felt that a development like that of the 1930s ought not be repeated, for both economic and political reasons. This explains why during the Second World War their governments in exile, together with representatives of Luxembourg, took the initiative of the setting up of a customs union, Benelux, and why they led the way in promoting European economic integration in the immediate post-war years.

4.5. *The Scandinavian countries*

The Scandinavian countries were characterized by a relatively short and modest setback in the 1930s compared to most other countries in the Western World. Denmark saw no years with her GDP below the 1929 level, in Norway, GDP was below its 1929 level only in 1931 and in Sweden, this was the case in 1931-33. The average annual growth rates during the period 1929-39 were for Denmark 2.5 per cent, Norway 3.2 per cent and Sweden 3.0 per cent.[12] For Norway and Finland especially, the period represented a substantial step forward compared to other European countries.

The Scandinavian countries – including Finland – had, in common, open economies with close ties to Great Britain and Germany. However, due to differences in the composition of exports, their foreign trade, including their terms of trade, developed differently during the 1930s. The Swedish economy took advantage of a favourable business cycle when armaments were increased from the middle of the decade onwards, whereas Norway and Denmark had the disadvantage of poor freight rates. Denmark's greatest problems were in her foreign trade, and Danish expansion during the 1930s was based on a home market protected by quantitative restrictions. Thanks to their export industries, metals and metal products, Norway and Sweden had more room in which to expand their economies than Denmark. For Denmark, dependence on agricultural exports and home market industries led after the Second World War to a profound need for structural adjustment in her economy.

Already in the early 1930s, a debate took place in Sweden concerning the need for an active fiscal policy to ease the slump. The Swedish Social Democrats put forward arguments in favour of such a policy during an election campaign in 1932, and their programme under the title: "Can we afford to work", must be considered as applied Keynesian theory. Whether or not the favourable Swedish growth rates in the 1930s can be regarded as the impact of new ideas concerning economic policy has been a matter of discussion. At least part of the explanation can, as suggested above, be found in the favourable conditions for the Swedish export trades in the second half of the decade.

4.6. Italy, Spain and Portugal
(See Chapter 15, sections 6 and 7.)

---

12. Finland saw negative growth rates in 1930-32. In 1933, GDP was back at the 1929 level. The annual growth rates were 3.9 per cent during 1929-38, but fell due to the Winter War in 1939-40.

4.7. The USA

Of all the western industrialised countries, the USA experienced the greatest setback. From 1929 to 1933, GDP fell by 29 percent. This should be viewed against the background that the American economy in the peak year is supposed to have been 20 per cent below full capacity. If this is true, the American economy when it reached the bottom in 1932-33 was down as far as below 50 per cent of its capacity.

Before the presidential election in 1928, the Republican candidate, Herbert Hoover (1874-1964), had campaigned on the basis of the slogan: "prosperity for ever", yet less than twelve months after his election the stock market collapsed. In accordance with the prevailing economic and political philosophy of the time, little was done to prevent the deepening of the crisis, apart from increases in customs duties. The next presidential election took place in the midst of economic crisis in November 1932, and the Democrat, Franklin D. Roosevelt (1882-1945), was its victor. The inauguration was not to take place until March 1933, according to the rules then in force, and in spite of urgent calls from the outgoing president, Roosevelt did not want to see him.

After a period of more than four months, in reality without government in the depth of a national crisis,[13] the new president took over, stating in his inauguration address that: "all we have to fear, is fear itself". A bank holiday was declared to save what remained of the banking system and the new administration set out to launch its "New Deal". The New Deal was a mixture of short-term measures to fight the crisis there and then, and long-term policies to improve public infrastructure and to initiate a federal social security programme. The introduction and continuation of the programme indicated a new acceptance of the responsibility of a society towards its people.

The operations of the short-term policy were to a great extent of a psychological nature, a major point being to bring expectations of continued price falls to an end in order to get private investment started afresh. The price of agricultural products and the incomes of farmers were subsidised, and the dollar was devalued, not because of the balance of payments, but to encourage price increases. Immediate emergency measures were taken to assist the mass of needy, unemployed without access to any kind of assistance apart from charity.

---

13. It had already at that time been realized that the procedure was inappropriate. In January 1933, an amendment to the constitution was passed, stating that the inauguration after future elections should take place on January 20th.

Among the more far-sighted reforms must be mentioned the Social Security Act of 1935, establishing an old age pension scheme for workers, based on obligatory insurance and supplemented by federal and state funds. Part of the Act was a modest unemployment insurance scheme, which covered fifty million workers by the end of the 1930s. Roosevelt was criticised by his Republican opponents for leading the nation along the road to Socialism – a forecast that has not been fulfilled so far. The boom initiated by the outbreak of the Second World War and the following years of high growth brought the development of social security to a halt until new initiatives were taken under the Kennedy and Johnson administrations in the 1960s.

After the re-election of President Roosevelt in 1936, the economy suffered a new recession in 1937-38, and it was not until at the outbreak of the Second World War, that GDP was back at its 1929 level. The American economy entered the 1940s with unused resources that were going to be crucial for the defence of democracy during the coming years.

5. Lack of international cooperation

At the time of the economic crisis of 1929-30, there was no such thing as an international economic relief agency. The League of Nations had no permanent body to handle economic affairs, conferences were called on an ad hoc basis and permanent institutions both at global and regional levels were lacking.

Influenced by the deepening crisis, an *Economic World Conference* was called in 1932, to be held in London during the summer of 1933. Just before the opening of the conference it was announced that the USA devalued the dollar. This was not due to American balance of payments problems, and it was clear that the American move would aggravate the problems of the USA's trade partners and thereby the problems of world trade. The London conference was therefore paralysed from the outset and marked, in reality, the end of wider, international attempts to fight the crisis – until the problems were solved or changed by the outbreak of war.

If global initiatives were few and far between, and inadequate, not to say totally lacking in practical effect, the same can also be said of regional initiatives to alleviate the effects of the crisis.

The Ottawa Agreement of 1932 established a system of customs preferences covering present and previous members of the British Empire. The preferences – known as the Commonwealth Preferences – were made possible not only by lowering existing internal duties, but also by raising duties on goods from third countries. So it could be argued that the overall effect of the system was a reduction in international trade, not an increase. This explains why paragraphs were written into the GATT agreement after the war to prevent new free trade areas and customs unions having similar effects. Through its arrangements, Great Britain indicated that it had closer ties to those overseas areas beyond the Seven Seas than to the countries across the English Channel and the North Sea. Experiences of this sort were among the stumbling blocks when France vetoed the acceptance of Great Britain into the European Community in the 1960s.

Already in 1922, Belgium and Luxembourg had created an economic union consisting of a customs and a monetary union, *the Beluxunion,* (chapter 9, section 6.4). This was followed in 1932 by an agreement between those two countries and the Netherlands,[14] later to be known as *the Benelux agreement.* However, Great Britain and the USA considered it a breach of existing obligations under international law (the most favoured nation clause) by the three countries. This issue was brought before the International Court by Great Britain, which ruled in favour of Britain by not approving the agreement. The outcome seems strange, considering that Britain at the very same time was establishing its own preferential area.[15]

In 1930, a convention was set up between Belux, the Netherlands and the three Scandinavian countries: *the Oslo Convention;* the initiative for which came from the Netherlands.[16] The central theme was an obligation to consult the other countries if a country planned to increase its customs duties. Attached to the agreement was a protocol stating that the participants should seek to cooperate concerning their economic policy. It goes without saying that "hard" obligations were few or non-existent. So, in close-up, the Oslo agreement can be seen as proof that even among small, friendly and closely related nations it was impossible to establish close cooperation in the depths of the crisis.

14. Known as the Ouchy-agreement. J.Viner (1950, 30f).
15. The argument of Great Britain was that the parties to the Ouchy or Benelux-agreement were separate nations, whereas the parties to the Ottawa-agreement could, by tradition and history, be considered members of the same Commonwealth!
16. Kindleberger (1990, 135 and 144).

In 1931, negotiations took place between *Austria and Germany* concerning the establishment of a customs union. The plan met with opposition from France, along with an outright threat to withdraw French loans to Austria. The plan was then set aside for a while – until the annexation of Austria in 1938 by Nazi-Germany.

Part IV
Reconstruction
and years of high growth
1945-73

The introduction to Part III finished by characterizing the years from 1914 to 1945 as a period of "bad experiences". Part IV, Reconstruction and Years of High Growth, is the story of whether – or rather how – those experiences were made useful. The answer lies, in part, in the words "reconstruction" and "high growth".

Chapter 11, From Vienna, 1815 to San Francisco 1945, describes some essential features of development in international cooperation. Special emphasis has been laid on the differences in attitudes towards international economic cooperation as they materialized in the Covenant of the League of Nations of 1919 and in the Charter of the United Nations of 1945. The difference in time between the two is only twenty-six years. Nevertheless, there is literally a world of a difference between them. From here the exposition goes on to describe the concrete steps taken as part of the preparations for peace in 1944-45. Among the more far-sighted was the creation of a new order as far as monetary matters were concerned, which was done within the Bretton Woods-system. Another major goal was to prevent new trade wars and bring down the obstacles to international trade and the international division of labour. This was to take place through the GATT agreement.

Chapter 12, Reconstruction and Marshall Aid 1945-50, takes as its starting point an account of the situation at the end of the war. The background to the Marshall Plan, proposed in June 1947, is explained and its subject matter described. A major feature of the Marshall Plan was that the recipient countries were made responsible for the distribution of means. This was done through the OEEC, which was set up for this purpose. Among the functions taken up by this new body was also the liberalization of trade and payments between the member countries.

Chapter 13, National developments 1945-50, describes the major aspects of development in Great Britain, Germany, France, Belgium, the Netherlands, the Scandinavian countries, Italy, USA, and Japan.

Chapter 14, Prolonged growth 1950-73, discusses the positive interaction between high economic growth and ongoing international economic integration, especially within the framework of the Treaty of Rome. The period is characterized by its extraordinarily high and steady growth rates. This development is analyzed with reference to the results of so-called growth calculations. Finally, chapter 15, National Developments 1950-73, deals with the same countries as chapter 13, plus Spain and Portugal.

Chapter 11

From Vienna 1815 to San Francisco 1945

What will history books of the year 2050 consider to be the most important events of the mid-1900s? Will it be the high growth rates, the Cold War or the beginnings of an ecological catastrophe? Or will it be the breakthrough of new types of international cooperation within the framework of the UN and the EC/EU that will stand out as the foremost contribution to history? Perhaps the latter.

There is, however, no doubt that relations between countries have followed new ways and rules since the Second World War. The years 1914-45 and the tragedies of "the great showdown" of that period caused a revolt against the anarchy that dominated the international scene. It is this development, concluding with the conference in San Francisco during the summer of 1945 when the UN and a number of affiliated organizations were founded, which is the subject matter of this chapter.

The concepts and trends dealt with fall, on the whole, outside the scope of economic history as it is generally considered, belonging rather under the "International Organization" heading of social sciences. Nonetheless, taking the increased importance of international cooperation into consideration, it seems reasonable as an introduction to the rest of this book to give a short account of the history of the international organizations.

1. New forms of international cooperation

Bilateral cooperation was the predominant type of international cooperation before 1945 when rights and obligations were agreed upon between pairs of countries. The opposite of this is *multilateral* cooperation where the individual country participates in an agreement among a group of countries, thereby obtaining rights and taking on obligations towards the rest of the members of the group. As a leading example of the first type, bilateral cooperation, traditional trade agreements such as the Franco-British customs agreement of 1860 may be cited. Within the same sphere, but an example of a multilateral agreement, is the GATT, the General Agreement on Tariffs and Trade, originally set up among some twenty countries after the Second World War.

Multilateral cooperation offers a number of advantages both of a practical kind and of a wider economic and political importance. If twenty countries granted one another MFN-treatment through bilateral agreements (treatment as Most Favoured Nations), it would take 190 agreements; clearly a rather complicated affair. If the number of countries increased to 150, it would take more than eleven thousand bilateral agreements, many of which, of course, would be insignificant. It is more important in a wider sense that the advantages of international trade under the multilateral system are considered as a whole. If the countries seek to balance the advantages and disadvantages of their mutual relations between themselves, pair by pair, there is then every likelihood that the result will be a dramatic fall in international trade. It was precisely the bad experiences of the 1930s that now promoted the rise of multilateral economic cooperation. Finally, it can offer smaller countries the possibilities of merging their interests and political power and so offsetting the influence of the great powers.

The change from bilateral to multilateral agreements meant a change in the character of diplomacy. Traditional diplomacy, built on negotiations directly between two governments, was now supplemented and replaced by *conference diplomacy*. To serve conference diplomacy and to handle current business between conferences, international organizations with *permanent international secretariats* were created with their own permanent staffs, building close relations to the respective organizations. Besides the traditional legations and embassies, a new type of diplomatic representation, the *permanent mission*, appeared as seen first at the League of Nations in Geneva after the First World War and, later on, in conjunction with the United Nations, the OEEC/OECD, EC/EU, EFTA, etc.

By then the number of countries participating in international cooperation had increased substantially and this, along with the rise of multilateral cooperation, led to a distinction between *global* and *regional* cooperation. Before 1914, European and global cooperation were almost identical in that substantial areas outside Europe were colonies and had limited mutual economic connections. The main exception to this was the USA and other countries of the Americas. The USA, however, through the Monroe Doctrine had purposely chosen to stay out of European affairs and opposed any European interference in the Western Hemisphere. It was not until the end of the Second World War that the distinction between regional and global cooperation became important.

Finally, the obligations undertaken were wider in scope and affected populations more directly than previously because countries actually *relinquished sovereignty*. Cooperation within the framework of traditional treaties implied that governments undertook the rights and obligations under the treaties. It was not the individual, private exporter who obtained the right to most favoured nation-treatment in the foreign country. It was his government as a party to the treaty according to traditional international law. Under the new type of cooperation, as seen in the EC/EU with the so-called regulations, the system works differently. Here, the decisions taken by the community are directly binding on its citizens, just as they themselves can go to court to protect their rights. Having reached this stage, international cooperation in essence means that the nation state in this particular respect has ceased to exist and has been superseded by a federation.

2. The Concert of Europe

Features of development in international cooperation since the Napoleonic Wars include:

a. the appearance of a small group of great powers and formal recognition of their priority in international cooperation,

b. the organization of international conferences and the establishment of permanent international bodies where participation at a regional or global level is open to all; international society has become universal,

c. the creation of permanent secretariats to run the day-to-day affairs
of the international organizations,

d. the establishment of permanent international judicial bodies.

At the end of the Napoleonic Wars in 1814-15, the European powers
met in Vienna to establish normal conditions in Europe. Normal conditions meant, above all, that the frontiers between the countries were
put back to what they had been in 1792 before Louis XVI was forced
off his throne. The participating great powers (Great Britain, France,
Austria, Prussia and Russia) agreed to unite in order to prevent a similar development from being repeated and to ensure that things remained as they had been before the great revolution. Such conferences
were recurrent features of the 1800s and known under the names of
The Holy Alliance and the Concert of Europe.

The Holy Alliance was born at the Congress of Vienna. It was meant
as a personal relationship between the heads of state to solve problems
between their countries and was open to "minor" monarchs as well.
The Russian Czar took the initiative and any decisions taken would, if
necessary, remain secret. The entire idea seems to have been a mixture
of good intentions and mysticism. The life span of the alliance covers
the first years of repression after the Napoleonic Wars. Between 1815-
22, four meetings were held. Great Britain remained outside, the formal reason being that participation in secret international agreements
was against British traditions since such agreements had to be approved by Parliament. To this could be added the wish to feel free to
pursue an expansionist policy overseas. The Pope was invited as well,
but abstained from participation saying that the Holy See was placed
above temporal princes.

Of longer duration were the recurrent great power conferences
known as *the Concert of Europe*. Meetings were held "according to
need", without prior agreement about the time and place for the next
one, and totalled more than thirty in the 99 years before the First
World War. Some of the conferences were called during very dramatic
situations such as the Paris conference in 1856 at the end of the Crimean War and the one in Berlin in 1878 concerning borders in the Balkans. As a peacekeeping institution, the Concert of Europe seems to
have been a success. Wars in Western Europe were few and relatively
short in duration throughout the 1800s compared to the years before

and those to come. As such, it seemed that the obvious thing to do was to try to continue such conferences within the framework of the League of Nations. From the great power conferences of the Concert of Europe, direct parallels were drawn to *the Council* of the League with its permanent members and, from here, to *the Security Council* of the United Nations with its five permanent members. The new factor introduced by the League of Nations was that the institutions were made permanent, had a fixed meeting place, set rules of procedure and permanent representatives who could be called upon at short notice.

From the middle of the 1800s onwards, another type of international institution developed. The background to this was the growth of international communications related to the spread of railways, telegraph lines, etc., which caused a need to define and administer common norms, to share costs and so on. This was done by setting up new *international administrative bodies,* early examples of which were the International Telegraph Union (established in 1865) and the International Postal Union (1874), which served common goals across borders. Unlike traditional diplomats serving their home countries, the civil servants of the new international bodies served a common, international purpose and these administrative bodies were to form the foundation for the present great international secretariats serving the United Nations bodies in New York, Washington DC and Geneva as leading examples, and not forgetting the staff of the EC/EU in Brussels.

A third element in the development of modern international organization was the *Hague system,* named after the city where two conferences took place in 1899 and 1907 when the Russian Czar took the lead. In principle, "all countries" were entitled to participate. In practice this meant 24 participants in the first conference and 44 in the second. As mentioned above, independent states, on the whole, were only found in Europe and in the Americas, so it is fair to say that participation was general. From those two conferences, lines can be drawn directly to *the Assembly* of the League of Nations and *the General Assembly* of the United Nations where all the member states can state their opinion on the matters dealt with and where each has a single vote.

Besides giving currency to the idea of international society, the Hague conferences can be seen as the origin of *the International Court.* The declared purpose of the two conferences was to limit spending on armaments, prohibit gas warfare, the dropping of bombs from hot air balloons, etc. As time and events were to show, the results within this sphere were limited. More successful, however, were the endeavours to promote international jurisdiction where countries could give notice of their willingness to let judicial conflicts be settled by a court of arbitration. The composition of the court, where the appointment of judges was first to be decided upon when a concrete matter was taken to the court, in this respect differed from ordinary, national courts. This also meant that a country having joined the system would actually be able to block a case from being taken up by the court. An advantage, however, was the multilateral nature of the system. At the 1907 conference, it was suggested that a permanent court be set up with its judges appointed in advance. However, due to problems with the appointment of judges and the outbreak of war in 1914, these plans were first realized in 1920 with the creation of the International Court as part of the League of Nations. This institution was transferred to the United Nations Organization after the Second World War.

3. The Inter-Parliamentary Union, IPU

Generally, the international cooperation so far mentioned took place between governments and was dominated by narrow national interests. Parliamentarians trying to cooperate across borders, whose aim was, in part, the same as inter-governmental cooperation to prevent violence and wars, followed a somewhat different approach. To this, however, should be added a wish to promote democracy and international understanding through the use of far-sighted measures.

The Inter-Parliamentary Union, IPU, was founded in 1889 on the initiative of British and French parliamentarians. Originally, it was a private society consisting of individual members of parliaments, but now is a union of parliaments represented by their members. The fact that the union – in principle at least – has been independent of government interests has given it wider opportunities to take initiatives and place matters on the agenda. The IPU was, from an early point in time, actively involved in the creation of an international court and a global peacekeeping organization.

Scandinavian parliamentarians have been active in the work of the IPU – the Dane, Fredrik Bajer (1837-1922) and the Norwegian, Christian Lange (1869-1938) were both awarded the Nobel Peace Prize. The son of the latter, Halvard Lange (1902-70), was the Norwegian minister of foreign affairs after the Second World War and, as such, led an active Norwegian foreign policy in the United Nations.

The IPU now holds semi-annual sessions organized in a way that makes it possible to move between different continents. In keeping with the idea of promoting democracy, it is not a condition of admission to live under democratic rule and conferences have been held in Peking and Havana. The IPU has its secretariat in Geneva, though its functions are few and its size modest.

4. The League of Nations

The aim of the League of Nations was to secure peace. It did not succeed and the verdict of history is clear: the League was a failure.

It has been said, somewhat unkindly, of both the League of Nations and the UN that they were created "to prevent the war which had just ended". The League was set up to prevent "the accidental war", the outbreak of which could be caused by the automatic nature of mobilization plans and the lack of political and diplomatic control. This explains why the Covenant of the League contained articles to enable the Council to postpone the outbreak of war. This might have prevented the First World War. The United Nations was designed to prevent "the intended war", where an aggressor simultaneously became involved in hostilities with the five permanent members of the Security Council, France, Great Britain, the USSR, the USA and China; and envisages an aggressor corresponding to that of Nazi Germany or Japan in the 1930s.

However, it is not this aspect of the work of the League that is the topic of this section; it is its economic functions – or rather lack of them – which will be dealt with here.

4.1. High politics, not economics

The economic provisions of the Covenant were few and easy to mention. Article 23a states that the member countries: "...will endeavour to secure and maintain fair and humane conditions of labour for men, women and children". This provision corresponded to existing treaties, and its realization was eventually entrusted to the ILO, the International Labour Organization. Furthermore, it was decided that the members should take steps: "to secure and maintain freedom of communications and of transit and equitable treatment for the commerce of all Members of the League" (Art. 23e). This can be said to have meant a "mild" obligation among the members to offer one another most favoured nation treatment. Finally, the Covenant included rules concerning economic sanctions towards countries breaching international peace. They were meant as part of the peacekeeping policy and not as part of economic policy. In practice, economic motives conspired to prevent their effective use.

It seems proper to point out that according to present-day opinion there was just about a total lack of economic provisions in the Covenant of the League of Nations, and a comparison with the Charter of the United Nations (section 5) will prove this. It is amazing that it was possible to draft two texts so radically different from one another within a period of only 25 years. This says more about developments from 1919 to 1945 than many pages of written history.

The complete silence of the Covenant of the League of Nations concerning macro-economic matters such as employment and growth can hardly be a cause for wonder. The silence of the Covenant was in full accord with the spirit of the time and the then predominant opinions on economic policy. The turn of the century had seen the birth of a formalized economic theory according to which price theory could form the basis for a coherent theory covering the goods markets, factor markets, money, capital and exchange markets. This type of system would inevitably move towards a state of equilibrium, and so all that was left for economic policy decisions were micro-level issues such as the protection of workers, regulation of working hours, etc.

4.2. International cooperation

The years before the First World War saw a number of initiatives to promote international cooperation at a practical level like the International Postal Union mentioned in section 2 of this chapter. This work was now carried on and strengthened under the League of Nations:

> "The lights which guide ships up to the quays of Hamburg or Buenos Aires; the signs which warn the motorist on the roads of Italy or Sweden; the standards which allow doctors in Sydney or in Cairo to use the medical experience of Paris and New York – a thousand such

Fig. 13: The newly built Geneva headquarters of the League of Nations. It never really came to serve its original purpose as the home of a new, peace keeping body. USA never joined, and Germany walked out after the Nazis came to power. Since the Second World War, the impressive buildings have served as the meeting place of a great number of international conferences such as, among others, the GATT.

practical details were planned and executed by the technical agencies of the League."

This salute to the League from one of its previous high-ranking servants – the author had been deputy secretary general of the League – concludes as follows:

"A still more convincing tribute is the fact that each of the special organizations set up by the League and extinguished by its death has been re-established by the United Nations."[1]

To prove this statement, a short review is given below of the history of some of the existing agencies and bodies under the United Nations.

1. F. P. Walters (1952 I, 176-77).

The *International Labour Organization (ILO)* can be traced back to the turn of the century when the initiative was mainly taken by Germany, in part because of fears of social dumping due to higher German standards in social security and labour protection. The field of cooperation is reminiscent of the so-called social dimension within the EC/EU. The ILO was set up according to separate provisions of the Covenant of the League and was integrated directly into the work of the League. From the very outset, it was stated that the secretariat of the ILO should be domiciled at the same place as the League, which brought the organization to Geneva where it has since remained. As an early and typical example of the results of the ILO, the Washington Declaration of 1919 introducing the 48-hour working week could be mentioned.

Under the United Nations, the *Transport and Communications Commission* was formed, building on cooperation established before 1914 and strengthened during the period of the League of Nations. As the name of the commission and one of the above mentioned quotations indicate, the aim of this was to facilitate transport and communication. The present *World Health Organization* (WHO) can be traced back to the International Health Office established in Paris in 1908 and carried on under the League as the Health Organization. At an early point in time after the First World War, the importance of its existence was proved through efficient participation in fighting epidemic diseases in Eastern Europe. The UN`s *Commission on Narcotic Drugs* dates back to the Opium Convention of 1912. In the League of Nations, a committee on the Traffic in Opium and other Dangerous Drugs handled the problems. The problem was, then as now, that the producing countries were less inclined to participate in efforts to reduce production. This was the case not only for producers of opium and other narcotics, since even a medicine-producing country like Switzerland hesitated until 1925 to join the Opium Convention. The present position of *UN High Commissioner for Refugees* dates back to the Refugee Organization created under the League in 1921. As a final example, *UNESCO* can be mentioned. In 1922, a committee was organized under the League to deal with matters concerning "Intellectual Cooperation". It was the outcome of a Franco-Belgian initiative and opposition and scepticism were widespread. Its aim was to promote education, the fine arts and spiritual activities. The means placed at the committee's disposal did not quite match the composition of the committee, which was at the

Nobel Prize level. With its first members including Albert Einstein (1879-1955) and M. Curie (1867-1934), the League allocated less than five thousand pounds sterling for the financial basis of the committee's activities. The organization set up its headquarters in Paris thanks to a special grant from the French government. So, when the budget problems of UNESCO now and then are on the agenda and in the headlines it is not really a new phenomenon.

As the 1930s progressed and the shortcomings of the League as a peacekeeping institution became ever more obvious, a new way of looking at international cooperation and peacekeeping efforts developed. Instead of seeking to solve international conflicts through mediation and the like after their outbreak, as the League did, the rise and escalation of such conflicts should be prevented through increased economic integration across national borders. Peace among nations was to be promoted in the same way as it had been within nations: through inter-dependence and a wish to avoid the losses and costs caused by open conflict. As part of peacekeeping policy this is known as *functionalism*. It was not through solemn declarations and statements that peace would be secured and not through threats of the use of force either. "Working international agencies will create a system of mutual advantages which will assume too great a value in the eyes of the beneficiaries for them to contemplate disrupting it by permitting the resort to war".[2]

There are two major reasons for referring to the functional approach as a tool in peacekeeping policy. Firstly, it had substantial influence on the drafting of the Charter of the United Nations at the end of the Second World War and, secondly, it played a role in the process of European integration after 1945. An early example of this was the creation of the European Coal and Steel Community (ECSC) in 1950-52. Secondly, part of the functional approach is the idea that there would be a spillover effect, that cooperation would pave the way for more cooperation or, as stated in the preamble to the Treaty of Rome, there shall be "an ever closer union".

The functional approach is sometimes seen as the counterpart to a federalist approach. Whereas the starting point of the federalist view is the writing of a constitution to be gradually supplemented by practical

2. I.L.Claude jr. (1963, 378). Particularly worthy of mention is the pioneering work of David Mitrany, A Working Peace System, London and New York. Royal Institute of International Affairs. 1946.

cooperation, the functional approach takes the opposite course. It starts with practical undertakings, which eventually might lead to a constitution.

The League of Nations and its results have been described in negative terms, and it could be objected that its successor, the United Nations, has shown shortcomings too. More important, however, is, where the United Nations has done better, part of the explanation is that it had the experiences of the League to learn from. It should be pointed out that a number of persons participating in international cooperation after the Second World War had, in fact, served for shorter or longer periods in the League of Nations. Among these was Jean Monnet, one of the key figures of European integration in the 1950s. In his memoirs, he describes how important his experiences during the First World War and his years in the League of Nations were for his later efforts towards European integration.[3]

As the practical work of the League intensified throughout the 1930s, this caused a growing need for a central, coordinating body. The result was a proposal for a "Central Committee for Economic and Social Questions". This was put forward in the summer of 1939, just as war broke out in September. Further attempts were stopped, but substantial elements of this idea reappeared in the provisions concerning the *Economic* and *Social Council* (ECOSOC) of the United Nations.

The League of Nations was born as the result of a war that cost 25 million human lives, and it was to die only twenty years later as the result of the outbreak of a war that would cost more than 40 million lives. In spite of all its failings it is proper to quote the following, written after the Second World War by the previously mentioned deputy secretary general of the League:[4]

"Although the League's span of life was short and troubled, its success transitory, and its end inglorious, it must always hold a place of supreme importance in history. It was the first effective move towards the organization of a world-wide political and social order in which the common interests of humanity could be seen and served across the barriers of national tradition, racial difference or geographical separation."

3.   J. Monnet. Memoires. 1976.
4.   F.P.Walters (1952 I, 1).

5. The United Nations. A different approach

It is outside the scope of this exposition to give a detailed description of the birth of the United Nations. Here the major effort will be made in pointing out the profound differences between the League and the United Nations in so far as their economic provisions are concerned. The specific initiatives taken at the end of the war are dealt with in the next section.

By the outbreak of the war in September 1939, the League had definitely run its course, though the formal survival of its headquarters in Geneva until 1946 is another story. The future system of international cooperation had to be placed within a new framework, unrelated to the League and its long list of defeats. For one thing, the position of the two new superpowers made its continued existence impossible – the USA had never joined the League and the USSR had been expelled as a last, empty gesture in December 1939 following its attack on Finland.

Traditionally, the foundation of the United Nations is traced back to the Atlantic Charter, presented in August 1941 as the result of a meeting between Franklin Roosevelt (1882-1945) and Winston Churchill (1874-1965) off the coast of Newfoundland. After the Japanese attack on Pearl Harbor in December 1941, this was followed by the "Declaration of the United Nations", which became the legal basis of the allied coalition – and the name of the coming world organization.

From the beginning, the Anglo-American initiative for creating a new world organization was met with scepticism by the USSR, having been expelled from the previous organization shortly before. However, in the autumn of 1943, at a meeting of foreign ministers of the three great allies, the Soviets accepted the idea of forming a peacekeeping organization. In the summer of 1944, a conference was held in Dumbarton Oaks, Washington DC, to outline the primary features of such a body. The USA and Great Britain were in favour of enlarging the functions of the new organization to economic and social matters, whereas the USSR wanted to restrict its work to matters concerning security policy. This can be seen in relation to the Communist and Marxist theory of catastrophe: if one expects – and waits for – the breakdown of the Capitalist system as a step towards Socialism, there can be no reason to participate in rescue operations to save the system – quite the contrary. To this should be added, at a more practical level, the fear of interference in internal Soviet economic matters. The over-all result was that the USSR accepted that the new organization should enter the sphere of economics – and would itself stay out of this area.

At another conference in July 1944 at Bretton Woods in New England, it was agreed to establish an International Monetary Fund (IMF) and an International Bank for Reconstruction and Development (IBRD), normally referred to as the World Bank. To ensure co-ordination, and in accordance with the pre-war proposal, it was agreed to establish within the UN framework a council to deal with economic and social matters. This was done by giving the new Economic and Social Council a coordinating function in relation to the *Specialized Agencies*. This meant that the essential questions concerning the economic provisions of the coming world organization were solved before the opening of the final conference in San Francisco in April 1945. At the opening of the conference 43 countries participated and a few more were invited during its course.[5] After ratification by a sufficient number of countries, including the five permanent members of the Security Council, the statute came into force on October 24, 1945, which has since been considered the birthday of the UN and is celebrated as UN-day.

Already in the preamble – the solemn opening declaration of the statute – the member countries express their will: "to promote social progress and a better standard of life in larger freedom, and ... to employ international machinery for the promotion of the economic and social advancement of all peoples". In special chapters, provisions follow concerning "International Economic and Social Cooperation" (Chapter IX), "with a view to the creation of...higher standards of living, full employment, and conditions of economic and social progress and development..." etc. In the next chapter, the rules concerning the Economic and Social Council follow, describing its composition, its functions and powers.

The short quotations given above illustrate the difference in spirit at the close of the First World War and at the end of the Second. Now the Charter, as opposed to the Covenant, expresses a political responsibility for the level of employment, and the Keynesian current is felt be-

5. Among the original participants from Western European countries were France, the United Kingdom, Belgium, the Netherlands, Luxembourg and Norway. Denmark was invited after the opening of the conference and was accepted as member number fifty.

hind the text. On the other hand, the Charter gives no answers to the question of the future of tariff-protection, exchange controls, quantitative restrictions, etc. Provisions of this sort were dealt with by the new specialized agencies under ECOSOC.

In practice ECOSOC was never given the function of a coordinating body as far as these institutions were concerned. What was left for the UN itself were matters concerning Third World problems, including questions of development and assistance. However, the creation of the Bretton Woods and the GATT systems marked precisely the difference between the lessons learned in 1918 and 1945. The most important of those new institutions are dealt with in the concluding sections of this chapter.

6. Preparing the peace

Among the pressing economic problems to be dealt with on an international level at the end of the Second World War, the following should be mentioned (the name of the international organization set up to deal with the matter in question is given in brackets):

a. an assistance programme to be started at the end of the hostilities (UNRRA, United Nations Relief and Rehabilitation Administration),

b. a solution to the global long-term problem of food supply (FAO, Food and Agriculture Organization),

c. arrangements for reconstruction and economic development (IBRD, International Bank for Reconstruction and Development = the World Bank),

d. a solution to problems concerning international payments through the creation of an appropriate international monetary system (IMF, International Monetary Fund = the Fund),

e. a lowering of trade barriers (ITO, International Trade Organization and GATT, General Agreement on Tariffs and Trade – only GATT came into being).

After the First World War, civilian populations suffered far greater losses than during the war itself due to malnourishment accompanied by epidemics. One influenza epidemic especially, known as the Spanish flu in Europe, cost millions of lives. In order to avoid a repetition of this, *UNRRA* was created. Another foreseeable problem was the vast number of refugees. Here UNRRA could assist as well, though at first the need was expected to be of limited duration. As far as the first area was concerned – supplying food and combating epidemics – UNRRA fulfilled its task. However, the problem of the return of refugees proved more intractable and the job was more or less impossible to complete. Many in Eastern Europe, especially people from eastern parts of Germany who had fled from Soviet troops, did not want to return.

The functions of the *FAO* were of a more long-term nature. Here, the major task was to increase the supplies of foodstuffs in "underdeveloped countries", as developing countries were called in the early post-war years. European countries made an important contribution through research and development into the creation of new and more resistant types of crops and the spread of knowledge concerning more efficient methods of agriculture. The FAO has its headquarters in Rome.

The *IBRD* (World Bank) was, as the words "reconstruction" and "development" denote, meant to have a double function. "Reconstruction" dealt with areas and countries hit by war damage, while "development" dealt with developing countries and the problems of "catching up". Eventually, it turned out that the Bank would concentrate on the latter. The Marshall Plan took up reconstruction in Europe on a large-scale basis as far as external financing was concerned. The main function of the World Bank was financing, or guaranteeing the financing, of basic investments (transport facilities, power stations, energy supply networks) in developing countries.

The *IMF* (the Fund) concentrated on short-term financing and its main partners were and still are the central banks of the member countries. The breakdown of the system of fixed exchange rates in the early 1970s meant a reduction of the functions of the Fund. Since then, the fall of the Communist system has given the Fund new tasks in assisting the economic transformation of those countries.

GATT was born as a temporary body to supplement a new international trade organization, the ITO, but since the ITO never came into existence, GATT turned into a permanent body. It almost reached its fiftieth birthday before being superseded, or rather supplemented, by the new World Trade Organization (WTO). GATT, as now the WTO, had its secretariat in Geneva, while the eight successive customs conferences under GATT were held in different places.

Of the five areas mentioned under points a to e, the two most important to Western Europe have been those dealt with by the IMF (the Bretton Woods system) and by GATT.

7. The Bretton Woods System

The lessons of the 1930s had shown that a well-functioning payments system is a prerequisite for an advanced international division of labour. Reorganizing the international financial and monetary system was considered an urgent matter from the outset. Early on, during the war, the British and the American ministries of finance considered the matter, with J.M. Keynes playing a leading role on behalf of the Treasury.

The subject was split up into two subtopics. First, there was the question of securing *long-term* international financing within sectors expected to be short of private financial resources. This would mainly be within the sphere of infrastructure such as railways, harbours, power stations etc. Second was the need for the re-establishment of a well-functioning international monetary system, including the necessary *short-term* credit possibilities for the central banks. After preparatory talks and investigations, these two fields of interest were the subjects of a conference in July 1944 in the American provincial town of Bretton Woods, New England. Keynes was appointed chairman of the committee dealing with the supply of long-term capital, which resulted in the establishment of the IBRD, the World Bank. His major interest, however, was with the other committee, the chairmanship of which the USA had reserved for itself. Here, the outcome was the establishment of the IMF.

Although both the Bank and the Fund were results of the conference in Bretton Woods, the *Bretton Woods system* only refers to the IMF, the aims of which were:

a. to secure stable exchange rates to prevent competitive devaluations;
   this was intended to facilitate a coordinated policy on business cycles and to strengthen the price mechanism as an allocative device,

b. to ensure the supply of sufficient international liquidity to carry out
   commercial international transactions and to solve temporary liquidity problems without resorting to exchange adjustments,

c. to abolish the trade and exchange restrictions of the 1930s and to
   prevent their renewal.

To meet these goals under a and b, the participants had first of all to
give prior notice of their exchange rates in terms of the US dollar.
Those rates were adjustable in case of persistent and substantial balance of payments difficulties ("to correct a fundamental disequilibri-
um"). Second, the participants were given drawing rights on the Fund
and, as part of this, the Fund was given the right to make recommendations or stipulate specific conditions concerning the economic policy
of the countries receiving loans from the Fund.
    Implementation of point c – the abolition of the restrictions inherit-
ed from the years of crises and war – proved to be the most difficult.
The possibilities for Western Europe of generating dollar incomes during the early post-war years were small or non-existent, so a general
opening up of European imports from the Dollar-Area had to be postponed for at least a dozen years. There was, however, an urgent need to
reduce the restrictions on intra-European trade and, to this end, it was
necessary to substitute the existing bilateral trade and payments system with a regional, multilateral system covering Western Europe.
The establishment of such a system was initiated in 1949-50, as described in relation to the OEEC. So it could be argued that the Bretton
Woods system came into force among the OEEC-countries already in
the early 1950s. It was not, however, until 1958 that the European currencies were made convertible into US dollars. Therefore, in a wider
sense, it took until the end of the 1950s before the Bretton Woods system came into force. Moreover, it lasted only until the early 1970s, operating, all in all, according to the original intentions for a mere dozen
years.
    When it is said that the Bretton Woods system aimed at a system of
complete freedom of exchange markets across borders, it is a statement

that needs qualifying. The freedom was at first only intended to cover current transactions of the balance of payments – that is, transactions related to the earning and spending of income (on goods, services, interest, etc.) – whereas capital transactions (all sorts of loans and investments) could still be the subject of regulations and restrictions. It was this distinction that was dropped in the 1960s with the result that those free moving means, being subject to sudden transfers from one country to another, grew dramatically and caused the final breakdown of the fixed exchange rates system in the early 1970s.

8. The foundation of GATT

Apart from exchange controls and the QRs (quantitative restrictions), the 1930s left a heritage of high customs duties. The USA and Great Britain had already agreed during the war that those problems were to be dealt with, but for practical reasons this could not be accomplished at a concrete level until the end of the war, being eventually resolved at conferences in Havana and Geneva between 1946 and 1948.

In Havana, a treaty was drafted concerning an *International Trade Organization (ITO)*. According to the treaty the participants were obliged to:

a. offer all other participants most favoured nation (MFN) treatment, so that the contracting parties could thus ensure one another equal conditions in international trade and reduce the risks of commercial wars,

b. participate in regular conferences where countries with a major trade interest could demand negotiations to be conducted with the trading partners in question, and institutional machinery to reduce tariffs was to be established,

c. ensure that the agreements so reached should be in force during fixed periods, common to all participants; and that during those periods there should be no possibility for raising tariffs,

d. abstain from the use of quantitative restrictions (QRs) and export subsidies.

According to the treaty, participants shared the common goal of full employment, although nothing was said about how this goal was to be achieved. Furthermore, the ITO charter contained provisions concerning the control of monopolies and the establishment of international commodity agreements, especially concerning raw materials and agricultural products (primary products). To satisfy the wishes of the USA, restrictions on the import of products of agriculture and fisheries could be imposed if they were part of a policy of simultaneously reducing the production of the importing country itself. Likewise, export subsidies were legalized for those commodities if their purpose was to prevent a fall in the market share of a given country. Both these provisions were to cause problems later on in the treatment of agricultural products under the GATT.

Already since the preparatory talks held during the war concerning future international cooperation, the USA had sought to limit discriminatory practices, whereas for Britain it was important to safeguard its special relations with the countries of the Commonwealth, including the customs preferences of the 1932 Ottawa agreements. The question was settled between Roosevelt and Churchill with the result that the USA gave in to British wishes, which paved the way for the acceptance of similar requests or more far-reaching arrangements. During the war, the governments in exile of Belgium, the Netherlands and Luxembourg had drawn up plans for a true customs union, the future Benelux. So, when the final drafting of the rules of the ITO and GATT took place, the USA had to accept the existence of customs unions and free-trade areas as exceptions to the general rule of MFN treatment.

In parallel with the conference in Havana, negotiations were opened in Geneva in 1947 concerning tariff cuts and agreements. The results of these negotiations were written into a *General Agreement on Tariffs and Trade*. This agreement, *GATT*, was meant to serve as an interim measure until the ITO could enter into force. For this reason, there were no provisions concerning the organizational aspects of the cooperation. In a formal sense, GATT had no organizational basis and no members, but only, as they used to call themselves, contracting parties. As for its temporary status, things turned out differently. Both liberal and protectionist members of the US Congress lost interest in the ITO and, furthermore, a first step had been taken through the GATT arrangement, so Congress never ratified the ITO. It was not until 1994, that GATT acquired its organizational superstructure and that new areas of cooperation were included under the new *World Trade Organization, the WTO.*

Chapter 12

Reconstruction and Marshall Aid 1945-50

1. The state of affairs in 1945

The economic and political conditions in Western Europe were in many respects fundamentally different after the Second World War by comparison with those after the First:

a. material destruction was far greater. This was due to air warfare and the movement of the war fronts over large distances covering vast areas. As a result, the German withdrawal in 1944-45 caused further great damage in Western Europe from Sicily to the North Cape, while damage in Eastern Europe was even greater and accompanied by outright genocide,

b. the foreign policy situation was entirely different as the Soviet Union, like the USA, had obtained superpower status and wanted to take advantage of its new position. At the same time, the USA was abandoning its isolationist policy. As a result, the political influence of even the larger countries of Western Europe was severely reduced, the area becoming little more than a buffer zone between East and West,

c. the previously liberal attitude towards economic policy had been replaced by a new and more interventionist approach. This was due to the years of crisis in the 1930s and the years of war and a war economy. This influenced government control of private businesses, the size of taxes and public expenditure, as well as the role of macroeconomic policy. New ideas concerning the international economy had paved the way for bestowing new functions upon the United Nations and its affiliated bodies such as the IMF and GATT,

d. a shift to the left had taken place in European countries, as expressed by the results of general elections held shortly after the war and liberation from the Germans. The contribution of the USSR to the defeat of Nazi Germany was met with admiration and gratitude. Pre-war scepticism towards the USSR and Communism had, in wide circles, been replaced by a sense of recognition of the economic and military accomplishments of the system. There was also the participation of Communists in the resistance movements, after the German attack on the USSR in June 1941. All this served to make life easier for left-wing movements and more difficult for some of the parties on the right, whose credibility had been undermined by their politics during the preceding years and by their soft stance towards Fascism and Nazism,

e. the reality of the military and moral defeat of Germany was beyond doubt. Unlike 1918, Germany in 1945 was an occupied nation under the control of enemy armies and their representatives. It was an open question how Germany would once again obtain self-determination in domestic and foreign affairs; any answer would require new and previously untried methods in international politics,

f. none of the countries in Western Europe had the strength to be compared with the two superpowers. France had suffered a military and moral defeat in May – June 1940, and Germany was, for many and obvious reasons, out of the reckoning, Great Britain, although undefeated and among the victorious nations, was exhausted after years of war and after shedding most of its former empire. Western Europe had doubts about its capacity to handle its own fate and what balance to strike between the two superpowers.

The differences between the "before" and "after" situations must include a further point: the existence of the atom bomb. There are two reasons why this was not included among the points above. Firstly, the existence of the atom bomb was not known of until after VE Day and, secondly, it had no direct effect on the economies of Western Europe until the USSR carried out its first nuclear test in the autumn of 1949. After then, however, it would serve to accelerate European rearmament, including that of Germany, and the entire process of European integration.

2. Supply shortages 1945-47

As far as supplies were concerned, the economic situation in 1945 and
the first two post-war years were characterized by shortages in almost
all material respects. There were housing problems, especially in larger
towns that had been hit by air raids. In the major cities it was necessary
to clear up the ruins simply to enable traffic to circulate. Bridges and
railways were destroyed and there was a shortage of railway equipment
and rolling stock. A single intact bridge over the Rhine was all that the
Allies encountered in March and April 1945. Hardest hit were the outputs of raw materials and manufacturing industry as mineshafts and
dams had been destroyed when the Germans retreated. Mines and
farmland below sea level had been flooded, so that even an agricultural
country such as the Netherlands suffered from famine in 1944-45. It
was far more than just a transient crisis as far as the supply of food was
concerned, for this shortage had an impact on lifestyles and consumption in a much broader sense. Not only were the vanquished affected;
the victorious and the formerly occupied countries were affected as
well. A few countries managed to get through the period without much

Table 12.1: GDP in fixed prices (1938 = 100). 1945-50.

	1945	1946	1947	1948	1949	1950
UK	116.6.	111.5	119.9	113.4	117.6	121.4
Germany	85.9	49.1	60.3	71.4	83.2	95.2
France	54.5	82.9	89.2	96.4	109.5	117.7
Italy	60.7	79.4	93.4	98.7	106.0	114.6
Austria	48.8	57.0	62.8	80.0	95.1	106.9
Belgium*	89.3	94.6	100.2	106.2	110.6	116.6
Netherlands	54.6	92.1	106.6	118.0	128.4	133.0
Switzerland	127.7	136.4	152.9	155.9	151.7	158.8
Denmark	94.2	108.8	115.0	118.8	124.1	133.1
Finland	98.8	106.8	109.3	118.0	125.1	129.9
Norway	97.8	108.3	120.7	130.3	132.8	140.1
Sweden	124.2	137.8	141.2	145.6	150.9	158.8
USA	204.6	165.4	160.6	166.8	166.9	181.2

* The figures for 1945-47 based on interpolations.
Source: A. Maddison (1991, Table A7)

material suffering. This was the case for Denmark and the non-occupied neutrals, Sweden and Switzerland, where problems were of a less serious nature.

During the war, talks had taken place as to whether large reparations should be demanded from Germany. Great Britain was opposed to the idea, though at first the USA had its doubts. The Secretary of State for Finance in the Roosevelt cabinet, Henry Morgenthau jr., advocated a plan known by his name, according to which Germany would be kept down to the level of a supplier of primary products. France, which had suffered greater and more widespread material losses than in 1918, advocated, like the USSR, the dismantling of industrial plants, etc. Great Britain was consistently opposed to such ideas on a broader scale, although it wanted to confiscate what remained of the German commercial fleet. The new British Labour government expressed a wish that German "big business", including its metal industries, should be nationalised and brought under political control. Under pressure from the USA, the British government had to abandon this idea a year after the end of the war, in return for the USA taking over a larger share of the expenses of the occupation of Germany.

The USSR had suffered great losses within its own borders – beyond any doubt greater than those of its western allies – and for this reason wanted to uphold its right to demand reparations and confiscations. This was to cause the later German Democratic Republic, GDR, in Eastern Germany substantial losses and delays in its reconstruction as entire industrial plants, railway tracks, etc., were dismantled and shipped to the East. The French had arguments and wishes similar to those of the USSR. They had, however, only been included among the occupying powers as a result of an invitation from Great Britain and USA, and had been offered a portion of what was originally intended to be part of the American zone of occupation. The two countries sought to put a damper on French wishes and managed on the whole to do so. To sum up, the overall conclusion is that reparations only had a long-term impact in the Soviet occupation zone. The three Western zones participated in the Marshall Plan from 1948 onwards and took advantage of the American economic assistance it provided. The presence of American troops had a similarly positive effect, with substantial expenditures being paid for in dollars.

The supply situation was so ominous that for the first two to three years the European economies still had the character of those of wartime as far as rationing and regulations were concerned. The production of equipment for the armed forces had stopped, but resources were so scarce that their allocation could not be left to market forces and the free choice of consumers. As far as "strategic" goods like coal, oil, petrol, fertilizers and foodstuffs were concerned, the European sources had almost dwindled away to nothing because of war damage, while suppliers from areas like the Middle East, the Americas, etc., required payment in dollars. Dollars, however, were in short supply, reserves having been depleted during the war, and this led to the creation of a new term: *dollar gap*.

When industrial production got off the ground again in 1946, the pressure on supplies of energy and raw materials increased, with the somewhat surprising result that households felt the shortage to an increasing degree. The shortage of fuel was particularly hard felt during the long cold winter of 1946-47. As far as food was concerned, rationing was continued until the end of the 1940s, and even longer for some goods.[1]

3. Command economies prolonged

As mentioned above, there were many good reasons for not returning to a decentralized market economy in the immediate post-war years. The fact that populations accepted that restrictions had to continue for some years must be seen as the effect of a change in the general attitude towards the economic system. In 1918-19, the predominant sentiment was in favour of as rapid a return to pre-war conditions as possible, whereas the general attitude in 1945 was in favour of a break with the past. If there was a shift on the political scene in 1945, it was to the left. The USSR and its economic system were met with goodwill and positive expectations, which tended to draw the Social Democratic parties towards the left. In Italy, the Communist party gained one third of the votes and in France, one fourth. A striking example of the shift to the left was the general election in Great Britain in the summer of 1945. Here the Conservatives, with their great wartime leader, lost to a La-

---

1. Out of many examples two will be mentioned. In Great Britain, meat was still rationed in the early 1950s. In Denmark cars until the mid-50s were sold only upon presentation of a special license issued by the Ministry of Trade to doctors, engineers, salesmen, etc.

bour Party that presented a programme including substantial nationalizations and a major reform and extension of the social security system.

Evaluated at a distance of over fifty years, it is open for discussion
how widespread and lasting the effects of post-war nationalization
were. The British nationalizations can be seen in an ideological context, while in the rest of Western Europe they should rather be considered as part of the confiscations of industrial plants belonging to Nazi
collaborators like the Renault factories in France, the steel and aluminium works in Norway constructed during the German occupation and
German property in other European countries. Apart from the British
nationalizations, economic ideology seems to have been of only minor
importance.

It is hard for later generations to understand that Western Europe
during four to five post-war years practised an economic system that
came close to direct planning with the use of goods allocations stipulat-
ing in physical terms the supply and the uses of material for production. Countries that suffered less during the war, finding themselves in
a stronger position after the war, soon came under domestic pressure
to reduce government control. This was the case in Belgium and Sweden.

4. The Marshall Plan

4.1. Background to the aid

Essential aspects of *the economic conditions* in Western Europe have
been presented in the preceding sections. Table 12.1 confirms that
economic progress was slow in the leading European industrial countries around 1947. Especially the developments in early 1947 should
be noted when the winter was long, cold and wet, and fuel and all
kinds of energy sources were in short supply. Frost and rain spoiled
the winter crops, while drought reduced the summer crops. Meteoro-
logically, it was a year of records as well as a catastrophe.[2] If net investments were to be sustained, it would mean substantial cutbacks in
the importation and supply of the most basic consumer goods. Two
years after the end of the war, populations on the brink of starvation

---

2.   That the wine harvest was of exceptional quality did little to improve the overall situa-
     tion.

would face further reductions in already strict rationing. In 1948, even with a favourable harvest, total grain production in Western Europe was 10-15 per cent below pre-war levels. At the same time, the population had increased by almost 10 per cent. This corresponded to a drop in per capita production of 20 per cent,[3] to which should be added the loss of traditional supplies from Eastern Europe. How would the populations react to prolonged developments like this? Would it threaten the speed of reconstruction – and perhaps the political stability – of Western Europe?

Apart from these problems, caused by specific and it was hoped temporary situations, Europe had to face a structural problem. Until 1914, Western Europe had enjoyed substantial net surpluses on its overseas investments. This was especially true of Great Britain, but also of France, the Netherlands and, to a lesser extent, Belgium. Those overseas incomes had made it possible for Western Europe to finance its trade deficits. The First World War had already changed this and the international financial crisis in the 1930s was partly caused by deficits in overseas trade. The inter-war period witnessed, in effect, the beginning of the dollar gap. The Second World War, its financing and war damage, meant a further deepening of the problem which could not be put down to the special circumstances of 1947.

As for *political conditions,* the relations between the USSR and the three Western powers of occupation in Germany had deteriorated throughout 1946 and the first months of 1947. Normal economic relations between the Eastern and the three Western zones were never established, which meant a loss of expected supplies of food from the mainly agricultural east to the industrial zones in the west. Furthermore, the USSR started confiscating and dismantling industrial plants in their zone. In the USA, this was taken as proof that the export of industrial goods from the west to the east was synonymous with continued assistance to the USSR. Besides the problems concerning supply and strictly economic relations, there were problems at a deeper political level. At meetings between Great Britain, the USA and the USSR during the last months of the war at Yalta and Potsdam, the two Western powers had placed the USSR under pressure to allow free elections in the liberated countries of Eastern Europe. Nothing came of this, and political life in those countries was organized in what turned into one-

3. Danish Ministry of Foreign Affairs (1949,20).

party systems. In the Soviet zone of occupation, this was accomplished in April of 1946 by uniting the Communist party and the former Social Democratic Party.

Considered from a western point of view, it appeared that the USSR wanted the countries that had been liberated by the Red Army, including East Germany, to be shaped according to Soviet ideas. On their side, the Soviets had growing fears that their Western allies would be soft on a future, reconstructed Germany. Taken together, this meant that a political, and potentially a military, confrontation was building up where the western and eastern zones met. As Winston Churchill expressed it in his speech in Fulton, Missouri, USA in March 1946: "From Stettin in the Baltic to Trieste in the Adriatic, an iron curtain has descended across the continent." It has later been questioned how aggressive the Soviet policy really was at the time, and whether it was guided less by an aggressive urge for further advances towards the west and more as a defensive move intended to protect the Soviet frontiers against potential German rearmament and aggression?[4]

Attention must now be turned towards *the motives* behind Marshall Aid. First, however, a comment on the matter must be made. The countries of Western Europe, as mentioned earlier, had seen their languages enriched by a new expression after the Second World War, the "dollar gap". With this in mind, the idea of accepting support from American taxpayers to finance the import of sorely needed goods must have seemed a rather obvious foregone conclusion – but was it?

When the American Secretary of State, George Marshall, in a speech at Harvard University on 5th June 1947 presented the thought, he was not introducing a plan but a sketch, a declaration of intent. Money was to be granted by Congress, so the size and the conditions of the appropriation by the Republican majority were as yet far from clear. There were many questions to be answered. How much would be presented as a gift and how much would be a loan? How far could the USA be expected to interfere in the domestic affairs of the recipients? Would the assistance open up possibilities for American takeovers of the most profitable industries in the recipient countries?

---

4.   Churchill's speech was delivered in President Truman's home state, Missouri, in the presence of the president. Truman was unaware beforehand of the impression the speech would make so he hastened to invite Stalin to visit the USA and Missouri as well. This visit never took place. R.H.Ferrell (1994, 234f).

Would the cooperation among the recipients be on the basis of majority decisions and thereby mean some sort of transfer of sovereignty?
Would the possibilities for trade with countries in Eastern Europe be
reduced – important questions for countries such as Denmark, Norway and Sweden? Such questions could only be answered in time: after the conditions had been stipulated by Congress and by a system of
treaties.

For Great Britain and the Scandinavian countries, it was crucial
that the cooperation between the participants was of a traditional, inter-governmental character so that they could not be overruled by a
majority vote, and for the latter, that participation did not exclude
closer Nordic economic cooperation. For Sweden it was particularly
important that participation did not have any negative effects on relations with Finland.[5]

A meeting was called in Paris at the end of June 1947 to which the
countries of Eastern Europe were invited, the Soviet Union being represented by its foreign minister. At the meeting, he announced that he
considered the plan to be an aggressive step by the USA and, as a result, further participation was limited to Western Europe.[6]

In the autumn of 1947, the Western European countries drew up a
plan for the future organization. In December, preparations on both
sides of the Atlantic were so advanced that President Harry S Truman
(1884-1972) could present the plan to Congress, which finally accepted
it in the spring of 1948 under the title of the *European Recovery Programme (ERP)*. At the same time, a convention concerning European
Economic Cooperation was set up in Paris whose sole signatories were
the countries receiving Marshall Aid. Distribution of the aid was left to
a new administrative body, the *Organization for European Economic
Cooperation (OEEC)*, with headquarters in Paris; and whose members
included only the recipient countries, not the USA. Shortly afterwards, bilateral agreements between USA and each of the OEEC-
countries were signed, all of this in a very tense atmosphere.

If, during this period, the American president felt a need for assistance to have his plans accepted by the American public and Congress,

5. Finland was not among the recipients of Marshall aid. However, she later became a
   member of the OEEC.
6. Spain was excluded because of its system of government, whereas Portugal was
   accepted.

the Soviet Union provided all the help he needed. The tightening of Communist regimes in Eastern Europe continued, culminating in a Communist take-over in Czechoslovakia in February 1948. This aroused particular excitement since it was the country in the East that had been closest to becoming a democracy before the Second World War. After the economies of the three Western zones in Germany were merged, the new tri-zone was incorporated into the Marshall Plan. In June 1948, a monetary reform took place introducing a new Deutsche Mark, soon to be known as the D-Mark. In reaction to this, the USSR established a blockade, barring access by rail and road to the three Western zones in Berlin. In the West, this was perceived as an attempt to force the West out of Berlin and, in the long run, perhaps out of Germany altogether. It seems true to say that this represented an early crisis highpoint in what had by then come to be known as the Cold War.[7]

American motives behind the Marshall Plan were numerous, as will become plain. It had cost lives and money to save the Western democracies from Fascism and Nazism, and were they now to be lost to Communism? After 1918, USA had withdrawn from Europe and returned to its policy of isolationism, but later on during the 1920s it had invested considerable sums in Europe, including Germany, which had all been lost. This must have been in the minds of the decision makers behind the Marshall Plan.

Besides these laudable motives – to protect democracy and western political ideas – motives of a more narrowly self-interested nature no doubt played their part as well. The aid was originally set at a total of 23 billion (23,000 million) dollars, which corresponded to annual contribution of roughly 2 per cent of the current GDP of the USA at that time. The American economy was in a mild recession in 1947, and an increase in exports corresponding to 2 per cent of GDP would have an expansionist effect on the economy. A substantial part of the appropriation could be expected to be spent on agricultural products, which would be welcomed by the farmers in the Mid-West and the tobacco growers of Virginia! Other special interests were also to be catered for, as the aid was given on condition that half of the goods

---

7. From June 1948 to May 1949, when the blockade was lifted, a total of 277,804 flights brought in 2,325,809 tons of goods to supply 2,250,000 Berliners in Western zones. R.H.Ferrell (1994, 259).

delivered under the plan would be shipped in American vessels. This condition seems odd as the aim of the assistance was to solve the dollar problem and it was exactly within the area of shipping that countries like Great Britain, the Netherlands, Norway and Denmark were competitive.

4.2. Character and size of the aid

The word *programme* in the title of the law – the European Recovery Programme (ERP) – indicates that the idea was something more than just financial assistance. It was not, however, presented as a detailed plan intended to serve as the basis for a planned economy in Western Europe. Rather, it was to be characterized as help for self-help as the European countries were to distribute the means made available among themselves. From the outset, the assistance was meant to be temporary and was supposed to enable the recipients, through mutual endeavour, to abolish the restrictions in intra-European trade inherited from years of crisis and war. The USA took, as its tradition dictated, a critical stance towards internal trade barriers in Europe and the recovery programme directly stated their wish to liberalize trade among the recipients. A final condition attached to the aid was that the participants in the programme should seek to stabilize their economies, which included the monetary conditions needed to avoid inflation. The background for this was that the war left most countries in a situation where they had an abundant supply of money – combined with a shortage of goods.

The assistance was scheduled to cover a period of four fiscal years beginning in July 1948, and a temporary appropriation was granted in order to ship wheat already at the beginning of that year while, at the other end of the programme, some assistance was offered after June 1952. In the later stages of the programme it was difficult to distinguish between civil and military assistance. In actual fact, the size of the Marshall Aid is estimated to have totalled 13 billion dollars, 10 – 11 billion less than estimated at the outset. Of the total assistance, Great Britain received 25 per cent, France 21, Italy 12 and Germany 11 per cent. Further down the scale, the Netherlands had 8,4 percent, Austria 5.2, Denmark 2.1, Norway 1.9 and Sweden 0.8 percent (though this was given as a loan). Finland had to remain outside the programme due to pressure from the USSR.

Assistance peaked during the years 1949-50. In Denmark's case, assistance in 1949 amounted to 2.6 per cent of Danish GDP, which corresponds fairly well with the relative size of the assistance given to other recipients. Due to the nature of the assistance – goods of "strategic" importance for production – the impact of the aid on current production was greater than the figures indicate. It has since been argued that the importance of the aid was exaggerated and that Europe already had some good harvests from 1948 onwards. This criticism seems to forget the desperate situation prevailing in Europe in 1947-48. Furthermore, in evaluating the effect of the aid and the plan, another aspect has to be taken into consideration, which is the effect on the liberalization and reshaping of European trade.

The plan has been subject to two fundamental points of criticism. It was claimed by Communist parties in Western Europe that the primary aim of the programme was to bring the European economy under American control. Had this been the case, the programme would have had a different nature because by far the most assistance took the form of food, raw materials for agriculture and industry, transport equipment, etc., and was offered as a gift. Had the main purpose been to interfere with, and take control of, European businesses, the assistance ought to have been offered in the form of complete factories and industrial plants, kept under American ownership. This was not the case. Later in the 1950s, when the high growth of the golden years was under way, American private enterprise invested heavily in the OEEC countries, but that is quite another story.

According to another, but entirely different, line of criticism, the aid programme was redundant. According to this point of view private capital movements could have overcome the dollar gap, though it is in order at this point to remember that the political situation in Western Europe in the years 1947-50 was most unfavourable for attracting private foreign investments in Europe.

There was the Communist takeover in Czechoslovakia, the Berlin blockade, the first Soviet test of an atom bomb in late 1949 and, finally, the outbreak of the Korean War in 1950. These events do not appear to have provided a favourable background for substantial private foreign investments. More important, what was most needed during the first post-war years were foodstuffs, raw materials, transport facilities etc., all things which were not normally financed through direct investment.

5. The OEEC, its structure and functions

The Organization for European Economic Cooperation was set up by a special convention of the European participants in the Marshall aid programme. The USA remained outside the organisation, but did send a "special representative". The aim of the organization was twofold: to *distribute the assistance* between the member states and *to liberalize trade and payments* among the member countries. To those two main aims, a third was added: the promotion of *further European integration*, though opinions were more divided on this point and the attitudes of the member countries were less clear.

From the very beginning, two different points of view existed as to what sort of cooperation was needed. The bolder view envisaged a more advanced type of cooperation, according to which the governing body of the organization, the Council consisting of representatives of the national governments, would be granted wide powers including the possibility of taking decisions by majority vote. This would give the cooperation a supranational or federal character. Opposed to this was the more cautious view held by a group of members consisting of Great Britain and the Scandinavian Countries which favoured a more traditional type of inter-governmental cooperation, so that no participants could be forced to accept decisions against their own will and vote. The dividing line in this matter was to be found later within the EEC, but at this stage, however, traditional procedure was upheld.

To serve the Council and the participants, a secretariat was established with its own permanent staff recruited from the member countries. Something similar to this had been seen in relation with the United Nations, but the OEEC, however, had far wider functions than the United Nations. So it seems fair to say that the secretariat of the OEEC saw the birth of a new type of international civil servant in charge of central functions as far as the economies of the member countries were concerned. Furthermore, member states established permanent representatives attached to the organization to handle day-to-day contacts. Finally, a number of committees and subcommittees were set up, manned by ministers and experts from the member countries. All in all, this meant that the OEEC came to serve as a training college for what was to take place later in the 1950s under the EEC in Brussels.

In the autumn of 1948, the members were asked to draw up long-term programmes covering the period 1948-52 for the reconstruction of their economies. The very idea of having such plans proves the difference in the attitude towards economic policy by comparison with the situation in the early 1920s, even more so as the idea reflected an American wish to ensure that the means were spent in an appropriate way. A new tool in this type of work was national accounting, giving a better understanding of the economies of the member countries. Thus, a by-product of the Marshall Plan was the promotion of coordinated national accounting in Western Europe.

The long-term plans proved that there were substantial risks of overlap in the expansion of industries. This gave rise to a confrontation between two, substantially different, attitudes, one favouring a solution on the basis of central planning and the other in a decentralized market economy. According to the first line of thought, the members should set up and coordinate detailed investment plans. According to the second viewpoint, the organization ought to work towards liberalizing trade between the members as soon as possible, to open markets up to international competition and to take advantage of the overall improved international division of labour. Although most European countries were still affected by the leftward shift after the war, it seems fair to say that it was the latter, market-oriented line that the OEEC followed from 1949-50. Judged with hindsight, it seems that the overall composition of investments was not too well chosen; at least in the 1950s it turned out that Europe had developed surplus capacity within the iron and textile industries which were hampered by overseas competition.

6. Abolition of restrictions

The years 1949-50 saw great changes and progress for the European economies. 1948 saw the first good harvest and by 1949, the most pressing problems of supply had been solved on a preliminary basis. It was time to deal with problems of a more structural nature, including the "normalization" of foreign trade. In September 1949, sterling was devalued by 30 per cent against the dollar. This was done to overcome the British dollar problem and, later on, it was claimed that this was too drastic a step. The British measure was followed by similar steps taken by the Scandinavian countries and the Netherlands and, shortly afterwards, it was decided to start liberalizing trade and payments within the OEEC-area.

This step gave rise to problems of a more fundamental character vis-a-vis the USA, as the time was still not ripe for a liberalization of European imports from the dollar area; the persistent dollar gap was a hindrance to this. Since the USA was in favour of rapid liberalization of intra-European trade, the only solution to this dilemma being temporarily to accept discrimination in the OEEC-countries against American exports. This problem was not to be solved until the introduction of the so-called external convertibility in the OEEC countries at the end of 1958.

6.1. Liberalizing the movement of goods
In the autumn of 1949, a general scheme to liberalize the movements of goods between the OEEC-countries was introduced. Until that time, the freeing of exports and imports had been on an ad-hoc basis. Now, imports were divided into three groups – agricultural products, raw materials, and other (that is to say: industrial) goods. Within each of those three groups, 50 per cent, calculated on the basis of imports in 1948, was to be liberalized, which meant they were exempt from quantitative import restrictions. The countries could decide on their own how the lists of those goods should be drawn up and the percentages of those lists were gradually increased to 90 per cent.

The lists dealt only with private importation – government imports were almost by definition kept outside the system. It did not make much sense to liberalize imports as long as the government had reserved an import monopoly for itself. Unfortunately, this was the case for agricultural products in several countries including Great Britain. For countries like Denmark and the Netherlands, this meant a fundamental bias in the entire system of freeing trade. In addition to this, the OEEC in practice did not deal with the problem of tariff protection, so the Benelux and the Scandinavian countries as a low tariff area were left more open to competition than the rest of the OEEC-countries.

6.2. Liberalizing payments
The reestablishment of a multilateral system of payments was the second major long-term aim of the OEEC. The background to this was to

be found in the restrictions (exchange control) and bilateral agreements of the 1930s in the exchange markets. If a more advanced international division of labour was to be realized, it was not enough to liberalize the movements of goods – payments had to follow suit.

In early 1950, it was decided to establish *the European Payments Union, EPU*. The core of the system was that the EPU undertook the task of serving as a clearing institute between the central banks of the participating countries. This meant that it was the overall position of the individual member country towards the rest of the members that was of interest, not all the bilateral balances. There was also a system of limited drawing rights, but this was not the essential point.

With those three steps, all taken within a few months in 1949-50 – the devaluation of sterling and other currencies, the beginning liberalization of the movements of goods and of payments – a foundation was laid for the growth to come. To this should be added the reorganization of German economic and political life. Parallel to this, initiatives were taken to introduce new types of European economic and political integration.

7. Preparing for further integration

It is a striking fact that most of the initiatives for European economic and political integration originate from, and have been taken by, Germany's small neighbours, Belgium, the Netherlands and Luxembourg, as well as the fourth neighbour to the west, France. This has meant that Great Britain and the Scandinavian countries have been in a situation where they had to respond to those initiatives from the South – without taking any substantial initiatives themselves. It is no surprise that it has been like this because internal European conflicts for centuries, but particularly in the 20th century, have been felt more strongly by those four neighbours of Germany than by the her Northern neighbours. Similarly, Germany did not take any initiatives in the process of integration. As the former warmonger and the final loser, Germany was precluded from taking initiatives of its own. This did not mean that Germany took less interest in the initiatives, quite the reverse. After the Second World War Germany saw a path to independence through giving up a portion of its sovereignty within the framework of a new European community. Freedom and recognition could be obtained by giving up part of its own freedom.

In 1929-30, the French foreign minister, Aristide Briand (1862-1932) made a proposal in the League of Nations to establish a union of European states within the framework of the League of Nations. According to the plan, a common economic policy should be pursued, aiming at the establishment of a common European market, including a customs union. The nature of the cooperation was unclear; at the same time, it was stated that it would be of a federal character – though without loss of sovereignty for the members! Somewhat like the later Treaty of Rome, it was meant as "a first step" aimed at something broader. The introduction of the plan was overshadowed by the economic crisis of the 1930s and, in reality, was buried in various subcommittees of the League until finally taken off the agenda in 1937. It deserves to be remembered as the first broad governmental initiative towards European integration. For this reason it seems natural that the French government, when presenting the plan for a European Coal and Steel Union in 1950, took the opportunity to mention the previous French initiative.

Influenced by the military collapse of France in May-June 1940, Winston Churchill in his capacity as prime minister stated at the time that: "there shall no more be two nations, but one Franco-British union". Taken as it stands, it was a far-reaching statement, though it ought to be seen in the light of the problems of the day. Britain was the only country left to fight Nazi Germany at the time and wished to maintain France, and what was left of French resistance including the French overseas territories, as its ally.

In the immediate post-war years, initiatives were taken in many countries to adjust their constitutions. In order to make closer integration possible, the transfer of functions and powers from national bodies to new international bodies had to be made legal. Such adjustments were made in France in the constitution of the Fourth Republic of 1946 and the Italian constitution of 1947. The 1949 German "constitution" – the term was avoided for political reasons – spoke of a transfer of powers to international authorities.

It would, however, be misleading to conclude that these adjustments could be taken as a preparation for the European integration to come in the 1950s. They should primarily be seen in relation to the Charter of the United Nations and its peacekeeping functions.

In 1952, the Inter-Parliamentary Union adopted a resolution stating that each national delegation should work in their respective parliaments towards adjustments of the national constitutions in order to make participation in international cooperation as efficient as possible. It is worthwhile mentioning that this took place after the creation of the European Coal and Steel Community so the resolution must have covered regional integration as well. The same can be said of the adjustments to the Dutch and the Danish constitutions in 1953, which were directly inspired by the current developments in European integration.

Chapter 13

National developments 1945-50

The common characteristics of the period were discussed in Chapter 12. The following account deals only with the specific problems and developments of the countries in question.

1. Great Britain

Unlike the First World War, the Second was followed by a fundamental change in the economic policy of Great Britain and its underlying ideology. This was evident from the result of the general election to Parliament in summer 1945, when the Labour Party won a clear majority. It was also reflected in the legislation introduced by the incoming Labour government involving far-reaching reforms in social security, extensive nationalizations, along with a break-up of the Empire by giving colonies their independence.

Contemporary observers found it astonishing that Winston Churchill, the incarnation of the victory of democracy, lost this election when his position as an international leader and statesman was at its zenith. One explanation offered suggests that the British gained a sense of a shared destiny during the dark years of the war. This brought the working and middle classes closer to one another; while the Conservatives were blamed for the experiences of the inter-war period when they had been in office.

Since the beginning of the century, British *social security legislation* had developed as a mixture of working men's insurance, paid for through premiums, and tax-financed social security. In 1942, at a time when Great Britain was the only country in Western Europe fighting the Germans, a report was presented, which outlined far-reaching social security reforms. The key person behind this was the economist, William Beveridge (1879-1963), professor and director of the London School of Economics. The report, entitled the "Beveridge Report" has been seen as a milestone in the development of social security and the welfare state. In many respects its conclusions and suggestions were similar to contemporary or earlier legislation in Scandinavia, though this is less generally known. William Beveridge was also the author of a report entitled: "Full employment in a free society", published in 1944. Based on the new Keynesian ideas, it sketched out a policy describing how to secure full employment after the war. Between them, these reports provide a complete programme for a society with jobs for all according to their working abilities, and which would secure good living conditions for everyone.

The proposals of the Beveridge Report were enacted by Parliament during the first couple of years after the war. Under the title of the National Insurance Act, a number of existing acts were merged, grants standardized, participation made obligatory and responsibility for the administration handed over to the government. Half the expenses were to be financed through the general budget, the other half through premiums. An important principle behind the reform was that the payments and services in general should be offered without reference to the recipients' incomes, which corresponded to the Swedish idea from the 1930s of "the home of the people" – Folkhemmet. Under the National Health Act, treatment in the primary health sector, by doctors and dentists, and the secondary sector, at hospitals, was made free of charge. Participation in this scheme was voluntary, but the conditions, however, were considered so favourable that more that 95 per cent of the British population joined the programme within a year.

The second part of the reform policy involved extensive *nationalizations*. While social security reforms had broad support, the government faced sharp opposition in the Parliament to this part of its programme. The motives behind the proposals were mixed and involved sectors of the economy, which, on the whole, were capital-intensive. It is a central part of Socialist ideology that this part of the economy deserves special attention. There was, furthermore, a wish among Labour politicians and economists to preserve the wartime planned economy in order to secure the efficient use of scarce resources. Moreover, it would be easier to make the nationalized sectors of the economy part of the planned demand management. This need for a new, active business cycle policy was used as an argument for the nationalization of the Bank of England as well. There were also more specific arguments. An outdated mining industry needed to undergo thorough modernization and public utilities had to be brought under government control to secure efficient planning. The same was true of the transport sector, which comprised railways, road haulage and airlines. The proposed nationalization of the iron and steel industry met the strongest opposition, and here the confrontation of ideologies was clearest and at its strongest. In opposition, the Conservatives and the Labour Party respectively promised to de-nationalize or re-nationalize, when they were returned to power.[1]

It should be noted that, contrary to what took place in France, Britain did not see the introduction of formalized long-term plans outlining the development of the economy in the future. On this point, the policy of the Labour government meant no fundamental change in the British tradition of a decentralized economy, so the overall impression of the period is that the government soon became bogged down in solving a number of short-term problems, including those related to the dollar gap.

The reforms of the Labour government after the 1945 election have since been strongly criticized, in particular the reforms within social security. Instead of taking part in the dynamic developments dominating continental Western Europe in the 1950s and 1960s, Britain set out on a course characterized by what was already christened in the 1950s, the "Stop-Go" policy. This meant economic upturns were stopped at an early point of time to protect the balance of payments and avoid inflation. The result was that the economy had no chance to start a process of long-term growth. According to this line of criticism, the entire country, including the trade unions, was encouraged to harbour unrealistic expectations concerning the strength of the British economy, and this was to hamper the country for decades to come. Against this, it could be argued that the "hard line" policy of confrontation, with lockouts and general strikes in the 1920s, had not resulted in the long sought for dynamism.

---

1. When they were back in power, the Conservatives de-nationalized the industry in 1951 and Labour re-nationalized it in 1967.

2. Germany

In reality, 1946-47 saw the complete separation of the three Western zones of occupation from the Soviet zone. The description below covers only those three zones – the future Federal Republic of Germany. The Germany spoken of here refers only to West Germany.

Of the countries of Western Europe, Germany was the one with the greatest difficulties in bringing production up to pre-war levels, partly because of political and administrative disorganization, partly because of the extensive war damage. A great and pressing problem was that of housing the population, including the vast number of refugees flooding in from the East. In addition, there was the loss of capital due to Allied confiscations during the first year after the war. A serious problem in establishing an administrative and political system was the lack of experienced personnel not tainted by a Nazi past. The initial setting up of a new system was accomplished through the establishment of administrative and political bodies at local level, but the recovery of the economy was hampered by lawlessness, corruption, the black market, etc.

The planned exchange of industrial goods for agricultural goods with the Eastern zone did not happen, with the result that the people in the Western zones suffered from food shortages. In order to improve the utilisation of resources, the British and the American zones were united from the beginning of 1947 in a "dual-zone" with a common administration, and in 1948 the French zone followed suit. The new "tri-zone" joined the Marshall Plan and in June of the same year a far-reaching monetary reform took place. The background to this was that the monetary system and the monetary economy at that time had suffered a total collapse and had been replaced by a system of barter, with cigarettes as the most widespread means of payment. The previous, and now valueless, Reichmark was replaced in the new tri-zone by a new Deutsche Mark, the D-Mark. This laid the basis for a normally-functioning monetary economy; and what was later to become known as the German economic miracle – the Wirtchaftswunder – was about to begin.[2]

---

2. The creation of the tri-zone and the ensuing monetary reform was considered by the Soviet Union to be in breach of the mutual agreements concerning the occupation status of Germany and was met by a blockade of the western allies' access to Berlin. See Chapter 12, section 4.1.

Following the establishment of the tri-zone and the monetary reform, a conference was called among representatives of the "states" or Länder to draw up what was in effect a new German constitution. The result was the creation in 1949 of the Federal Republic of Germany. In parallel with this, the Soviet zone of occupation was transformed into the GDR, the German Democratic Republic, known as the DDR, Deutsche Demokratische Republik. In West Germany, great care was taken not to use the word "constitution" as this term had to wait for a united Germany, including East Germany.

In August 1949, the first election was held to the new "Bundestag" in Bonn, where it was to remain for fifty years. Two parties came out as by far the largest, first the Christian Democratic Union, the CDU, followed by the Social Democrats, the SPD. Konrad Adenauer (1876-1967) was appointed chancellor and remained in office until 1963. He had been mayor of Cologne in the 1920s, but during the Nazi period, he had stayed out of politics and public life. In his time as the political leader of his country, he saw the nation change from being an occupied country to one whose status put it among the leading states in Western Europe and the democratic world.

3. France

After the defeat and retreat of the German army, France was left with a double problem. First, came that of material reconstruction after severe war damage and second, the moral and political recovery needed after the defeat in May-June 1940 following a German offensive lasting only six weeks, and resulting in the collaborating wartime Vichy-regime. Addressing this second point became the life mission of Charles de Gaulle (1890-1970).

In June 1940, the Third Republic, established in 1871, was dismantled and a government, which collaborated with the Germans, set up under the leadership of the French hero of the First World War, Marshal Phillipe Pétain (1856-1954). As leader of the Free French Forces, de Gaulle established contact with the resistance movement in France, including its Communist cells. His position during the last years of the war as the self-appointed leader of a government in exile was transformed after D-Day in June 1944 into that of the official leader of a liberation government. He held this position until January 1946 when he withdrew in opposition to a proposed constitution for the new Fourth Republic. In de Gaulle's opinion this gave too much power to parliament and not enough to the president. A hasty settling of scores, when eight thousand persons are presumed to have been executed without proper trials and sentencing, had accompanied the liberation itself.

As was the case for the rest of Europe, political life of France saw a shift to the left at the end of the war, leading to calls for *nationalizations* in business. As in Great Britain, this caused a to and fro process between nationalization and de-nationalization, involving merchant banks, insurance companies and other financial corporations, civil aviation, parts of the automobile industry, etc.

Another aspect of this trend was the introduction of *economic planning*. At this early stage it can be seen as part of the policy of reconstruction. However, unlike most other countries in Western Europe, France carried planning beyond this initial interim stage. A special Planning Commission was established and Jean Monnet was appointed as its first head. He had previously been a leading official of the League of Nations and was later to become known as one of the founding fathers of the European Communities.

The theme of the first plan was predictable enough. It included the reconstruction of the infrastructure within transport and communications, of power stations, the reestablishment of mines, iron and steel works, etc. Behind these immediate plans, however, there were visions of a break with the stagnation of the pre-war years. The result was the special French type of economic planning, so-called indicative planning, characterized by less formality and detail than the Soviet type of planned economy, but nevertheless aiming at the harmonization of a policy and pursuing some common, main goals. An important element in this indicative planning is networks of informal relationships between members of the staff in the central planning institute, high-ranking civil servants in the ministries and leaders of financial institutions and businesses. An important contribution to this was the establishment of the École Nationale d'Administration (ÉNA), as the top ranking institution in addition to existing courses of education in economics and political science. A number of leading personalities in French and European politics have graduated from this institute, including several French presidents and prime ministers as well as leading figures in the Commission of the European Community.

The first plan was intended to cover the years 1946-50. In order to make it correspond better with the Marshall Plan the period was extended by a year. The second plan had, as its major theme, a strengthening of research, modernization of manufacturing industry and structural reforms in agriculture.

Like Britain, France implemented *social reforms* in the early postwar period, but the results, however, differed substantially. France continued the continental tradition of compulsory insurance schemes for employed personnel, paid for through premiums. Unlike the British schemes, they did not include the entire population, with the result that parts of the French population were left outside the system including the self-employed, a rather large section of the population. This said, it must be added that the level of the grants, services and benefits offered could be characterized as relatively high – as were the premiums paid.

4. Belgium and the Netherlands

After the breakdown of the German lines of defence in Northern France in August-September 1944, the German withdrawal from the major part of Belgium took place rather rapidly and left the area relatively undamaged. The same could not be said of the Netherlands where liberation did not happen until early spring 1945. As part of the German defence and retreat, substantial areas were flooded. So despite the country's traditional rôle as a producer of food, it had to face outright famine during 1944-45. Another difference between the two neighbouring countries was the fate of their colonies during the war. Whereas Belgium had retained its substantial incomes from the Belgian Congo, the Dutch colonies in the Far East had been occupied and plundered by the Japanese and there had been uprisings against the mother country.

Considering the favourable economic conditions in *Belgium* at the end of the Second World War, it might have been expected that Belgium would have regained in the immediate post-war years what she had lost in terms of economic growth in the 1930s. However, this was not the case. On the contrary, Belgium was among the countries of Western Europe, when measured over the period 1938-50, produced the lowest growth rates. This was 1.3 per cent compared to 2.4 per cent for the Netherlands and Denmark and 2.8 per cent for Norway, all countries also occupied by Germany during the war. The explanation for the low growth rates is not to be found in the structure of the Belgian economy. Belgium had basic industries like coal mining, building materials and textiles, all products in heavy demand in the post-war years. In addition, Belgium was just about the only European country possessing substantial dollar reserves in the post-war years. There was the fundamental basis for a rapid modernization of its industries through the importation of industrial equipment from the USA, but this only happened to a limited extent.

The economic policy of Belgium during those years was later criticised as being short-sighted. Rather like what took place in Sweden in 1945-46, import restrictions and rations were lifted as part of a general and understandable post war optimism, with the import of American cars, Coca Cola, etc., as the outcome. Instead of renewing industrial plant and equipment, the Belgians had ample supplies of ladies' nylon stockings![3] The result was that Belgian investments remained low compared to those of the rest of Western Europe, at just 15-16 per cent of GDP.[4]

Initially, Belgium was not supposed to receive Marshall Aid, and the Belgian government suggested that Belgium could supply goods to other European countries under the plan and be paid by the USA in dollars – a somewhat odd proposition, considering that the whole idea behind Marshall Aid was to overcome the European dollar shortage. In 1950, Belgium did ask for direct help and what she received was, in contrast to the original request, used almost entirely for the mining industry. So she missed her chance to modernize other, more promising, sectors of her economy.[5] It seems fair to conclude that Belgium threw away the opportunity to modernize its economy in the early post-war period. Furthermore, when she only devalued her currency by ten per cent in September 1949, while Britain and followers devalued sterling by thirty, the foundation was laid for a prolonged crisis in the 1950s.

The position of the *Netherlands* in the post-war years can be characterized briefly as being the opposite to that of Belgium. She had experi-

---

3.   C. P. Kindleberger. Europe's Postwar Growth: The Role of Labour Supply. 1967.
4.   Crafts, N. and G. Toniolo ed. (1996, 181).
5.   Ibid.

enced a loss of productive capacity due to war damage and a shortage of foreign exchange, but the other side of the coin was reconstruction at record speed and high growth rates up to 1950.

Several explanations have been given for this, some of which are controversial. In the immediate post-war years, strict public control and regulation of the Dutch economy was maintained. Under the leadership of a central bureau of planning, the economy almost took on the character of a centrally planned economy. The leader of the bureau was the future Nobel Prize winner, Jan Tinbergen.[6] Unlike Belgium, wartime restrictions were continued with a view to regulating consumption and investment. Furthermore, a policy of consensus was decided upon, based on tripartite talks between government, trade unions and employers. The aim was a stable development in the labour market, including modest wage increases. Political life as well was characterized by cooperation including the Social Democrats and the Catholic parties. Unlike Belgium, the Netherlands managed to follow a strict fiscal policy aimed at balancing the budget.

The Netherlands received substantial amounts of Marshall aid. From 1948 to 1951, the assistance corresponded to 4.9 per cent of GDP. Together with Austria, she was the country receiving the most aid in proportion to her GDP. When Britain devalued in 1949, the Netherlands followed sterling all the way down and, in doing so, took another route from the one she had chosen in the early 1930s. Since neither Germany, Belgium nor France devalued as much as Britain, the Dutch economy entered the 1950s in a favourable position in terms of competitiveness, while at the same time a relaxation of the policy of restrictions was introduced, as it was in the rest of Western Europe.

5. The Scandinavian countries

The Second World War did not represent such a distinction between a period of low and high growth rates for the three Scandinavian coun-

---

6. Jan Tinbergen (1903-94) received the Nobel Prize together with the Norwegian economist, Ragnar Frisch (1895-1973), in 1969, when it was presented for the first time. They had been working within the same fields and both men had inspired the generation of economists participating in the formulation of economic policy in the post-war years. Both had their original professional education outside economics: Tinbergen was a physicist and Frisch a goldsmith. Both had taken an interest in national accounting and the formulation of mathematical models of economies in the 1930s. A brother of Tinbergen, Nicolas, received the Nobel Prize for his work in biology.

tries as it did for the rest of Western Europe. Norway and Sweden had fairly high growth rates during 1929-39: 3.2 and 3.0 per cent respectively, with Danish growth rates during the 1930s somewhat lower at 2.5 per cent on average. As far as economic policy and political life were concerned, the need for change was not felt in the same way as in most other countries. Social Democrats had been in office before the war and continued once the war was over.[7]

Norway suffered the greatest losses during the war. The size of the merchant fleet had been halved and fighting during the German retreat from Northern Norway caused great damage in a poor and remote part of the country. As far as supplies were concerned, Sweden was better off, holding international reserves and possessing an orderly internal economy. In Denmark and Norway, the German occupying forces had opened accounts in the central banks, granting themselves unlimited drawing rights upon them. To put it another way, the expenses related to the occupation and exports to Germany were paid for by printing banknotes. The result in both countries was, as in other liberated countries, a monetary situation, which ran out of control. It resulted in the unhappy combination of a shortage of goods and an ample money supply, which made the macro-economic regulation of the economy through ordinary monetary and fiscal policy impossible in the first post-war years.

At the time of liberation in May 1945, *Denmark* had 250.000 refugees mainly of German origin, to whom were added about 200.000 German soldiers, corresponding in total to 10 per cent of the national population. The soldiers walked home during the summer of 1945, but the refugees remained in Denmark for several years because the occupying forces in Germany wanted Denmark to take on the responsibility for feeding them until Germany could do so herself. The last refugee left Denmark in 1949.

To illustrate developments in the second half of the 1940s, two reports on economic policy deserve mention. The first was the result of a study group established by the Ministry of Finance during the war consisting of a small group of professors of economics who reported on "post-war economic problems". In the short run, they thought that wartime regulations ought to be continued and a monetary reform, in-

---

7. In Denmark for shorter periods, 1945-47 and 1950-53, replaced by governments of a more liberal approach.

cluding the confiscation of part of extraordinary wartime incomes, should be undertaken. In the longer term, the report advocated a Keynesian type of economic policy based on a combination of strict fiscal policy and a slack monetary policy – high taxes, low interest rates – all with a view to lowering consumption and increasing investment.

The other report was the result of a study group consisting of younger economists set up by the Social Democrats. Their report: "The Future of Denmark", advocated continued government regulation of the economy based on a high degree of investment control and central planning. Concrete suggestions concerning nationalization, however, were few and modest in nature. Whereas Great Britain and France undertook substantial nationalizations in the immediate post-war years, the Danish labour movement concentrated on what was called "economic democracy", otherwise known as worker participation, in the running of industry. In October 1945, the Social Democrats suffered a defeat at the general election, and the programme was partly blamed for this. When the Social Democrats returned to government in 1947, the programme was taken off the agenda. If asked, which of the two reports came closest to the policy pursued in actual fact, it has to be that of the Professors' Committee. It should be added that the Danish social security system underwent a substantial reform in the 1930s, which may explain why initiatives concerning social policy in the post-war years were concentrated on the victims of the war and occupation.

For the first four to five years after the war there was little room for manoeuvre in economic policy due to an ample money supply combined with a shortage of foreign exchange. In order to avoid inflation and secure a fair distribution of the consumption of essentials, it was necessary to continue wartime regulations and rationing of many goods. To secure the imports of goods needed for reconstruction, it was also necessary to implement import restrictions. Controls were lifted for a while in 1945-46, but the outcome was a loss of exchange reserves, mainly spent on less-than-vital consumer goods available for export from Great Britain.

Danish agriculture enjoyed favourable conditions during the first post-war years due to a general shortage of food. Problems, however, did arise as some of the equipment and raw materials used in agriculture such as fertilizer and oilcakes were imported from the dollar area, whereas the sales of production took place within the sterling area.

When Britain devalued in late 1949 to overcome her dollar shortage, this meant a substantial worsening of the Danish terms of trade when money earned in sterling had to be exchanged for dollars at a higher price. Further problems piled up in 1950 due to an increase in the prices of raw materials caused by the Korean War. The five-year period after the liberation in the summer of 1945 ended with Denmark facing critical conditions, which was not the case for the other Scandinavian countries.

The economic situation of *Norway* at the end of the war resembled that of Denmark: supply shortages, surplus purchasing power and worn-out real capital. On top of that, in contrast to the situation in Denmark, Norway suffered from food shortages. Germany, as part of its economic plans for "Neuropa", had endeavoured to develop the Norwegian economy into a supplier of industrial raw materials for German manufacturing industry. The background for this was above all hydraulic power, which supplied electricity for the production of aluminium, other metals, uranium and fertilizer. Sabotage and air raids had delayed the construction of the plants. However, at the end of the war, plants that did exist could be taken over by the Norwegian government and explains why the immediate post-war period saw more nationalizations in Norway than in its two Scandinavian neighbours.

A Norwegian government in exile operating from London existed in parallel with a collaborating government headed by Vidkun Quisling (1887-1945) After the war his surname and rôle during the war gave rise to a new term for a traitor all over the world. At the end of the war a coalition government replaced the collaborating government until a general election could be held in October 1945. Out of 150 seats in parliament, the Labour Party "Arbeiderpartiet" gained 76 and formed the government, continuing to do so until 1965.

Just as the Danish Social Democrats had suggested the establishment of a planned economy, the Norwegians presented a similar proposal suggesting a three tier system consisting of councils set up at enterprise level, at industry or trades level and, finally, at national level. Whereas the Danish proposal was put aside after the defeat of the Social Democrats in the October 1945 elections, it was enacted in Norway. This laid the basis for a Socialist type of economic policy of corporate character – that is to say, a policy formulated by cooperation between different economic groups. Besides this institutional set-up, the restrictions and regulations of the preceding years of crisis and war were retained. Part of these consisted of strict price controls and the control of production, as well as the categories and quantities of goods. As part of this policy, national accounting was introduced partly as a means of planning investment activities.

Somewhat reluctantly, Norway joined the Marshall Plan in 1947. The reluctance was due to doubts as to the possible implications of such a move for her foreign policy, traditionally based on neutrality. There were, furthermore, initial doubts as to whether the Norwegian type of planned economy could be continued were Norway to join the programme. As for the first problem, growing east-west tensions soon solved that as Norway was shortly after to become a member of NATO. As for the second question, the OEEC decisions to liberalize foreign trade would cause problems in upholding the strict regulation of the economy.

The situation in *Sweden* at the end of the war differed substantially from that of the rest of Western Europe, Scandinavia included. The supply situation had seen no major changes[8] and there had been no direct damage caused by war. Some trades such as the aircraft and car industries for example had even had the opportunity to modernize. Where countries liberated from German occupation had to enforce strict regulations due to the abundance of money and the shortage of foreign exchange, Sweden found herself in a position in which the more rapid normalization of the tools of economic policy was a real possibility. This favourable situation gave rise to pressures for the rapid rescinding of wartime restrictions. In 1945-46, import controls and restrictions on the construction of housing were relaxed and the Swedish crown was re-valued by 16 per cent to reduce inflation. These steps caused a heavy drain on the exchange reserves and the policy of restrictions was subsequently revised. From 1949 onwards, the situation was so "normal" that the major emphasis in macro-economic policy was put on fiscal and monetary policy where Sweden came to serve as a laboratory in the coming years. Sweden ended rationing and wartime regulations sooner than Denmark or Norway.

---

8. In return for Swedish supplies of iron ore to Germany during the war, Germany accepted limited traffic across the North Sea to Swedish ports. All in all, more than two hundred return freight passages took place. This secured, besides raw materials, a modest supply of consumer goods such as coffee and tobacco. E Wigforss (1954, 270f).

The term "Folks Pension" became part of Swedish legislative language in 1935, and during the war an extensive social security reform was prepared.[9] This resulted after the war in legislation introducing full "old age pensions" for all and a general health insurance scheme including free treatment at hospitals. There were income subsidies for all families with children, unrelated to the size of the family income. What was to become known after the war as the "Swedish model" within social security developed in the years immediately after the war.

It seems reasonable to claim that Sweden from the end of the war was a "social laboratory" as far as the rôle of the public sector in a private capitalist country was concerned. This was also true in the area of fiscal policy, which meant fine-tuning with the aim of adjusting not only the level, but also the composition, of investment.

A further sector where Sweden delivered a pioneering performance in those years was in labour market policies. Here, two trade union economists presented reports suggesting what was to be called an active labour market policy.[10] The idea was that with increased mobility between trades and regions, it would then be possible to maintain a higher overall level of employment at a given level of pressure upon wages and prices. To administer the system, a labour market board – the AMS – was set up. The idea can be said to be a forerunner of the structural and supply side policies introduced at the end of the years of high growth in the 1970s.

6. Italy

Although there was severe fighting as the Germans retreated in 1943-45, Italian manufacturing industry in Northern Italy managed fairly well. More serious was the damage to the infrastructure such as roads, bridges, railways and harbours. However, thanks to an ample supply of labour, reconstruction took place rapidly and by 1949-50 it was so advanced that GDP was back at its pre-war level.

The Fascist regime was to have some lasting effects on the institutions of society. This was especially true in the case of the huge, ineffective public sector, inherited as a result of the employment policy of

9.   The committee preparing the reform was headed by Tage Erlander (1901-85), the later prime minister for 23 years, 1946-69.
10.   Gosta Rehn (1948) and R. Meidner (1948).

the old regime. It was also true in the case of the extensive nationalizations, including that of the financial sector, undertaken by the previous
regime. As a result of bank crises in the 1930s, the government had acquired a number of leading industrial firms during the period and
united them in a governmental investment society (the IRI), which
survived the end of both the regime and the war. In addition to this,
the new, democratic Italy inherited a tradition of close cooperation between business and government, so in these two respects there was a
high degree of continuity between pre-war and post-war Italy.

In 1947, a reform of the constitution was decided upon, one of
whose major goals was to prevent the concentration of political power
that had occurred in Fascist times. This was to be achieved through
extensive parliamentary control of the government. The background
for the frequent governmental crises and changes of government in Italy[11] is partly rooted in this constitution. This apparent lack of continuity, in reality, was combined with a high degree of continuity as far
as the gallery of leading politicians is concerned. From 1946 to 1981,
all prime ministers were recruited from the Christian Democrats, and
there are examples of politicians who have been members of more than
twenty different governments.

As in France, the Communists held a leading position in political
life at the end of the war, thanks to their contribution to the resistance
movement. However, because of the previous period of dictatorship in
Italy, no established political movements existed to counterbalance the
Communists. Consequently, a Communist threat was felt more
strongly in Italy than in the rest of Western Europe, including France
where the Communist movement was equally strong. It seems fair to
conclude that the Communists left an important mark on the economic
development of Italy in the post-war years. This is true in the case of
the continued nationalizations and the influence of trade unions, which
for many years were organized according to political and religious loy-
alties. Support given to the Communist party was greater in Italy than
in the rest of Western Europe, France included. Italian Communists,
however, were less attached to the USSR, which in the 1960s gave rise
to the term "Euro-Communism", referring to a local, national Communism.

11. The country's fiftieth government since the Second World War was formed in 1990.

In 1947, Italy joined the IMF and in 1948 the OEEC, and in this way opened the path to the internationalization of its economy. The Italian trade policy of those years can be seen as a break with 75 years of protectionism. It was, however, more difficult to relinquish the tradition of governmental interference in domestic economic policy, as will be explained in chapter 15.

7. Spain and Portugal

Readers are referred to chapter 15, section 7.

8. The USA

Table 12.1 might leave the impression that the USA had to live through a period of widespread unemployment during the first years after the war, but this was not the case. The figures should rather be read to mean that during the last years of the war the USA had put in an extraordinary effort to use its resources, and when the war ended had changed down a gear to a more normal level of activity.

Already in August 1944, after the consolidation of the invasion of France, steps were taken in the USA to prepare for the transformation to a civilian oriented economy. At that time the war effort involved about 40 per cent of the nation's total resources, or 40 per cent of GDP. There were reasons to fear that a sudden drop in a demand component of that size would cause a severe fall in total activity levels and a correspondingly sharp economic recession. This did not happen, however, because there was a great amount of saved up purchasing power and postponed spending due to wartime restrictions. This was especially the case for durable consumer goods, including automobiles. Supplies of these were rationed during the war and already by that time they were a major component in American household budgets. There was also a great need for house building and business investment as part of the transformation to peacetime.

The extent of the change in traditional ways of looking at the economy caused by the experiences of the 1930s and those of the war can be seen from the acceptance of Congress in 1946 of *the Employment Act*. According to this, the President would appoint a Council of Economic

Advisors, present an annual economic report to Congress and a report by the Council of Advisors. All this can be seen as the recognition of the need for an anti-business cycle policy and therefore a breach of the traditional peacetime "laissez-faire" ideology.

However, the steps taken the same year by Congress to repeal wartime price and wage controls were rather different. Between 1946-48, annual price increases averaged 10 per cent, which by American standards was an unusually high figure. After this, a dampening of the cycle was felt as a stabilization of prices and production, and growing unemployment occurred. This recession, however, was short-lived as tax cuts, Marshall Aid and growing military expenditure due to East-West tension took the economy upwards once more. The outbreak of the Korean War in June 1950 took it into an outright boom.

By 1950 the USA had held the position for half a century as the nation with the strongest economy in the world. Throughout those fifty years, it had achieved higher growth rates in both total and per capita terms than the countries of Western Europe; or, to put it differently, the position of the USA had been further strengthened. In this respect, the years around 1950 mark a dividing line. Over the next twenty-five years, Western Europe was going to experience the highest growth rates both in absolute and per capita terms. As the leading nation of the world economy, the USA peaked around 1950.

9. Japan

As previously mentioned, China and Japan responded differently to the expansion of the European countries during the second half of the 1800s. Whereas China had desperately tried to isolate itself from the Western powers then dividing the country up into spheres of interest, Japan had begun to transform its economy according to western patterns.

Its military institutions were modernized on the lines of the German model for the army and the British model for the navy. The reform of the army resulted, after a war with China in 1894-95, in the annexation of the island of Formosa and the attachment of Korea to Japan as being within its sphere of interest. The modernization of the navy proved its value a few years later when in the war with Russia in 1904-05, out of a Russian fleet of 35 warships, 33 were sunk within two days of their arrival in the waters between Japan and Korea. According to the peace treaty, Korea and Southern Manchuria became Japanese protectorates, and the victory over Russia raised Japan to great power status. Although this did not give Japan any direct influence on European politics, it meant a change in the European balance of power in favour of Germany at Russia's expense. So far, Japan had no direct influence on the European economy.

During the First World War, Japan participated on the side of Britain, France and Russia, against the Central powers, Germany and Austria. In practice, this meant the occupation of some of Germany's concessions in China. In 1927, a political revolt took place, which resulted in a strengthening of the power of the army and high finance. The occupation of Manchuria followed in 1931 and, in 1937 open war broke out against China, which lasted until the collapse of Japan in August 1945.

The direct reason for Japan's involvement in the Second World War was its wish to secure its supply of strategic raw materials. In the summer of 1941, it invaded French Indochina, causing the USA to prepare a naval blockade against Japanese imports of oil and oil products. Japan's situation was reminiscent of Germany's in the sense that it lacked important strategic raw materials. The attack on Pearl Harbor on 7th December 1941 should have secured Japanese command of the Pacific, but within six months the US navy gained the initiative after the battle of Midway and the slog from island to island began towards the main Japanese islands. After the two atomic bombs were dropped in August 1945, Japan signed a declaration of unconditional surrender on 2nd September 1945.

1.6 million Japanese soldiers were killed, 0.3 million were missing and another 0.2 million civilians were killed. Compared to the losses suffered by Japan's enemies, those figures are modest. The Chinese in particular suffered great losses during the eight years of war and occupation, and if the years from the outbreak of the war in Manchuria are included, it comes to fourteen in all. The end of the war meant the return of a great number of Japanese from the former occupied territories, with the result that the population in Japan itself remained constant in spite of the number of killed and missing.

The sector of the Japanese economy that suffered the greatest material damage was housing, followed by shipping. Thanks to the structure of Japanese manufacturing industry, which was composed of

many small firms supplying parts for final products, manufacturing industry was not too badly hurt, although shipyards, steel works and
power stations had suffered substantial damage. The peace terms involved withdrawal from all areas conquered and occupied since the
First World War. The USA's view was that since Japan had caused the
war, it should be held responsible for its consequences and no assistance for reconstruction would be offered. On the contrary, Japan
would have to help in the reconstruction of its former enemies.

To ease the transition from war to peace, the USA decided to allow
the Emperor to remain as head of state, but from now on holding an
entirely different position in society and in the eyes of the population.
His sacred position as the Son of Heaven was abandoned and, consequently, so was the absolute obligation of the Japanese to obey his will.
Part of the process of introducing democracy was an education reform
according to which schools, instead of teaching obedience towards the
Emperor, were to teach the pupils independence.

Several economic reforms were implemented and, as in Germany,
laws and measures were introduced to prevent the previous monopolies from dominating economic and political life in the future. A land
reform took place, giving farmers (and former tenants) the option of
buying their land at very low prices. An exchange reform took place in
1949, simplifying the system of exchange rates in foreign trade. The
existing system, consisting of many different exchange rates against
each currency (to be selected according to the purpose of each transaction),[12] was replaced by a conventional exchange rate system with the
dollar exchange rate fixed at 360 yen to the dollar.

Contrary to its original intentions, American policy towards Japan
was relaxed on two occasions during the period 1945-50. The first time
was in 1947-48 because of the advance of Communist China and the
second came in the summer of 1950 with the outbreak of the Korean
War. This second point in time marked the beginning of the extraordinary growth that the Japanese economy has achieved since the Second
World War.

---

12. The system served as a differentiated scheme of export subsidies and import taxes.

Chapter 14

Prolonged growth
1950-73

The period covered by this chapter has come to be known as the *golden age* among economists. The limits of those golden years are unusually distinct. In 1950, post-war reconstruction had finished and production in most Western European countries had reached or surpassed pre-war production levels. The outbreak of the Korean War signalled the start of a boom – a period of growth of exceptional strength and duration. At the end of the period in 1973, growth was brought to a sudden halt with a dramatic increase in energy prices as the signal factor.

The exceptional nature of the period 1950-73 can be seen from Table 14.1, illustrating the growth rates in successive sub-periods from 1870 to 1994. The growth rates for the 1950-73 era were four to five times as high as the growth rates for 1913-50 for those countries that had served as battlefields – Austria, Belgium, France, Germany and Italy. For the Scandinavian countries, and Great Britain and the Netherlands as well, the difference was substantially smaller.

In the period up to 1950, growth rates in the larger European countries had lagged behind those of the USA, but after 1950 this changed. Growth in Western Europe, except for Great Britain, was now superior to that of the USA. This can be seen as part of a general trend in the economic development of western industrialized economies in which the difference in GDP per person is reduced. This phenomenon is known as "convergence" or "catch up" and will be discussed both in this chapter and in chapter 19 in relation to developments after 1973.

1. Growth and growth factors

1.1. Growth accounting

As mentioned earlier, the OEEC in its early stages had contributed to a wider use of national accounting. With a view to standardization, a working group was set up under the United Nations and came up with "A System of National Accounts", SNA, which has since been improved on in several new versions. Consequently, most industrialized western countries have had roughly comparable national accounts from the beginning of the 1950s. The direct aim of the new statistics was to assist in conducting economic policy. Since the figures existed, however, it seemed obvious to take advantage of them as a tool for economic historians; so this led to a good deal of use – as well as abuse.

A primary use for the new standardized figures was to explain the differences in growth rates. This covered both differences between countries within the same period as well as differences between periods for the same country. Two outstanding examples will be looked at here. Early in the 1930s, the Russian-born American economist, Si-

Table 14.1: Annual change (per cent) of GDP (fixed prices). 1870-1994.

Per cent p.a.	1870-1913	1913-50	1950-73	1973-94
Great Britain	1.9	1.3	3.0	1.8
Germany	2.8	1.3	5.9	2.1*
France	1.5	1.1	5.0	2.1
Italy	1.9	1.5	5.6	2.4
Austria	2.4	0.2	5.3	2.4
Belgium	2.0	1.0	4.1	2.0
Netherlands	2.3	2.4	4.7	2.2
Switzerland	2.1	2.6	4.5	1.1
Denmark	2.7	2.5	3.8	1.9
Finland	2.7	2.7	4.9	1.9
Norway	2.1	2.9	4.1	3.4
Sweden	2.2	2.7	4.0	1.4
USA	3.9	2.8	3.6	2.4
Japan	2.3	2.2	9.3	3.4

* Excl. previous DDR.
*Source:*A. Maddison, 1991. Table A6, A7 and for 1973-94 OECD National Accounts 1960-94.

mon Kuznets (1901-85), had begun setting up national accounts for the USA. He continued his work after the Second World War, drawing comparisons between the level and composition of GDP in different countries and between the growth rates. In 1971, he was honoured for his work by being awarded the Nobel Prize. In the same year he published a major work: "Economic Growth of Nations". A key point in his analysis is the importance of the so-called sectoral shifts between agriculture, industry and services.

Another work, built on a different method of analysis, was published in 1967 by a team of economists and statisticians from a number of countries headed by the American economist Edward F. Denison (1915-). This survey covered the years 1950-62 and dealt with the USA, Belgium, Denmark, France, Germany, Great Britain, Italy, the Netherlands and Norway. Denison's analysis of growth rates and growth factors was based on a macro-economic function of production where growth was explained on the basis of the growth in the supply of labour and capital. In calculating the labour supply, a number of corrections were incorporated to allow for changes in the number of working hours in the year, changes in the level of education, etc. In calculating the growth of the total factor supply – obtained by adding the growth of labour and capital – the two factors were given weights of 0.7-0.8 for labour and 0.3-0.2 for capital; with the sum of the two weights adding up to one. The theoretical explanation for the selection of those weights is that they correspond to the shares of each of the two factors in total national income and, as such, they have been taken as expressions of the relative importance to total production of the two types of factors. It is obvious that many difficulties had to be overcome, including the problems involved in calculating the total size of national wealth.

On the basis of these estimates, figures for the relative growth in total factor inputs can be approximated. At a constant level of overall factor productivity, the growth in production should correspond to the relative growth in factor inputs. The estimated growth figure can then be compared to the actual growth figure, measured on the basis of the actual GDP-figures, with the result usually being that the actual figures are somewhat higher than the calculated figures. There exists an "unexplained" residual, known as the third factor, which can then be interpreted in a number of different ways. The existence of the third factor can be explained by increasing returns from economies of scale (not considered in the model), increasing international division of labour, structural change (such as sectoral shifts), use of new natural resources (like North Sea oil and gas), importation of new technology, etc. The existence of such factors cannot be doubted, but what is in question is how their actual importance is to be quantified – a point which the originators of the figures make no attempt to hide.

1.2. The special character of the period

The work by Edward Denison only covered the first half of the golden years. The British economic historian and former OEEC/OECD economist, Angus Maddison, undertook more recent work. His results were published in "Dynamic Forces in Capitalist Development, A Long-run Comparative View" (1991). The calculations cover France, Germany, Great Britain, Japan, the Netherlands and the USA. The exposition is comparative in two respects as it compares the growth of the six countries as well as the growth within each country over three successive periods of time: 1913-50, 1950-73 and 1973-87. This enabled Maddison to compare the years of high growth with the preceding and the subsequent period and to point out the special characteristics of the golden years.

A fundamental explanation according to Maddison of the outstandingly high growth rates in Western Europe and Japan during those years is what he terms "exceptional supply-side factors". It can also be explained by the existence during that time of some *once-and-for-all advantages* in the economies of these countries, which included the following points.

a. *High investments:* in Western Europe, the weak business cycle of the 1920s and 30s, and the disruption of international trade, etc., had kept investments at a low level. Meanwhile, technological progress had been substantial, causing a high potential demand for investment.

b. An abundant *supply of labour:* although this point is less clear, a fall in unemployment implies in itself an increase in work hours and for that reason would temporarily lead to a higher growth rate in factor inputs. To this should be added the impact of increased participation rates, especially for married women, and a higher level of education. This development will, however, at least in part be counterbalanced by a long-run tendency towards a decrease in the annual number of working hours per employee.

c. Before and during the Second World War, a "technology gap" had appeared between the USA and Western Europe (point a.), which meant that great potential was to be found in Western Europe – and Japan – for the *importation of technology*, leading to an increase in overall factor productivity.

d. *Structural change:* a corresponding transfer of labour to sectors with higher productivity, the primary example of this being the transfer of labour from agriculture to manufacturing industry. The possibilities for such a shift were great after 1945 since the crises of the 1930s had caused hidden unemployment in farming and small businesses.

e. *Increased international division of labour:* the inter-war years had seen the growth of protectionism, especially during the 1930s, with its quantitative restrictions and exchange controls, so the importance of international trade as part of the GDP had dropped by a third. The restoration of the international division of labour could temporarily cause exceptional growth rates while the change to a higher level of international trade took place.

The expression, "once-and-for-all advantages", deserves comment. An increase in the level of employment, participation rates or the level of the international division of labour in themselves constitute permanent advantages. The same can be said of structural changes and sectoral shifts. However it will also cause special increases in growth at the time they were occurring. An example of this would be a young farmer leaving farming in order to move to the city for good, who would represent a *special* increase in production compared to the previous period. In principle, the same can be said of all the points from a to e.

In addition to these points dealing with factor supply and allocation, there are also some *conditions of a political and institutional character,* which should be noted as part of the explanation for the extraordinarily high growth rates.

f. *A flexible labour supply:* for a high level of employment to be maintained in such a dynamic economy without causing increased inflationary pressure, a flexible labour market was necessary. On the whole, this condition seems to have been fulfilled in Western Europe until the early 1960s, but from then on there was a tendency towards growing wage increases. An additional explanation for the relative stability of wages could be that until the 1960s, labour and their organizations still suffered from money illusion – that is to say, they still concentrated on *nominal* wage increases.

g. The existence of a *stable but flexible exchange system:* what is meant by stable is the stability of exchange rates while flexible means an appropriate amount of international liquidity. From the middle of the 1960s there were increasing signs of instability due to differences in price development, increased amounts of "hot money", and a liberalization of international capital movements combined with an occasional shortage of liquidity.

h. In addition to those advantages, which explain the growth of production, there were *favourable terms of trade* vis-à-vis third world-countries from the middle of the 1950s. Western Europe, as a whole, took advantage of the relative decrease in the price of raw materials and energy. This caused problems in some regions (for example coal and iron mining areas), but the overall effect seems to have been positive.

1.3. Results of the growth calculations [1]

The main conclusion of the calculations is that the extraordinary high growth rates in the period 1950-73 can be explained by an extraordinary increase in factor productivity combined with an increase in factor inputs, especially the amount of real capital.

In Germany and France, growth rates increased from a level of 1 per cent (1914-50) to 5-6 per cent (1950-73), an increase of 4-5 percentage points. Out of this rise, 1.5 percentage points, or one third of the total augmentation, can be explained by increases in factor inputs, mainly real capital such as machinery, plant, transport infrastructure, etc. The remaining increase in growth, corresponding to somewhere close to 3

---

1.   The figures are based on the calculations in A. Maddison (1991) as presented in Chapter 5, table 5.19 of his book.

to 3.5 percentage points, can be explained by increased productivity in a wider sense, including the growth factors mentioned under points c to e above.

For Great Britain, growth rates were far lower. According to the calculations, this can be explained by a lower growth of productivity at 1.3 per cent, or between half or a third of the increase of productivity that took place in France and Germany. This means that the chief explanation of the low growth rates in Britain as compared to those on the Continent is the low increase in factor productivity. Of the Netherlands' growth rates of 4.7 per cent, 2.4 per cent are explained by increased productivity. The extreme Japanese growth rates, which were higher than 9 per cent per annum for a period of more than 20 years, are explained by very high levels of investment combined with high productivity increases.

In the USA, average growth rates during the years 1950 to 1973 amounted to 3.6 per cent, of which 1.1 per cent, according to the calculations, could be attributed to increased factor productivity. This growth component played a far smaller rôle here than in continental Western Europe. This supports the impression of a substantial European importation of technology during those years.

This development can also be seen as the result of so-called convergence. Behind this expression lies the general observation that between countries, and regions within countries, with close mutual relations, the earnings of the factors of production, and thereby the GDP per capita, will tend to settle at approximately the same levels. From a theoretical point of view it can be argued that such a "smoothing out" of the earnings will take place. Reasoning along those lines is part of the new growth theory and can be considered as a supplement to the calculations referred to above.

2. Growth and integration – an interaction

The years of crisis in the 1930s had been characterized by low growth rates and a decrease in the volume of international trade by a third or more compared to its previous level. It is tempting to ask the question of whether in the period of high growth there was a causal relationship between high growth rates and ongoing economic integration and vice versa. The first "cleaning up" of the restrictions left over from the

1930s and the war was initiated by the OEEC in the early 1950s, leaving customs duties, special arrangements concerning agricultural produce and raw materials, and Non-Tariff Barriers, NTBs, to be dealt with at a later stage.

2.1. The impact of integration on growth

The growth of the division of labour is included in the analysis of growth rates from the period 1950-73. To quantify the impact of this factor is, however, a doubtful undertaking. In the early 1950s, import and export quotas[2] were as low as two-thirds of their pre-1914 levels, but at the end of the period of high growth the figures were back at their old levels. The growth of international trade in the 1950s is essentially explained by the abolition of the regulations from the 1930s. On the other hand, the growth of trade in the 1960s could be explained to a high degree by tariff cuts within the European Communities and the European Free Trade Association (EFTA), as well as tariff reductions for industrial products agreed upon in GATT.

Apart from Japan, the countries of Western Europe enjoyed the highest growth rates in foreign trade (including their internal trade), which brings us to the question of the impact of integration on growth. The estimates that attach the greatest importance to the liberalization of trade during the period 1960-70 suggest that this may explain a third of the average annual growth, corresponding to about 1.5 percentage points.[3] These calculations, furthermore, cover the period when the abolition of internal duties took place within the EC and EFTA. Calculations by Angus Maddison lead to the conclusion that increases in foreign trade only added 0.3 – 0.4 percentage points to growth rates in France, Germany and Japan, constituting less than one-tenth of the total growth, and far less than the above-mentioned figures. Only in the case of the Netherlands was the impact of increased foreign trade close to 1 per cent of growth. The difference between the two sets of estimates is so wide that it may be concluded that it is impossible to reach an agreement as to the size of the impact of the growth of trade. It is the author's impression that the Maddison calculations underestimate what may be termed the more remote conse-

2. Defined as total import (or total export) as a fraction of GDP. Normally expressed in per cent.
3. R.A.Batchelor, R.L.Major and A.D.Morgan, reproduced from J.Foreman-Peck (1995, 288).

quences of the process of economic integration, merely noting those effects as "increased productivity" without any further exploration or explanation.

2.2. The impact of growth on integration

The European Coal and Steel Community (ECSC), was agreed upon in 1950-52, the European Economic Community, EEC, and EURATOM in 1955-57, and the European Free Trade Association (EFTA), in 1959-60. As far as the first three – later to be united in the European Communities – are concerned, the high growth rates of the golden years cannot have been a major underlying cause behind the setting up and signing of the treaties. At the time, the world was still not aware of the new economic climate of continued high growth and full employment, though the situation was somewhat different by the end of the 1950s when EFTA came into being. Then, high employment in industry reduced fears of increasing foreign competition and concomitant economic adjustments. It is certain that continually high growth rates in the EC had a direct influence on the British application for membership to the EC in 1961 as Great Britain's growth rates were only half of those of the EC countries. High growth levels within the EC must, in general, have increased neighbouring countries' interest in membership.

High growth had a more direct impact on *the speed* of the process of integration once it began. The Treaty of Rome came into force at the beginning of 1958 when it laid down a transitional period of 12 years, after which internal free trade should have been established and a common external customs tariff realized.

A former member of the first EEC Commission stated in his description of the early years of the Community that: "the generally favourable economic and employment situation permitted an accelerated dismantling of internal tariffs and early adaptation of national tariffs to the common external tariff".[4]

The reduction of customs duties between the six countries started in early 1959, and as the process gathered speed, three-fifths of the customs duties on manufactured goods had been eliminated by mid-1963, bringing about the reduction of internal customs duties two years be-

4.   Hans von der Groeben (1985, 147f. and 193).

fore schedule. Since EFTA had set up a timetable for a parallel dismantling of its internal tariffs, the EFTA countries had to speed up their plans as well and here too the high level of activity in manufacturing industries encouraged the process.

The conclusion of this seems to be that high growth had no major impact in the early stages of integration between 1950-57, whereas continued high growth rates had an effect on the ensuing integration efforts. As growth benefited from integration, so the process of integration benefited from growth, and this reciprocity must be singled out as one of the highlights of the golden age.

3. The Bretton Woods system, its grandeur and its fall

Even before the end of the Second World War, the framework for the coming international monetary and exchange rate system had been designed. The core of the system, later to be known as the Bretton Woods system, was the fixed, though adjustable, exchange rates which were notified to the International Monetary Fund by the participating countries and their central banks. The devaluation in 1949 of sterling and a number of other European currencies had brought about a more realistic rate of exchange against the dollar. From 1950 onwards, convertibility was established between the currencies of the OEEC countries, while restrictions against the dollar were continued.

This situation was bound to be unacceptable to the USA in the long run since it established a systematic discrimination against American exports to Western Europe. As the 1950s progressed, the dollar gap diminished due to growing European competitiveness and American capital exports to Europe. By the end of 1958, when corrections took place in European exchange markets,[5] it was made clear that discrimination against the dollar could not continue, so the convertibility between European currencies was extended to include US dollars. The Bretton Woods system had, so to speak, only been partially implemented for eight years. Now it was to be fully applied.

The Bretton Woods system must be deemed a success. For a period of almost twenty years, from the devaluation of sterling in 1949 to the renewed British devaluation in 1967, exchange markets were charac-

5.   A devaluation of the French Franc after the return of de Gaulle.

terized by a high degree of stability. Major exceptions were the French franc and German mark, which moved respectively downwards and upwards. During the last half of the 1960s, a tendency towards temporary imbalance and disturbances was felt and the system had to give way to a managed or "dirty float" of the exchange rates. Among the factors behind this development were:

a. An increase in world trade had caused a long-term increase in the demand for international liquidity for transaction purposes. US dollars served as the leading international means of settlements. The USA was still on the gold standard, but gold reserves were not increasing, and the USA did not want to increase the dollar value of its gold reserves by increasing the price of gold (in dollars). The system drifted into a deadlock situation, which was called the "Triffin dilemma", after the Belgian-American economist Robert Triffin. The dilemma consisted of a divergence between the constantly growing need of other countries to keep short-term balances in dollars and the growing difficulties for the USA in securing the value of the dollar. The ratio between the USA's gold reserves and its short-term obligations was steadily falling, causing growing fears concerning the future of the dollar.

b. When the Bretton Woods system was established, it was only intended that part of international payments – such as payments related to international trade in goods and services – should be liberalized, while it was to be possible to retain government control of payments on the capital account. With the passage of time, this distinction turned out to be difficult to apply in practice. To begin with, long-term capital movements were liberalized, followed gradually by short-term movements. This led to an increase in the amount of "hot money", which damaged an important precondition for the functioning of the entire system and suffered a breakdown in consequence.

c. After ten to fifteen years of high employment rates, the rate of wage and price increases was growing, though not to the same degree in all countries. This caused fundamental changes in the competitiveness of different countries and a growing need for exchange rate adjustments. Additionally, this in turn caused recurrent waves of speculation.

d. The USA, from the 1950s onwards, had a substantial net export of capital related to its overseas investments and the expansion of its industries. From the end of the 1960s those capital expenses were added to by a deficit on the current account, partly due to the costs of the Vietnam War, which meant a further drain of American exchange reserves, including gold, and so increased uncertainty over the value of the dollar.

e. Pressure on the dollar was further increased by the appearance of two new leading currencies, the German D-mark and the Japanese yen. Both countries maintained strict economic policies, ensuring surpluses on their balance of payments, so no initiatives to strengthen the dollar emerged from either of those two leading economies.

Frequent and increasing speculative movements and crises in the exchange markets characterized the years 1966 to 1973. Central banks with strong currencies felt obliged to buy up currencies under pressure. If a crisis resulted in the devaluation of a weak currency, the central bank with the stronger currency suffered a loss when it had to sell the devalued currency back at a lower price. This provided the strong country with an argument for letting its currency float. That means, in principle, that the central bank does not interfere in the exchange market, and the exchange rate is purely the result of market forces. In practice, governments and central banks tend to interfere from time to time, a so-called "managed float". From the point of view of a central bank it is apparent that floating has the advantage that the bank is not under any obligation to buy a threatened currency with the risk of having to sell it at a loss afterwards.

It was arguments of this sort that led the German Bundesbank to decide in May 1971 to let the D-mark float, which was followed in September by the USA abandoning the obligation of the Federal Reserve System to sell gold. In December, under the Smithsonian agreement, the US dollar was devalued, the Yen and D-Mark re-valued and the margins within which the exchange rates could move according to the rules of the IMF were enlarged to 2.25 per cent from the registered exchange rates. The room for adjustment is larger than first appears because if a currency at one end of the exchange rate spectrum were to switch places with its counterpart at the other extreme, it would mean a change of roughly 9 per cent in the exchange rate between the two.

For the members of the EC, this margin was too wide. One reason for problems was caused by the system of agreed, fixed, agricultural prices. Furthermore, exchange adjustments of that size would introduce uncertainty into the functioning of the internal trade between member countries. A number of EC countries, along with a few other Western European nations, decided to introduce a special system where the margins for exchange rate fluctuations were limited to half of that introduced by the Smithsonian agreement; namely 1.125 per cent above or below the registered rate. This system was named "the snake within the tunnel" and can be considered to be a forerunner of the EMS, the European Monetary System (EMS), which started in 1979.

The snake could be characterised as an attempt to organise a block-float, grouped around the German mark. The group of participants was, however, rather unstable. In addition to Germany, its steady participants included the Netherlands and Denmark. In 1973, the US dollar was floated permanently, providing the death blow to the Bretton Woods system, though this, however, did not leave the IMF without responsibilities. It still had a role to play in procuring credit and keeping up the moral standards of governments. This was felt by Great Britain, among others, later in the 1970s.

4. From OEEC to OECD – Organisation for Economic Cooperation and Development

By the end of the 1950s, the OEEC had fulfilled its original functions – the distribution of Marshall Aid, the liberalization of intra-European trade and payments and, finally, the introduction of currency convertibility against the dollar. To this should be added the progress of European integration taking place outside the OEEC. At this stage, Great Britain tried to use the organization as a tool to prevent discrimination between the six members of the coming customs union of the EEC and the remaining members. France finally brought this to a halt in autumn 1958. It should also be noted that the USA was sceptical at the time about special European cooperation on trade policy that excluded the USA. It seemed as if the organisation in its current form had outlived its purpose.

At the same time, a number of common problems united the industrialized countries on a global basis. These included domestic problems such as business cycle policy and external problems relating to non-industrialized countries. In response to this state of affairs the organisation changed its name in 1960 to the *Organisation for Economic Cooperation and Development, the OECD*. The USA, Canada, Australia and New Zealand joined the organization, followed shortly afterwards by Japan. From then on its functions were, on the whole, consultative. As the importance of the EC has grown, the importance of the OECD in European matters has decreased. What is left is an exchange of information between countries. The general public is aware of the frequent country reports in which the organization evaluates the economic policy of individual member countries. Equally well known are the semi-annual reports, Economic Outlook, on the economic development of the group as a whole. An idea of the different aspects of the organization's work may be gained by browsing through a list of its publications.

5. GATT – half a success

GATT – the General Agreement on Tariffs and Trade – was set up in 1947 as a temporary body awaiting the setting-up of the International Trade Organization, ITO. As this never happened, GATT nearly celebrated its fiftieth birthday before being replaced or rather supplemented by a new organization, the World Trade Organization, WTO, at the end of 1994.

During those 47 years, seven tariff conferences took place within GATT. Five were held before 1973, of which the last, the Kennedy Round, was the most successful. Since then, the Tokyo and Uruguay Rounds have been held. To label GATT as "half a success", in the title of this section, is a polite exaggeration in the case of its early years. Firstly, only industrial products benefited from tariff cuts while agricultural products and raw materials were generally outside the agreement. Secondly, it was only the most advanced industrial countries, that is to say, the countries of Western Europe and North America, which gained substantially from these efforts. Thirdly, the negotiations centred on tariff cuts, whereas all forms of hidden protection, the Non-Tariff Barriers, NTBs, were ignored.

The first four conferences that took place in the 1950s and the beginning of the 60s, produced poor results. In the early 1950s, interest was focused on the abolition of quantitative restrictions. The individual European countries did not wish to cut tariffs as they were preparing their entrance into a coming European customs union or free trade area, and the EC, in its early stages, did not want to make substantial cuts in the common external tariff. A widespread conviction of high and steady economic growth was needed to overcome the fear of increased competition. Finally, the USA had changed its own trade policy at the beginning of the 1950s, giving up its free trade policy as American farmers at that time felt a growing need for protection. The USA sought a waiver for itself, which allowed it to practice quantitative restrictions on agricultural products and hereby reduced American pressure for general tariff cuts.

From the early 1960s, a change in the position of the USA could be seen. Discrimination against its exports to the EC and EFTA countries was felt to an increasing degree, while at the same time the American balance of payments position was deteriorating. Furthermore, for reasons of foreign policy, the USA wanted to strengthen its ties to Western Europe in creating what the newly elected president John F. Kennedy called an Atlantic Partnership.

Consequently, in 1962, after Britain applied for membership of the EEC, the Kennedy administration presented to Congress what was to become the "Trade Expansion Act". According to this, the president was granted the power to carry through across-the-board tariff cuts. That meant general tariff cuts, and not restricted to specific items in the tariffs. The Act, as passed by Congress, went so far as to authorize the total abolition of tariffs if the EC countries and the USA accounted for 80 per cent or more of world trade, and allowed tax cuts of up to 50 per cent for other items (excluding agricultural products). The proposal would, if realized, have meant something close to the creation of a North Atlantic Free Trade Area for industrial goods. However, this part of the Act lost its meaning when, early in 1963, France vetoed Great Britain's application to join the EEC.

The negotiations based on the Trade Expansion Act, known as the Kennedy Round, took place from 1963 to 1967, at which time the law and the powers given the president expired. The result was that the overall level of tariffs for industrialized countries fell by a third and, if viewed from their point of view, the result was a success. In a wider context, however, there were some severe shortcomings. Agricultural products were not included and the same was true for Non-Tariff Barriers, while the so-called "voluntary export restrictions" were still being forced upon overseas textile producers and, soon, also on car manufacturers.

Even if the tariff cuts were non-discriminatory, their effects were not and this was realized even while the Kennedy Round was under way. It was argued within the United Nations that developing countries ought to have special customs preferences in order to promote their export industries. However, the overall reduction of customs duties on industrial products had reduced the importance of such measures. By the end of the Kennedy Round, it was obvious that future GATT negotiations had to be given a new, wider scope to prevent the bias involved in previous negotiations. The first attempt to do so was made at the Tokyo Round, starting in 1973, and continued in the Uruguay Round, which began in 1986.

6. Towards the end of the growth period

In Table 14.2, figures concerning growth rates, inflation and unemployment in OECD-Europe and the USA during the last years of high growth are shown. The question is, do these figures indicate the approach of a change in the economic climate?

Growth rates in Western Europe were still very high, at a level of 4-5 per cent and reflected on the surface a high degree of stability. No signs of sudden forthcoming change can be seen here, and the same can be said of the unemployment rates, down at 3 per cent. More suspicious are the figures concerning consumer prices where a constant level of employment corresponded to a growing level of price increases. If this continued it would be hard, not to say impossible, to sustain high employment figures in the longer run, though one way of doing this could be through the use of an incomes policy; that is, direct government intervention in the setting of wages and the prices of goods.

A somewhat similar picture, though less clear and more unstable, can be seen for the USA, where, as in Europe, the reaction was to supplement traditional fiscal and monetary policies with the direct control of wages and prices. It was at this stage, and in reaction to those attempts, that the monetarists proclaimed Keynesian policy to be dead.

Table 14.2 Average annual percentage increases in GDP and consumer prices and average unemployment rates, OECD-Europe and USA, 1966-73.

Per cent	OECD-Europe			USA		
	GDP	Prices[1]	Unemploy-ment [2]	GDP	Prices[1]	Unemploy-ment
1966	3.8	3.8	2.5	5.1	2.9	3.6
1967	3.3	3.3	3.0	2.2	2.8	3.7
1968	5.0	3.7	3.3	4.2	4.2	3.4
1969	6.1	4.0	3.0	2.4	5.4	3.4
1970	4.8	5.1	2.9	-0.3	5.9	4.8
1971	3.3	6.6	3.1	2.8	4.3	5.7
1972	4.2	6.5	3.5	5.0	3.3	5.4
1973	5.8	8.6	3.2	5.2	6.2	4.7

1) Consumer prices. 2) Calculated as the average for France, Italy, Great Britain and Germany
Source: OECD, Economic Outlook, div. nos.

The field within the world economy that saw the most obvious changes during those last years of high growth was that of exchange rate policy. The restructuring of the economic regime from a system of fixed exchange rates (with restrictions on capital movements) to one of floating exchange rates (under free capital movements) can be taken as a sign of the beginning of new economic conditions. The same can be said of the growing interest in incomes policies. During the early 1970s it was apparent that a change in the foundations of economic policy was under way, though that an entire epoch was close to its end was not as yet understood.

Chapter 15

National developments
1950-73

For the countries of Western Europe as a whole the period 1950-73 was characterized by exceptionally high growth rates with a number of inter-related reasons being responsible for this as described in the previous chapter. This chapter concentrates on the more specific nature of developments in Western European countries, supplemented by an outline of those in the USA and Japan.

1. Great Britain

After six years of Labour government, the Conservatives returned to power in 1951 under the leadership of the now seventy-seven year old Winston Churchill. Their rule was to last, under changing prime ministers, until 1964, after which followed fifteen years with governments of changing colours, but with the relations between Britain and the European Community as a leading theme throughout this period.

In British terms, both before and after, these years stand out due to their unusually high growth rates (Table 14.1). However, by comparison with those of other countries during the same period, these growth rates lagged far behind. Depending on which of those two perspectives one chooses to view this period from, opinion will be more or less positive.

Why was it that Britain did not experience the period of high growth in the same way as the countries on the Continent? Many answers have been offered, but before looking into some of them it seems proper to draw attention to the fact that at the time of the outbreak of the First World War, Britain was one of the countries in the world with the highest per capita GDP. If there is a general tendency – and there

seems to be – for the income levels of industrialized countries to converge, then the countries at the higher end of the scale must be expected to have relatively low growth rates. This, however, does not of
course explain why countries lower down overtook a country – like
Britain – at the top of the list.

Some of the explanations for this belong to the world of psychology.
It has been argued[1] that the ambitious social security policy of the first
post-war years and Britain's role in the Allied victory gave the population a false impression of the strength of the British economy. From
there, explanations go on to more direct economic matters such as the
strength of the trade unions and their opportunities to prevent or delay
measures designed to rationalize production, which resulted in frequent strikes, problems in delivering export goods on time, etc. At a
more objective level, it should be noted that British industries in the
interwar period had problems in adjusting their products to their markets.

A major problem was posed by the recurrent balance of payments
crises and here too it can be said to have been the continuation of problems of the pre-war and early post-war periods. Even if the US dollar
took over as the key currency after 1945, sterling still played an important role in the world economy. Despite the fact that the current account of the balance of payments normally did not show major surpluses, now and then the opposite was the case, long-term capital exports still took place thanks to the import of short-term capital. In this
way Britain and the Bank of England retained their position adopted in
the early 1930s, occasionally experiencing withdrawals from its reserves of international liquidity (US dollars, marks and yen), while
Britain's own assets remained of a long-term nature. This laid the basis
for crises involving hectic speculation against the pound and hasty in-
troductions of economic squeezes.

It was this sort of policy, alternating between contraction and expansion, that was termed "stop-go" policy. A consequence of this was
that business constantly had to face an unstable economic climate,
making it difficult to achieve high levels of long-term investment. A
look at a few figures will bear this out. Britain only succeeded on two
occasions during the twenty-three years of high growth, in achieving

---

1.   Among others C. Barnett (1986, 11 ff).

growth rates of 3 per cent or more for three successive years. This happened in 1953-55 and 1959-61.

Speculation against sterling intensified during the 1960s. The last adjustment against the dollar had taken place in 1949, and since then the French franc had been devalued and the German mark had been re-valued. In autumn 1967, sterling was devalued by 16.7 per cent (14.3 per cent according to the British method of noting exchange rates), and this step was accompanied by restrictive policies and a drop in growth rates, all under the watchful eye of the International Monetary Fund. Between 1969-72, British growth rates averaged 2.1 per cent compared to 4.9 per cent in OECD Europe (including Britain). While the rest of Europe, more or less, finished the golden age with a continuation of high growth, Britain experienced a downturn already in the late sixties.

2. Germany

Germany had little experience as a democracy when the German Federal Republic (BRD) was established in 1949. The fourteen years from the beginning of the Weimar Republic in 1919 to the Nazi take-over in 1933 were all they knew of such a system. The experiences of those years had been far from positive, but, in spite of this, political life in the reborn Germany showed a maturity dominated by stability and a will to engage in political cooperation. Those were the preconditions for what came to be known as the German economic miracle, the "Wirtschaftswunder", when the high growth rates of the years of reconstruction continued after reconstruction itself had been completed. From the establishment of the Federal Republic in 1949 until 1969, the government was led by the CDU, the Christian Democratic Union. Between 1969 and 1982, the leadership of West Germany was in the hands of the Social Democrats, the SPD and, finally, from 1982 to 1998 it rested once more with the CDU, now under Helmuth Kohl (1930-). In any terms this may certainly be called stability, which is a very different story from that of France in the 1950s – not to speak of Italy throughout the entire period.

In its domestic policy, Germany took advantage of a consensus based on a pragmatism inspired by the bad memories of the policy of confrontation that resulted in the Nazi take-over in 1933. Another factor having a similar effect was the division between East and West Germany and the pressure caused by the fact that West Germany was the easternmost outpost of the democracies. From the point of view of foreign policy, the Federal Republic had the advantage that the western democracies soon needed their former enemy as an economic partner and military ally.

One aspect of the policy of consensus was a high degree of stability in the labour market, where wage pressure was held back, along with price increases, and there was a high rate of return on investments. Part of the explanation for this may be found in the memories of the galloping inflation after the First World War and the social and political disorder it caused. Furthermore, the German labour market had a high degree of trade union participation, which, under the given conditions, promoted the consensus policy. In terms of the growth of the absolute size of its GDP (as compared to GDP per capita), the Federal Republic had the advantage of a substantial immigration from East Germany, supplemented by a vast number of immigrants from the Balkans.

The average annual growth rates during the period 1950-73 amounted to 6.0 per cent, which brought Germany to the top of the list among the countries of Western Europe. This happened, however, in such a way that a dividing line may be drawn in 1960. In the decade 1950-60, the average annual growth rate was 8.0 per cent, compared to 4.4 percent during the remaining thirteen years of the period of high growth. For the majority of the countries mentioned in table 14.1, their period of greatest growth was the opposite. In general a tendency may be discerned – though a weak one – towards an increase in growth rates after 1960, so the answer to the question of what was special about the German "economic miracle" ought to be looked for in the 1950s.

On the basis of growth calculations, the explanation for the high growth rates may be found in three main factors: an increased supply of capital, an increased supply of labour and an increased factor productivity. According to the previously mentioned calculations by Edward Denison concerning the years 1950-62, the major cause of high growth was an ample supply of factors. Germany's growth in productivity seems to have been in line with that of France and Italy, somewhat above that of the Netherlands, Denmark, and Norway, and substantially above that of Great Britain.

3. France

The relationship between French political and economic life constitutes a paradox: the political scene was dominated by instability, while the economy was characterized by high and stable growth.

From May 1947 to May 1958, the time of the return of de Gaulle, France had twenty different governments as the result of recurrent parliamentary crises, which corresponds to an average government lifetime of just over six months. The nation had to live through two deep crises related to the liquidation of its colonial empire during those eleven years. The first was the war lost in Indochina between 1947-54, and followed by a civil war in North Africa in 1958-62, which ended in the creation of a new nation, Algeria. After that, internal conflict ensued in 1968, which bordered on a revolt that began among students and workers in Paris before spreading across the country as a general strike. It was, indeed, a stretch of history containing explosive factors and deep changes.

Against this stands a picture of economic development dominated by high and stable growth rates. Throughout the period 1950-73, the average annual growth rate amounted to 5.0 per cent. There were no years with a growth rate below 2.5 per cent and only three years showed growth rates under three per cent. The political instability does not seem to have been mirrored at all in the economy of the country, a state of affairs which may be better understood when seen in association with the stability lying below the political surface. This stability manifested itself primarily in the staff of the central administration and, closely linked to this, by financial institutions and leading circles in business, which more or less constituted a "brotherhood". There was a shared past in a small number of elitist educational institutions, with the national school of administration, the ENA, as the prime example. Even in periods with frequent changes of governments, such as during that prior to the return of de Gaulle in 1958, there was a high degree of continuity in economic policy.

This was seen in the continuity of economic planning in a second plan (1952-57), aimed at an increased effort concerning education, research and development, as well as house building. A third plan followed (1958-61), concentrating on the competitiveness of France within the Common Market, which was meant to be realized from 1959 onwards when the French market for industrial goods was to be opened up to German industry. Planning was continued in a fourth and a fifth plan, but with a shift to the right in French politics these were less precise in their description of the aims of development.

Behind the actual policy there lurked some fundamental contradictions. The course of events in Indochina and North Africa laid claim to resources, as did the wish of de Gaulle that France, in order to be influential in international diplomacy, should have its own nuclear force; its "force de frappe", including the necessary rockets, advanced aircrafts, etc. Other programmes were designed to make France independent of American technology in such fields as nuclear power, data processing, television and telecommunications.

All those plans meant considerable public and private expenditure in research and development, and these large investments had to be financed at the cost of immediate private consumption. This was accomplished through a policy based on high returns for big business and widespread wage differentials where low-income groups fell behind, especially within the public sector. There were, furthermore, structural reforms in agriculture, causing a great number of small farms to disappear. Taking all this into consideration, it is not surprising that the high and stable growth rates were accompanied by a good deal of political tension resulting in frequent strikes and "work to rule" actions, particularly in the public sector such as railways, the postal service and at airports. In the area of small business, similar problems were felt when farmers blockaded motorways around the great cities of France.

Although the change to the political system following the return of de Gaulle in 1958 does not seem to have had great implications on growth rates, it is appropriate to mention some of the events of that year.

On 1st June, de Gaulle took office as prime minister and in September, the constitution of the new Fifth Republic was approved. In November, an election for the National Assembly took place, giving the Gaullists and the right-wing parties 75 per cent of the votes. Finally, in December, de Gaulle was elected President of the Republic for a period of seven years, beginning on 1st January 1959. This is worth mentioning not only because of the effects this had on developments in European integration in that year, but in the ensuing decade.

For French foreign policy, including its stance towards European integration, the change in the political system had a clear impact.

France displayed an increased will to prove to the rest of the world that France wanted to play a new and leading role in international politics. In November 1958, de Gaulle let it be announced that the ongoing negotiations concerning a British proposal for an enlarged European free trade area should be stopped because they were leading nowhere.[2] In this manner de Gaulle had marked, at a time of a national crisis, that he was prepared to act as a leader in European politics. The crisis in Algeria was accompanied by a sharp rise in inflation, which by 1958 had reached a level of 15 per cent and resulted in December in a devaluation of the franc of 16 per cent. This was accompanied by a currency reform where one hundred "old" francs were substituted by one new franc.

In spring 1969, de Gaulle left French politics almost as suddenly as he had returned in 1958. He had emerged from the 1965 presidential election in a weakened position and the student revolt and general strike of 1968 led to a loss of his authority. At the same time the position of his prime minister, Georges Pompidou (1911-77), was strengthened. Finally, he lost a referendum and, to everyone's surprise, withdrew to Ireland.

4. Belgium and the Netherlands

In both countries, the period of high growth was characterized by thoroughgoing structural changes. As far as domestic matters were concerned, Belgium came close to the closure of its centuries-old coal mining industry, while for the Netherlands this period meant a sharp reduction in the share of agriculture in production, employment and exports. As far as foreign relations were concerned, both countries had to relinquish their overseas possessions. Belgium made a hurried exit from the Congo in 1960, while the Dutch East Indies had become by mutual agreement the independent state of Indonesia in 1949. As far as economic growth during this period is concerned, Belgium, with an average growth of 4.1 per cent, found herself lagging behind her neigh-

---

2. The later Danish Prime Minister, J.O. Krag, has described the circumstances in detail. The news concerning the decision of de Gaulle arrived just as a meeting of ministers dealing with the matter was in session. The French minister of information, however, did not announce the news in the meeting, but outside! One can imagine the reaction of the meeting's participants, not least the British.

bours France, Germany and the Netherlands, with growth rates of 5.0, 6.0, and 4.7 per cent respectively.

For *Belgium,* the period 1950-73 can be divided into two distinct parts, which were the years up to the late 1950s and the succeeding years leading up to the first oil crisis. Throughout the 1950s, the average annual growth rate was 3.0 per cent, compared to 4.9 per cent during 1960-73.

As previously mentioned, in September 1949, Belgium only devalued its currency by a third compared to the devaluations of a number of its Western European competitors. The result was an increase in the Belgian franc's value of approximately 20 per cent compared to these countries, including the Netherlands. There was no basis for the Belgian decision in the level of costs in the country, so Belgium went from having a strong external economy in 1945 into a diametrically opposite situation where it constantly needed to keep an eye on the balance of payments and foreign exchange reserves, which eventually resulted in a stop-go policy.

Part of the problem was an unsuccessful fiscal policy. Whereas most countries in Western Europe ran surpluses on their budgets during those years as a means of promoting investment, Belgium, once again, moved in the opposite position. An explanation for this may lie in the existence of conflicts between regions and trades, making it easier to agree on government expenditure than on taxes.[3] As a counterbalance to its slack fiscal policy, Belgium had to practice a tight monetary policy resulting in high interest rates, which kept investment low. Another problem was the reluctance to abolish the measures introduced in the 1930s in favour of Belgian agriculture and mining industries, which took the form of subsidies and schemes in favour of trades and firms facing growing competition within the Benelux area.

In this matter, a change took place at the end of the 1950s. First, the Belgian economy took advantage of a high external and internal level of demand during those years and, second, it finally realized – in spite of strong regional opposition – that the coal-mines had to close. Third, participation in the European Economic Community made it clear that Belgian trades and industries were going to face increased competition in the near future, pushing the economy towards a more dynamic attitude. All in all, the Belgian economy adjusted with unexpected speed

---

3.   Krafts, N. and Toniolo (1996, 177 and 184).

from the end of the 1950s onwards, resulting in significant increases in productivity.[4]

Whenever the problem of combining full employment and modest wage increases was discussed in the 1950s and early 1960s, "the Dutch case" was normally brought forward. What could not be done in other countries seemed to be possible in *the Netherlands*. There, a policy of consensus was begun in the immediate post-war years and carried on throughout the 1950s and early 1960s.

For the foreign trade of the Netherlands, this meant a strengthening of its competitiveness, paving the way for an adjustment of its export trades in favour of goods characterized by a higher degree of processing, including products from agriculture, gardening and horticulture as well as from manufacturing industries. The effect of modest wage increases was high returns on invested capital, resulting in a high level of investment.

As far as costs were concerned, the Dutch economy was well equipped to meet the challenge from the establishment of the Common Market of the Six. Furthermore, there were the advantages to Dutch agriculture resulting from the CAP, the Common Agricultural Policy then being set up, which resulted both in freer access to the markets of the other member countries and a higher price level for its products.[5]

In 1963-64, two events occurred of major importance to the Dutch economy. In 1963 huge deposits of natural gas were found in a Dutch area of the North Sea and, in 1964, a wage explosion occurred with increases as high as 15 per cent in real terms.

The discovery of natural gas meant an abundance of energy, causing the growth of energy-consuming industries such as chemicals, steel and specialized hothouse gardening. This new energy situation generally led to more capital-intensive production. It also marked the end of the period of modest wage increases. Although the new access to natural resources was, in overall terms, a boon for the Dutch economy, it was not without short-term problems in the form of increased pressure

4. It is tempting to compare the Belgian and the Danish economies. Denmark also saw a substantial increase in its growth rates from the late fifties onwards – the result of an adjustment of its economic policy – making room for more dynamic development, including the growth and modernization of its manufacturing industries.
5. To be fair to the first commissioner of agriculture in the EEC, the Dutchman Sicco Mansholt, it should, already at this stage of the exposition, be pointed out that he was in favour of a lower price level than that which was actually fixed.

on costs. This phenomenon gave rise to a new term, the Dutch disease, which was also felt in Norway some ten years later. Nonetheless, growth rates stayed at a high level, but were now concentrated within the newly emerging trades, supplemented by the public sector.

5. The Scandinavian countries

On looking at Table 14.1, it is a striking fact that the post-war growth rates of the three Scandinavian countries were lower by comparison with pre-war rates than those of most other countries in Western Europe. The "delayed growth" achieved in the latter countries had been partly accomplished by the Scandinavian countries in the inter-war years and during the war.

Just as German political life in those years was characterized by a high degree of stability, this was also the case in the Scandinavian countries, most obviously so in Norway and Sweden where Social Democrats were in power throughout the fifties and into the sixties, and in Sweden right up until the seventies.

In Denmark, the picture was not quite as stable. A Liberal-Conservative coalition was in power between 1950-53, after which a government lead by the Social Democrats followed in 1953-68. It is, however, difficult to discern the actual differences in the policies pursued by the consecutive governments.

A common characteristic of the three countries was the relatively high growth of the public sector during this period. Measured in terms of the income of the general (including local) government as a percentage of GDP, the three countries distinguished themselves from the rest of Western Europe by the end of the period. Whereas total taxes for OECD Europe in 1974 corresponded to 38.8 per cent of GDP, the figures for Denmark were 48.4, Norway 48.5 and Sweden 48.8. In spite of these high figures, it should nonetheless be mentioned that rather few nationalizations took place in the businesses and industries of the Scandinavian countries. Although half the flow of income was reserved for general government, production itself to a high degree was left in the hands of the private sector. A well-known remark by a Swedish politician was: "What matters is not who owns the cow, but who milks it!" Norway saw the highest number of nationalizations, which in part can be explained by German initiatives during the Second World War and in part by the relatively strict Socialist tradition of the Norwegian Labour Party. In the end, these nationalizations must be considered as unsurprising since they were mainly concerned with the utilization of natural resources.

A tendency towards increased growth rates common to the three countries can be seen around 1958, which saw a general upturn in the business cycle. From 1960 the free trade area for industrial products (EFTA) was established and adjustments made to the Nordic economies to suit the new international conditions. All in all, the three countries had a favourable start to the 1960s with average growth rates between 1959-64 at 5.5 per cent for Denmark, 4.7 per cent for Norway, and as much as 6.2 per cent for Sweden.

1957-58 stands out as a line of demarcation for the economy of *Denmark*. Previous years had been characterized by balance of payments problems and "stop-go" policy, where emerging upswings gave rise to a shortage of international reserves and a tightening of economic policy. In 1958, net international debt was brought down close to zero – more precisely to 1.9 per cent of GDP. In this way, the problem of servicing old international debt was overcome and it was recognized that a far-sighted, long-term economic policy was both possible and necessary because of contemporary developments in European economic integration.

As late as 1958, agricultural products still made up 55 per cent of total Danish exports, but developments during the 1950s made it clear that this type of export was facing increasing problems both in terms of quantity and price. What would be the effect of the Common Market of the Six? Would Danish manufacturing industries, producing mainly for the home market and protected by import restrictions for 25 years, be able to adjust?

Two factors can explain why the impact of approaching European economic integration was so great. The first was the composition of Danish exports in terms of goods and target countries and the second was the division of Western Europe into two separate trade areas, the six members of the European Economic Community and the remaining countries of Western Europe. Livestock production leaves fewer possibilities for adjusting the composition of production for different types of products than industrial production does. The production of

butter and cheese is necessarily accompanied by the production of cattle for slaughter as well as dairy cows, just as the production of bacon is
associated with sows.[6] However, whereas butter and bacon were mainly sold to Great Britain and other countries outside the EEC, cattle
were mainly sold to Italy and pigs and dairy cows to Germany. So the
only satisfactory solution for Danish agriculture was to unite the markets for its major export items, which especially meant uniting the
British and German markets. The prospects for this, however, were
poor, and to this may be added that the future of the CAP, the Common Agricultural Policy, was still undecided. There were indications
that the future price of grain might be high, though the effect of this on
the price and sale of animal products was unknown.

Between 1950 and 1958, employment in manufacturing industry
was nearly constant at 320.000, but during the next five years until
1963 it increased to 400.000 or by 25 per cent. During the same period,
the use of labour in agriculture decreased from more than 310.000 to
230.000,[7] a fall of a quarter. As is apparent, the years when European
integration began within the frameworks of the EEC and EFTA
formed a very dynamic period in Danish economic history reminding
of developments in Belgium at the same time.

In the area of social security, this period saw a number of reforms
partly inspired by pre- and early post-war Swedish legislation. The
more outstanding reforms actually concerned short-term payments
such as benefits for the ill and unemployed. Here, exceptionally high
levels of benefit and long periods of entitlement were introduced, giving rise to doubts and debates caused by the sharp increase in unemployment after the oil crises of the 1970s.

The years 1949-52 were good ones for *Norway*, which achieved annual
growth rates ranging from 3 to 5 per cent. The country had a substantial dollar income and experienced the very opposite of a worsening of
its terms of trade – unlike more unfortunate countries such as Denmark. The Korean War was accompanied by higher freight rates and
increased prices for raw materials. Nevertheless, the period saw a
thorough change of economic policy in Norway where, since 1945, pri-

6. In the language of economists, one may speak of "joint production", where the produc-
    tion of one particular item necessarily results in the production of other goods, perhaps
    even in fixed ratios. Besides livestock farming, most examples are found within the che-
    mical industry. A common textbook example is beef and hides.
7. Measured in so-called whole-year-workers.

ces had been kept down by a combination of price controls and government subsidies. However, the continuation of this policy was made impossible by price increases due to devaluation in September 1949 and the outbreak of the Korean War in June 1950. Furthermore, decisions taken in the OEEC to start liberalizing foreign trade, including the gradual abolition of quantitative import restrictions, made it impossible in practice to uphold the policy of the early post-war years. In the years 1951-53, the Labour government had to accept the new situation in the form of annual price increases of as much as 25 per cent, and a relaxation of the foreign as well as the domestic policy of restrictions.

From the beginning of the twentieth century, structural changes in the Norwegian economy had been under way, reducing the relative importance of forestry and fishing and increasing that of shipping. Furthermore, hydraulic power had opened new possibilities for the production of metals and fertilizer (Norwegian saltpetre). On the whole, these growing sectors of the economy were characterized by a high capital-labour relationship. If the exodus from farming and other traditional trades were to continue, it would be necessary to provide new occupations that could absorb this surplus labour force.

Norway, just as Denmark, therefore faced the problems involved in establishing an export-oriented manufacturing industry almost from scratch. In the case of Northern Norway, however, special problems were involved as geographical proximity to the Soviet Union in the northernmost areas made the presence of a Norwegian population and an active business life necessary. From an economic point of view, it was a complicated problem to find the ways and means of allowing a local population to make a living on the basis of local, natural resources. One way of accomplishing this was to modernize the fishing industry so catches could be sold frozen, pre-packed and prepared for direct sale to consumers.

An economy such as the Norwegian is characterized by a large need for real capital. This is the case for hydraulic power, sea transport, mining, and metal processing. Furthermore, geographic and climatic conditions are such that heavy investments are necessary in infrastructure and housing. The development of the Norwegian economy in the first long period after the Second World War could only be accomplished through a comparatively high level of investment. During the 1950s, the rate of investment to GDP was as high as 35 per cent, compared to 20-25 per cent in most other countries in Western Europe.

Fig. 14: Hydraulic power had opened up new possibilities for the production of metals and Norwegian saltpetre. Here is a view of the Flomfjord saltpetre factory, 1963.

Considering this, the deficits in the Norwegian balance of payments were relatively modest, and it was only in the late forties, during the period of reconstruction, that the deficit reached a level above 5 per cent of GDP.

Throughout the 1950s and 1960s it was, as stated earlier, a major goal of economic policy to reduce the relative importance of, and dependence on, primary trades. In view of this it seems odd that the development of the Norwegian economy during the 1970s and 1980s went in exactly the opposite direction. In the 1960s, the rights to extract oil and natural gas in the North Sea had been divided up among the countries bordering the area. In 1969, oil was found in the Ekofisk field situated in the Norwegian zone. Even before the first energy crisis, OPEC I in 1973-74, oil discoveries were such that it was profitable to start extracting oil. In 1972, the state-owned Statoil Company was established to produce oil in cooperation with other firms, including foreign ones. At this stage, it was important for the Norwegian government to ensure that the oil was brought ashore in Norway with a view to establishing a local refining industry, etc. All this, of course, meant further demands for vast investments in the Norwegian economy.

In autumn 1972, the Norwegian people – like the Danes – had to vote Yes or No in a referendum on the question of joining the EEC. The result was a No, supported by a majority of 53.5 per cent of the votes cast. When Denmark produced a majority of Yes-votes a week later, two of Norway's closest trade partners, Great Britain and Denmark, had taken a different line on the question of European integration. Consequently, there was a widespread feeling that Norway was facing a period of crisis and economic downturn in the years to come. Nonetheless, the period turned out to be one of unusual growth at a time when the rest of the industrialized world was suffering in the throes of recession.

By 1950, *Sweden* had, with the exception of a few months during the summer of 1936, been led by Social Democratic governments since 1932. This stability continued during the entire period of high growth and beyond. It was not until 1976 that the opposition formed a government. By that time, Sweden had been governed by the same party which had been in office for 44 years, in some periods with absolute majorities, and headed by only three prime ministers: Per Albin Hansson (1885-1946), Tage Erlander (1901-85) and Olof Palme (1927-86): a record hard to beat in any democratic society.

The development of the Swedish economy around 1950 is reminiscent of that of the Norwegian economy. There was a devaluation in 1949 which, combined with price rises due to the Korean War, caused total price increases of 20-25 per cent during 1951-52. As in Norway, it was impossible to keep prices down through subsidies and price controls. Furthermore, Sweden was subject to external pressure from the OEEC to liberalize its remaining restrictions in foreign trade, and similar internal pressure from Swedish export-oriented industries.

The outcome of this was a change in the early fifties in the underlying strategy of Swedish economic policy. The interests of export trades were promoted, although a tendency to favour trades with a higher added value through fiscal and monetary policy made itself apparent. For the metal industries, this meant increased interest in the production of means of transport, cars, lorries and ships, and for the woodworking industry it meant an increased interest in the production of furniture. On the whole, these products were at the upper end of the quality scale.

A striking feature of Swedish developments was the fact that industrial expansion during those years took place mainly within a few, but large plants. The ten largest firms in manufacturing industry were responsible for a third of the total export of goods. Another interesting point was the multinational character of Swedish firms. In 1960, Swedish companies employed 106.000 persons in their foreign branches and by 1970 this figure had increased to 183.000.

Two aspects of the Swedish economy during those years deserve special attention. These were the high and constant level of employment along with the overall balance on foreign trade. The counterpart to the first aspect was a low level of unemployment, generally around two per cent of the total labour force, and the primary problem felt in the labour market was a constant shortage of skilled, highly-qualified labour. Two means were used to remedy the situation. Firstly, Sweden was opened up to immigrants and, on average, 15.000 entered the country per year throughout the entire period of high growth. The second means employed was Sweden's "active labour market policy", whose original aim had been to reduce unemployment through increased mobility between trades and geographical areas, but which changed in the course of time into the prevention of a labour shortage.

The second aspect of the Swedish economy worthy of mention was the satisfactory development of the balance of payments, which meant that Sweden financed her investments out of current savings. On the whole, Sweden did not have to worry about her balance of payments during those years. In terms of economic growth this meant that no need was felt for "stop-go" policies.

Increasing incomes and prices in the early 1950s led to a need for increased pensions to secure a higher degree of compensation than that offered by existing schemes, and resulted in a government proposal for a Common Supplementary Pension Scheme, the ATP. According to the plan, the idea was to secure for all members of the labour force a pension that corresponded to sixty per cent of what they earned during the fifteen years of their highest income. It was to be financed through obligatory contributions, which were to be put into a huge pension fund. This scheme corresponded in two respects to traditional Swedish social security policy for it was directed at everyone and financed through premiums. The new elements in the plan were the idea of saving the money in a special fund for later reimbursement and the decision to vary the premiums and pensions according to income. All in all, the suggestion gave rise to ideological conflicts, especially in respect of the idea of creating a single huge pension fund. The matter was eventually settled by referendum. A Social Democratic proposal, in line with the above-mentioned description of the plan, faced two proposals of a more traditional and liberal character. The Common Supplementary Pension Scheme obtained close to fifty per cent of the votes and was translated into reality in a slightly modified form. In Swedish business life there was a widespread fear that the scheme would mean the introduction of what was called "funding Socialism," that is, a socialisation of large parts of business where a central fund would obtain decisive blocks of shares, leading to subsequent ownership of the firms in question. This fear was allayed by the decision that the fund had to invest in bonds etc., which could neither give it a direct say in the management of the businesses nor provide it with any direct ownership of firms. This, however, has since been altered.

In the early 1930s, Swedish economic policy, supported by Swedish economic theorists, had the character of what might be called a pre-Keynesian economic policy. This was continued and refined after the abolition of wartime restrictions in the early 1950s. At that time, Sweden was considered by the rest of the world to be a laboratory as far as the use of fiscal policy for fine-tuning was concerned. Not only was the setting of the overall level of demand one aim of this selective policy, but also that of the composition of demand down to the distribution of investment between different industrial branches.[8] In addition, Swedish business banks and the financial sector remained under the strict control of the central bank, the Riksbank, which guided the placements of the financial institutions through its directives; in short, through a system of credit control and rationing.

While the 1950s can be seen as a period of transformation and structural change in Swedish economic life, the 1960s took on a consolidating character. Investments changed in character in the sense that business investment decreased in significance and welfare investment, including investments in housing, grew in importance. The appearance

8. This was done through a system of tax deductions, the build up of investment funds within the individual firms and the release of the means of such funds. Assar Lindbeck (1975, 107ff).

of new, overseas producers applying pressure upon the markets of raw materials, including metals, was also felt in Sweden. In this lay the origin of a coming balance of payments problem. Similar trends could be observed elsewhere in the shape of increasing domestic cost levels and increased foreign competition for the Swedish textile and shipbuilding industries. At this time, however, all these things were still bubbling under the surface. As the energy crisis of 1973-74 hit Western Europe, Sweden was still among the strongest countries as far as international currency reserves were concerned.

6. Italy

For Italy, as for the rest of Western Europe, the years 1950 to 1973 marked a period of exceptional economic growth. If a particular feature is to be singled out, it has to be the fact that the growth in Italy was unevenly distributed from a geographic point of view. Put bluntly, the differences between the South and the North of Italy not only persisted but deepened.

Already around 1900, industrialization had begun in Northern Italy in a triangular zone, covering Turin and Milan to the north and Genoa to the south. It was from here that industrialization spread from 1945 onwards to neighbouring areas to the east and south. Development was encouraged by high rates of savings and investment, an ample supply of labour, moderate wage increases and correspondingly high profits. As for the structure of the trades, a substantial part of the expansion took place in small businesses, which were favoured by tax legislation, public grants, supported by local communities, etc. The common characteristic was, however, that development occurred mainly in the North.

This does not mean that no initiatives were taken to promote growth in Southern Italy. In the 1950s, major importance was attached to the development of infrastructure, including means of communication and institutions within health and education. In spite of such initiatives, the level of income in the South had difficulty keeping up with that in the North. The harmonization of incomes, which might have been expected, did not happen at all, unlike in France.

Just as Italy is a dualistic society from a geographical point of view, it may also be considered to be so from the point of view of the relationship between the private and public sectors. In the private sector, there are highly competitive firms producing for example office equipment and cars. These exist side by side with inefficient and overstaffed businesses within the public sector, such as the postal service and telecommunications. The above-mentioned disparities could also be described in terms of the differences between the non-competitive and the competitive sector of the economy, which were laid open to foreign competition as a result of changes in Italy's trade policy after the Second World War, including their membership of the OEEC.

Throughout the 1950s, the economy was characterized by an ample supply of labour and a split in the labour movement into different trade unions according to religious and political affiliation. From the middle of the 1960s onwards, growing wage pressure was felt, culminating in 1969 in what became known as "the hot autumn". The three hitherto distinct types of trade union – the Communist, the Socialist and the Christian – united, which gave them more power. The result was increased pressure on wages and increased influence for the unions on hiring and firing policies, one of whose aspects was that former employees enjoyed an advantage over other job seekers when their previous employer was hiring workers once more. All in all, the system meant a reduction in labour market mobility.

Along with these changes, there was an extensive reform of the social pension schemes, which included a rise in the benefits and a change in the financing according to which a smaller share was to be covered through premiums and a greater share through taxation. However, it turned out to be difficult to reach agreement on the tax-side of the reform, with the upshot that Italy faced serious problems on the brink of the first oil crisis. There was growing pressure on wages and an increasing government budget deficit, which resulted in a correspondingly rapid rise in public debt.

7. Spain and Portugal

It was not until the middle of the 1970s that the two countries of the Iberian Peninsula embarked on a process of democratization after years of dictatorship. For both countries, their systems of government had meant difficulties in their relations with the surrounding world and for their economic development.

This was especially true in the case of *Spain* where, as the result of the Spanish Civil War, 1936-39, General Francisco Franco (1892-1975) established a dictatorship of a Fascist character. During the Second World War, Franco observed benevolent neutrality towards Germany, receiving Hitler as his guest shortly after the German occupation of France. By the end of the war, Spain met hostility from a broad range of countries, including the USA, which eventually resulted in the 1946 adoption of a UN resolution declaring an economic boycott of the country. Due to increased East-West tension, the USA gradually softened its stance toward Spain and Franco, opening the way for private American investment in the country. In 1953, an agreement was signed granting the US Air Force bases in Spain in exchange for economic support. This agreement and the presence of US troops seems to have had little effect on the character of the regime and the economic system, which was still mainly based on self-sufficiency.

European Economic integration during the late 1950s seems to have had a more direct impact on economic policy under the Franco regime. Spain's economic isolation became increasingly obvious and oppressive the more progress was made in European economic integration. In 1962 it was announced that the Community would not have any contact with the country under its existing regime. Because of Spain's growing economic isolation and General Franco's increasing age, Prince Juan Carlos (1938-) was appointed successor to Franco as Head of State in 1969. This step was seen as an indication of the impending liberalization of the political system.

From an economic point of view, the civil war of the 1930s and the ensuing world war had meant a great reverse for Spain's development. It was not until 1950 that her GDP reached its 1929 level. A chronic problem was the shortage of foreign exchange, which resulted in a highly protective import policy. On this issue, the 1953 agreement with the USA provided a certain relief. The country had been kept outside the Marshall plan and the OEEC, but as a first step towards acceptance it was admitted in 1958 to the OEEC, the IMF and the IBRD.

However, an obligation to liberalize the foreign trade of the country was attached to those admissions. The period 1960-73 was a golden age as far as economic growth was concerned, with average annual growth rates as high as 7.3 per cent, compared to 4.7 per cent for OECD Europe as a whole. Among the countries of Western and Southern Europe, only Greece and Portugal experienced similar growth rates of 7.7 and 6.9 per cent respectively. A major factor behind the sudden upturn was the increase in earnings from tourism. From 1959 to 1973, the annual number of foreign tourists went up from 4 million to nearly 35 million. As well as the growing income from this source, there was also the income from the homeward transfers of a growing number of Spanish migrant workers in other European countries.

Portugal also entered the post-war period with a well-established Fascist dictatorship. Accordingly, the economy was organized in a corporate fashion, meaning that the setting of wages and the allocation of capital were decided in cooperation between the government (i.e. the regime) and the (government-controlled) organizations within business and the labour market.

At the end of the Second World War, the Portuguese economy was even more backwards than that of Spain, with fewer modern industries and almost half the Portuguese population was still occupied in agriculture. The home market was too small and too poor to form the basis for an export industry with the exception of a limited textile production based on cheap labour.

It is fair to say that Portugal was met with more openness than Spain. This may be explained by the fact that the Portuguese regime did not come to power by means of a civil war, nor was it as closely connected to German Nazism and Italian Fascism as Spain was. The country was among the recipients of Marshall Aid from 1948 and, from the very beginning, was a member of the OEEC, a NATO member from its beginning in 1949, and one of the seven countries joining the EFTA (European Free Trade Association) in 1959-60. This greater international acceptance meant that the country started developing sooner after the war than Spain, although it had to start from an even lower economic level.

The late 1940s and the 1950s were characterized by improvements in infrastructure (communication and power stations), and may be seen as a transitory stage with average growth rates as high as nearly seven per cent, increasing throughout the period. Growth calculations indicate that an increased supply of capital may explain as much as half of the growth, the rest being primarily due to an overall increase in factor productivity, in part because of sectoral shifts from agriculture to urban trades.

The dictatorial regime seems to have left its mark on the economy in several respects. The level of wage increases was exceptionally low – about two per cent a year – during the period of high growth. It was not until the late 1960s that Portugal began to build up public debt, brought about by the struggle against liberation movements in the country's colonies.

When President Antonio di Salazar died in 1970, after 38 years in power, his successor began softening the regime, but it was not until 1974 that the regime was replaced by democracy, following the so-called Carnation Coup.

8. The USA

Compared to contemporary Europe, the growth rates of the USA during the period 1950-73 were lower and less stable. According to growth calculations, the fact that they were lower can be explained by a lower rate of increase in productivity levels. That they were less stable is apparent from the existence of three periods of different levels of growth rates: 1950-53 (6.0 per cent p.a.), 1953-60 (2.1 per cent p.a.), and 1960-68 (4.5 per cent p.a.). After this, a period with substantial year-to-year changes followed; similar periods and corresponding changes cannot be found in the figures for OECD Europe.

After a weakening of economic growth during 1947-49, the American economy saw three years of high growth due to the Korean War. The high level of activity was accompanied by unacceptably high price increases with the result that the economic policy of the rest of the 1950s pursued a primary goal of keeping price rises at a minimum level. In that respect, the policy was a success for the annual rate of inflation was kept below 1.5 per cent. However, growth rates at an average of 2.1 per cent were low as well, and far below those of both Western Europe and even those of the USSR.

This was part of the explanation why the candidate of the Democrats in the 1960 presidential election, John F. Kennedy (1917-63), repeatedly stated during his campaign the need "to get this country moving again". After his – extremely narrow – victory, he suggested a number of initiatives, the majority of which were not accepted by Congress until after his assassination and he was succeeded in November

1963 by Lyndon B. Johnson (1908-73). The best known of these was the proposal to send a man to the moon and back – a firm response to the Soviet space programme. In terms of domestic policy, the introduction of "medicare" – a health programme for the aged – can be seen as the greatest social reform since Franklin D. Roosevelt's New Deal. The "war on poverty" programme, though, was less successful and later stopped.

From 1965 onwards, the economy was stimulated by the growing Vietnam War, which caused renewed price rises and a worsening of the balance of payments. In 1969, the Republican, Richard M. Nixon (1913-94), was elected president without bringing about any change in the economic stabilization policy. The war in Vietnam was intensified, as were the deficits in the federal budgets and balance of payments. This triggered off a series of failed attempts (table 14.2) to stabilize the economy through incomes policy and tax increases.

In addition to this, there were problems related to the position of the dollar; because the development of the American balance of payments from the beginning of the 1960s had foreshadowed future problems. According to American terminology, the net-position of the balance of payments reflects the so-called "basic balance" (not the current account, as in other countries), and this basic balance indicates changes in gold reserves and net exchange assets. The position of the basic balance gives an impression of the changes in the international liquidity of a country –including its gold reserves. Any eventual deficit in the basic balance must be paid for through a reduction of the international liquidity of the country in question, which was what happened to the USA during those years.

The 1960s finished with growth rates close to zero (for 1970, - 0.3) without the desired fall in inflation, which was at a level of 5-6 per cent. Furthermore, in 1971, the current account of the American balance of payments came out showing a deficit, which may be seen as the background to the introduction in August 1971 of an extraordinary import duty of ten per cent along with the suspension of the obligation to sell gold. In December of the same year, this was followed by a decision taken at "the Smithsonian meeting" to widen the limits of exchange rate adjustments within the Bretton Woods system. It was during this period that economists started to have doubts about the Keynesian economic recipe, though, so far, monetarist theories had no direct impact on American economic policy. That change, which placed more responsibility on monetary policy, did not take place until the end of the 1970s.

During the first half of the 1900s, it was said that when the American economy sneezed, the European economy would catch pneumonia; the explanation being that the America represented such a large market for European goods. The same dependence, however, was not felt in Europe during the years 1950-73, or at least not to the same extent. The previously mentioned changes in American growth rates in 1953, 1960 and 1968, are not to be found to anywhere near the same degree in Western Europe, and only during the years 1957-58 can a close connection between developments in the USA and Western Europe be seen. So, all in all, it seems fair to conclude that the health of the European economy was no longer as dependent on the American economy as it had been previously. This does not mean, however, that the USA had only marginal influence on the European economy during this period. The four examples described below will show that this was not so.

Part of the idea behind the Marshall Plan was to promote the transfer of American technology and know-how to Europe, and this was continued in the following years through the copying of American management styles, the establishment of close relations with American research and teaching institutions and via direct American investments in Europe. The 1950s and 1960s were the decades when American multinationals gained a foothold in European business.

Another field where the position of USA had substantial consequences for Western Europe was in trade policy. There, its effect was a double one, which operated in two directions at the same time. Although the USA took the initiative to implement tariff cuts on manufactured goods, at the very same time the USA had a waiver within GATT allowing it to impose quantitative restrictions on the import of agricultural goods, and so contributed to the continuation of agricultural protectionism for decades to come.

A third sphere, that deserves to be mentioned, is European integration. To Americans, the division of Europe into a great number of economic entities surrounded by customs walls, passport controls, etc., by tradition seemed rather odd. Even more so as the Americans thought of Western Europe as an ally in the Cold War where a strong, common Western European economy was preferable to a weak, divided Western Europe. So, for many reasons, the USA has been sympathetic to European integration, even if it was to cause discrimination against American goods; though it goes without saying that the less discrimination, the better.

Finally, the collapse of the Bretton Woods system in the early 1970s needs to be mentioned once again. Here, the development of the American balance of payments in the 1960s was undoubtedly part of the explanation of what happened subsequently. However, as pointed out and expressed by the "Triffin dilemma", the entire idea of a specific, national currency as the key global currency was an illusion in the long run. Seen in that light, it was only a question of *when* the Bretton Woods system based on the US dollar would break down, since it was bound to happen sooner or later.

9. Japan

It was not until 1953 that the Japanese GDP reached the level it had been at in 1939-40. Consequently, the growth of the early 1950s may be seen as the end result of reconstruction. However, the outbreak of the Korean War in June 1950 meant a fundamental shift in the conditions of the Japanese economy, which makes it reasonable to begin the description of the Japanese economy during the golden years at this point of time.

In June 1950, the Cold War was transformed into a regular military confrontation when troops from North Korea, supported by Communist China, crossed the 38th parallel, which was the line of demarcation between North and South Korea. This was seen by the Americans as a Soviet-Chinese attempt to gain control of the entire Far East, and the response was a massive American military build-up and a counterattack based on a Security Council resolution within the framework of the United Nations.[9] From Japan to the southernmost part of Korea, the distance across the Tsushima Straits is nearly two hundred kilometres. Japan suddenly changed its position from being an occupied nation to being the base for extensive American military operations. For Japan, this meant unexpected income in "hard" foreign exchange that

---

9. The USSR was boycotting the Security Council at that time and so did not veto the resolution.

could be used everywhere, which widened her economic room for manoeuvre. As a result, the tight deflationary policy following the exchange reform of 1949 was eased and the economy given freer rein.

At the political level, the new situation made the USA want to
change the status of the country through a peace treaty, which was
done without the participation of the former ally, the USSR, in 1952.
The consequence was a reduction in American interference in Japanese domestic affairs. One result of this was that control over the cartels, the pre-war Zaibatsu, and industrial mergers was eased which, in
practice, meant their re-establishment. Another aspect was that policy
towards the trade unions was tightened, causing a worsening of the
workers' situation.

From 1950 to 1973, the Japanese GDP increased more than seven-
fold, corresponding to average annual growth rates of 9.3 per cent. To
compare, the other wartime loser, Germany, had growth rates of 5.9
per cent throughout the same period. Unlike Germany, however,
whose growth rates declined in the 1960s, Japan's increased from 8.4
per cent from 1950 to 1959, to 9.9 per cent from 1960 to 1973. Calculated on the basis of per capita figures, the relationship between the
growth rates of the two countries remains the same at 8.0 per cent for
Japan and 4.9 for Germany between 1950 and 1973, which implies that
the difference was not due to any special increase in the Japanese population.

To explain the high growth rates of Japan, it is proper to refer to
chapter 14, section 1, Growth and Growth Factors, where a number of
the general characteristics of the period of high growth are mentioned.
The questions to be then raised are, first, which of those factors were
felt to an unusual degree in the case of Japan and, second, are there any
special conditions additional to these factors that can explain the exceptional Japanese growth rates?

As for the supply of factors of production, Japan, to start with, had a
very high level of savings, resulting in a very *high level of investment*.
The explanation for this is a high share of profits, and other non-wage
incomes, and a high rate of saving from those incomes. Furthermore,
the rate of household savings had been high due to the absence of an
advanced social security system. As far as the *labour input* is concerned,
the number of working hours only saw a modest reduction, while the
standards of education were significantly raised. According to the calculations by Angus Maddison already mentioned, the growth of the

quantity and quality of factor input in the case of Germany can explain an average annual growth of 2.4 percent (through the 1950-73 period), while the same component in the case of Japan explains an annual growth of 5.5 percent. Lastly, sectoral or *structural shifts* in the labour force, from agriculture to manufacturing industry, also added considerably to overall growth.

To those quantitative factors, other factors of a qualitative or institutional character must be mentioned. A typical example would be the close ties between government and business, which constituted an informal system of planning along with a common career pattern for high ranking personnel in civil service and financial institutions. This system, reminiscent of French indicative planning, was then combined with an opaque system of subsidies for export trades, along with a corresponding system to protect Japanese firms on the home market. At the centre of this was the *MITI, the Ministry of International Trade and Industry,* though it must be said that the characteristics presented above were closer to the truth in the 1950s than in the 1960s. The acceptance of Japan, first into the GATT and then in 1864 into the OECD, meant that Japan had to increasingly adapt to international norms as far as trade policy was concerned. For that reason, it is generally understood that certain adjustments took place in its trade policy around that time.

A problem for Japan in the early stages of its return to the world economy was to ensure that a low price level for its export products was combined with a high or at least acceptable, level of quality. In order to achieve this, permanent quality control was established through cooperation between the MITI and the business organisations in question. To mention a leading example, this was the case for photographic equipment and optical instruments, with the aim of Japanese products reaching the standard of those from the USA and Germany. A further explanation of the export success was the existence of a large home market for goods such as consumer electronics. Due to extremely high rents, Japanese apartments are generally small, which provides an incentive to reduce the size of television sets, radio and amplifier systems, etc.[10] After these had been developed for the home market, they were subsequently offered for export at highly competitive prices.

10. Michael E. Porter (1990, 404).

The competitiveness of Japanese exports gave rise to the introduction of all sorts of import restrictions in the old industrial countries. One way of doing this was to make Japan accept what were called voluntary restraint agreements, where the exporting country had to control and eventually restrict its exports of a given export item. Such arrangements were, to a wide extent, reached in the case of textile exports and, later on, cars. In this respect, Japan has shared the fate of other newly industrialized countries.

Part V
European integration
1950-73

Just as the years between 1950 and 1973 marked a watershed in the general economic history of Western Europe after the Second World War, this also applied to the history of European integration. In 1950, the French Minister of Foreign Affairs, Robert Schuman (1886-1963), presented the plan subsequently named after him, which led to the creation of the European Coal and Steel Community (ECSC). Great Britain, Ireland and Denmark joined the European Communities, EC, in 1973, thereby increasing the number of members from six to nine, though the admission of Great Britain in particular was to give rise to digestive problems in the years to come. There were further internal ones in the shape of inflation, balance of payments difficulties and growing unemployment in the wake of the first energy crisis of 1973-74. The years between 1950 and 1973 may be considered to be the period when a European carcass was designed and built, while the putting into practice of a genuine internal market and the fulfilment of the wish to set up an Economic and Monetary Union were left to the future.

It is a recurrent theme of this work that foreign policy and defence issues, as well as economic motives, have been major factors behind the process of European integration. The evidence for this in 1950-57 is explained in *chapter 16, The Birth of a Community 1950-57*. The positive attitude of the USA towards initiatives which, in themselves, led to discrimination against American exports, may be seen as an effect of the Cold War along with concerns about developments in the balance of nuclear arms in those years. It was important for the USA to have Western Europe as an economically powerful ally, and this economic power was to be created and promoted through integration. The significance of foreign policy issues for the process of integration was amply demonstrated at the time of the fall of the Berlin Wall in 1989 and the collapse of the Soviet Bloc in 1991, as will be explained in chapter 21.

Chapter 17, The First Fifteen Years 1958-73, deals with the implementation of the central provisions of the Treaty of Rome. The subheading "An emergency solution" covers an account of the reaction of the non-EC members of the OEEC to EC activities, which led to the establishment of EFTA, the European Free Trade Association. Another principal theme of this chapter is the recurrence of crises caused, in the main, by France as the Community progressed from one stage to the next in the transitional period. French policy during the almost eleven years of de Gaulle's presidency was guided by a will to translate into reality only what was stated explicitly in the Treaty, such as the setting up of a Common Agricultural Policy, and no more.

Another aspect of French policy during those years was the reluctance, if not outright opposition, towards British and other applications for membership. Great Britain and its three associates, Ireland, Denmark and Norway, all applied twice for membership in the course of the 1960s and encountered the French veto as related in *chapter 18, Enlargement with Obstacles*. Enlargement, therefore, had to wait until de Gaulle's retirement from office. Chapter 18 also deals with the sad fate of the initiatives for special Nordic economic cooperation. However, upon sober reflection, the economies of the Scandinavian countries from the outset were not complementary and were even less so in the 1950s. The plain truth about Nordic economic cooperation is that it was not until the establishment of EFTA, initiated by Great Britain, that realistic initiatives were taken for the establishment of free trade between the Scandinavian countries; and even then agriculture and fishing were excluded.

Chapter 16

The birth of a community
1950-57

1. Two perspectives

In the spring of 1950, following an initiative by the French government, talks began which resulted in the creation of the European Coal and Steel Community (ECSC) just two years later. On 1st January 1958, the treaties of the European Economic Community (EEC) and EURATOM came into effect. In less than eight years, six countries, which at various periods in European history had been at war with each other, had united together to enter into a new and previously untried form of cooperation.

The history of this can be written from two widely different perspectives, depending on the views taken of its development and the driving forces behind it.

It can be viewed from a more narrow perspective as an economic success story about the creation of a common market whose aim was to facilitate the trade not only of products, but also capital, labour, etc, as well as the establishment of a common agricultural policy. This represents one way in which to interpret the treaties and their consequences for European unity. However, its history can be given a much wider dimension, where it becomes the story of the utilisation of the costly experiences of the Western European countries in the preceding years. Chapters 8-10 describe the Europe that generations of middle-aged Europeans born around the turn of the century had to look back on in 1945. There had been ten years of war (1914-18 and 1939-45), eleven years of bungling (1918-29) and ten years of economic crisis (1929-39). This perspective portrays the story of a desire to promote *an ever closer union*.

Shortly after the end of World War II, an optimistic feeling of peace had been rapidly replaced by an increasing East-West tension. The process of European integration during this period can therefore also be seen as the result of external factors where foreign and defence politics played a decisive role in giving integration momentum. To what extent did the Communist coup in Czechoslovakia in February 1948 influence the development of cooperation within the OEEC, formed in spring 1948? To what extent was the establishment of the European Coal and Steel Community (ECSC) affected by the Soviet Union's transformation into a nuclear power in autumn 1949 and the outbreak of the Korean War in 1950? How crucial were the Suez Crisis and the Soviet Union's demonstration of power against the Hungarian uprising in October and November 1956 for the establishment of the European Economic Community (EEC) at the beginning of 1957?

The rest of the chapter examines these two perspectives – both the narrower economic aspects of cooperation as well as the wider issues, which in certain situations were decisive factors in dictating the policy towards integration. An outline of the motives and methods used to promote integration will be given, together with a brief description of the creation of the European Coal and Steel Community (ECSC) and later the European Economic Community (EEC) and EURATOM. No attempt will be made to give a detailed description of the contents of the various treaties, although some principles behind them will be identified.

2. The policy towards integration – motives

Ever since the end of the 1940s, concerted efforts were made to promote both economic and political integration between Western European nations. Political integration in this respect is thought of in terms of cooperation on foreign policy and security issues. With the decision of Western European countries to join NATO, including West Germany's involvement in the defence alliance, cooperation in foreign issues was essentially removed from the sphere of Western European integration. Even though the Western European countries found the solution to their defence concerns within the framework of NATO, it would nevertheless be appropriate to recognise the importance of such foreign policy considerations in the motives behind the process of integration. This process aimed at:

a. promoting the economic growth of member states,

b. preventing internal European military conflicts,

c. preventing renewed German aggression,

d. integrating a rebuilt Germany into Europe,

e. strengthening Western Europe against Soviet aggression,

f. strengthening the position of Western Europe between the two superpowers,

g. promoting human rights and democratic forms of government.

Additional motives included those determined by the individual aims of each member state. For example, the governments in France and Italy around 1950 were eager to minimise the influence of strong Communist parties in national politics. To this may be added the wish of the individual countries – most obviously in the case of France – to strengthen their position in international politics.

These motives have all played roles of varying importance, in various mixes from country to country and at various times. Taking Western Europe as a whole, the narrow economic motive towards promoting economic growth was most strongly held by Britain, Ireland and the Scandinavian countries. In contrast, the wider goals as listed above were held relatively strongly by Germany's neighbours to the west and by Germany itself, which saw integration as a way of regaining her place as an equal partner in international affairs. The desire for a strengthening of the position of Western Europe between the two superpowers through the process of European integration was without doubt felt most strongly by the previous European great powers, especially France. The desire to promote democracy meant that Spain, Portugal and Greece were not allowed to join the Community as long as they maintained their dictatorships. In this respect, continued pressure was placed on these governments to move towards a more democratic form of government.

3. The policy towards integration – methods

The policy of integration incorporated in a schematic form the following views of how cooperation should take place:

1. as to the *type* of cooperation: through traditional government integration (confederal cooperation) *versus* supra-national integration (federal cooperation),

2. as to the *scope* of integration: through sectoral integration (sectoral cooperation) *versus* general integration (general cooperation), i.e. designed to encompass foreign policy and security issues.

For a closer understanding of the term "*traditional government integration*" (confederal cooperation), it is necessary to understand what is meant by the well-known term from international law: "self-governing society". This means a society that, in relation to its citizens, acts as the highest judicial power. As long as the citizens remain within the bounds of the society, its constitutional organ alone has the power to impose burdens on its citizens and lay down rules of law. Each country through its government can make agreements with the governments of other countries, which each is obliged to respect. If these agreements are then to become legally binding *in* the respective countries, the provisions must be "transformed" into national law, a process to be implemented through the national legislative body. If this concerns, for example, a treaty that gives foreigners access to the labour market on the same terms as the native citizens, the treaty must be accompanied by the adoption of national legislation, which in the respective countries transforms the provisions of the treaty into national law. The core of traditional governmental cooperation means, as the term implies, that cooperation only directly concerns the governments and only indirectly, through legislation, encroaches upon the rights and duties of citizens in the participating states.

In contrast to traditional government integration is "*supra-national integration*" (federal cooperation). This form of cooperation implies that the decisions taken have the effect of law "directly", or immediately, in the member states. It is not necessary for member states to transform the decisions into national law through special legislation. In other words, under federal-style cooperation, the national authorities no longer function in the areas involved as the highest judicial power in relation to its citizens, but are superseded by the federal authorities. Consequently, in those areas affected, a completely new state is brought into existence, a federal state.

The second distinction outlined above concerns *the scope of integration*. If it were to be confined to specific areas of economic and social life, such as the import duties on industrial goods or defence only, this would be described as *sectoral integration*. From such a limited and well-defined cooperation, a smooth transition can be made towards more comprehensive cooperation, such as an economic and monetary union. In case it goes even further and incorporates, in addition to economic matters, foreign policy and security issues, it becomes proper to speak of *general integration*.

An agreement on sectoral integration can be so thorough in its description that there is no further need or wish for additional supplementary provisions to include new topics. In contrast, agreements can be formulated that describe the scope of cooperation in purely general terms, accompanied by declarations urging broader cooperation. An example of the first type of agreement is reflected in the creation of EFTA, whose aims were clear to all parties involved from the beginning and where no provision was made for an expansion of its activities at a later date.

The treaty for the establishment of the European Economic Community (EEC) differed completely because it was already evident in the first two lines of the treaty's text, which stated that member states are determined to establish the foundations of *an ever closer union* among the European people. It was from the very beginning clear that there was more union to come.

The distinctions outlined above under points 1 and 2 intersect each other in such a way that four combinations emerge: a) confederal, sectoral integration; b) confederal, general integration; c) federal, sectoral integration; and d) federal, general integration. Such a sharp division of cooperation into four separate categories can give a misleading picture of the reality. The truth is that European integration and the development of the integration process since the Second World War have shown characteristics of all four categories. The justification for the categorization lies in its usefulness in indicating tendencies in the development of cooperation in the form of movement between "the categories".

An example of a) *confederal, sectoral integration* is what has been taking place within the OEEC/OECD and EFTA, and in a number of the UN-affiliated economic institutions (IMF, GATT etc). On security issues, integration of this type has taken place within NATO, bearing in mind that the operative side of NATO in the form of a joint command has supra-national elements. An example of b) *confederal, general integration* was evident in the type of integration advocated by France during the period of de Gaulle under the title of the "Europe of the Fatherlands". The idea was to include foreign and security policy as well as cultural policy in a general sense. On the other hand, it was the intention that this should be implemented at government level in the form of decisions reached in unanimity at meetings of the respective heads and leaders of the member states.

Examples of c) *federal, sectoral integration* include the European Coal and Steel Community (ECSC) and the European Economic Community (EEC). Behind the latter's treaty declaration "to establish the foundations of an ever closer union", lies a manifesto that can be interpreted as an indication of a desire for the development of a federal, general form of cooperation (c.f. point *d*). In the 1970s, initiatives were taken to organise regular meetings between the heads and leaders of EC member states, so called summits, which meant that the driving force behind EC cooperation was in reality removed from the EC treaty's organs and placed in the hands of their respective governments. These issues will be examined in more detail in chapter 21, which focuses on the treaty of the European Union, the Maastricht Treaty. As examples of d) *federal, general integration* in Western Europe, Germany and Switzerland may be mentioned and – outside Europe as a pioneer – the USA.

This chapter will confine itself to simply stating that EU cooperation is characterised by a sectoral-federal economic element and a less developed sectoral-confederal foreign and security policy element. The problem that arises concerns whether a strengthening of the sectoral-federal economic element, through the establishment of an economic and monetary union, will promote integration in such a way that foreign and security policy, as a result of a "spin-off" effect, will devel-

op a federal character and thereby draw the cooperation towards federal, general integration.

In addition to the above distinctions there is a further one which
concerns the process of decision-making; *unanimous* versus *majority
decision-making*. Under the latter a country might be obliged against its
will expressed by its own vote. Even if the system of majority voting in
principle can be said to conform to confederal integration, in that the
decisions taken still have to be transformed by the national parliament,
it will be felt as federal. A long-standing tendency of EC cooperation
has been the growing use of majority decisions. The assessment of how
much the integration policy has contributed to the development of a
supra-national form of cooperation depends on two components: the
frequency of decisions of a federal character and the extent to which
majority decisions are permitted.

4. The European Coal and Steel Community (ECSC)

4.1. The establishment

During 1948-49, a series of events took place in rapid succession culminating in a serious deterioration of East-West relations. In February
1948 a Communist seizure of power took place in Czechoslovakia under dramatic circumstances. In March a defence agreement, the Treaty of Brussels, was signed between Britain, France and the three
Benelux countries. In April 1949 the Atlantic Pact was signed, partly
as a result of the Soviet blockade of routes into Berlin in 1948-49.

Parallel to these events was the development of the "European
Movement" due to efforts of leading politicians to promote European
economic, cultural and political integration. Following a proposal from
a group of politicians, including Winston Churchill, a conference was
held in The Hague in May 1948 to discuss European integration. Here
it was decided that proposals be put before the national parliaments of
each country for the establishment of a new European organ, the
Council of Europe.[1] Sceptics of this plan included Britain's Labour
government and the Social Democrat governments in the three Scandinavian countries. A heavily diluted proposal won support in May

---

1. For the distinction between the Council of Europe, the European Council, and the
    Ministerial Council or just the Council see chapter 21 section 2.

1949 from ten nations: the Benelux countries, France, Ireland, Italy, Britain, Norway, Denmark and Sweden. The Council itself was composed of government representatives, each with the right of veto. An advisory Assembly, whose members were appointed by the national parliaments, was attached to the Council. The stage was now set for a strained working relationship between the Assembly's more pro-integration members and the Council. This was evident regarding the creation of the two European cooperation organs in 1948-49, the OEEC and the Council of Europe, neither of which satisfied the hopes of the "Europeans".[2]

The defence of Western Europe in 1948-49 was characterised by a reduction of Western conventional forces balanced by the USA's monopoly of nuclear arms. A decisive shift in this occurred in autumn 1949 when the USSR conducted its first atomic bomb test causing a need for the swift reinforcement of conventional forces in Western Europe, particularly in West Germany. Less than five years after the end of the Second World War and the defeat of Nazi Germany, Germany's neighbouring countries found themselves in the situation where they required German support to defend their borders.

This was the background for France's proposal in spring 1950 for the creation of a European Coal and Steel Community (ECSC). It was no surprise that the proposal encompassed coal and steel, as these were essential to any rearmament programme. If the German coal and steel industries were to play a role in rearmament, which was a necessity, it would have to be brought under some form of joint control, but in a way that was acceptable to Germany. The plan was drafted by the head of the French Planning Committee, Jean Monnet, who, as previously mentioned, had experience of working in the League of Nations as well as the Allied administration during both the First and Second World Wars. The plan was put forward by the French foreign minister, Robert Schuman, after whom the plan was named. Participation was open to any country, but of the European producer and consumer countries only six joined, namely France, Germany, Italy and the three Benelux countries.

Britain was invited to join, but after brief consideration declined. At that time Britain was Western Europe's largest producer of coal and steel. Nevertheless the British government was only informed of the

2.   D.R.Urwin (1995, 33pp).

plan after the German and the American governments and, when it was informed, only had 24 hours to decide whether or not it wished to participate in a forthcoming conference.[3] Consequently, the atmosphere in which the British government approached the invitation was strained and not conducive to a decision in favour of its acceptance.

A serious obstacle for Britain was the French demand that cooperation should have a supra-national character, that it should allow for the possibility of direct intervention in the coal and steel industries of each member state, and that majority decisions should be permitted. Ever since the creation of the OEEC in 1948, Britain had resisted the demand that cooperation should have a supra-national character and was determined to maintain this position. In addition, Britain may have feared that participation could create difficulties for its recently nationalised coal and steel industries, whose development was a central feature of the Labour government's economic policy. Participation could also interfere with Britain's desire to protect its overseas economic and political interests at a time when the Empire was being dismantled. Finally, just as Western Europe in May-June 1940 had been overrun in a mere six weeks, it was feared this might happen again. Britain, therefore, would be better served by not having its coal and steel so closely associated with the rest of the European coal and steel industries.

The eventual outcome was that Britain decided to remain outside the concrete discussions that began in June 1950 concerning the creation of a Coal and Steel Community. With regard to the outside world's attitude towards the negotiations, it is worth noting that the USA, in the light of the deterioration of East-West relations, including the Korean War, accepted the plan and the accompanying opportunity to utilise the German economy to strengthen defence in the West. The Scandinavian countries adopted Britain's policy. The grouping of the European market segments, which was to remain for the next 23 years, had taken shape.

The negotiations were initiated in Paris in June 1950, scarcely a week before the outbreak of the Korean War. In view of the scope of the issues and the fact that an attempt was being made to reach agreement on previously untried solutions, the negotiations were conducted with remarkable speed. In April 1951 the treaty for the European Coal

---

3.   J.W.Young (1993, 32)

and Steel Community (ECSC) was signed in Paris, paving the way for the process of ratification by the national parliaments to begin. This proved to be a drawn out affair. In France, nationalist Gaullists on the one hand and Communists on the other voted against the treaty. In Germany the Social Democratic Party (SPD) voted against the treaty on the grounds that participation could impede German reunification. The smoothest process of ratification took place, as expected, in the Benelux countries, although there were doubts in the Netherlands concerning the absence of Britain. In April 1952, the French Senate gave approval and the treaty came into effect in July 1952, two years after the start of negotiations.

4.2. *The institutions*

For posterity, the European Coal and Steel Community (ECSC) has attracted interest first and foremost because certain principles had been set out that would later be applied to the framework of the European Communities (EC).

At the centre of the Community was the High Authority, which had nine members, two from each of the larger member states, Germany, France and Italy, and one from each of the smaller states. They were appointed for six-year periods, organised in such a way that the periods were staggered. The members were independent of their home governments, and were forbidden to receive instructions from outside bodies regarding the execution of their duties. The High Authority was allowed great freedom to act on majority decisions. The individual governments were represented in the Council of Ministers, which had some supervisory control over the High Authority. The two organs later came to correspond to the Commission and the Council in the European Economic Community (EEC), although it should be noted that the High Authority had relatively more power in the ECSC than the Commission of the EEC.

In addition, three other organisations were created: the Assembly, the Court of Justice and the Advisory Committee. The Assembly was equivalent to the later Assembly (Parliament) of the EC/EU and, as in that body's early stages, not an obligatory part of the creation of general rules of law. In this respect, the conflicts of authority within the present European Communities (EC) can be traced back to the establishment of the Coal and Steel Community. The Court of Justice was set up to settle conflicts involving private companies, governments and the Community. The Advisory Committee was composed of represen-tatives from business and the labour market, and continued to exist in the EC/EU in the shape of the Committee for Economic and Social Affairs.

Questions regarding the working language of the Community and the place of residence of the High Authority proved to be a stumbling block from the beginning. The eventual outcome saw the acceptance of four working languages – Flemish, French, Italian and German. As re-gards the question of residence, it was decided that the High Authority would temporarily reside in Luxembourg until a more permanent so-lution could be found. However, no formal final decision on this issue has ever been reached.

The object was the coal and steel industry. A common market for its products should be created, and the Community would be given wide-ranging powers to regulate prices, production, distribution, etc. As this concerned a field of business with a high degree of concentration and a tradition for price fixing, cartels, etc., the Community was given ex-tensive powers over individual companies and enterprises. Seen in an economic context, cooperation affected areas of economy where it would be difficult to rely on market forces, and in that respect a prob-lematic area had been chosen in which to initiate cooperation. The awareness that it was a difficult area to operate in, with sharply fluctu-ating market conditions, was soon confirmed, firstly, in connection with the recession that occurred in the aftermath of the Korean War in 1953 and in the late 1950s when the Community found itself burdened with vast stocks of coal.

With the creation of the European Economic Community (EEC) on 1st January 1958, the need for separate organs for the Coal and Steel Community diminished. Consequently, a partial integration of the in-stitutions rapidly took place, although the High Authority continued to exist until 1967, at which time, through the "Merger Treaty" of 1965, it became part of a single system under the EC, the European Communities.

5.   Failed plans

The outbreak of the Korean War, in June 1950, resulted in an in-creased fear of a Soviet attack on Western Europe, and a desire in the

USA to transfer military resources in Europe including Germany, to the Far East. In September the USA set out proposals for a German contribution to the defence of Western Europe in the form of Germany's entry into NATO. The thought of German rearmament would clearly lead to apprehension and be met with resistance throughout Europe, not least in France, and reaction to the American proposal was swift. In October 1950 the French Minister-President René Pleven (1901-93), put forward a proposal for the establishment of a European defence alliance, the *European Defence Community (EDC)*. Known as the Pleven Plan, the proposal attempted to facilitate German rearmament in such a way that there was no question of the formation of independent units of German troops with their own command structure. This was to be achieved by preventing the creation of any purely German divisions. The practicability of such a proposal was very doubtful.

The proposal discriminated against Germany as the other member states, in contrast to Germany and in addition to their contribution to the so-called European army, were allowed to build up their own national forces within NATO. The fact that Germany agreed to the proposal was due primarily to the efforts of its newly-established government which, in return for its consent, demanded – *and received* – a guarantee that its occupied status should be lifted and that Germany should be given sovereignty over its foreign affairs. The USA was reluctant to accept the French proposal, whilst Britain preferred to solve the issue of German rearmament through NATO. In general, the French proposal was regarded by the outside world as directed as much against German as against Soviet aggression.

In May 1952, the six members of the Coal and Steel Community signed a treaty on the EDC. What remained was to have the treaty ratified by the respective parliaments of the six countries. During the negotiations on the Defence Community it became clear that such a Community would be a fragile construction without any clear agreement for cooperation in foreign affairs. To compensate for this, a proposal was put forward in September 1953 by the Belgian Prime Minister Paul-Henri Spaak (1899-1972), that the idea of a *European Political Community (EPC)* should be considered. The result was ready in spring 1954 in the form of a proposal that would serve to help coordinate activities in both the Coal and Steel Community and the Defence Community.

In 1953-54 the procedure to ratify the EDC treaty began in earnest. Britain, which was not a part of the European Defence Community (EDC), desired a solution to the question of German rearmament where Germany's contribution to the defence of Western Europe would be channelled through NATO. As Germany soon after became a member of NATO, French interest in the EDC lessened, primarily because France's special role as the link between Germany and NATO no longer applied. At the same time, Germany experienced a strengthening of its economy when the German "Economic Miracle" (Wirtschaftswunder) began to take effect. The outcome of this was that the French National Assembly, the last parliament still to ratify the EDC treaty, never approved it. Quite simply, it was never put to the vote. At the end of August 1954, the French Minister-President Pierre Mendès-France (1907-82) was forced to accept that there was no longer any justification for ratifying the treaty, and the plan was dropped.

The solution to the question of German rearmament was that Germany and Italy agreed to comply with the provisions of the Brussels Treaty, signed in March 1948 by Britain, France and the Benelux countries. The aim of the treaty was now modified towards strengthening European unity. This meant that there would be mutual consultations, that Britain would promise to keep her troops in West Germany and, finally, that West Germany and Italy would join NATO as equal members. Besides the European Defence Community (EDC), the plan for a European Political Community (EPC) was also overtaken by events beyond its control. The agency for cooperation within the widened provisions of the Treaty of Brussels changed its name to the *Western European Union (WEU)*, under which it led a rather low key existence for almost 40 years until the early 1990s when plans for political cooperation within the framework of the EU gathered more momentum.

6. The creation of the Treaty of Rome

6.1 The road to Messina

By winter 1954-55, the impetus for the integration process had clearly disappeared. This was true first and foremost in France where political life was characterised by civil unrest, military defeat in the country's overseas territories, accompanied by economic and political strife on the domestic front. The Coal and Steel Community had a successful beginning, yet initiatives for expanding integration into the field of foreign and security affairs had, as already mentioned, failed. In this situation it seemed wise to continue with more realistic plans where greater support and enthusiasm could be generated – and which simultaneously had the built-in potential to develop into something as yet undefined.

Recognising a weakening of interest in European integration, the EPC pioneer, Belgian's foreign minister Paul-Henri Spaak, backed an initiative by the Benelux countries in May 1955 to issue a joint memorandum proposing the creation of an economic union. Support for Spaak's proposal came from the Dutch foreign minister and Luxembourg's prime minister, both of whom had served with Spaak as ministers-in-exile in London during the Second World War when they had also all played a role in drafting the agreement which led to the creation of the Benelux treaty. Behind the initiative was also the ever-present Jean Monnet, chairman of the ECSC's High Authority. According to the proposal, the ECSC should call a meeting and Britain would be invited to attend. This wish for Britain to participate reflects the desire amongst the Benelux countries to maintain contact across the North Sea and the English Channel.

The conference was opened in Messina on 1st June 1955 and began with the proposal of the Benelux countries. The meeting followed the procedure of a meeting of the ECSC's Council of Ministers and took place at ministerial level. The British government was indeed represented, although only by civil servants, which could only be interpreted as a sign that Britain did not afford the matter great importance. The meeting concluded with the establishment of a civil service and expert committee, but which was placed under political chairmanship. The chairman appointed was none other than the initiator of the proposal, Paul-Henri Spaak, whose work, approximately 20 months later, resulted in a ceremony to sign the Treaties of Rome creating the European Economic Community (EEC) and the European Atomic Energy Community (EURATOM).

That the enormous task of drafting a treaty for a European Economic Community (EEC) proved possible in such a short period of time, and that sufficient support could be found, can only be explained by the extraordinary circumstances in which it took place. However, only two factors will be highlighted here: a "technical" factor and a "political" factor, where the latter was clearly the most influential.

By using the term "a technical factor" to explain how the work could be carried out so swiftly refers to the fact that some of the preparatory work had already been completed. Discussions had previously taken place in GATT and OEEC concerning an elimination of customs duties and quantitative restrictions. Under the Customs Cooperation Council, a new customs nomenclature (Brussels's nomenclature) had been set up. Negotiations had taken place on a Dutch-French initiative on the issue of a future European agricultural policy under the heading "The Green Plan" – without any hope of its sprouting. The creation of institutions to represent a new and enlarged Community could, in general, be modelled on those of the Coal and Steel Community. A working platform was chosen where efforts focused on formulating some overall principles, while attempts to find detailed solutions to problems were postponed until a later date. Finally, the participants had some prior knowledge of each other through previous work in OEEC, ECSC and GATT meetings.

From here attention turns to the other side of the matter, namely the political explanation for the swift completion of the negotiations. There was undoubtedly a desire amongst leading politicians for the negotiations not to become bogged down in small details. To this should be added the dramatic political events abroad that took place in autumn 1956 when, for the first and only time, a superpower, the USSR, directly threatened the use of atomic weapons.

6.2 *From Messina to Rome*

It is worth noting that the working platform chosen has continued to be used since that time. According to the Messina Resolution of 2nd June 1955, a ministerial conference was to be arranged for the purpose of studying how a customs union and an organisation for atomic energy could be established. In order to help facilitate this process, the above mentioned expert committee was charged with presenting findings to the ministerial conference, and worked on this matter from July 1955 to March 1956. Britain participated in the initial stages in the work of the committee, but withdrew after becoming concerned at the proposed scope and character of cooperation. The expert committee's findings became known as *the Spaak Report*. A central feature of the report was that there was an imperative not to become bogged down in small details for fear of becoming stranded in the various sub-committees. A characteristic feature was the creation of a common customs tariff with external customs duties. A simple and practical calculation formula was adopted in which the duties for individual positions in principle were to be determined as an average of the basic duties in the four[4] customs regions.[5]

While the plans set out in Messina had been relatively diffuse, they had in the meantime become much more specific, focusing on the establishment of economic cooperation, where the creation of a common market was a central feature, as well as the development of cooperation on the production and utilisation of atomic energy. Alongside the committee's activities, attempts had been made in the respective member states to gain support for the plans from politicians, union representatives as well as representatives of the business community. As a central figure in these efforts we once again meet Jean Monnet, now former chairman of the ECSC's High Authority, but ever present and much involved as head of the Action Committee for the United States of Europe, a private society of influential individuals representing a cross-section of society in the six countries. Consequently, by the time the Spaak Report was submitted for review in spring 1956, the ground had already been prepared in the individual countries involved.

The Spaak Report was first taken up for review in the ECSC Assembly and a couple of months later in the Council of Ministers at the end of May 1956, almost one year after the first meeting in Messina. A decision was taken by the Council to charge the ministerial conference with the task of preparing a draft treaty on the basis of the content of the report. During preparations for this, dramatic and explosive events of a foreign and security nature took place in October and November 1956. Britain and France intervened militarily in connection with Egypt's (The United Arab Republic) nationalisation of the Suez-Canal at the same time as war broke out between Egypt and Israel. These events in the Middle East took place precisely at the moment when the Soviet army stamped out an uprising in Hungary, which gave the Soviet leader Nikita Kruschchev (1894-1971) the opportunity to remind the politicians and people of the West that the Soviet Union possessed

4. Benelux, France Italy and Germany.
5. This attempt to create a customs union should be compared with the concerted, yet fruitless, efforts of the Nordic countries at the same time to set up a common external customs tariff. The Nordic procedure differed in terms of its attempt to negotiate on each product without formulating a guiding principle. See chapter 18, section 8.

rockets and nuclear weapons that could reach Western European cities. Within days, the USA intervened in the Anglo-French military involvement in Egypt and the actions of the two European powers were condemned in the United Nations with the support of both the USA and the USSR.

These events represented a real awakening for the Western European countries to their true standing in world politics where all depended upon the will of the USA and the USSR. The texts of the two treaties were completed by the six countries in the midst of these violent outside events. The Kremlin made it clear that the Soviet Union was prepared to use military means to maintain control over its vassal states. At the same time, the UN headquarters in New York made it clear that the two former leading world powers, Britain and France, as well as the rest of Western Europe, would be relegated to the sidelines when important global issues were on the agenda. Consequently, the serious negotiations for wider economic cooperation in Europe were heavily affected by motives reaching beyond the question of tempo for the elimination of customs duties and the establishment of a common customs tariff. In February 1957 the two treaties for the EEC and EURA-TOM were finally negotiated. On 25th March 1957 both treaties were signed in Rome, what may be seen as reminiscent of the coronation ceremony of the Holy Roman Emperor, Charlemagne, in the same city on Christmas Day 800 AD, and whose empire once stretched as far as the new European Community.

6.3. Ratification and implementation

From here on, the procedure to ratify the treaty could begin. In the constitutions of the six countries, preparations had already been made to permit participation in a form of cooperation that involved the transfer of power to supranational organs. In July 1957, the necessary approval was given by the parliaments of Germany, France and Italy. Belgium and Luxembourg followed suit in November and the Netherlands at the beginning of December. The treaty could therefore come into effect on 1st January 1958, a date that can be rightly regarded as the Community's birthday.

The degree of support in the parliaments of the six countries must be regarded as having been solid. Resistance stemmed predominantly from extremist groups, either nationalist parties on the right of the political spectrum or Communist parties on the left. In Germany the Social Democratic Party (SPD) had altered its position so much during the 1950s that they voted for the treaty together with the government party, the CDU. Support for the treaty was weakest in France where the Gaullists, Communists and certain radical groups (centred on the former prime minister, Mendès-France) voted against ratification. In the National Assembly votes for and against were three to two in favour of the treaty. As mentioned earlier, two separate treaties were at stake, one for the EEC and one for EURATOM, the latter appearing to have been assigned greater importance during the 1950s than since. The strong degree of support in Germany in favour of the treaties can be partly explained by the inclusion of the field of nuclear energy. At the same time, the potential presented by the opening of markets for agricultural produce was a strong argument in both France and the Netherlands. In addition, an expectation existed of a general stimulation of the economies of each of the six countries. Consequently, benefits were to be gained by each country from ratification.

The fact that the treaties were swiftly drafted and passed relatively smoothly through the respective parliaments did not mean little consideration was given to the outcome. This can be testified to by the applicant countries which later petitioned Brussels to join the Community and were expected to declare loudly and clearly that they "accept the treaty as it stands"; a condition that proved difficult to accept for Britain, Denmark and Norway in the 1960s. The explanation for the exalted status of the treaty's text is in reality clear for all to see. It was considered paramount that any enlargement of the Community as a result of the entry of new members, large or small, must not be allowed to damage the established legal relationship between the present members. For that reason the text of the treaty cannot be altered according to suit wishes of newcomers, with the consequent necessity of the short, unconditional declaration of acceptance. Any applicants with particular problems have so far been offered nothing more than certain provisional concessions or exceptions.

As time has passed, by now more than 40 years, an impression has developed that the Treaty of Rome first and foremost came into existence as a result of internal magnetic forces between the participants. Although this is a delightful thought, the populations of that time did not interpret it like that. For the people who lived through this period, the newly born Community was, to a great extent, the result of the perceived threat of war and conflict against the background of a menacing outside world during a dark period of Europe's history. Economic historians should not ignore such a perception.

7. The Treaty – contents and principles

It falls outside the scope of this study to examine in detail the 248 articles of the Treaty of Rome with their accompanying protocols.[6] Instead, only certain primary aspects behind the treaty's economic provisions and the Community's institutional framework will be identified.

7.1. *An efficient market economy*

In principle, the treaty concerns a decentralised, market-oriented economy. That it aims at a decentralised, market-oriented economy can be seen from the fact that much of the treaty focuses on how price formation in the Community can be made to function efficiently. The term "price formations" is used here in its widest sense, covering not just goods and services, but also factors of production. The efficiency of price formation was to be achieved through the provisions regarding "*the four freedoms*": the free movement of goods, labour, capital and services, to which can be added the right of establishment. By offering the best possible conditions for price formation, the ground would be prepared within the Community for economic efficiency. In economic terms, economic efficiency was to be achieved through the optimal use (allocation) of resources (labour, capital and know-how) aimed at optimising the size and composition of the output. The Community is, as will be seen, based on central thinking within the theory of foreign trade and welfare theory, focusing on the question of optimal allocation. From this it seems fair to conclude that the EEC treaty was designed for countries with decentralised market-oriented economies, although this was not stated explicitly in the treaty.[7]

A related question is whether or not the treaty's provisions presume private capitalist ownership in business life. This is not in fact the case. It is well-known that extensive public ownership has existed in business life in France and Italy since the 1950s, particularly in the car manufacture, the oil industry and the banking sector. However, it

---

6.   In the absence of any indication, the references apply to the Treaty of Rome, i.e. the text of the 1957 treaty.

must be assumed that publicly owned enterprises were to comply with the treaty's requirements.

Although Articles 1-8 of the treaty fell under the heading "Part I, The Principles", nothing is mentioned about the two highly important questions referred to above concerning the choice of the economic structure of society. This should come as no surprise as there was no reason to bother either the negotiators or the parliamentarians with politically explosive issues like these.

Without anticipating the debates following later alterations to the treaty, it should perhaps be highlighted that the 1992 Maastricht Treaty added a provision (Article 102a) which stated that the Member States and the Community shall act in accordance with the principle of an open market economy with free competition, favouring an efficient allocation of resources. Whether this addition to the treaty text should simply be taken as a clarification of the original text or incorporates a shift in the character of the obligations is difficult to determine.

As regards the goals of the Community, Article 2 of the treaty states that it shall have as its task to promote throughout the Community a harmonious development of economic activities, a continuous and balanced expansion, an increase in stability, an increase of the standard of living, and closer relations between the States belonging to it. In other words, the goal was to promote economic growth and to avoid the extreme periods of depression like those experienced during the 1920s and 1930s.

In order to give an idea of the means used to achieve these goals, it is appropriate to outline the main content of Article 3. It should be noted that the text of the treaty outlines its provisions in a more brief and concise manner than that found in most textbooks.

According to Article 3, the goals of the Community are to be achieved through:

---

7. Jean Monnet expressed the following opinion in 1962: The large market does not prejudge the future economic systems of Europe. Most of the Six have a nationalised sector as large as the British and some also have planning procedures. These are just as compatible with private enterprise in the large market as they are within a single nation. (Article in the Journal of Common Market Studies, 1 (1), 1962). In contrast to this statement is an extract from a speech made by Margaret Thatcher to the College of Europe in Bruges, September 1988, where she confronted the Community: "My third guiding principle is the need for Community policies which encourage enterprise. If Europe is to flourish and create jobs of the future, enterprise is the key. The basic framework is there: the treaty of Rome itself was intended as a Charter for Economic Liberty. But that is not how it has always been read, still less applied." The two contrasting statements are taken from B.F.Nelsen et al (ed) (1994, 20 and 49).

a. the elimination, as between Member States, of customs duties and quantitative restrictions on the import and export of goods,

b. the introduction of common customs duties and a common trading policy towards third countries,

c. the removal of obstacles to the free movement of persons, goods, services and capital between member states,

d. the introduction of a common policy in the sphere of agriculture,

e. the introduction of a common policy in the sphere of transport

f. the introduction of a system ensuring that competition in the common market is not distorted,

g. the implementation of measures to facilitate a joint co-ordination of economic policy between member states, and to help prevent problems regarding the balance of payments,

h. the mutual approximation of the laws of the Member States to the extent required for the functioning of the common market.[8]

The article continues with provisions for the establishment of a European Social Fund and a European Investment Bank, as well as for the association of "the overseas countries and territories", i.e. past and present colonies. Adjustments have since been incorporated in the formulation of the points together with a series of new points. The original points in the following section will be referred to in the past tense.

The provisions under points *a, c, e-f* as well as *h* concerned efforts to promote a smooth and efficient market economy, and thereby secure uniform price conditions and minimise market imperfections. The provisions only made sense as already outlined in a decentralised market economy. Point *b*, regarding the introduction of a common customs tariff, had a more dual purpose. The existence of a common customs tariff would serve to promote uniform price conditions among member

8. Up to and including the Single European Act, the term "Common Market" has been used. However, it was replaced by the term "Internal" or "Single Market" following the ratification of the Treaty of the European Union.

states. In contrast, other motives lay behind the fixing of the level of the customs duties; for example, the member states could offer each other preference in relation to non-member states. A common customs tariff would, particularly in the early phase, serve to strengthen the Community's identity. In addition, a common customs tariff could be used to benefit certain branches and business sectors at the expense of others.

Only point *g* directly concerned relations at the macro level, where member states should coordinate their policies to prevent too great deficits or surpluses on their balance of payments. No mention was at this point made of anything that would later be discussed under the heading EMU, an economic and monetary union. Furthermore, the provision was allowed to gradually disappear into the background. As a country with a substantial surplus over long periods, Germany cannot be said to have complied with the requirements of this provision. When the Community attempted to coordinate a common anti-depression policy after the first oil crisis, nothing emerged except for a solemn declaration. Point *d* about a common agricultural policy was dealt with under articles 38-47, without offering any greater clarity. As regards the aim of the common agricultural policy, the treaty stated that it should ensure a fair standard of living for the agricultural community and simultaneously ensure consumers of reasonable prices for supplies (Article 39.1e). It could hardly have been expressed in more unclear terms.

Where the Treaty of Rome offered the most clarity concerned the establishment of a customs union. As a simple rule for fixing the common customs duties it was decided, as mentioned, that they were to be calculated as an average of the basic duties of the four customs regions. The French and Italian duties lay above the average whilst German and, particularly, the Benelux duties lay below. Both the desire for a common customs tariff and the internal elimination of customs duties was to be achieved according to a set timetable, which could, however, be deviated from to a certain extent. In reality, the process of establishing a customs union was achieved in less than ten years, a year and a half earlier than planned. No serious reference was made in the treaty to the forthcoming common agricultural policy. The French undoubtedly had expectations of acquiring new markets, especially in Germany, while German industry definitely saw opportunities to break into the heavily protected French market for industrial goods.

7.2. The institutions

As mentioned in section 3, the European Coal and Steel Community (ECSC) served as a prototype for the institutional framework of the European Economic Community (EEC). Its area of jurisdiction was, however, much wider as the Treaty of Rome encompassed all aspects of the economy. This could suggest that the member states were not so keen to relinquish national self-determination. Consequently, the supra-national element was weaker in the EEC than in the ECSC. This was especially evident in the fact that the EEC Commission was given fewer wide-ranging powers than the High Authority of the ECSC.

To offer a brief outline of the Commission and the Council of the EEC in terms of national institutions, it should be noted that the Council is equivalent to the legislative authority while the Commission corresponds to the executive, the government of the EEC. The role of the Commission from the very beginning was rooted in its power of initiative. The third element in the system was the Assembly, whose name was altered in conjunction with the ratification of the Treaty of the European Union (Maastricht Treaty) in 1993 to the more melodious sounding European Parliament, which according to its own members is a real parliament, although at a rudimentary stage. According to the Treaty of Rome, the Assembly was described as being an advisory body, but which retained the power in theory to discharge the Commission. If any tendencies in the development of the relationship between these three organs should be highlighted, it would have to be said that power became more and more vested in the Assembly (the European Parliament). That such a development came as no surprise to the authors of the treaty is apparent from the inclusion of certain provisions in the original treaty that opened up for direct elections to the Assembly.

It was decided that the provisions of the treaty should be implemented over a twelve-year period, divided into three stages of four years each. This method of dividing into stages, where the provisions regarding a wide range of issues were to be implemented by certain deadlines, had the objective of ensuring a balance between the advantages and disadvantages for the individual countries. In addition, it would become easier to measure how far the process in each country had come, and to put pressure on less compliant member states. Provisions were made for the three stages to be extended, but not for longer than to a total period of 15 years. If everything went according to plan, the Treaty would have been fully implemented by 1st January 1970 – which was indeed the case. However, this was not achieved without drama. Both the transitions to the second and third phases in 1962 and 1966 respectively, gave rise to difficulties for – and with – France.

As a counterbalance to the provisions regarding implementation, such treaties usually contain provisions regarding expiry and notification of renunciation of membership. For the ECSC the treaty was due to expire after 50 years in the year 2002, whilst no provision for winding up was made regarding the EEC. In this sense, a new and everlasting entity was born into the international Community on New Year's Day 1958. On the other hand, a member state can no doubt dissociate itself from the group once its membership no longer has any real meaning.

With the exception of the provisions concerning the customs union, the provisions of the Treaty of Rome primarily had the character of declarations of intent. It was therefore difficult for outsiders to form a reasonably clear picture of what the creation of the Community would mean in the long-term, and therefore also difficult to know how to relate to this innovation in European politics.

8. The Community's wider aims

In the first lines of its preamble,[9] the EEC Treaty opens with the declaration that the member states are determined to lay the foundations of an ever-closer union among the peoples of Europe. No attempt is therefore made to hide the intention of member states to develop something more than just a broad economic arrangement. However, regarding the development of the Community, the content of the treaty does not cover a period of more than 12-15 years set as the transition period.

This preamble, as mentioned at the beginning of the chapter, paves the way for two principally different interpretations of the aims of the treaty and the Community.[10] A *wide interpretation* is that member states have not only entered into a well defined economic cooperation, but

9. The technical term for the solemn foreword that normally accompanies large-scale treaties. It includes a basic declaration of intent with an explanation of why the states have agreed to abide by the provisions of the following treaty.
10. An analysis and comparison of the two perspectives can be found in H.von der Groeben 1987, p. 26.

have decided to join what is called the "the dynamics of the Community" (c.f. the declaration of 'an ever closer union'). This conjures up the image of Columbus' voyage across the Atlantic where time alone would show what would happen and whether, as it turned out in his case, the journey on the whole would be successful. The *narrow* interpretation is less imaginative, revolving around what could most suitably be described as the establishment of a "customs union with dressing", where the dressing comprises the free movement of labour, capital and services, the right of establishment and a common agricultural policy.

Having outlined the main differences between these two perspectives of the aims of the treaty, it becomes clear that the perspectives indicate something essential about the differences in the attitude in Western European countries towards the treaty and cooperation within the Community.

The original member states as a whole, and for most of the time in principle, have spoken in favour of the internal dynamics, i.e. a development of the Community after the deadline for the transition period specified in the Treaty of Rome had been reached. An exception to this interpretation was evident in France during the premiership of de Gaulle from 1958 to 1969, when France took the position that the provisions of the Treaty of Rome would indeed be implemented, but that no further development was necessary. The development of increased cooperation, specifically a political form of cooperation, should not become an issue for the Community and its institutions in Brussels. As will be described in more detail later, this view was virtually reflected in the policy pursued by the Community during the period 1973-85.

In 1973, three new countries joined the Community, of which Britain and Denmark took the clear position that they preferred "a customs union with dressing" – a form of cooperation of a well-defined economic content, equivalent to what they had agreed and signed up to in 1972. Ireland's policy on this issue was less clear. Like the countries of Southern European who later joined the Community, Ireland had benefited from considerable development funding in connection with the intensification of cooperation and, as is generally recognised, the study of motives is a difficult field.

Of the Community's four primary institutions, it has been through the Council that the governments of the member states seek to exert their influence on the development. The Council's attitude to the degree of dynamics came to reflect the predominant views of the member states. The Court of Justice was, in principle, apolitical and its task was to exercise legal judgement in matters affecting the Community. In reality, it must be said to have supported the dynamics through rulings that reflected the view that the Community's rules of law should be given priority over those of the member states in the event of any conflict between the two sets of laws.

Supporters of a dynamic development, where the Community constantly assumed greater powers, are to be found first and foremost and at all times in the Commission and the Assembly (the European Parliament). According to the Treaty of Rome, the Commission not only has the duty of taking initiatives, but also the power of initiative regarding issues where it deems it necessary. This implies that a Chairman of the Commission with support from members of the Commission will be able to raise particular issues for debate and the adoption of policy. Such was the case during the first chairmanship of the Commission of Walther Hallstein (1901-82) and again from 1985 under the former French finance minister, Jacques Delors (1925-). The European Parliament in practice has been composed of members who have primarily been recruited amongst politicians with a positive attitude towards increased integration. In this respect, the Danish representatives have been an exception. On the other hand, the Parliament's powers are so limited and of such a negative character that initiatives originating from this body can only be expected to receive attention if they find support in national politics. This was the situation in 1984 when the initiatives that led to the agreement on the Single European Act were taken.

When attempting to determine the driving forces behind the integration process, it should be remembered that behind the organs mentioned is a large body of civil servants who, through a long process of recruitment, over the years have developed a personal attachment to the Community. Experience has shown that in these circles an understandable spirit has grown up where the prosperity of the Community is afforded its own unique importance. Therefore, in any study of the forces exerting an influence on the direction of the Community, this factor cannot be ignored.

Chapter 17

The first fifteen years
1958-73

If the history of the European Communities[1] from 1958 to 1993 were to be split up into stages, the fifteen years described in this chapter would come out as the most dynamic as far as concrete, accomplished results are concerned. This was especially so during the first twelve years covering the transitional period of the EEC. This period corresponds with the years when growth rates peaked, and both for growth rates and the speed of the process of integration, 1973 can be said to mark a dividing line. As for the process of integration, ten lean years followed. It was not until 1984 that the process speeded up again, this time as a reaction to growing unemployment, inflation, and low growth rates, implying a weakening of the relative position of the EC compared to the USA and the Far East.

The dynamism of the fifteen years from 1958 to 1973 was based on the economic aspects of integration, while political integration took place outside the institutions of the Community. That was because France during the period of de Gaulle's presidency took the stance that political cooperation in a wider sense – foreign policy, security issues, and cultural policy – should take place directly between governments and be kept away from the institutions in Brussels, Luxembourg and Strasbourg.

---

1. In 1965, it was decided to merge the institutions of the ECSC, the EEC and EURA-TOM. At the same time, the system had its name changed to the European Communities, EC. It was not until the signing of the Maastricht treaty that the term "the European Union" was formally introduced. In this chapter, the term "EC" will be used, even when only the EEC is being spoken of.

1. The beginning

In view of the size of the task, the Community had an easy and positive beginning. While some of the explanation for this can be found in the favourable economic climate, a good deal is related, however, to the fact that the key persons, politicians and civil servants of the governments and the Communities, knew one another beforehand and thus were aware in advance of the attitudes of their colleagues towards the pressing problems that were being dealt with.

A high-ranking civil servant from the West German Ministry of Foreign Affairs, Professor Walter Hallstein, was elected the first chairman of the Commission.[2] He had participated in the process from the creation of the European Coal and Steel Community (ECSC) and throughout the 1950s, he had worked closely with the German chancellor, Konrad Adenauer. He was known for his positive and active approach towards European integration. By selecting Hallstein, the Council indicated that it would accept an active approach by the first Commission. It should be noted that this took place before the return of de Gaulle to French and European politics, and that de Gaulle later managed to have Hallstein removed from the Commission. The nine members of the Commission were recruited from among politicians and civil servants. Of the first, mention must made of the former Dutch minister of Agriculture, Sicco Mansholt, who was appointed commissioner for agriculture; and of the latter, the Frenchman Robert Marjolin, a former secretary general of the OEEC. Along with those, there then followed a number of civil servants recruited from the same circles.

According to the Treaty of Rome, it was the responsibility of the Commission to put forward proposals that would form the basis for the decisions of the Council. The speed, therefore, with which the Community got underway rested heavily on the Commission. Hans von der Groeben, the other German member of the first Commission besides Hallstein, wrote as follows about his impressions of his fellow members:[3]

---

2. His name is related to "the Hallstein doctrine", according to which Germany ought to break off diplomatic relations with countries officially recognizing East Germany, DDR, as an independent state. As will be understood, the significance of Hallstein's position in international politics stretched beyond the matters of the Community.
3. H. von der Groeben (1987, 31).

"All members were convinced of the political importance of their task. They did not look upon the Commission as a technical subsidiary body or as a General Secretariat. The Commission was determined to push ahead with the process of integration, not only in the economic field, but also from the institutional and political aspects, and to this end make use of all weapons and methods provided by the Treaty and to employ all the opportunities for further development."

Just as the final negotiations concerning the Treaty of Rome had been speeded up by foreign policy matters in October and November of 1956, the same thing happened again at the start of the Community. The treaty was to enter into force on 1st January 1958, after ratification. Only a couple of months before, the USSR had launched the first satellite, the Sputnik, into orbit around the globe. It was thus made clear that the Soviet Union had at its disposal intercontinental rockets capable of reaching the great cities of the USA, which led to a revaluation of American strategy for the defence of Europe and of its own territory. The existing strategy had so far been based on what was called "massive response", according to which an attack by the Soviet Union on Western Europe based on the use of conventional arms would be met with the extensive use of nuclear weapons. As part of the strategy, this had to be made clear to the USSR beforehand.

Consequently, the situation altered after October 1957. As the threat of atomic warfare reached American cities, the background to the strategy changed. Was it realistic to expect that the USA would risk its great cities and millions of lives in order to defend Western Europe? Now it was no longer a question of massive nuclear retaliation, but rather of retaining the possibility of answering an attack through conventional means. It was hoped that the use of the "heavy stuff" could be avoided, by presenting a realistic defence based on conventional weapons. This in turn proved to be of great importance for the development of European politics, including the development of the Community.

An increased dependence on conventional weapons – so called flexible response – would increase the burden and costs of the defence of Western Europe. In so far as integration stimulated the economy of Western European countries, it would increase their possibilities of carrying the costs of defence themselves. Seen from the other side of the North Atlantic, this would add to the willingness of the USA to accept economic discrimination through European customs unions and free trade areas. Whereas the USA, possibly assisted by Great Britain, might have tried to delay the realization of the Community through the GATT and OEEC, their interests actually went in the opposite direction. This line was further strengthened after the inauguration of John F. Kennedy as American president in 1961.

Another aspect of this development has been touched upon previously, dealing with the problems of the French economy and foreign policy. On 1st June 1958, de Gaulle returned as French prime minister, and was soon to become president. He had no confidence in the will of the USA to defend Western Europe, nor did he have any faith in the will and capacity of Great Britain to do so either. Since Germany for many reasons was prevented from having nuclear weapons, it was France – and only France – which was able to offer Western Europe the necessary security. However, this meant that France had to spend the resources necessary to obtain the position of a nuclear power, in addition to which, in the late 1950s, France had to finish off a costly war in North Africa. The conclusion was that France would take a positive stance towards the realization of the economic aspects of European integration as stated in the Treaty of Rome, and strive to obtain the maximum possible amount of benefits from it, including trade in agricultural products. In order to retain French influence, not to say dominance, Great Britain should be kept at a distance, closer political integration was not to take place within the framework of the Community or other supranational bodies; and cooperation was to be kept at the inter-governmental level. The consequences of the latest developments within foreign policy were, therefore, increased French goodwill towards the economic aspects of the Community along with increased scepticism towards the development of its political aspects.

2. Bridge building or sabotage?

As a result of the rapid conclusion of negotiations concerning the EEC and Euratom, Western Europe faced a situation in early 1957 characterized by a split between the six members of the Community and the remaining Western European countries. In the case of the more economically advanced countries, the division can be said to have been between the Six and the "Six non-Six", comprising Austria, Denmark, Great Britain, Norway, Sweden, and Switzerland.[4] In this fashion, the starting shot had been fired for hectic activity in an attempt to avoid new types of discrimination among the countries of Western Europe. From the beginning, four out of the six common market countries, the Benelux plus West Germany, were anxious about their prospects. The influential, liberal minister of economy, also considered the architect of the West German economic miracle, Ludwig Erhard (1897-1977), looked with scepticism upon the protectionist tendencies in the Community's policy because his liberal beliefs made him favour an open Community. Similar ideas were found in the Benelux-countries with their tradition of close relations with Great Britain (especially in the case of the Netherlands). In direct opposition to this, the greatest resistance to a broad European trade arrangement was found in France – and this was so even before the return of de Gaulle in spring 1958.

In autumn 1957, the British government took the initiative within the OEEC to establish a committee to investigate the possibilities of forming a European free trade area, and Reginald Maudling, a member of the British government, was elected as its chairman. It was clear that the situation was urgent because the members of the EEC had to start cutting their internal customs duties on 1st January 1959. If discrimination was to be avoided among the countries of Western Europe, there was only about one year in which to accomplish this. It can be said of the work in the so-called Maudling committee that there was a high level of activity but little movement. There are good reasons for taking a closer look at the background to this, since it was to leave its stamp on European integration for more than a decade.

The British suggestion was to create a free trade area with the customs union of the EEC countries as one of its participants.[5] This free trade area was, on the whole, to exclude agricultural products, which, as a product category, would be kept outside the abolition of the internal customs duties. Furthermore, Britain wanted to continue its preferential arrangements with the Commonwealth countries, dating back to the Ottawa Agreement of 1932. As part of this, Britain wished to

4. Finland was not included in the group. Due to her delicate position between East and West, she was excluded from participating in a full-scale cooperation with Western European countries.
5. While it is possible for a country to be a member of a customs union and a free trade area at the same time, or of two free trade areas at a time, it is impossible to be member of two customs union at one time – applying two different customs tariffs.

maintain its access to agricultural products at world market prices. Finally, she was in favour of liberal "rules of origin" within the free trade area, opening up for possibilities of exporting goods produced on the basis of cheap raw materials imported from third countries to other members of the free trade area. The description given here can be criticized for its lack of detail, but as a brief account it seems fair enough. Anyone participating in such negotiations was there to take care of national interests, and while the British proposals went a long way in this respect they showed little understanding for the problems of others.

From the beginning of 1958 onwards, the Commission was made a member of the Committee, represented by its chairman Walter Hallstein. To the Commission, the British proposal must have been seen as such a watering down of its coming customs union, that it could be seen as an attempt to sabotage the entire idea of the Community. From the point of view of the Commission, it was exactly the creation of a customs union that would give the Community an identity of its own at this stage. To bring the Community into a free trade area at this early point in time would amount to killing it in the cradle; or, as it was expressed at the time: the Community ran the risk of being dissolved like a lump of sugar in a cup of tea!

France was opposed from the very start because from the French point of view it all looked very British. Great Britain was trying to get the best out of membership of two free trade areas: a special overseas system and a European system, where both were tailored to suit British interests. British industrial products would have access to markets in Western Europe, while agricultural products from Western Europe were denied similar access to the British market. According to the French, Britain sought to have the best of both worlds without paying for either.

Germany, the Benelux countries (primarily the Netherlands) and the Scandinavian countries were not as sceptical about the plan. General sympathy was felt for plans involving steps toward tariff cuts, although Denmark had similar misgivings to the French regarding the exclusion of agricultural products from the free trade arrangements. On this point, the Netherlands was in a better position as a result of its participation in the coming common agricultural policy of the EC, the CAP.

It is a widely held opinion that the distance between the French and the British positions was so great that there was no real chance of finding a positive solution. However, the weak French governments during those months in 1957-58 did not have the necessary strength to make a decision to conclude the meetings and get it over with. In June 1958, de Gaulle was back as prime minister and in the autumn a new constitution was agreed upon, aiming at a high degree of presidential government. Finally in November, as described earlier (chapter 15, section 3), during a meeting of the Maudling committee – though outside the meeting room itself – de Gaulle let his Minister of Information announce to the press in a way that humiliated the negotiators, that the proceedings were at an end.

Consequently, the proposal was taken off the table. Now, more than forty years later, it seems clear that European integration at the time was at a crossroads. If the British approach had been followed, it seems likely that things would have developed in the way predicted by Hallstein and the Community would have been watered down from the outset. As it turned out, the position of de Gaulle and France meant support for the development in the long run of a federal type of integration represented by the Commission and its federalists, and in direct opposition to the wishes of France at the time. At the hour of destiny, France had a decisive influence upon the nature of European integration.

On 1st January 1959 the first tariff cuts were implemented among the Six, though adjustments to the external common tariff were not to take place until the beginning of the second transitional stage, three years later according to the plan. The first internal tariff cuts corresponded to a tenth of the existing tariffs. To reduce discrimination at a critical point in time, the Council decided that the internal reductions should apply to non-member countries as well whenever the duties of the Common Tariff were lower than existing national tariffs. The argument behind this was that those customs duties had to be reduced regardless. In this way the Community showed goodwill and reduced fears beyond its borders at a vital time.

3. European Free Trade Association, EFTA
– an emergency solution

Already during the negotiations of the Maudling committee concerning a "greater" European free trade area, special contacts had been established between the "Six non-Six", i.e. Great Britain, the three Scandinavian countries, plus Austria and Switzerland. After the collapse of the negotiations, it was natural for these countries to investigate the possibilities of realizing among themselves what was impossible to bring about on a larger scale. The result of this was the establishment of the European Free Trade Association, EFTA.

EFTA in many respects was a strange construction. Geographically speaking, the countries were spread out over Western Europe, with Great Britain and the Scandinavian countries forming a core area, to which were added Austria and Switzerland to the South and, as a seventh, Portugal to the West. Considered as an economic entity, each of the seven countries, apart from Portugal, had closer ties to the Common Market as a whole than to any of the EFTA countries. From a political point of view, it was a mixed assembly. Great Britain, Denmark, Norway and Portugal were members of NATO. Portugal was ruled by one of the worlds oldest existing dictatorships under President Salazar. Austria, Sweden, and Switzerland were neutral, though for distinctly different historical reasons. As for the size of the respective populations and their respective economies, there were extreme discrepancies. Out of a total population of 89 million, 53 million lived in Great Britain, including Northern Ireland, and 36 million resided in the remaining six countries. By comparison, the population of the EC numbered 167 millions, distributed more evenly between the member countries.

These facts are put forward to underline that EFTA, from a British point of view, was an unsatisfactory solution from the very beginning. Both from a political and from an economic point of view, Britain's interest in this grouping was of a marginal nature compared to her interests in the real Six. However, at that time, the establishment of EFTA was seen by many as a well-nigh perfect solution to a problem that could not be solved. It is also worth noting that Sweden, after the birth of the EFTA, was likely to accept the paternity, although acknowledging that without British consent there would have been no reason to start negotiations. However, it was in fact the case that Sweden early in 1959 took the initiative by making enquiries of her future EFTA partners and called a meeting in June at Saltsjoebaden outside Stockholm. An arrangement like EFTA offered Sweden, as a neutral country, the conclusive advantage that it contained no declarations of any kind concerning foreign policy. For Sweden, as for Austria and Switzerland, it had been a constant obstacle that this was the case with the EC. However, it was a different situation altogether for Great Britain, Denmark and Norway who were members of NATO. So, while a solution within the framework of EFTA had the character of an emergency solution for the latter countries, it was an almost perfect answer for Sweden. If the seven member countries and midwives of the EFTA were to be ranked according to their degree of satisfaction, the Swedish Ministry of foreign Affairs, the UD, would undoubtedly easily come in first.

In all essentials, the EFTA treaty was negotiated within a couple of weeks in June 1959, the result being a smaller edition of the free trade area negotiated the year before in Paris. Agriculture and fisheries were kept outside the agreement, so its outcome was confined to industrial products. Denmark obtained a special concession from Britain securing zero duty on bacon as opposed to the previous level of 10 per cent, and in addition there were some symbolic arrangements with Sweden and Switzerland.

In spite of the presence of three neutral countries, Finland was not allowed by the USSR to join as a full-scale member, which illustrates the sensitive nature of East-West relations prevailing at the time. However, a solution was found through an agreement of association, which resulted in what was called the *Fin-EFTA*. In reality, this meant that the "Seven" from then on became the "Eight".

While the EC as outlined in the Treaty of Rome, as mentioned earlier, could be characterized as *a customs union with dressing*, and opening up for a deepening of the integration, the EFTA must be characterized as *a free trade area without dressing*. This means that there were no provisions concerning the free movement of capital, labour, etc. and no hints concerning a "next step". In terms though of the establishment of the free trade area itself, the treaty followed the provisions of the Treaty of Rome concerning the establishment of the customs union.

Considering what it was meant to be, a free trade area for industrial goods and created as an emergency solution, EFTA was a success. To the six, or rather seven, small EFTA countries, their participation stimulated foreign trade and participation in the international division of labour. The treaty came into force on 1st July 1960 and existed with all of its original members until 1973 when Britain and Denmark joined the EC. These thirteen years will always stand out in economic history as a period of exceptional growth and dynamism. Having made such a contribution, and as an emergency solution, it did not do badly at all.

4. Early successes and failures

To judge from the speed with which the customs union of the Six was realized, the Community was a success from the outset. According to the original plan, internal customs duties were to have been abolished at the beginning of 1970, but this had already been accomplished by July 1968, eighteen months ahead of schedule. However, the treaty had other provisions and there problems were indeed abundant.

The provisions for the creation of a "common market" were aimed at what have been called *the four freedoms*: the free mobility of goods, persons, capital and services, supplemented by the free right of establishment. With a view to realizing these goals, the transitional period saw the issue of a steady flow of regulations and directives. A field where substantial results were attained was the liberalization of the capital market, but this was also part of a global movement and not a specifically EC phenomenon. Apart from bringing down internal customs duties, overall results in realizing the four freedoms were poor.

Even the free movement of goods encountered difficulties. However, the treaty had foreseen the rise of such problems and for this reason contained provisions prescribing the reduction of government subsidies, the harmonization of taxes and all sorts of levies, the harmonization of legislation etc., all with a view to securing the creation of a well-functioning internal market. Nevertheless, the member states met great difficulties in practice in living up to the prescribed aims. If checks at internal borders were to be abolished, those barriers had to be done away with. There was, however, still much to check and control. Despite the good intentions of the treaty itself, the term *neo-mercantilism* was used to describe the tendency to allow new types of protectionist measures to replace earlier forms of customs protection. Furthermore, the energy crisis in 1973-74 and the ensuing slowdown of the economies aggravated the problems.

The Community, around about New Year 1961-62, because of French initiatives, had already faced a confrontation intended to block federalist tendencies in the cooperation. In accordance with her economic interests, France was prepared to accept the achievement of the economic provisions of the Treaty of Rome, but, as a matter of principle, preferred cooperation to develop as traditional inter-governmental cooperation and extend the efforts to include foreign policy and security issues. With this in view, after the election of de Gaulle as president for his first seven-year term, France in 1961 took the initiative to organize meetings between the heads of state (i.e. de Gaulle) and heads of government (i.e. the PMs) of the Common Market countries.[6] A committee was established to suggest how closer political cooperation could be established. The French ambassador to Denmark, Christian Fouchet, who was supposed to be able to spare the necessary time, was appointed chairman. A report was presented in the autumn of the same year containing four institutional innovations, all kept at governmental level and beyond the reach of Community institutions. The proposals included the establishment of:

a. a council, consisting of the heads of governments and ministers of foreign affairs, note that the chairman of the EC Commission was not to be included

b. a secretariat based in Paris consisting of civil servants from the participating countries; once again, Brussels and Luxembourg were kept at a distance,

c. four standing committees to deal with matters concerning foreign affairs, defence, trade and cultural policies respectively,

d. a European Assembly, appointed by the parliaments of the individual member countries.

Had a proposal along these lines been accepted and implemented, it is hard to see how there would have been any space left for the young and efficient institutions in Brussels. In reality, all the common market countries, apart from France, seem to have been opposed to the developments outlined above. They still wanted their security interests to be taken care of through NATO. Four of the countries, the Benelux and Italy, may have feared Franco-German dominance in such a set-up,

6.   Seen in relation to what was put on paper some twenty years later (in the Single European Act, 1984), we find here the ingredients for what was to become the European Council.

without independent, supranational institutions like the Commission and the Court of the Community to counterbalance the two.

The result was that the work of the Fouchet committee came to a halt in 1962. Interest was now directed towards the negotiations to accept Britain as a member. There was a widespread feeling that they ought to reach a conclusion before such far-reaching matters could be decided upon. Those negotiations ended on 14th January 1963, as the result of a French veto. On the 22nd there was another demonstration of French strength as a Franco-German agreement of cooperation was signed by de Gaulle and Chancellor Adenauer, dealing exactly with the four points mentioned in the Fouchet plan. It was this agreement that came to form the basis for the *Paris-Bonn axis* (or Bonn-Paris axis, if viewed from Germany). After these preparatory manoeuvres, it was not until 1974 that regular, scheduled meetings between the heads of states and governments commenced, and not until 1987, with the entry into force of the Single European Act, that those meetings were instituted through a treaty.

5. The Common Agricultural Policy, CAP

5.1. The principles

From the very beginning of negotiations concerning the coming Community, it was made clear that agriculture should be included in a co-ordinated manner with other sectors of the economy. It was, however, equally clear that it might be difficult to bring this about. Two strong arguments spoke in favour of including agriculture, in spite of the expected difficulties: Firstly, the prices of agricultural products are a vital cost factor for the rest of the economy. To prevent differences in the conditions of competition, a common price level should be sought. Secondly, three of the member states, namely France, Italy and the Netherlands, had a substantial export of agricultural goods, including garden produce, fruit, wine etc. If the opening-up of trade were to take place in a balanced manner, these goods had to be included.

It was likewise recognised beforehand that it would be complicated to find solutions. Each member state had its own agricultural policy, with substantial regulation of the sector. This was done according to different principles, and at different price levels. One common characteristic, however, was that all schemes included some sort of subsidy.

For that reason the establishment of a common policy would most likely result in substantial changes in the advantages and disadvantages for the member states, and of groups within the states. An inherent danger would be that the sum of the national producer interests would lead to a solution with a high level of subsidy, a sort of lowest common denominator. A special problem was caused by the great differences in the conditions under which identical products were produced. Efficient farms in the Netherlands, Northern France and Northern Germany were to compete with small farms situated in the mountains of Southern Germany and in Alpine France. If the support had to be offered through prices, then prices and costs might be high.

According to the Treaty of Rome, the Commission was obliged within a period of two years to present proposals for a Common Agricultural Policy, CAP. With a view to this, a conference was held in July 1958 in Stresa in Northern Italy. The result was the approval of some guidelines, which the Commission was to follow in its further work. Among those goals were the free movement of agricultural produce across borders and the survival of family farms. It was up to the Commission to transform the recommendations of the conference into concrete proposals. The Commissioner for agriculture was the former Dutch Minister of Agriculture, Sicco Mansholt (1908-95). In his case, his personal background and experience was from a country with an efficient, export-oriented agriculture. To understand the problems Mansholt had to face, it should be remembered that these were of a different nature to those faced, for instance, in relation to the creation of the customs union. There, the obligations under the treaty were mainly of what might be called a negative nature with the ultimate goal of abolishing internal customs duties. Within agricultural policy, however, the problem was that widely different systems of subsidy had to be coordinated and fused together into a common system. Within the area of manufacturing industry, different Non-Tariff Barriers, NTBs, were practised, along with semi-secret systems of subsidy, of which shipyards were a good example. Those problems however were not put on the agenda until the middle of the 1980s at the time of the Single European Act. In agriculture, on the other hand, these problems had to be dealt with at this early stage.

As a starting point it was decided that the coming CAP should function *via the price system*, not through quantitative regulations such as product rationing, etc. This did not mean, however, that it could be concluded that prices would be the outcome of market mechanisms as the interaction of supply and demand.

One possibility was an arrangement where consumer prices were lower than producer prices, which would correspond to the British deficiency payment system. Under this system, there would be no need for support buying. There was, however, a risk of incurring great expenses involved in the financing of the difference between producer prices and lower consumer prices. Countries and economic units, like Britain, which needed to import agricultural produce, would normally implement arrangements of this sort. France was opposed to the idea, arguing that agriculture wanted "fair pricing, not subsidies". Another possibility was to let producer prices and consumer prices be identical, but at a level granting farmers a "reasonable standard of living" as prescribed by the Treaty of Rome; this price level was expected to be above world market prices. As long as the Community was a net-importer of agricultural goods, imports could supply the budget of the Community with income through duties and levies. In case output exceeded internal demand, the Community would have to provide assistance in buying up surplus production. For the consumers, this arrangement would most likely mean food prices above world market levels, all depending on the prices to be set for the farmers. Furthermore, in the case of production within the Community being at a level above demand, this would mean further expenses for taxpayers in order to cover the net expenses of the CAP.

Apart from the principle that the system should be "market oriented", as explained above, three wishes or demands were formulated:

a. a common or internal market for agricultural products should be established,

b. goods produced within the Community should take advantage of a community preference,

c. the entire system should be built on the principle of financial solidarity.

Point a. corresponds to the idea that agricultural produce, just like goods from manufacturing industry, should be allowed to pass from one member state to another without the payment of duties and similar levies. From this would follow a common price level for food; an important aspect of the system.

Point b. aimed at ensuring that prices within the Community would be above world market prices as the common tariff did for industrial products. Within agriculture, however, the problems were more complicated. A final solution had to await the working out of the system, including the variable levies, which were to come. Those levies corresponded in principle to the levies under the old British sliding scale of the 1830s and 40s. According to the system, a minimum import price is fixed, a threshold price, and if foreign goods are offered for sale below this price, a variable levy corresponding to the difference up to the threshold price then has to be paid.

Behind the fixing of the threshold price, lies the intended producer price. The administrative function of the threshold price is to form the basis for calculations of import levies, to prevent imported goods being sold below the prices of goods produced within the Community. A separate question is how high those (guaranteed) prices should be? If they were fixed at a high level, the Community would be faced with an obligation to buy a surplus production at the guaranteed prices.

Point c. prescribes financial solidarity because there would be both net-gainers and net-losers among the member states as the result of the CAP. Such differences and imbalances were not to be used beforehand as decisive arguments against the suggested arrangements. The entire question of advantages and disadvantages following from participation in the Community is so large that it cannot be considered as a question involving isolated sections of the overall cooperation. The principle of financial solidarity could therefore be taken as a mutual promise not to take costs too seriously when the CAP was given a concrete shape. For northern producers, the major interests were in grain and related products, while those of the south also included wine, citrus fruits, and vegetables.

5.2. The enactment

Based on the principles described in the preceding section, the Commission presented its proposals for concrete regulations, etc. in summer 1961. It is outside the scope of this exposition to give a detailed description of the proposals: suffice it to say that within the field of vegetable production there are ample possibilities of adjusting production by switching between different crops. Under a system of central price fixing – and this was what was about to come into effect – the prices would be set so that an appropriate price structure was created. This was not only to be the case for cereal and vegetable products. In order to secure a balanced composition of the outputs, the relationship between the prices of vegetable and animal products was also to be balanced. Here, the start began through a proposed scheme for grain and so-called "grain products", with pork (bacon, ham, etc.) and poultry (chickens and eggs) as leading animal examples.[7]

As far as the price of grain was concerned, the two largest producer countries of the Community, Germany and France, had enjoyed a high price level since the late 1800s, due to protectionist policies. During negotiations, it turned out that the German government was under strong pressure from their farmers' organization (the Bauernverband), which also represented the less efficient farms in Southern Germany. It is a mistake to believe that it was mainly France at this stage that advocated high prices because, as a potential exporter of agricultural goods to countries outside the Common Market, France had some worries in accepting the high German prices.

By the end of 1961, the first four-year stage of the transitional period came to an end, which meant that a number of problems had accumulated and were awaiting solution. In the next four-year period unanimity would still be required when decisions were taken on the future rules of the Community. However, France had already at this stage decided to opt for a large package deal and, by the end of 1961, the Council of the EC had still not reached a solution. To keep the door open for a solution and not merely prolong this first stage, "the clocks were stopped". After a prolonged New Years Eve, a compromise was reached and the clocks were re-started on 14th January 1962. The Community was then ready to celebrate the New Year by accepting a regulation introducing the beginning of the CAP. After the next four-year period it would turn out that it was possible to heighten the drama even more, as explained below in relation to the Luxembourg-compromise.

With the decisions of January 1962, the guidelines for the CAP had, on the whole, been agreed upon. During the process, a change in the

---

7.   The cost of producing one kilogram of pork or chicken is closely related to the price of grain. A similar relation is not found in beef production, etc. For this reason, the first proposals did not cover cattle, beef, butter and other products based on livestock.

positions of the parties had taken place. Long-term goals in favour of structural changes represented by Mansholt and the Commission had given way to short-term interests represented by the ministers of agriculture and representatives of the farmers. Although by far the majority of agricultural goods produced in the northern areas of the Community were covered by the decisions, many goods were not, in particular produce from the Mediterranean areas. So, when some authors state that an agricultural policy was not agreed upon until 1968, this is partly correct. It seems more correct, however, to state that the Community never had a coherent agricultural policy, but rather a row of costly "here and now" solutions that came to form the CAP.

6. The Luxembourg Compromise

6.1. The subject-matter of the crisis

If the transition in 1961-62 from the first to the second stage of the transitional period had caused problems, the transition to the third stage, 1965-66, threatened the very existence of the Community as outlined in the Treaty of Rome. Three main issues were on the agenda at the same time:

a. the increased use of majority decisions after the transfer to the third stage,

b. the future of the financial system of the Community, including the financing of the CAP, one aspect of which was whether the Community should be granted "income of its own",

c. the Assembly, now preferring to be called The European Parliament, was exerting pressure to strengthen its competence.

The first point, the use of the majority vote, was in itself a decisive step towards a federal type of integration. Even the major member countries of the Community might then be overruled. This was a price which Germany was prepared to pay, but which the France of de Gaulle was not, especially since France was opposed to the changes under the two next points, namely giving the Community its own financial sources and to assigning more power to the Assembly.

The question of financing the Community had to be solved if the CAP was to be carried out and extended into the future. This confronted France with a dilemma. While France took advantage of the – costly – agricultural policy as it had developed, there was French scepticism at the same time about offering the Commission more financial power by giving the Community automatic incomes which were not to be decided upon annually by the Council.

Closely related to this was the third point, the desire of the European Parliament for increased power. According to the Treaty of Rome, the competence of the Assembly was strictly limited and it was, in reality, simply an advisory body, reminiscent of an Assembly of the Estates General in the first half of the 1800s. The Treaty of Rome, however, had an article that opened up the possibility of direct elections of the members of the Assembly. If this were to serve any purpose, then the Assembly would have to be given more influence. This, however, was a frightening prospect – to have a Commission and a Parliament with their own, automatic incomes and a Parliament with increased influence on the legislation of the Community, all at the expense of the Council and the governments of the member countries.

In spring 1965, the Commission had prepared a package aiming at simultaneous solutions to all three sets of problems. According to the package, a temporary decision that the revenue from customs duties and variable import levies were to form the income of the Community was to become permanent. The Assembly should, like the Commission, have a greater say in budgetary matters, and, finally, the existing temporary agricultural policy should be made permanent as the Common Agricultural Policy of the Community.

The package proposals were leaked to members of the Assembly before it was officially presented to the Council, causing the chairman of the Commission, Walter Hallstein, to give the Assembly an outline draft since talks concerning the package already had started. The French saw this as an attempt by Hallstein to go behind the Council's back as well as the national governments. The overall position of France was that she was opposed to the package's federal ingredients and in favour of those involving an extended economic cooperation, including the CAP.

The existing, temporary arrangement for the financing of the CAP expired on 1st July 1965. At a meeting of the Council on 29-30 June,

France suggested that the temporary financial arrangement should be prolonged until the end of the transitional period in December 1969. This meant that the entire case could be taken up again at that time. The suggestion found no support among the rest of the members of the Council, whereupon the French representative, the minister of foreign affairs, Couve de Murville, declared that the negotiations had suffered a breakdown. This turned out to be the beginning of "the policy of the empty chair". France withdrew from the Council, abstained from sending representatives to the meetings of the Council, which might be considered a breach to her obligations under the Treaty of Rome, and called its permanent representative in Brussels back to Paris. All was done with a view to opposing a federalist development of the Community and to soften up its five co-members.

6.2. The solution to the crisis

The absence of France from the supreme body of the Community lasted for seven months, a period that stands out as being very critical in its history. The termination of the crisis is not free from reminders of the meeting in 1807 between the Russian Czar and Napoleon. Since an agreement could not be reached as to where to meet, the two notables met on a raft on the river Nyemen. Something similar was now arranged with de Gaulle as the organizer. France would not come to Brussels, would not see representatives of the Commission and would not even appear at a meeting of the Council. Finally France gave way and a meeting was held in Luxembourg in January 1966 without the participation of the Commission.

The reason why France agreed to participate in a meeting of the Council was to be found in domestic problems at this time. At the close of 1965, de Gaulle's first term as president expired and a presidential election was to take place in November – during the period of "the empty chair". A keen candidate for the presidency, Francois Mitterrand (1916-96) had decided to run for office. Seven years earlier, de Gaulle had won the necessary majority on the first ballot, but this time he had to fight a second round in which he obtained 55 per cent of the vote. Although re-elected, his position from the beginning of his second term was substantially weakened and the opposition strengthened. The trades and industries of France, and especially French agriculture, looked with anxiety at a government gambling for national-political reasons with their economic interests at stake in the decisions to be taken within the Community. France and the policy of de Gaulle had, in fact, been caught up in the functionalist effect of integration, according to which economic integration has a tendency to pave the way for still more integration.

At the end of January 1966, a solution was found according to which a majority of the proposals put forward by the Commission were accepted. The Community was awarded its own regular income, primarily to finance the CAP, the Assembly obtained some limited concessions and, finally, it was decided to proceed to the third stage involving extended use of majority voting; though attached to this was a French reservation, later known as the Luxembourg Compromise.

6.3. *The veto and the Luxembourg Compromise*

The term, the "Luxembourg Compromise", in the language of the Community does not actually refer to the package agreed upon in the meetings in Luxembourg in January 1966, but to the introduction of a special rule of procedure meant to modify the way the rule functioned in majority voting. The resolutions decided upon in the Council included a decision to proceed to the third stage and what followed from this in terms of voting procedures. However, in deciding this, the Council took note of a declaration that meant in reality that matters should not be taken to a vote unless all members of the Council were prepared to abide by the result. This rule was only to apply when *very important interests* of one or more partners were at stake, and to this was attached a declaration according to which France reserved for herself the right to decide what would be considered cases of very important interests. The Luxembourg Compromise, as an exemption from the Treaty, was never tested in court. So far, the member countries in practice have been reluctant to overrule a member in matters of such claimed importance. However, years later when Britain as a member tried to veto a decision concerning the CAP and referred to the Luxembourg Compromise, France declared that the matter was not so important to Britain! France apparently being the most qualified to decide in this matter.[8]

It is interesting to look at the overall impact of the crisis and its solution. The Commission emerged weakened and, at a personal level, de

8.   J. W. Young (1993, 142).

Gaulle forced through the replacement of its active and dynamic chairman, Walter Hallstein. One of the points of criticism, which he faced, was that he – just like heads of state – had introduced the custom of holding formal receptions when new chiefs of mission arrived in Brussels. This was too much like the beginnings of a European presidency and was to be nipped in the bud. Hallstein left the Commission in 1967 when the institutions of the three separate communities (the ECSC, the EEC and the Euratom) were merged through the Merger Treaty. That the Council came out strengthened was felt in terms of increased direct cooperation between the governments of member countries. All in all, it seems fair to conclude that the events in 1965-66 meant a setback for the federalist forces in Europe.

Opinions are divided concerning the economic aspects of the compromise. The acceleration of the internal tariff cuts was upheld and a final decision on the CAP made possible. On the other hand, the establishment of what would later be known as "the internal market" came to a halt. From then on, a less advanced model of the Community was aimed at.

7. The 1969 Hague summit

7.1. *Reduced speed*

With its decisions of January 1966, the Community had secured for itself within a limited area the necessary conditions to allow it to continue its work. Formally, it changed its name with the entry into force of the Merger Treaty to the *European Communities, the EC*. The former Belgian commissioner, Jean Rey (1902-83) was elected as the new chairman of the Commission.

In practice, the work of the Commission now concentrated on the administration of the four freedoms – the free movement of goods, persons, capital and services. The results were modest; reports were written, but no efficient steps were taken to harmonize the taxes and levies of the member countries. Early in 1967, it was decided that the remaining internal customs duties should disappear by July 1968, eighteen months ahead of schedule. In order to secure a balance between industry and agriculture, it was decided that the CAP should formally come into force at the same time, and now extended to include remaining products.

All in all, it seems fair to conclude that decisions on the future development after January 1967 waited for a change of leadership in French politics. This came unexpectedly in May 1969 when de Gaulle made a change in the French constitution the subject of a referendum, which he lost, and in consequence, resigned. His successor was his prime minister, Georges Pompidou. The Gaullists remained in office, though in a milder version.

7.2. *Movement again*

By the end of 1969, the twelve-year transitional period ended. According to the Treaty of Rome, the transitional period should have seen the coming into force of the measures necessary for the realization of the Common Market. This required making a general survey of the status of the Community. To this should be added that the change of French president eventually opened up new possibilities to get the Community moving again.

It was the new French president himself who took the initiative to call a meeting between the heads of states and governments. The meeting took place in December 1969, later known as the Hague meeting. The background to the meeting was a number of unsolved problems, which had accumulated throughout the 1960s:

a. Great Britain, followed by Ireland, Denmark and Norway, had submitted applications for membership of the EC. France had opposed the British application during the de Gaulle years and negotiations had been brought to a standstill,

b. no final decisions had been taken on the question of the future incomes of the Community,

c. there was growing pressure from the Assembly for increased influence.

In addition there was the fact that international monetary affairs were going through a period of growing uncertainty, including instability among the currencies of the members of the Community. Furthermore, a new Social Democratic government in Germany under Willy Brandt (1913-92) had engaged in an open and more positive policy towards the East. The consequence of this being

d. there was felt a need for increased macroeconomic cooperation among the member states, including talk of the eventual creation of an Economic and Monetary Union (EMU)

e. closer cooperation concerning foreign policy and security issues.

On all five points, the decisions reached at The Hague may be characterized as positive, though it only became apparent later that the solutions to points d and e would run into problems. As for a, it was decided to resume negotiations with Britain and her fellow applicants. In the case of b it was decided during 1971-74 to grant the Community its own permanent income from customs duties, import levies and a value-added tax, VAT, constituting up to 1 per cent of a harmonized VAT-basis. In spring 1970, this was confirmed by an agreement that included point c, granting the Assembly increased influence in budgetary matters. In support of point d, it was decided that an Economic and Monetary Union should be established and come into force by 1980. With a view to this, a committee was appointed under the chairmanship of Pierre Werner (1913-), prime minister of Luxembourg. As for point e, a committee was appointed to investigate ways to promote the establishment of closer political cooperation. This committee was chaired by a Belgian civil servant and later member of the Commission, Etienne Davignon (1932-).

The appointment of these committees – later known respectively as the Werner and the Davignon committees – can be seen as the beginning of a period *rich* in initiatives towards a strengthening of the Community, though *poor* in results. It was not until 1983-84, under the influence of a prolonged European economic crisis, that sustainable initiatives were taken such as the Single European Act of 1985-87. The Werner report was presented in late 1970 and must be deemed to be very ambitious. It suggested the establishment of an Economic and Monetary Union, including a European central bank, and specified in precise terms the dates for the accomplishment of the various stages of the plan. In this respect, the Werner plan appeared more ambitious and precise than the Delors plan of the early 1990s.

The Hague meeting stands out as a major event in the history of European integration, partly because decisions were taken on important matters waiting to be solved such as points a – c, and partly because "summit meetings" were used from now on when important matters

Fig. 15: EU summit of heads of states and governments in Paris, October 1972. A declaration was agreed upon concerning the creation of a European Union. Great Britain, Denmark and Ireland were, in their capacity as coming members, invited to the meeting. The first two were later to delay the process of integration.

were at stake. For the Community and the Commission, this might be a doubtful, not to say a dangerous development. Meetings held outside the institutions of the EC reduce the possibilities for the Commission to take initiatives. This was what actually happened during the 1970s, so in that respect the spirit of de Gaulle was still present. A period followed when European integration to an increasing degree contained elements of traditional inter-governmental cooperation.

The follow-up to the Hague meeting is referred to chapter 21, section 1. Here it is sufficient to say that both the Werner and the Davignon Reports were put aside for the time being.

Chapter 18

Enlargement with obstacles

1. Britain alters course

On 1st July 1960, the dismantling of the customs duties between the EFTA countries began. Only eight months later the British government was considering an application for membership of the EC. How could this seemingly swift change in the British position towards European integration be explained when there was no change of government and it was led by the same prime minister, Harold Macmillan (1894-1986)?

Four reasons will be put forward:

a. in January 1961, John F. Kennedy was inaugurated as president of the USA,

b. economic development in Great Britain lagged further and further behind that of the EC,

c. the relative importance of the Commonwealth countries to British exporters was declining,

d. there was the prospect of the Common Agricultural Policy coming into being.

Of all those factors, the new president of the USA, and with him the changes to its security policy, may have had the most direct impact. Shortly after his inauguration in January 1961, John F. Kennedy was asked what the greatest surprise had been for him upon moving into the White House. His answer was that: "The only thing that surprised us when we got into office, was that things were just as bad as we had been saying they were."[1] Part of the background to this comment was an acknowledgement of the fact that American defence capability was such that the USA, in practice, would be unable to answer even limited aggression through the effective use of conventional force. Surveys showed that the USA had only 10 divisions that were operational at short notice and that the transport capacity of the air force was so limited that it would take a month to transfer a division by air to the Far East. The conclusion was that USA was unable to meet an attack that fell below the nuclear threshold. For this reason, the USA urgently needed to release some of its economic and military resources from their involvement in the defence of Europe. To compensate for this, Western Europe would have to strengthen its economy and increase its contribution to the common defence of democracy. One way of doing this was through an enlargement of the EC. As will be seen, the situation in 1960 was reminiscent of the situation ten years earlier when a similar pressure existed and contributed to the creation of the Coal and Steel Community.

The American-European policy sketched above was first presented as the "Grand Design", meaning that it had both an economic and a security dimension. Later, it was presented under the title "Atlantic Partnership", including a plan for Atlantic tariff cuts under the Trade Expansion Act. As part of this plan, the USA was in favour of a strengthening of the EC, but an EC that included Great Britain.

To this motive for a change in the British attitude towards the EC, the three other points mentioned above may be added. The member countries of the Communities had growth rates about double that of Britain. At the beginning of 1961, Britain was once again going through a crisis in her balance of payments, necessitating a slowdown of the economy. If the British economy was to take advantage of the dynamics of the European economy, the EFTA solution was inadequate. The area was simply too small compared to that of the EC. Here was a market of 170 million, compared to the 36 million of the EFTA partners.

Changes in the economic position of Britain were further underlined in 1960-61 by the fact that the British exports to Europe for the first time exceeded exports to Commonwealth countries. This trend

---

1.   T.Sorensen (1965, 294).

caused British industries to take an increasing interest in economic ties with Europe.

Finally, the prospects concerning the CAP should be mentioned. The first plans had by then been outlined and did not look too promising from a British viewpoint. It seemed likely that the outcome would be a rather high price level combined with substantial Community preferences. If Britain was to join the EC regardless, she might just as well do so in time to exert an influence on the CAP.

2. Futile negotiations

In August 1961, the British government, followed by Ireland and Denmark, presented its application for full membership of the Community. An application from Norway followed in 1962.

At the opening of the negotiations, Britain presented three leading intentions:

a. to reach a satisfactory solution concerning her future relations with the Commonwealth countries,

b. to have an influence on the future agricultural policy the CAP,

c. to secure the existing free trade arrangements with her EFTA partners.

The problems in relation to the CAP were not due to British agriculture, but to macroeconomic problems. Britain and British consumers for more than a century had access to food at world market prices. A CAP built on high, guaranteed prices to farmers, and corresponding Community preferences, would mean a substantial increase in Britain's import costs for food. Since Britain was a net-importer of food this would mean a deterioration of her terms of trade at a time when there were more or less constant balance of payments problems. Moreover, the growing cost of food would be very visible to British consumers and cause the general public to oppose British membership of the EC.

From the very beginning it was obvious that Britain was sceptical about the federal aspects of the Community. This had been the case every time European cooperation had been on the agenda. At this point, there was complete agreement with the French position under de Gaulle. The main problems were, as indicated, the future relations with the Commonwealth countries and the agricultural policy. But, additionally, there were some far-reaching problems concerning foreign policy and security issues.

According to the Treaty of Rome, any enlargement of the Community demanded the acceptance of all of its member countries, thus giving each member the power of veto. It was this right that France availed herself of under de Gaulle in January 1963. As the case had been four years earlier, at the time of the Maudling committee, the negotiations were terminated in a manner humiliating to the rest of the participants. Once again, the French announced at a press conference – this time held by the president himself – that the negotiations should be terminated. This was done in a language differing substantially from what was usual among elderly statesmen. One of the reasons mentioned for interrupting the negotiations was that Britain was inhabited by islanders, that its population was "insular", and had its main interests beyond the seas.

Behind the rhetoric and the insults, arguments concerning security policy combined with a wish to maintain French dominance within the Community were to be found. It was an important part of the security policy of de Gaulle that Western Europe should have its own nuclear weapons, as well as the necessary means of delivery. Because of the economic costs, Britain had been forced in autumn 1962 to give up the idea of having its own rockets. At a meeting on the Bahamas between President Kennedy and Prime Minister Harold Macmillan (the "Nassau meeting"), an agreement was reached whereby the USA would place Polaris missiles at the disposal of Great Britain for use on British ships on condition that they should only be launched with the approval of the USA.

It is generally believed that this was the stumbling block, which de Gaulle took as proof of Britain's lack of will to act as a European nation. If Western Europe was to hold a position of world influence between the two super powers, corresponding to the size of its population and its economic power, it ought to have nuclear weapons of its own. But Britain, through its recent agreement with the USA, had made it clear that she was willing to give up final control over her own nuclear weapons. For internal as well as external reasons, Germany was precluded from becoming a nuclear power so responsibility for the security of Western Europe rested with France.

In addition to this, another argument against British membership of the EEC to be borne in mind was the future influence of France on European affairs. Any enlargement of the Community bringing in Britain – most likely with some followers – would reduce French influence, primarily over Germany, and thus reduce the relative strength of France within the Community. For France to have a major impact on developments during the transitional period, it was important to keep Britain at arm's length. The negations concerning the CAP and other matters had been complicated enough in 1961-62, when the clocks in Brussels were stopped. Similar things might happen again, as they actually did, during the period of "the empty chair", during 1965/66. There were no reasons to confuse matters further through the presence of Great Britain during the period of transition.

It has been asked whether Great Britain could have avoided the breakdown in 1963 through a greater degree of compliance? The answer is: "Probably not". This was shown four years later in 1967 when Britain applied again. This happened under a Labour government with Harold Wilson (1916-) as prime minister. While the Labour Party had then been overwhelmingly opposed to the application in 1961, a change had taken place. The background to this once again was the high growth rates of the Community, compared to the problems in the British economy, as well as the prospects concerning the CAP. By far the majority of the Conservatives were now in favour of membership, so the overall attitude of Parliament was far more positive.

In summer 1967, Britain made her new application at a time when the British economy was troubled by increasing difficulties, including growing doubts about the future of sterling. In November 1967, the pound sterling was devaluated by 16.7 per cent. This enabled de Gaulle once again to announce that this was not the right time for Britain to join the Community, so that the British application, along with others, was set aside pending consideration at some later time.

3. Enlargement at last

After the de Gaulle's retirement in April 1969 and the Hague meeting in December, negotiations could begin anew, with this time the Conservative Edward Heath (1916-) as prime minister.[2] Britain's bargaining strength had been further worsened by the fact that the Six had now reached a final agreement on the CAP and the principles for its financing.[3] At the opening of the negotiations, Great Britain had to agree that: "we take the treaty as it stands". According to Community philosophy that now included the regulations, etc., concerning agricultural policy and the financial directives. Another problem, which appeared on the horizon, was the report by the Werner committee. Here, plans had been drafted for a future Economic and Monetary Union, including a European central bank – ideas far from British thoughts concerning European cooperation. It is outside the scope of this exposition to go into details concerning the negotiations and their outcome. A British acceptance in principle of the CAP overcame the main difficulty in relation to France. However, political problems arose at home. Both major parties, Labour and the Conservatives, were divided on the matter. In order to avoid deep and lasting conflicts within each of the two parties it seemed necessary in the opinion of many to give their MPs and parliamentary candidates a "free vote" such as also happened in Norway and Denmark.

After the consent of the Parliament had been obtained, the accession documents were signed in Brussels on 22nd January 1972 at a ceremony where Ireland, Denmark and Norway signed as well. These three countries all announced that the final national decision would rest on a referendum. The Labour party asked the same from Britain, but the Conservatives refused, arguing that this would be contradictory to British traditions of representative democracy. After their referendums, Ireland and Denmark were able to join, but Norway had to pull out of the agreement because her voters decided against membership. So, on 1st January 1973, the Community was enriched by the inclusion of three new members, Great Britain, Ireland and Denmark.

Only thirteen months later, in February 1974, Labour replaced the Conservatives and Harold Wilson was back in office. During the election campaign Labour promised to re-negotiate the conditions of accession and put the result to a referendum, although this was a most

2.   In his previous capacity of Lord Privy Seal, Edward Heath had been the leader of the British negotiating team through 1961-63. Since then, he had enjoyed great respect on the Continent for his efforts to bring Britain into the Community.
3.   The revenue of custom duties and variable levies on agricultural products, plus a VAT of 1 per cent.

exceptional step and against all British tradition. The changes, which the British brought back from the re-negotiations, were minor, but favourable to the government and its endeavour to keep Britain in the Community. The world market prices for food were high during the period, which helped in keeping the costs to Britain of the CAP down. The Werner plan and its strict timetable for the creation of an Economic and Monetary Union broke down, so the plans for a European Central Bank disappeared for a time below the horizon. Negotiations concerning the future relations to the former British colonies had a positive outcome, resulting in the Lomé convention, corresponding to similar arrangements for the former colonies of the original Common Market countries. On 5ht June 1975, the referendum was held and even members of the government had a "free vote". With Harold Wilson and Edward Heath as the leading spokesmen in favour of membership, the share of Yes-votes was as high as 67 per cent.

After this, the British internal conflicts over European integration seemed to be over. However, a few months later, the "European" in British politics, Edward Heath, was replaced as leader of the Conservative Party when Margeret Thatcher (1925–) was elected to replace him. New turmoil waited ahead.

4. The three companions

Great Britain's repeated applications were bound to raise questions in other "non Six"-countries as to their position towards the EC. For some countries, the result under the given circumstances could be predicted in advance. As already explained, Austria, Switzerland, Sweden and Finland for foreign policy reasons were prevented from presenting applications for full membership. What they could hope for was some sort of association containing a free trade arrangement. Spain, Portugal and Greece, because of their backward economies and undemocratic governments, were excluded for the time being. This left Ireland, Denmark and Norway as applicants for full membership.

4.1. Ireland
The Irish application in 1961 came as a surprise. Ireland had stayed out of the Second World War[4] and later out of NATO, declaring itself neutral. However, its economic ties to Britain were close because Ire-

land's lop-sided, predominantly agricultural economy made her highly
dependent on trade with Britain. Half its imports came from Britain,
which took in return as much as 70 per cent of Irish exports. It was an
open question whether the Irish economy would be considered developed enough to be admitted as a full member of the Community. Seen
through Irish eyes, membership would support both her independence
and her economy, especially in view of the advantages following from
the participation in the CAP and access to the EC regional development schemes.

For constitutional reasons, a referendum was necessary before
membership of the Communities could become a reality. The vote in
favour was 83 per cent – a convincing result.

4.2. Denmark

To the Danish government, a solution which united the British and the
German markets within a single market including agricultural products brought close the realization of years of wishful thinking, particularly since there were signs that this would take place at a high price
level. At this point, reality surpassed expectations. It is fair to say that
Danish considerations centred on the economic aspects of the question. The matter of European integration was spoken of as "the market
problems", the parliamentary committee dealing with the question of
integration was the "Market Committee" and, for long periods of time,
the government had a "Minister of Market Affairs".

When the Danish government learned that the British government
was considering the possibility of applying for membership of the EC,
a letter was sent by the minister of foreign affairs to the British government, stating that Denmark was prepared to take similar steps. The
outcome was that the Danish government delivered its application in
Brussels on the same day as the British.

It is outside the scope of this chapter to go into detail on the negotiations as they took place throughout 1961-63, 1967 and finally 1970-
72. The political process had some similarities to that of Great Britain.
There existed among the Social Democrats, as in the British Labour
Party, opposition to the idea of joining the EC. The opposition here, as
in Britain, was given a free vote, thus avoiding a split in the party. The

---

4. During the First World War, the Irish had shown open sympathy towards Germany as
    part of their fight for independence from Great Britain.

rest of the opposition was mainly recruited from the far left and the far right wings. The options presented were either to seek an association with the EC or to hope for some sort of a Nordic economic union. It was at that time unclear whether the EC countries would accept an association with a country fulfilling the economic conditions for full membership, and what the position of Danish agriculture would be under association.

A solution based on an intensified Nordic economic cooperation was in practice unrealistic because the other Nordic countries were not prepared to allow the efficient Danish agriculture to compete with their own agriculture, which was already struggling to make a living under unfavourable climatic conditions.

In September 1972, the Danish Folketing passed a law concerning Danish accession to the EC. The law had to be taken to a referendum, which took place in the beginning of October. 90 per cent of the electorate cast their votes and the result was 63 percent in favour and 37 against. This made Denmark ready to join the EC on 1st January 1973.

4.3. Norway

A few days before the Danish "Yes", Norway held its referendum. Here the outcome went against EC membership, with 53 per cent voting "No". In spite of many characteristics in common with Denmark, substantial differences existed as well. It should be remembered that Norway did not gain the position of an independent country until 1905. For four hundred years, Norway was in a union governed from Denmark, and then followed almost hundred years in a union with Sweden. Norwegians speak of this total of five hundred years as: "the five hundred years' night". In the 1950s, when European integration got underway, Norway had only existed as an independent nation for fifty years. The Norwegians had only recently escaped from their forced partnerships. How much importance arguments and feelings of this sort had is hard to say, but it seems likely that they were of some significance.

Due to unfavourable climatic conditions, agriculture in the major part of the country existed only thanks to protectionism and heavy subsidisation. Like Japanese agriculture, Norwegian agriculture is among the most highly subsidised in the world. The fate of Norwegian agriculture within the EC was at best unclear. A common fisheries policy was not formulated in detail, but there was a risk that fishermen from other EC countries would have increased rights to fish close to the Norwegian coast.

The German occupation during 1940-45 undoubtedly left Norway with deeper wounds than Denmark, which contributed to a more sceptical attitude towards joining a community with Germany as a leading member. Where changing Danish governments managed to concentrate the debate around economic matters, in an attempt to keep their electorates together, similar possibilities did not exist in Norway. Here, undoubtedly there was a stronger tendency to make the matter a question of the future of national self-determination, as opposed to its loss to some remote, federalist institutions. At a more ideological level, it was also a question of the future of the strict, Norwegian alcohol policy, which placed all dealings concerning alcohol under the authority of a state monopoly. What would happen in case of the abolition of customs control at the frontiers and the introduction of a free right of establishment?

It was not until the spring 1962 that Norway presented its application for membership in Brussels. From then on, negotiations were parallel to those of Denmark, apart from the uncertainty as to the future fisheries policy. Here a plan was not presented until 1972, shortly before the signing of the act of accession. After the accession had been confirmed by parliament, the Storting, a referendum took place in September 1972. Of the votes cast, 53.5 were against, and so the decision was taken to remain outside the EC. Some argued that if the Danish "Yes" had come before the Norwegian vote was taken, it might have made a difference to the result, and this may be so. However, when the Norwegians almost 25 years later had a chance to change their mind, the result was negative once again. It seems that the first "No" must be taken seriously.

5. The remaining EFTA partners

The British decision in spring 1961 to apply for membership in the EC caused a mixture of expectation and fear among her EFTA partners. Expectations arose among those like Denmark, which saw a solution to the economic problems caused by the economic division of Western Europe into two separate market areas. Fear arose among those, which, for foreign policy reasons or otherwise, were excluded from joining an enlarged Community. This was the case for the three neutral EFTA countries, Switzerland, Austria and Sweden, as well as Finland. Out of those four, it was undoubtedly Sweden that felt the most aggrieved – not to say offended – by the change of policy of the British government.

The result of their annoyance was pressure on the potential EC countries to apply only for an association with the EC, or at least for the continuation of cooperation between the current EFTA countries. At a meeting in London shortly before Britain and Denmark gave in their applications, an agreement was reached that the two applicants should negotiate on the assumption that a satisfactory solution would be reached for their EFTA partners. The French "No" and the resultant termination of the negotiations in January 1963 solved the problem for a time. When the matter was brought up again in the early 1970s, and Britain and Denmark were accepted into the EC, the promise from 1961 was kept and existing free trade continued. In 1989-90, the problem reappeared on the agenda once again, this time caused by the Single European Act, SEA, and the planned introduction of the internal market by the end of 1992.

The Danish application, presented in August 1961, caused Sweden to propose an Agreement on Nordic Cooperation. The proposal contained far-reaching obligations as to future consultations. In its original shape, it was unacceptable to Denmark, as it contained obligations that would be hard to live up to in case of EC membership. The result was a watered-down edition of the original proposal, signed in March 1962 in Helsinki. After the January 1963 breakdown of the negotiations concerning the enlargement of the EC, the basis for that agreement was lost.

6. Early Nordic cooperation

From 1875 to 1914, a Scandinavian currency union existed, based on a common price of gold in Danish, Norwegian, and Swedish kroner. Through parts of the 1800s, Norway and Sweden formed a free trade area, which was abolished at the close of the century. The First World War meant the breakdown of the gold standard and the Nordic curren-

Fig. 16: The mid 1800's saw the rise of a feeling of a Nordic brotherhood. Not least among students under the impression of mounting German pressure on the Danish border to the south. Here is a print of the departure of students from other Nordic countries after a gathering in Copenhagen in 1862.

cy union. In the middle of the 20s, although this time with a weakened Scandinavian currency union, the countries were back on the gold standard until 1931 when England "went off the gold".

In 1930, the three Scandinavian countries plus Belgium and the Netherlands signed the *Oslo convention*. Except for the name, there was nothing especially Scandinavian or Nordic inherent in the agreement. The scope of the convention was strictly limited, mainly consisting of obligations to consult one another if customs tariffs were increased. The cooperation between the "Oslo-states" during the 30s dealt primarily with their neutrality policy.

At the close of the Second World War there seems to have been a new, common feeling of community spirit among the Nordic countries. Seen against this background, it was a painful experience when Norway and Denmark joined NATO in 1949, while Sweden remained neutral. It seems that this caused a sense of guilt within the Danish Social Democratic Party, which was then compensated for by renewed, strong Nordic feelings. In any case, the leader of the Social Democrat

Party, Hans Hedtoft (1903-55), took the initiative in setting up the Nordic Council in 1952. Once again, Finland had to be excluded, but since the Nordic Council developed a tradition of not dealing with foreign policy matters, Finland was able to join a few years later.

Members of the Nordic Council are representatives of the parliaments and the governments of the five Nordic countries.[5] The council is a purely consultative body, and its primary spheres of interest have been within cultural policy, judicial harmonization, the creation of a common Nordic labour market and a Nordic passport union. As far as the promotion of Nordic economic cooperation on a wider scale is concerned, the results of the Nordic Council have been poor, not to say non-existent.

7. Failed Nordic negotiations

If it were asked when trade was made duty free between the neighbouring towns of Elsinore in Denmark and Hälsingborg in Sweden, separated by a distance of only eight kilometres, then the answer would be at the same time as trade between the two towns and Lisbon and Zurich was made duty free, namely after the creation of EFTA. The example is mentioned because it is symptomatic of the development of Nordic economic cooperation. Initiatives resulting in practical measures have come from outside of Scandinavia, while the initiatives the Nordic countries themselves have taken have lacked the necessary backing in practical politics.

Three separate initiatives after the Second World War have been taken at governmental level towards the creation of a special *Nordic common market*:

a. in 1947-50 within the framework of "the common Nordic committee for economic cooperation",

b. in 1954-57 within "the Nordic economic co-ordination committee",

c. in 1968-70 under the Nordic Council, with a view to establishment of "Nordek".

5. Supplemented by representatives of special regional entities.

The background to the first initiative was the Marshall plan and an American wish that the European countries should seek to integrate their economies. The initiative was partly inspired by the creation of the Benelux. The committee presented its report in 1950, which in reality meant the burial of the plans for a customs union. The major factor behind this was Norwegian fears of increasing competition from Swedish manufacturing industry and Danish agriculture.

The next initiatives were taken in 1954. Except for agricultural products, quantitative restrictions among the OEEC countries had on the whole been abolished by that time. But the customs duties were still untouched. Consequently, a new committee consisting of special ministers of Nordic cooperation was appointed. In 1956, Finland joined the committee, which did not facilitate the process of reaching mutual solutions. In 1957, a report was presented suggesting what in reality corresponded to a customs union, but excluding special "sensitive" sectors and branches such as agriculture, the fishing industry, textiles, footwear, etc. By this time, the Treaty of Rome had been signed and initiatives taken towards the creation of a great European free trade area. So, once again, external initiatives had replaced the special Nordic initiatives. Two years later, EFTA saw the light of day. This can be seen as the result of a Scandinavian, or rather Swedish initiative, but the outcome was not a specifically Nordic arrangement.

Denmark took the third initiative for special Nordic economic cooperation in early 1968. The background to this was the French "No" in late 1967 to the new applications of Britain and its associates to join the Common Market. The Danish proposal came as a surprise when it was presented at the annual session of the Nordic Council. Extensive reports were prepared, and at the end of 1969 a draft treaty was presented. Still, no agreements had been reached concerning agriculture, though this did not influence the presentation ceremony at the session of the Nordic Council in Reykjavik in early 1970. However, shortly before that, the EC countries at the Hague summit had decided to resume the negotiations with the applicants, so Nordek at once lost its momentum. In March 1970, the Finish government announced that they were not prepared to participate in the final signature of the treaty, which meant that the process of ratification was stopped before it had begun. By that time, the focus of events once again had moved to Brussels.

8. Why they failed

The idea of closer Nordic cooperation undoubtedly had broad support of the people of the Nordic countries. So why did the attempts fail? The explanation is to be found both in the economies of the countries and in their political traditions.

The economies of the Nordic countries are only complementary to a modest degree and were even less so a few years ago. Previously, their exports had been concentrated around a few items, where they had a substantial market share. For Norway and Sweden (plus Finland), this was first and foremost the case for products from the forestry industry, but also metals and specialised products from the metal industry. By far the major part of the markets for those products were found outside the Nordic countries, and distributed over a wide range of countries. Danish exports consisted mainly of agricultural products. Here, the Nordic countries could have formed a good market, but this was prevented by protectionist agricultural policies in the rest of the countries. It was quite simply that Denmark could not import and consume all the aluminium, ball bearings and the paper for newsprint produced in the other Nordic countries, while the latter did not want to buy the agricultural goods that Denmark was able to supply. Under such conditions, the prospects of reaching positive results were poor. These fundamental facts were, oddly enough, allowed to pass unnoticed for decades whenever the question of Nordic economic cooperation was on the agenda.

Table 18.1 shows the intra-Nordic trade in 1955 at a time when the trade in industrial products on the whole had been liberalized. For purposes of comparison, figures for the year 1988 and 1998 have been included. Of their total exports in 1955, only 14.4 per cent went to the other Nordic countries.[6] Of their total imports, 12.5 per cent came from the other Nordic countries. As will be seen, the Nordic countries were marginal trading partners at the macro level, although it might be objected that mutual trade has grown since then as indicated by the table's figures. However the level was still as low as 20 per cent.

To these economic explanations of why a closer Nordic economic cooperation was not realised, must be added some political and institutional explanations. These are concerned, firstly, with the special

---

6. Figures for Iceland are excluded, due to their insignificance for the overall picture.

Table 18.1. Trade among Nordic countries as per cent of their total foreign trade. 1955, 1988, and 1998.

Percent.[1]	Import			Export		
	1955	1988	1998	1955	1988	1998
Denmark	14.4	20.0	21.0	14.0	21.3	21.8
Finland	10.7	18.4	18.8	5.9	21.3	15.6
Norway	21.0	28.8	25.1	16.6	20.1	18.9
Sweden	7.4	19.8	19.4	17.8	23.1	20.3
Total	12.5	21.5	21.0	14.4	21.7	19.3

[1] Per cent of total imports and exports respectively.
Source: For 1955: Th. Kristensen, ed. (1958, 22) For 1988 and 1998: Nordiska Statistika Sekretariat (1990 and 1999).

Scandinavian methods of dealing with this type of problems and, secondly, with the political will to reach a result.

It was characteristic of the negotiations in the 1950s between the Nordic countries that they were conducted according to branches of industry. Behind this, we find a tradition in those countries for a consensus policy involving representatives of the government, of business and of trade unions. As a method of integration, the method involves the danger that the representatives of those who fear the impacts of integration are more likely to speak up than those who see a distant and uncertain advantage in an eventual integration.

The method distinguishes itself completely from the method used by the original Six common market countries when they prepared their common customs tariff. Here, as explained, they had the rule of thumb that the duty was calculated as a simple average of the tariff rates of the four customs entities that made up the coming customs union. Seen in a political context, this straightforward method is explained by the existence of a political will to reach a result. Such a will was never declared in advance when Nordic economic cooperation was put on the agenda.

The termination of the negotiations concerning Nordek points to a third complication in Nordic cooperation: the special problems of Finland and its great neighbour to the east. For centuries it has been a central theme in Swedish foreign policy to assist the Finns in maintaining contact with the West. The case has usually been presented as a matter of due regard for the Finns. However, Sweden, like Denmark, has had a selfish interest through the years in supporting Finland and avoiding anything which might endanger the position of Finland as an independent Baltic nation. This was simply to keep Russia/the Soviet Union at a distance. From this it followed that it was important to have Finland as a participant in Nordic cooperation, although the Finnish participation was subject to the realisation that cooperation could be carried no further than allowed by the USSR. The limited room for movement in Finish foreign policy thus set the limits on Nordic cooperation.

Part VI
Time of upheaval 1973-

The years of high growth had been characterized by stability in the conception of macroeconomics, based on Keynesian theory. On the whole, the economies of Western Europe had displayed a high degree of stability: high, constant growth rates, full employment and moderate inflation. There were, however, signs of increasing problems in combining the latter two factors. A general trend in Western Europe had been economic growth accompanied by an increase of the share of general government in GDP, caused by increased public expenditure on education, health care, and social welfare benefits. As for external relations, the golden years of the 1950s and 60s had been marked by rapid growth in the international division of labour which was accelerated by the establishment of the EC, EFTA and the results of the GATT and the IMF.

In most of these areas, a reaction set in during the 1970s and 80s. The Keynesian interest in demand management through fiscal policy was supplemented, not to say substituted, by a keen interest in the functioning of the market proper. For a time, this was referred to as "supply side" economics. Warnings were made against the cost of the welfare system through its impact on the general incentive to work and save. Trade unions came under increasing attack for their opposition to increased mobility in the labour market thus increasing what had become known as the "natural rate of unemployment".[7]

The high level of activity including the high level of employment had thus far supported the process of European integration and the growth in the international division of labour by reducing the resistance to increased international competition. Here again, the period after the early 1970s saw a substantial change. The energy crises of 1973-

---

7. The rate of (un)employment that can be combined with steady price development including a stable price level.

74 and 1979-80 meant temporary balance of payments problems along with increased inflation. There was, furthermore, increased competition from overseas manufacturing industries in areas such as consumer electronics and car manufacturing. At first, this meant a setback for the process of European integration as the individual member countries attempted to protect their national industries with all kinds of subsidies and Non-Tariff Barriers (NTBs). It was not until the mid-1980s, after years of nearly zero growth and ten per cent plus unemployment, that the realization grew that the future of Western European industries was a matter of common concern to be dealt with on a mutual basis within the EC. There are straight lines from that point on to the setting up of the Single European Act (SEA), the Maastricht Treaty, all the way through to the third and final stage of the Economic and Monetary Union (EMU).

Chapter 19, *Return to Normality, 1973 -*, points to the fact that the two decades following the first energy crisis were not as bad in historical terms as they were thought to be by comparison with the years which immediately preceded the oil crisis. "The present phase generally ranks as second-best" writes Angus Maddison, the British economist and historian, about the years 1973-89.[8] A comparison between the economies of the EC member states and the USA shows that, during those years, Western Europe saw a substantial increase in labour productivity whereas the USA only had a very modest increase. As for employment, the picture was reversed: a modest increase in the EC and a substantial increase in the USA. The conclusion is that the EC experienced what can be called "jobless growth" during those years which left 18 million unemployed out of a total labour force of 170 million in 1997.[9]

Specific problems and developments are dealt with in Chapter 20, *National Developments, 1973 -*. The political shift to the right is illustrated by the coming into office of Margaret Thatcher in Britain in 1979, Ronald Reagan in the USA in 1981 and Helmut Kohl in West Germany in 1982 along with corresponding shifts in Belgium and Denmark. Only one of the major countries, France, experienced a move, albeit temporary, to the left with the election of Francois Mitterrand as President in 1981 and the appointment of a Socialist government.

8.   A. Maddison (1991, 124).
9.   OECD. Historical Statistics 1960-97. Table D (OECD 1999, 22).

Chapter 21, *European integration 1973 –. Slowing down and movement again*, describes the unsuccessful initiatives of the 1970s, including the Werner Plan which outlined the establishment of an Economic and Monetary Union by the end of the 1970s. As mentioned above, it was not until the mid-1980s that more successful initiatives were taken. The collapse of the Soviet bloc after 1989 meant the rise of entirely new possibilities for enlarging the EC. Before this could take place, however, a need was felt within the EC, which now adopted the name of European Union, EU, to speed up the process of integration among the countries of Western Europe resulting in the Maastricht Treaty of 1992, the Amsterdam Treaty of 1997 and the entry into force of the third and final stage of the Economic and Monetary Union in 1999.

Fig. 17: In the evening of November 9, 1989, some of the transit points between East and West Berlin were opened for passage on foot and, in the following days, the Wall was opened up for car traffic. Three young Germans showing their legitimation cards, on their way to West Berlin.

Chapter 19

Return to normality
1973-

After several hours spent driving on a smooth highway, problems may be experienced on switching back to an ordinary, bumpy road. Similar feelings confronted the industrialized countries after 1973 as growth rates fell back to a more normal level than they had been at for the last twenty years or so.

Measured by the elastic yardstick of history, any evaluation of the period after 1973 may come out with different results. Compared to the previous period, the overall impression is that of deterioration in nearly all respects. Growth rates were down by half, rates of inflation were doubled or tripled, and rates of unemployment tripled or quadrupled. But, when compared to periods before 1950, the picture becomes quite different. As far as growth rates are concerned, the twenty years after 1973 compare with the best periods prior to 1950. As far as the development of prices is concerned, earlier periods had encountered serious problems due to falling prices – deflation. As for unemployment, the problems of the past are hidden in a statistical fog, although we know that unemployment in most countries was higher in both the 1920s and 30s.

Seen from an historical perspective, the distinguishing feature of the economy of Western Europe since 1973 has been a hitherto unseen combination of inflation, unemployment and growth. It is this combination that has given rise to the term "jobless growth". Others have mainly noted the jobless side of it and coined the term "euro-sclerosis".[1]

As for political ideology, the pendulum swung from the left towards the right. This could be seen from changes in the order of priority of

---

1.   N.Crafts and G.Toniolo, ed. (1996, 73-94).

ends and means in economic policy. Full employment was replaced by
stable prices as a leading goal. The theoretical rationale for this shift
was given through a new concept, "the natural rate of unemployment",
NAIRU,[2] that corresponds to the level of employment at which it is
possible to have a stable level of prices or rather level of price changes.
If employment exceeds this level, the necessary labour force can only
be called forth by wages exceeding the value of its marginal product,
thereby starting a process of accelerating price and wage increases. The
heritage from Keynes and the interest in the postwar years in securing
employment through demand management were replaced by an interest in the supply side of the economy, including an interest in wage and
price formation.

The two events having the greatest impact on the economies of the
industrialized countries in the short run were the two energy crises,
OPEC I and OPEC II, in 1973-74 and 1979-80 respectively. Initially,
OPEC I was accused of having caused the end of the years of high
growth. At a later time it was realized that factors of a deeper and more
permanent nature were at work behind the falling growth rates and increasing unemployment figures. Seen in relation to the outside world,
Western Europe has felt two major changes since 1973, the effects of
which we are not fully aware of yet. Firstly, a number of new industrialised countries emerged, the so-called NIC countries,[3] and, secondly,
the break-up in 1991 of the USSR and the Soviet block occurred. In
this respect, 1989, with the fall of the Berlin Wall, marks the beginning
of the end of an epoch. Both events have confronted Western Europe
with problems. How ought the West to react when industrial flagships
such as shipbuilding and the production of automobiles and household
electronics encounter efficient competition from overseas producers?
It was problems of this sort that led in the middle of the 1980s to the
idea of realising the internal market of the European Communities and
the Single European Act. Besides this, the West was confronted with
the question of its future economic relations with the former members
of the Eastern block; countries that have never or only for very short
periods experienced what it means to live in a democracy and to be
part of a market-oriented economy.

2. Non-Accelerating Inflation Rate of Unemployment.
3. The Newly Industrializing Countries were places such as South Korea, Taiwan, Hong-
    kong, Singapore and Thailand.

1. The energy crises

In 1973, and again in 1979, the oil exporting countries raised the prices of crude oil three to fourfold. On both occasions, increased oil prices were blamed for the ensuing setbacks to the economies of oil importing countries. Since then, the verdict has been modified. Instead of being seen as the reason for a prolonged crisis in the economy of Western Europe, the crises have been seen as catalysts, merely promoting processes that were inevitable in any case.

1.1. The impact of an increase in oil prices
For the purposes of analysis, the impacts of an increase in oil prices for the economies of the importing countries can be divided into three components: a loss due to a worsening of the terms of trade, a loss of wealth and a loss of production.[4]

The "terms of trade"-loss implies that a greater amount of export goods is required to pay for a given amount of imported oil. If the value of the import of the commodity in question (here crude oil) corresponds to 1 per cent of the GDP of the importing country, then the immediate loss due to a three to fourfold price increase corresponds to 2-3 per cent of GDP. After some time, the importing country will find substitutes, perhaps begin oil production itself, etc. This well tend to reduce the "terms of trade"-loss in the long run. The figures given in the example here correspond fairly closely to the loss felt in Western European countries after OPEC I. At that time, the annual growth rates were 4-5 per cent, which means that the increased oil bill corresponded to the increase of GDP over six to eight months, in itself not an alarming event. After OPEC II, the loss was somewhat lower and some new oil-producing countries like Great Britain and Norway even gained from the crisis.

The wealth loss can be seen as the result of an *economic* obsolescence caused by a change in the relative prices. A new power station, constructed for the use of liquid fuel, has to be adjusted to the use of solid fuel. Houses have to be insulated more, means of transportation with traditional engines scrapped sooner, etc. The wealth loss consists, as

---

4. The argument at this point corresponds to an analysis of the OECD after OPEC II. OECD, Economic Outlook no. 27, June 1980 contains a special section concerning "The impact of oil on the world economy".

will be seen, of the costs caused by the necessary economic adjustments.

The loss of production is the least tangible type of loss. Here, three causes for the existence of such a loss will be mentioned. Firstly, the increased expenses on imported oil will reduce expenditure in the oil importing countries on other goods, setting off a negative multiplier process in these countries. Secondly, in the cases where oil importing countries start pursuing uncoordinated contractive economic policies in order to protect their Balance of Payments, this will add to the loss of production, without having a substantial impact on their deficits vis-à-vis the oil producing countries. Thirdly, increases in oil prices will be likely to cause not only direct, but also indirect price increases. The wage earners will want compensation for the price increases. If this results in a contractive, anti-inflationary economic policy, a third type of self-induced loss of production will occur. Both after OPEC I and OPEC II, wage earners sought to escape from their part of the oil bill increases. There can be no doubt that this self-inflicted loss was the most costly of all those caused by the oil crises.

1.2. The development at OPEC I and OPEC II

During the last three months of 1973, the price of crude oil went up from three dollars per barrel to almost 12. Throughout the following six years, the oil price was nearly constant, while the general price level doubled. Then, in 1979, due to an Iranian revolution followed by a crisis between the USA and Iran, the price at first reached 36 dollars per barrel, eventually stabilizing around 30 dollars. A substantial part of the increases under OPEC II can thus be seen as compensation for the general inflation since OPEC I. To this it must be added that the exchange rate of the dollars in 1979-80 was down by 30 per cent compared to what it had been during the previous years, thus causing a further reduction in the real price of oil earned by the OPEC countries.

OPEC I seems to have had the strongest short-term effect on the growth rates (table 19.1), whereas OPEC II had the strongest long-term effect. The figures leave us with the clear impression that the wage increases were not solely, or even mainly, the product of oil increases, but of prevailing institutional factors.

The development in 1974-75 was seen at the time as a sort of economic canyon that had to be bridged before the economy could get back to normal again. The feelings about OPEC II were entirely different. This time, there were no expectations that the "good old days" were waiting around the corner. Here the countries were trapped in a slowdown, with annual average growth rates around 1 per cent from 1980 to 1983. The same period saw an increase in unemployment rates from a level around 5 per cent to 10 per cent, without causing a substantial reduction in wage increases in Western Europe.

Table 19.1. Annual increases in GDP and wages (per cent) and relative unemployment (per cent) for OECD-Europe and USA. 1973-83.

per cent	OECD-Europe			USA		
	GDP	Wages [1)]	Unem- ployment	GDP	Wages[1]	Unem- ployment
1973	5.8	13.3 [2)]	3.5	5.2	7.0	4.8
1974	2.3	15.9	3.7	-0.5	8.3	5.5
1975	-0.8	18.8	4.9	-1.3	9.0	8.3
1976	4.5	13.2	5.4	4.9	8.1	7.6
1977	2.7	11.2	5.7	4.7	8.8	6.9
1978	3.1	12.3	6.0	5.3	8.7	6.0
1979	3.6	11.7	6.2	2.5	8.5	5.8
1980	1.6	13.1	6.8	-0.2	8.7	7.0
1981	0.3	12.2	8.2	1.9	9.8	7.5
1982	0.8	10.7	9.4	-2.5	6.3	9.5
1983	1.7	8.0	10.3	3.6	3.9	9.5

[1)] Hourly earnings in manufacturing. [2)] For 1973, EC countries only.
Sources: For wages and unemployment: Historical Statistics 1960-85. OECD (1987). For 1973 OECD (1985). For GDP: OECD, Econ. Outlook no. 50, Dec. 1991.

2. Growth and growth factors

2.1. Jobless growth

On the basis of table 19.2, comparisons can be made between some central macro-economic indicators for the EU countries (EU-15) and the USA. During the years 1973-79, the labour force in the EU grew by 0.7 per cent annually, while total employment was nearly constant, growing by only 0.2 per cent annually. As will be seen, this corresponds to an additional supply of labour not being employed of rough-

ly 0.5 per cent a year. In spite of this modest growth in total employment, there was an average GDP growth of 2.5 per cent. As will be
seen, there has occurred a growth of labour productivity that amounts
to almost 2.5 per cent a year. Similar calculations based on figures for
the USA provide different results. Here, the growth rates of the labour
force, employment and GDP between 1973-79 were all at the same
level, around 2.5 per cent. In the USA, the increase in the labour force
was absorbed by the labour market, but in such a way that the average
labour productivity during those years was nearly constant.[5] Similar,
although less distinct, trends are found for the 1980s. In the USA, the
figures for the increase in the labour force and the level of employment
were identical. In Western Europe, the labour force on average grew
by 0.4 percentage points more a year than employment. Considered
over the years 1973-89, an increase in total employment of 5-6 per cent
corresponded to an increase in GDP of nearly fifty per cent. This is the
background for the statement that Europe during those years experienced what may be called *"jobless growth"*.

*Table 19.2: Annual increase in labour force, employment, and GDP (in fixed
prices). EU-15 and USA. 1973-79, 80-89, 90-93, and 94-98.*

	EU-15				USA			
	73-79	80-89	90-93	94-98	73-79	80-89	90-93	94-98
Total labour force	0.7	0.9	0.3	0.4	2.6	1.7	1.1	1.3
Total employment	0.2	0.5	- 0.4	0.6	2.5	1.7	0.7	1.8
GDP	2.5	2.2	1.4	2.4	2.6	2.4	1.8	3.8

Source: 1973-89 OECD Historical Statistics (1999). 1990-98 OECD Economic Outlook
no. 65 (June 1999).

One may ask the hypothetical question of how large the growth of
GDP would have been in the EC countries, if the growth in employment corresponded to the growth in the labour force, and if the growth
of productivity had remained unchanged. Instead of the achieved

---

5.   As will be seen from the table, this picture changed in the 1990s, when the USA experi-
      enced an annual growth of labour productivity of 2 per cent.

growth of nearly 50 percent, there would have been a growth of roughly 60 per cent. The calculation, however, is based on the presumption that the part of the labour market that did not find occupation would have had the same productivity as those who did. It seems likely, in fact, that in general they would have had a lower productivity. The conclusion to this – hypothetical – calculation is that the material losses due to the years of crisis are rather modest. The most serious aspect of the crisis concerns the sufferings of the persons and families more or less isolated from the labour market, to which may be added the long-term problems of the whole of society resulting from high rates of youth unemployment.

2.2. Weakened growth factors

As described in chapter 14, Western Europe had taken advantage of a number of "once and for all" advantages during the period of high growth such as the import of technology from the USA, increased international division of labour, sectoral shifts, a modest wage pressure, etc. For most or all of those points, the impact on future growth rates seems to have disappeared by the time of OPEC I and OPEC II. Although a worsening of the terms of trade due to increased oil prices was the immediate and visible reason for the slow down, that does not mean that other and deeper factors were not at work.

Estimates of the size of the real capital of a society or fractions of its capital are a complicated matter, both for theoretical and practical reasons. One method is to accumulate the investments over a given number of years, which are supposed to correspond to the average lifetime of the investments. This corresponds to what may be called the gross capital. If deductions are made corresponding to the current depreciations, a net figure is obtained. Relative changes can then be calculated by comparing current investments and the value of the stock of capital.

Table 19.3 contains figures concerning the relative growth of capital (gross) per person employed for the years 1950-73 and 1973-92. As will be seen, the figures are calculated separately for "machines, etc.," and for "non-residential structures". As far as investments in machines etc. are concerned, a substantial difference can be seen between the USA, Japan and the three European countries. The USA did not experience the damage of the Second World War, which may explain why the relative growth of the stock of "machines, etc." in the USA was so much lower during the period 1950-73. Table 19.3 points to a long-term

Table 19.3. Annual relative growth in stock of machinery, equipment and non-residential structures per person employed, 1950-73 and 1973-92.

Per cent. p.a.	Machines etc.[1]		Non-residential structures	
	1950-73	1973-92	1950-73	1973-92
USA	2.4	2.2	1.5	1.1
Japan	6.3	6.0	8.0	5.5
France	8.7	4.1	3.3	3.4
Great Britain	4.8	2.7	4.6	3.6
Germany	6.9	2.9	4.5	3.0

[1]"Machinery and equipment" incl. means of transportation.
Note. The figures are calculated as gross figures. See. the comment in the text.
Source: A. Maddison (1995, table 2.2)

trend according to which the European countries (and Japan) are approaching the USA as far as the amount of capital per unit of labour is concerned. Such a development could explain both why Europe has experienced a higher growth of labour productivity and why the growth rates of Europe tend to decline.

Observations of this sort have resulted in a "theory of convergence". According to this, economies working under similar conditions, such as the level of education and economic and political institutions, tend to converge towards the same level of payments to the factors of production, and thus the same level of income. This corresponds with the results of comparisons between the level of incomes in the individual states of the USA. Calculations indicate that the absolute differences of income (GDP per capita) tend to shrink by 2 per cent a year.[6] If this holds true across the Atlantic as well, it means that the growth rates in Western Europe will converge towards those of the USA, and towards one another. If the incomes per capita in A (USA) at the outset are double the incomes in B (Western Europe), this means that B at the outset will have an additional growth of 2 per cent a year compared to A. Had the difference only been 25 per cent, the additional growth due to convergence would shrink to 0.5 per cent.

---

6.   N.Crafts and G. Toniolo (1996, 19). This means that the difference of incomes over time is developing according to a geometric progression of a quotient of 0.98. After 25 years the difference will be reduced by nearly 40 per cent, after fifty years by 64 per cent or nearly two- thirds.

Based on similar considerations, we may speak of a "*convergence club*" in Western Europe. In order to make calculations of this sort, it is necessary to convert the GDP figures to the same currency; a rather doubtful manoeuvre. This is done by using the special Purchasing Power Parity (PPP) exchange rates, which are supposed to mirror the purchasing power of the currencies. Such a calculation made for 1992 would show that the following countries: Italy, the Netherlands, Sweden, Austria, Belgium, Norway, France, Denmark and Germany,[7] (ranked in order of growing incomes) fell within the 16,000-19,500 US dollar segment (1990-prices).

3. The economic climate

3.1. Reduced cyclical movements
The years of high growth were characterized not only by exceptionally high growth rates, but also by the high degree of stability of the growth rates. Changes took place, but were modest compared to previous periods. Around 1960, optimists among economists – such do actually exist – declared that "the cycle is dead".

Table 19.4. Annual year-on-year changes in growth rates of GDP (fixed prices) in percentage points, selected countries and sub periods. 1871-1992.

Pct.-points.	1871-1913	1922-29	1930-39	1951-73	1974-92	1983-92
USA	6.3	5.1	8.1	2.6	2.6	1.7
Great Britain	2.2	5.7	2.7	1.9	2.0	1.4
Germany	2.3	11.8	3.2	2.4	1.9	1.2
Italy	5.5	5.1	6.0	1.6	1.9	0.7
Belgium	1.5	3.2	3.9	1.7	2.3	1.2
Netherlands	n.a.	3.1	4.1	2.8	1.5	1.2
France	4.9	8.8	5.9	1.4	1.3	1.0
Denmark	2.1	5.4	1.9	2.9	2.0	1.0
Norway	1.6	6.4	4.5	2.0	1.6	1.6
Sweden	3.2	3.4	3.2	2.2	1.4	1.1

Source: 1870-1973 A. Maddison (1991 table A 6 –8). 1973-92 OECD., div. nos. of Economic Outlook and National Accounts, Main Aggregates Vol I. 1960-94.

7.   N. Craft and G. Toniolo, ed. (1996, 6).

With a view to judging the background for this statement, the size of the year-on-year changes in growth rates (measured in percentage points) between 1871-1992 are shown in table 19.4. The table confirms with a high degree of certainty that the economies have been stabilized. In Western Europe, the 1920s on the whole stand out as a period of instability. Since the Second World War there has been a general tendency for the annual changes to decrease. Especially the year-on-year changes during 1983-92 were low. Economies have been kept on a very short leash in order to prevent tendencies towards increased inflation. It should, however, be added, that such calculations are very sensitive to the quality of the input. This is even more so, the earlier the periods being considering.

3.2. The growth pattern 1973-98

The economic situation around 1970 must be characterised as diffuse and unstable because of the sporadic attempts to fight inflation. At the same time, there were fears of the consequences of the instability in international monetary affairs for jobs and production. In 1972, this resulted in a shift towards an expansionist policy, resulting in increased growth rates but also in increased inflation. Lastly, to this were added tendencies towards increased prices of raw materials and grain. The failure of the Soviet grain harvest caused great Soviet purchases of wheat in the world market, including from the USA. For many raw materials, prices had not been so high since the Korean War in the 1950s.[8] Already in the first half of 1973, the OECD countries experienced substantial price increases, even before OPEC I and the drastic increases in the price of crude oil.

With reference to table 19.5, it is possible to give an outline of the business cycles between 1973 and 1998. As far as medium-term development is concerned, six distinct periods can be singled out. What the table does not reveal is that the shifts between the periods can be registered somewhat earlier in the American economy than in that of Western Europe. OPEC I was followed by a sharp setback in 1974-75 followed by an upturn in 1975-79. Then came OPEC II, and another setback in 1980, with this one lasting for four years from 1980 until 1983. Then followed seven years with growth rates back around 3 per cent, only to be replaced by a new setback around 1991.

---

8.   OECD., Economic Outlook, no 50, Dec.1991, p. 3.

Table 19.5. Annual change (per cent) of GDP (fixed prices) in selected sub periods. 1973-98.

Per cent p.a.	1973	1973-75	1975-79	1979-83	1983-90	1990-93	1993-98
OECD	6.0	0.4	4.1	1.4	3.4	1.3	3.0
OECD Europe	5.8	0.8	3.5	1.2	3.0	0.7	2.4*
Germany	4.8	-0.6	3.9	0.5	3.1	1.6	1.7
France	5.4	1.4	3.5	1.4	2.6	0.2	2.0
Italy	7.1	1.3	4.9	1.5	2.9	0.2	1.8
UK	7.1	-1.1	2.8	0.5	3.2	-0.1	3.1
Austria	4.9	1.8	3.5	1.4	2.7	1.7	2.4
Belgium	6.0	1.4	2.9	1.3	2.6	0.8	2.5
Netherlands	4.7	2.0	3.0	0.3	3.1	1.5	3.2
Switzerland	3.2	-2.8	1.2	1.5	2.8	-0.4	1.0
Denmark	3.6	-0.8	3.3	1.0	2.2	1.2	3.6
Finland	6.6	2.1	2.5	3.4	33.3	-4.0	4.6
Norway	4.1	4.7	5.0	2.5	2.6	2.8	4.1
Sweden	4.2	2.9	1.2	1.1	2.5	-1.7	2.7
USA	5.2	-0.9	4.4	0.8	3.4	1.8	3.8
Japan	7.6	1.8	4.9	3.3	4.5	1.7	1.2

* EU 15.
Source: 1973-79 OECD Econ. Outlook no. 50, Dec. 1991. For 1980-93 OECD, National Accounts, Main Aggregates, vol. I, 1960-94. For 1993-98 OECD Econ. Outlook no. 66, Dec. 1999.

Another way of illustrating the development is through the unemployment figures. In 1974-75, the level of the unemployment rates went from 2-3 per cent to 4-5 per cent. After OPEC II, the rates went up to 9-10 per cent, a level at which they stayed during the 1980s. In 1990-91, a temporary, minor fall took place, followed by an increase to 11 per cent or more. A major factor behind the temporary decrease in 1990-91 was the reunification of Germany, causing an initial wave of hectic activity, followed by a contractive policy to curb price increases.

Leading macro-economic indicators for years have been the rate of unemployment, the position of the balance of payments and the rate of price increases. To these, a fourth indicator has been added since OPEC II; namely the size of the public debt (compared to the GDP). Around 1980, the average size of the public debt (calculated net) of the EC countries amounted to 21 per cent. In 1983, the figure was 31 per cent, in 1990, 34

Table 19.6: General government expenditures as per cent of GDP. 1960-96.

Per cent of GDP	1960	1968	1974	1987	1996
UK	32.2	39.3	44.8	42.9	43.4
Germany	32.4	39.1	44.6	47.3	48.6
France	34.6	40.3	39.3	50.9	55.0
Italy	30.1	34.7	37.9	50.8	52.9
Austria	35.7	40.6	41.9	52.4	53.8
Belgium	34.5	41.7	45.0	58.1	52.8
Netherlands	33.7	43.9	47.9	62.4	52.4
Switzerland	17.2	20.7	24.1	29.8	34.2
Denmark	24.8	36.3	45.9	57.3	61.0
Finland	26.6	32.8	32.0	46.3	59.4
Norway	29.9	37.9	44.6	49.2	45.8
Sweden	31.0	42.8	48.1	59.4	65.2
USA	26.8	30.3	31.7	36.3	35.5
Japan	17.5	19.2	24.5	32.7	36.5

Source: OECD, Historical Statistics, 1960-97, Paris 1999

per cent and in 1998 57 per cent.[9] The background to this was a combination of huge public deficits, caused by the economic setback and high interest rates. The growing public debt from the early 1980s was considered dangerous to future economic development. Firstly, the major public loans might have negative impacts on private investment, corresponding to the idea of "crowding out". Secondly, the high costs of the loans meant a growing pressure on public budgets at a time when the level of taxation was already considered a problem threatening future economic development. Thirdly, the budget position in 1992 was included among the convergence criteria to be fulfilled by EC countries wanting admission to the third stage of EU's Economic and Monetary Union.

4. Economic policy in transition

As far as the principles behind economic policy are concerned, a dividing line can be drawn about 1980. Keynesian demand management in

9.   OECD. 1999, I, annex table 35.

the late 1960s and the 1970s had been supplemented without success by incomes policies. Around 1980, the belief spread that more lasting results in bringing down unemployment and inflation could only be obtained through structural changes in the economy. In politics, this was reflected in changes in political leadership. In Great Britain, a Conservative government under Margaret Thatcher (1925–) took over in 1979. In the USA, the Republican Ronald Reagan (1911–) was elected in 1980, and in Germany, the Christian Democrat, Helmut Kohl (1930–) became chancellor in 1982.[10] Of the larger countries in Western Europe, only France moved to the left when Francois Mitterrand was elected president in 1981, although in the years to come he would have to cooperate with changing majorities in the National Assembly.

4.1. Time for a change. 1973-80

During the late 1960s and early 1970s, an increasing inflationary pressure was felt. At a given level of unemployment – say 3 per cent – an increasing level of inflation was realised; in the language of economists, the Phillips-curve relation[11] had broken down. Several reasons can be given for this. If the trade unions not only wanted compensation for already registered inflation, but also for anticipated inflation, this over time would result in accelerating inflation. If labour productivity did not grow as fast as it had in the preceding years, but the trade unions managed to maintain the relative wage increases, this would result in growing inflation too. Finally, the 1960s and early 1970s had seen a substantial increase in public expenditure and taxation. If taxpayers sought to keep up their level of disposable income, i.e. income after tax, this would be a third cause of increased inflation.

The 1960s and 70s had seen scattered attempts to keep inflation down through incomes policies; that is, direct intervention to keep down nominal wages and prices through wage and price control. On the whole, the results were poor or at best short-sighted. When an incomes policy was lifted, there would simply be extra pressure on wages and prices. As a result of this, interest in incomes policies seems to have vanished between OPEC I and II.

10. The same month Denmark had a coalition government lead by the Conservative Poul Schlüter remaining in office for more than ten years. In 1982 Belgium as well saw a change from a Socialist to a Liberal government.
11. A curve that shows the price- or wage increases as a function of the level of unemployment.

4.2. *Reorientation towards structural policy. 1980 –*

As well as such macro-economic problems, Western Europe had to face growing competition from overseas producers. It was first felt within the textiles sector, but from here it spread to the iron and steel industry, shipbuilding and car manufacture. A way of reducing the problem was so-called voluntary agreements according to which the overseas producers promised to restrict their export of the goods in question to specific quantities. Such agreements were among other goods made for textiles and for cars. Other ways of assisting national industries were cheap loans, tax rebates, and all sorts of Non-Tariff Barriers (NTBs). Such a development had been under its way before OPEC I, but was now speeded up. This caused the OECD to present a report in 1978 analyzing the extent to which such measures were practised. The study confirmed that their use was widespread.[12] The development in economic reasoning in those years can be illustrated by the following quotation from the preface of a publication on the same subject presented five years later by the OECD in 1983:

> "Faced with sluggish growth, unacceptably high unemployment and widespread inflation, and recognizing the inter-relationship between macro-economic performance and structural adjustment, the OECD Council at ministerial level approved in June 1978 "Some General Orientations for a Progressive Shift to More Positive Adjustment Policies". This move was part of a broader programme for concerted action to improve the world economic situation. The programme encompassed demand-management policies, efforts to improve the energy situation, measures to maintain an open multilateral trading system, and international monetary policies." [13]

The central theme is indicated by the words "...recognizing the interrelationship between macro-economic performance and structural adjustment...". A good macro-economic climate (high growth, high employment) will have a positive effect on the micro-economic climate (high mobility and willingness to adjust to changes) and visa-versa. Between those two levels of the economy, there will be interdependen-

---

12. Selected Industrial Policy Instruments, Objectives and Scope. OECD., Paris 1978.
13. OECD (1983, 5). Positive Adjustment Policies, Managing Structural Change. OECD., 1983.

ce. But this might also be of a negative character. The problem, according to the report, was then to interrupt such a negative relationship between the macro and micro-economic levels and replace it by a positive relationship.

As it stands, this can be seen as a "technical" comment on the economic and political situation in the early 1980s. A closer look reveals that it is more controversial. The wish to have a well-functioning micro-economy corresponds to a wish to have a well-functioning market economy, which includes the labour market. And here, the political alarm bells start ringing.

The economic-political ideas mentioned here appeared under several names, of which the most frequently used was *supply side economics*, to distinguish it from demand management policy. The difference may seem greater than it actually is. In Sweden, the idea of an active labour market policy was introduced as early as the late 1940s in order to supplement demand management and to reduce the risk of inflation under full employment.

Besides increased flexibility in the labour market, *decontrol* should take place in sectors under public control, including pricing, granting of concessions, etc. As a leading example of this, civil aviation can be cited; first in the USA and then in Europe. Another aspect of the structural reforms was *privatization*. Both Great Britain and France have seen examples of this, though Britain in particular under Margaret Thatcher.

The 1983 OECD report in 1989 was complemented by a report entitled: "Economies in Transition. Structural adjustment in OECD Countries". This report was more direct, containing recommendations concerning the different spheres of the economy such as the labour market, the financial markets, the public sector, including the public debt, and the high level of taxation.

5. Prolonged GATT negotiations

In 1973, the GATT countries convened for their seventh round of tariff negotiations called the Tokyo round after its first meeting's location. It went on for six years, which may be taken as proof of a lack of will to reach results. This may be explained by the fact that the conference coincided with the slowdown in the wake of OPEC I. The results seem to have been similar to those of the Kennedy round, achieving the reduction of customs tariffs by nearly a third. Once again, it was mainly the trade between the industrialised countries that benefited from the tariff cuts. The average level of tariffs for manufactured industrial products is estimated to have been reduced to 6 per cent after the conference.

At a ministerial meeting of the GATT countries held in Uruguay it was decided in 1986 to have another tariff-cutting conference. This time, the round lasted for eight years, finishing in 1994. The duration of the conference was mainly due to problems concerning agricultural products. As far as internal trade among the industrialised countries was concerned, the result was similar to that of the Tokyo round. The level of tariffs for manufactured goods was cut by another third, now down at 4 per cent, which, in an historical context, is an unusually low level, and in itself representing an exceptional degree of liberalization of foreign trade.

The problems at the conference were found in other spheres. The USA and the EC had a long-lasting conflict concerning agricultural products. Areas where the results were poor were in voluntary export control, stopping the widespread use of subsidies and Non-Tariff Barriers, discrimination in public procurement, trade in services, etc. Having registered the need to deal with these problems it was agreed to give GATT the formal organisation for which it had waited for almost fifty years, the World Trade Organization, WTO.

Chapter 20

National Developments 1973-

In chapter 19, a number of characteristics common to the countries of Western Europe were outlined. In this chapter, more specific aspects of the development of individual countries will be dealt with.

1. Great Britain

1979 saw a fundamental change in the economic policy of Great Britain. The "European" in British politics, former prime minister Edward Heath, was replaced by Margaret Thatcher as leader of the Conservative party. Under her leadership, the Conservatives returned to the government benches in 1979, and this marked the beginning of a period in British economic politics known as the "Thatcher experiment". In 1990, after a revolt in her party, she was replaced as prime minister by John Major (1943–), who remained in office until 1997 when election defeat brought to an end eighteen years of Conservative government.

By comparison with European traditions, the change of ideology upon the return of the Conservatives in 1979 stands out as unusually distinct. At the micro-level, an interventionist policy was replaced by one aiming at liberalization and increasing competition in business. At the macro-level, short-term demand management was replaced by a medium-term policy based on the announcement of goals for monetary expansion corresponding to the principles of orthodox monetarist policy. An important ingredient of the policy, falling between the micro- and macro-levels, was a weakening of the trade unions. The programme of the Thatcher government to an unusual degree is an expression of ideas brought forward in the wake of OPEC I and II.

Common factors for both the Conservatives and Labour were *internal* party conflicts on the subject of European integration. In the 1990s, the conflict deepened among the Conservatives, almost causing a split in the party. In 1997, Labour returned to power with Tony Blair (1953–) as prime minister, and he brought about a more positive attitude towards the EC.[1]

To Great Britain the oil crises meant that it became profitable to extract oil from the North Sea. Great Britain was the first country to venture into this area in 1975. By the time of OPEC II, she was self-sufficient and, from then on, a net-exporter. Out of the average annual GDP growth of about 1.5 per cent during the period 1973-80, a third or 0.5 per cent originated from the extraction of oil.

An important part of the policy of the Labour government between OPEC I and II had been attempts to control wage and price increases through incomes policies, combined with selective subsidies to certain industries. It was this policy, involving a partnership with the trade unions and widespread use of public subsidies, which the crusades of the Thatcher government targeted and confronted. To this it must be added that the Thatcher government presented an equally fierce critique of Britain's position within the EC. All of these points were brought up during the 1979 election campaign. After that her incoming government had the chance to test the programme in practice.

The public sector was to be reduced in order to decrease the marginal tax rates of persons and corporations alike. To promote dynamics and limit inefficiencies in business, extensive privatization should take place. To improve the functioning of the labour market, the trade unions were to be weakened and to ensure that the policy of the government was carried through at the local level, local government influence was reduced. One reason behind this was a wish to privatise the stock of houses and flats owned by the local authorities. As part of a strict monetary policy, priority in economic policy was to be changed in favour of stable prices at the cost of employment – in itself not something specific to British policy at the time. As far as the distribution of incomes and consumption was concerned, the changes in tax and housing policies and the cuts in the expenditure of local government must have been a burden for the lower income groups. As an extreme part of

1. For Britain and the EC, including the conflicts over the CAP in the 1980s, see chapter 21.

its tax policy, the government proposed a "poll tax" in 1989 under which an equal amount would be paid by all, with payment being made a condition for an individual to have the right to vote. This proposal, backed by the prime minister, caused such turmoil in her own party that it caused her downfall and replacement by the less extreme John Major.

One might ask whether the Thatcher experiment worked as intended and whether it brought Britain back onto the path of higher growth? The public sector of Great Britain before the change of government in 1979 was of a comparatively modest size, (table 19.6), and its composition does not seem to have caused special problems compared to other countries in Western Europe. During the 1980s, it was slightly decreasing calculated as a percentage of GDP at a time when the public sector of other countries saw substantial growth. This must be seen as the result of a tightening of the expenditure policy. On the taxation side, this was followed by a reduction in the level of marginal taxation as well as that of corporate taxes. As far as economic growth is concerned, the results of the Thatcher experiment are unclear. The period between 1980 and 1983 started with annual growth rates averaging 0.5 per cent. At the same time, the unemployment rate rose from 4 per cent to 10 per cent, a substantial increase compared to the rest of Western Europe during the same period. These years can be seen as the time when the trade unions had to "learn a lesson", which ended by making them more open to changes and adjustments. From 1983 to 1990, a period followed (see table 19.5) where the growth rates of Britain were slightly above the figures of OECD Europe – 3.2 per cent compared to 3.0 per cent. Then, from 1990 to 1993, a setback followed, with growth rates just below zero, compared with a 0.7 growth rate for OECD Europe as a whole.

If the aim of the Thatcher experiment was to trigger the release of hidden opportunities in the British economy, the result seems to have been a disappointment. As far as growth rates are concerned, Britain did no better during the 1980s and early 1990s than the countries on the continent. However, where growth rates had previously lagged behind the rest of Western Europe, they were now breaking even. Unfortunately, this was mainly due to a decrease in the growth rates on the continent and not to a substantial rise in British growth rates. Ranked according to GDP per capita, Britain found herself in the early 1990s as number eleven out of sixteen European OECD countries.

2. Germany

A spy scandal in 1974 caused a change of chancellor when Helmut Schmidt (1918-) replaced his fellow Social Democrat, Willy Brandt (1913-92). Eight years later, in September 1982, the coalition partner, the FDP (Freie Demokratiche Partei), gave up supporting the Social Democrats and turned to the CDU to form a government under the leadership of Helmut Kohl (1930-), who was to remain in office for sixteen years.[2]

By far the greatest political and economic event during the twenty years following the OPEC I was the reunification of Germany in 1990. To the former West Germany, this meant a short, hectic economic boom in 1990-91. It also meant a further strengthening of the position of Germany in relation to the rest of Europe and beyond. Of the twelve member countries of the EC at the time of reunification, Germany now represented 25 per cent of the total population and 30 per cent of the total GDP.

A special feature of the German economy during the 1970s and 1980s was the low rates of inflation. At OPEC I and II, the GDP-deflator[3] rose by 7 per cent (1974) and 5 per cent (1980), compared to 11 and 12 per cent for OECD Europe as a whole.[4] As will be seen, the price increases in Germany, especially after OPEC I, were modest. This can, however, be seen as part of traditional German policies due, first and foremost, to the experiences of inflation in the early 1920s. A result of the modest price increases during the 1970s was constant surpluses on the German BoP, resulting in a criticism of Germany for having an economic policy that was too tight.[5] In 1977, the G7[6] passed a resolution once again asking for expansionist measures in the countries with a surplus. As a result, Germany finally undertook such a policy in 1978-79, unfortunately just before OPEC II. The eventual outcome turned out to be a stronger pressure on the German economy than foreseen, including a deficit on the BoP and a decrease in the ex-

2. In modern German history only surpassed by Otto von Bismarck.
3. A measure of the price increases of the production of the country (its GDP).
4. OECD., National Accounts, Vol. I, 1960-87, table 31.
5. Germany, along with the USA and Japan, was expected to serve as a locomotive for getting the world economy moving. All three locomotives dropped out.
6. "The Great Seven" industrial countries, i.e. USA, Japan, Germany, France, Great Britain, Italy, and Canada. The group has been enlarged with Russia. The chairman of the Commission represents the EC.

change rate of the DM – partly due to a simultaneous rise in the US dollar after 1979.

Germany was therefore faced with economic problems in balancing her economy similar to those faced in most other countries in Western Europe. In 1981–82, she experienced a substantial increase in unemployment and zero growth, resulting in a growing distrust of the Social Democrat government, which was accused of being soft on the trade unions, pursuing a failed industrial strategy and a slack fiscal policy. As will be seen, this was a critique paving the way for a change in favour of structural changes corresponding to the prevailing trend. As a result of the crises, the coalition partner, the FDP, changed sides, turned to the CDU and in autumn 1982, a new coalition government took over with Helmut Kohl as chancellor.

Compared to the contemporary Conservatives in Britain, the German government moved cautiously, even though policies consisted mainly of the same sort of ingredients. These included a reduction of trade union influence, a decrease in public expenditure and taxes, privatization and smaller subsidies to industries. The result was a substantial improvement in the BoP, but as far as other macro-economic goals are concerned the results were modest. Growth remained down at around 2 per cent, and unemployment stabilised at 7 per cent.

Then, along with the fall of the Berlin Wall, a change occurred in the foundations of the economic policy. On 9th November 1989, it was announced that a few routes from East to West Berlin had been opened up for free traffic. This was the signal which began a chain of events that nobody, only a few weeks earlier, could have predicted would take place for many years to come. Nonetheless, amidst the joy and excitement, it was clear, that a difficult process was waiting ahead.

What lay ahead had never been attempted before. The former East Germany, the DDR, with its centrally governed, state-capitalist economy, was to merge with the market-oriented, private-capitalist economy of Western Germany, the BRD. This, sooner or later, would require the acceptance of the same currency, common legislation, a common tax system and all the remaining characteristics of another state. How was this to be done – and how quickly? The economic experts were in favour of a gradual solution bearing in mind the great differences between the two parts of the country. This corresponded to the methods preferred by Germany in the EC, where Germany had normally been a spokesman for long transitional periods.

In terms of the total area of the united Germany, the former DDR accounted for 30 per cent, and its population, for 21 per cent. Its proportion of total GDP is more complicated to calculate. If the exchange rates are fixed as one to one (one Ost Mark = one DM), then the GDP of the former East Germany corresponded to 14 per cent of the Germany's total GDP. Calculated on the basis of the same, overvalued exchange rate, the GDP per capita in the former DDR corresponded to 64 per cent of that in West Germany. A clearer idea of the differences is given by the relative productivity of the labour force. Here it is estimated that it was as low as 40 per cent of the West German productivity.[7]

To those differences should be added that at the time of reunification there was a substantial difference in the relative prices in the two Germany's. Goods for daily consumption were far cheaper in the former DDR, at around a mere fifth or even less, priced in Ost Mark. On the other hand, consumer durables cost three or four times as much and were generally of poorer quality. So, in consequence, both the level and the structure of prices had to be adjusted.

The first problem, the level of prices and wages, was met at an early point in time, in the form of the question of the exchange rate between the OM and the DM. If a low and "realistic" exchange rate were chosen, say two OM to one DM, it would support the competitiveness of the economy of the former DDR. However, this could have been considered unjust to those who, out of their current modest incomes, had managed to accumulate some savings in OM. Furthermore, the incomes of wage earners and salaried people would be cut in half after the introduction of the DM and would most likely cause a mass migration to the west, causing great housing problems in West Germany. If an exchange rate of one-to-one was introduced, the wage differences between the east and the west would be kept down, but so would the competitiveness in the east. This would result in increased unemployment and growing expenditures from the Federal budget. This second solution, though, would be seen as a gesture of a higher degree of solidarity towards their new fellow citizens so long as the necessary means could be supplied during a transitional period.

The two questions presented here, the exchange rate and inclusion in the economy of West Germany, were solved within a short period.

---

7.   Figures from OECD, Economic Survey, Germany (1990,46ff).

Elections to the Bundestag were held in March 1990 in Germany, including the former DDR. The result was a prolongation of the CDU government. After the election, an agreement was reached which meant that reunification was to be accompanied by an arrangement whereby one DM was exchanged for one OM as far as wages, salaries, pensions, interest rates and transfer payments were concerned. Financial claims would be met at a rate of two OM to one DM. However, every person was granted the possibility of exchanging up to 6.000 OM at a rate of one to one. Part of the arrangement was a plan to sell the formerly state-owned businesses and industries of the DDR. For this purpose, a new institution was created, the "Treuhandanstalt". In 1991, a total of five thousand previously state-owned firms were sold.

Initially, the fast solution to the reunification caused a brief boom in the German economy. However, it soon showed up pressure on the federal budgets and thus led to contractive economic policy. From growth rates of 5 to 6 per cent during 1990-91, 1993 saw a direct fall in the German GDP.

3. France

Due to the rules fixing the electoral period for the French president at seven years, there has been a high degree of stability in the top leadership in French politics. De Gaulle's successor in 1969, Georges Pompidou (1911-74), was followed after his death by the Gaullist, Valèry Giscard d'Estaing (1926-). After the 1981 election, his successor was Georges Mitterrand (1916-97), who was later re-elected in 1988 for a further period. It is within foreign policy that the French president has his greatest power. In matters of economic policy, the president is more dependent on the National Assembly. Until 1986, he had a Socialist majority and Socialist governments. Then, after their election defeat, he had the Gaullist Jacques Chirac (1932-), the later French president, as prime minister. 1988 saw a return to a government headed by Socialists.

The Mitterrand's first presidential period, 1981-88, began in the wake of OPEC II at a time of a fast growth in unemployment. With the later chairman of the EC Commission, Jacques Delors (1925-), as minister of finance, an expansive fiscal policy was initiated at a time when the general trend in economic policy was to do just the opposite. The

Table 20.1. Excess-inflation and –interest rate (per cent p.a.) of France compared to Germany. DM exchange rate (FF pr. DM, 1984 = 100). 1982-93.

	Excess-inflation	Excess-interest rate	DM exch.rate
1982	7.3	7.1	88.2
1983	6.5	6.2	97.2
1984	5.4	5.3	100.0
1985	3.7	4.7	99.3
1986	2.0	2.8	103.9
1987	1.1	3.8	108.8
1988	1.3	2.6	110.4
1989	0.6	2.1	110.4
1990	-0.1	1.7	109.8
1991	-0.6	1.0	110.7
1992	-3.4	1.1	110.1
1993	-1.3	0.5	111.4

Source: OECD. Econ Outlook., Annex-tables.

result was a worsening of the BoP, from –0.7 per cent of GDP in 1981 to –2.2 per cent in 1982. The resultant reaction was a reversal of the policy. Seen in a wider context, the French experience during 1981-82 corresponded to the simultaneous German experience, which meant that even the larger countries under the prevailing conditions would find it difficult or impossible to introduce an expansionist economic policy without running into obstacles. The conclusion that a successful economic policy has to be conducted beyond national level – that is, at a Community level – was soon to be reached by France and Germany, just as they would soon come to believe that such policy would have to be based partly on growing export demand.

That said, it is easier to understand why Jacques Delors, the leader of the unsuccessful French policy in 1981-82, was to be found in Brussels from 1984 onwards as a very active chairman of the EC Commission, working hard to realize the idea of an internal market within the EC and the establishment of an Economic and Monetary Union, the EMU. Hence a main theme in French economic policy from the mid-1980s was the preparation for French membership in a coming EMU as an equal partner with Germany.

During the more than twenty years of Gaullist rule from 1958 to 1981, the post-war elements of economic planning had been reduced.

So, when speaking of France, 'planning' refers to indicative planning, consisting of the announcement of some major medium-term targets for certain sectors of the economy.

Mitterrand wanted to reestablish the earlier policy. With the support of a Socialist majority in the National Assembly, a policy of nationalizations was introduced. As a result, 15 per cent of industrial production took place within nationalized firms, just as the leading banks were brought under public ownership. When compared to Britain and Germany, it seems that France followed a more active and aggressive policy of industrial development. French industrial policy, with the interaction between the private and the public sector, could be characterised as reminiscent of American industrial policy as seen, for example, in the Apollo-programme of the 1960s.

In 1987, the Single European Act, SEA, entered into force, followed in 1989 by the so-called Delors report suggesting the formation of an Economic and Monetary Union. In the long run, the plan might assist

Fig. 18: The French TGV trains can be seen as an example of French industrial policy, letting the government take the lead in technical innovation. At the same time, the new, rapid trains serve to keep the country together, with Paris as the hub of the system.

in strengthening the position of France within European economic and monetary matters. In the short run, it put considerable pressure on French economic policy to live up to the conditions for participation in a coming EMU. By tradition, France tended to have a higher rate of inflation than Germany. This difference now had to be reduced. In table 20.1, figures are found for the years 1982-93 concerning the excess-inflation and the excess-interest rate of France compared to Germany, and an index for the development of the exchange rate in FF of DM (FF per DM in 1984 = 100).

From the middle of the 1980s onwards, the excess-inflation decreased rapidly and since 1990, following German reunification, Germany has had a modest excess-inflation. The excess-interest rate was brought down close to zero, so in terms of a preparation for participation in the EMU, the policy could be seen as a success. What is less evident is that a high price was paid for this success in the form of unemployment rates up at 12 per cent in the first half of the 1990s.

4. Belgium and The Netherlands

In *Belgium,* the decade, 1973-82, was characterized by growing macro-economic problems, a growing public debt being the most significant one. OPEC I hit Belgium in the middle of a boom. In 1973, the growth rate was as high as 6 per cent. At the time of the increase of oil prices, wage increases had recently been agreed upon, and indexation of wages according to price changes was also part of the system. The combined result of this was a tendency toward increased real wages at a time when a worsening of the terms of trade confronted the country with a loss in real income.

This in itself was sufficient to cause problems for the competitive sectors of the economy. In addition there occurred a rise in the value of the Belgium franc, B.Fr., caused by Belgium's participation in the exchange rate cooperation ("the Snake") between the EC countries. The overall outcome was growing unemployment, an increase of the deficit on the public budget and a rise of the interest rate. To alleviate the pressure on traditional export trades like the textile and the glass industries, government subsidies were introduced, causing further pressure on the national budget, though without solving the long-term problems of those industries.

In 1979-80, OPEC II further worsened the existing problems without leading to more fundamental changes in economic policy. The long-term interest rate in 1981-82 reached a level of 15 per cent, and the net public debt rose as high as 94 per cent of GDP, and showed signs of further increase.[8] In 1982, Belgium experienced a change in government and a change in economic policy, just as a number of other countries did. The Socialists left the government benches, a devaluation of nearly 10 percent took place, accompanied by government interventions in wage- and price-fixing. By this time, public debt was stated to be close to 100 hundred per cent of GDP. During the 1980s, it kept growing, to eventually stabilise around 120 per cent of GDP at the end of the 1980s, with the net interest on public debt corresponding to nearly 10 per cent of GDP.

On the one hand, this situation called for a tight fiscal policy in order to prepare Belgium for a coming Economic and Monetary Union, but entailed the risk of putting renewed pressure on the wages. On the other hand, a slack fiscal policy would cast doubts as to the future of the exchange rate, and put pressure on interest rates and costs. To those economic problems, there were also difficulties caused by the state of relations between the different groups of the population living in various parts of the country. In 1989, a far-reaching change in the Belgian constitution took place, separating the country into three different regions with a substantial degree of autonomy, including matters such as industrial policy. At the same time as the country was participating in the process of European integration, it was going through a diametrically opposite development in its internal policy, which demanded the attention of a substantial part of the country's political will and resources.

Measured on the basis of GDP, *the Netherlands* survived OPEC I fairly easily, but met with substantial difficulties following OPEC II. Part of the explanation behind the Dutch development was the extraction of natural gas discovered during the 1960s. Originally, the plan had been to proceed slowly with the use of the gas, partly because of low energy prices at that time. In this respect, the price increases caused by the oil crises meant a change. The extraction of oil was speeded up and the

8.   General government net financial liabilities." OECD Economic Outlook (1996, Annex table 35).

export of natural gas took off. In the short run, this meant increased room on the BoP and the possibility of carrying through an expansionist economic policy after a brief setback in 1975. By the close of the 1970s, the direct contribution of natural gas corresponded to 6 per cent of GDP. As mentioned previously, the discovery of natural gas had side effects. Increasing wage pressure and a rise in the exchange rate at the cost of the competitiveness of other branches, brought effects which were known collectively as the "Dutch disease" (for the similar problem experienced by the Norwegian economy, please refer to the next section). In spite of attempts by the government to revive the tradition of an incomes policy, wage increases ran ahead of productivity increases. During the same period, a relatively large number of young people entered the labour force, with the overall result that the years around OPEC II saw a substantial increase of unemployment.

In 1982 and 84, the partners in the labour market independently concluded agreements with a view to slowing wage increases and unemployment. In 1983, unemployment peaked at around 11 per cent, falling to around 5 per cent in the early 1990s; a relatively low figure for an EC country at that time.

Already from the early postwar years, a strong Keynesian tradition had existed in the Netherlands, supported by the Economic Bureau of Planning. It has been argued that this tradition in the years around OPEC II was responsible for a delay in the adjustment of economic policy. This showed too little interest in deficits on the public budgets and the growth of government debt; a reduction of the budget deficits did not take place until the end of the 1980s.

A remarkable feature of the Dutch economy has been the stability of its currency, the guilder, against the DM, and, related to this, the small margin between the Dutch and the German interest rates. Considered against this background, the Netherlands was well prepared to join the Economic and Monetary Union of the EU.

5. The Scandinavian countries

As far as the overall economic climate is concerned, the period saw a substantial difference between Norway on the one side, and Denmark and Sweden on the other. Norway averaged growth rates of 3.3 per cent during the period 1973-93, compared to 1.7 per cent for Denmark, and 1.4 per cent for Sweden (table 19.5). On the whole, there seem to be substantial differences between developments in the three countries during these two decades. Denmark was hit hardest by the direct effects of OPEC I and II, while Sweden had to carry through the most dramatic and sudden changes in its economic policy at the end of the period. One way of illustrating the development of the internal relationship is by quoting the internal exchange rates. In 1973, the Swedish krona cost 1.39 Danish krone compared to 0.83 Danish krone in 1993. In 1973, the Norwegian krone cost 1.05 Danish krone compared to 0.91 Danish krone in 1993.[9] Although the relative purchasing power of the Swedish krona in 1993 was undoubtedly higher than indicated by those figures, they nonetheless reflect a fundamental change in the international position of the Swedish economy during those years.

1973 was an eventful year for *Denmark*. It started the year by joining the EC, and finished it with the oil crisis, followed by a general election, which lead to a fundamental change in the party-system in the Folketing. Parties never before represented in parliament now obtained more than one third of the seats. As far as economic policy is concerned, the years 1974-75 were characterized by confusion. Although the direct loss in terms of trade only corresponded to 2-3 per cent of GDP, or a seven to eight month increase in GDP at previous growth rates, the situation turned out to be so complicated to handle that growth rates were negative during 1974 and 1975 at –0.9 and –0.7 per cent, respectively. This may be explained by a combination of total wage increases of about 40 per cent within the two years, combined with an exchange rate policy where the Danish krone followed the DM, causing a substantial worsening of the Danish industrial competitiveness. To this must be added a temporary reduction of the VAT rate in 1974-75, in order to promote employment, which resulted in record high deficits on the BoP in 1976 and 77 (respectively 4.8 and 3.8 per cent of GDP). The response to this was an attempt to solve the double problem of increasing unemployment and BoP deficits by "twisting" the demand from goods likely to be imported, to goods and services which were not. Or, put in more direct terms, to move away from private to public consumption. The result of this was a fast

9.   OECD Economic Outlook, nos., 41 and 60, Annex tables.

growth of employment in the public sector, calling forth further labour supply without lowering the unemployment rates. On top of this, OPEC II occurred in 1979-80. This time, wage increases were kept at a much lower level through adjustments in the indexation of wages. Furthermore, successive minor downward adjustments to the Danish krone took place within the EMS cooperation. 1981-82 saw a sharp increase in the deficit on the public budgets and a corresponding increase in interest rates. In September 1982, the Social Democratic government resigned and a Conservative government took over without a general election being held.

The new government brought wage indexation to an end, prolonged existing wage agreements and introduced a tight fiscal policy. The combined effect of this, of previous devaluations and a sharp fall in the level of international interest rates, was a substantial increase in growth rates and a decrease in unemployment at a time when most of OECD Europe saw a deep and prolonged crisis.

This period was, however, followed by a growing deficit on the BoP, which reached 5.4 per cent of GDP in 1986. The background to this was a sharp and unforeseen increase in the private propensity to consume, met by fiscal measures to reduce the tendency to finance consumption through loans. The end of the 1980s and early 1990s marked a shift in the political focus from employment to the BoP. The latter changed from a deficit of the said 5.4 per cent in 1986 to a surplus of 3.3 per cent in 1992. During the same years, the rate of unemployment went up from 8 to 11 per cent, at which level it remained during the first half of the 1990s.

In September 1972, *Norway* decided by a tiny margin to stay outside the EC, and against the recommendations of the government. In the midst of fears of the economic effects of this outcome, an unexpected solution to their economic problems appeared. This was the discovery of rich oil and gas fields in the North Sea and, on top of that, a three to four-fold increase in the oil price, which made it profitable to extract the oil and gas.

In Norway, the years following 1973 were experienced differently than in the rest of Western Europe. In the 1980s, before a fall in the oil price took place, oil contributed nearly 10 per cent to the Norwegian GDP. This in itself was, of course an advantage to the economy, allowing for an expansionary policy in a period of international crises. However, it also involved problems, as mentioned in relation to the experience of the Dutch economy throughout the 1960s and 1970s. Since the 1930s, it had been part of Norwegian economic policy to expand manufacturing industry. In itself, the extraction of oil would be a step in the opposite direction. For this reason, the government wanted to bring the extracted oil ashore in Norway in order to establish related industries. Furthermore, the oil findings would most likely result in an increased wage pressure and an increase in the international value of the Norwegian krone, causing problems in other sectors of the economy. There was also the increased risk of vast changes in the external terms of trade to be added. In order to minimise this risk other competitive sectors, including a petrochemicals industry, were to be developed.

In 1979-80, oil prices almost tripled, which corresponded to an increase in the real price of oil of almost 100 per cent compared with the 1974 level. For Norway, this meant a sharp decrease in the real burden of the foreign debt accumulated during the 1970s in order to finance the new oil industry. Consequently, throughout the early 1980s, Norway still enjoyed good economic fortune. However, in 1986, the price of crude oil dropped to 11 dollars a barrel due to an increase in the Saudi Arabian supply of oil.[10] At the same point Norway experienced wage increases at an annual rate of 16 per cent at a time when the corresponding figure in OECD Europe was down at around 5 per cent. In this way the Norwegian economy had moved into a new stage where it faced BoP difficulties, reduced growth and unemployment rates going up from 2 per cent to 5-6 per cent.

The internal economy was characterised in the middle of the 1980s by a building boom caused by a slack monetary policy followed by a drop in the prices of property. In 1990-91, this was followed by an international setback resulting in a genuine bank crisis reminiscent of similar Swedish crises (see below). As a result of changes in the Communist block, Norway once again faced the issue of whether or not to join the EC. Once again, a referendum brought about a "No", while Norway's two neighbouring countries, Finland and Sweden, decided to enter the EC.

A brief description of the *Swedish* economy during this period would describe it as being slow to adapt to altered conditions. On the

---

10. The lowest absolute price since 1973 and less than half the real price after OPEC I.

positive side, it deserves mention that, until the end of the 1980s, unemployment rates were kept down at around 2 per cent; an exceptionally low level in comparison to the rest of Western Europe. However, Swedish growth rates were also among the lowest, and this tendency strengthened throughout the period (table 19.5). The continuously high level of employment corresponded, not surprisingly, to a poor growth in labour productivity. Seen in a wider context, the Swedish economy faced by the early 1990s substantial problems of adaptation and structural reforms, especially in view of their decision to seek membership of the EC.

Sweden entered the first energy crisis in 1973 with a record high surplus on its BoP. In view of this, the crisis and the ensuing worsening of the BoP were considered to be temporary, and to be financed through Sweden's international reserves. The decision was made to attempt to "leap over" the crisis and the reduction in international demand by implementing an expansionist fiscal policy. This decision, however, turned out to be based on a fundamental misunderstanding. Firstly, the terms of trade loss was not temporary, but permanent and had to be paid for regardless. Secondly, a concerted international effort to stimulate the international economy failed. Thirdly, the same can be said of expectations of an expanding market for traditional Swedish raw materials.

The reaction to this was the introduction in 1976 by a new Agrarian/Conservative government of subsidy schemes targeted at the endangered industries, combined with a devaluation of the Swedish Krona. Between 1977-82, a total of 30 billion Swedish kronar was spent in support to Swedish industries, of which half went to the shipbuilding industry. In 1981, a new devaluation of 10 per cent took place, followed by another devaluation of 17 per cent, this time carried out by a Social Democratic government. The idea was now to kick-start the economy by favouring the competitive sectors of the economy and transferring resources from the sheltered sectors. The policy worked for a couple of years, but then developments in employment and wages in the sheltered sectors overtook the progress in other areas.

Part of the explanation for this can be found in the developments in the capital market. During 1985, restrictions on the import of capital were relinquished and a financial deregulation was undertaken. This gave rise to what the Swedish minister of finance called "the great consumer festival", and an accompanying overheating of the economy. Once again, the economy was back in a situation where the high level of employment rested upon internal demand with accompanying BoP problems.

In 1991, Sweden applied for membership of the EC, although without plans to join the exchange rate cooperation within the EMS, and thus without plans for taking advantage of the mutual scheme of assistance within the EMS. Estimates of the government budget deficit for 1992 were as high as 11 per cent of GDP. At this stage, the government faced difficulties in obtaining foreign loans, which resulted in pressure on the Krona. The Riksbank then decided to float the Swedish krona with the result that it fell by 20 per cent against the EMS currencies, as mentioned at the beginning of this section.

The early 1990s marked a change in the strategy underlying Swedish economic policy. Employment – as the leading goal of economic policy – had to give way to other goals, including improving the BoP and a reduction of the deficits on the government budgets. In short, Sweden started preparing to live up to the criteria of a coming Economic and Monetary Union. This resulted in a sudden increase of unemployment rates in 1990-93 from 1.6 per cent to 8.2 per cent and a drop in the average growth rates over the same four years to –0.8 per cent.

6. Italy

Italy entered the 1970s with two problems that came to dominate her economy for the following twenty years:

a. a strengthening of the trade unions which resulted in increased wage pressure and reduced mobility in the labour market,

b. a public sector characterised by growing fiscal problems due to a lack of balance between expenditure and income from taxes.

Nonetheless, the evaluation of the twenty years following OPEC I may differ according to the selection of success criteria. Measured on the basis of growth rates (1973-94), Italy did best out of the four large EC countries, averaging 2.4 per cent, which was above the growth rates of France and Germany at 2.1 per cent each, and substantially above Great Britain's 1.8 per cent. (table 14.1). Considered over a longer period of time, Italy did relatively well in the first part of the period, but finished below the average of OECD Europe in the 1990s (table 19.5). Before OPEC I, unemployment in Italy was high in comparison to the rest of Western Europe, partly due to geographical differences between the north and the south. Unemployment saw a steady increase and stabilised at a level of approximately 10 per cent of the total labour force in the mid-1980s. It should however be remembered that since the number of self-employed was relatively high, real unemployment might have been higher. Compared with Spain, which reached a level of unemployment of 20 per cent at the same time, the figure seems modest. It should, however, be remembered that the Italian pension schemes were generally generous in granting pensions, including to persons of working age.

Price increases in Italy have been above the Western European average, and clearly above it throughout 1973-89. From 1974 to 1981, the annual rise of the GDP deflator was nearly 20 per cent, approximately twice the average increase in the rest of Western Europe.[11] This may be seen in conjunction with the development of public finance. Out of the nine member countries of the EC during the time of the energy crises, Italy – along with Belgium – was the country that experienced the largest budget deficits. In 1992-93, the Italian public debt corresponded to a whole year's GDP.[12] In Italy, shortcomings in the system of control to deal effectively with the taxation of a great number of small firms and shops were in part to blame.

Italy joined the European Monetary System from its very beginning in 1979. It was the hope of the government to thereby put the economy in a straitjacket, keeping inflation down and bringing the economy in line with the rest of the EC countries. Unsurprisingly, this hope was not fulfilled. The Italian Lire had to adjust several times within the system and was given a wider range of movement than the rest of the currencies.

Judged on the basis of the convergence criteria of the EMU within the EC in the early 1990s, which set narrow limits to central macro-

---

11. OECD, Historical Statistics, 1987.
12. In Belgium the debt at that time corresponded to the GDP for 15 months.

economic indicators (chapter 21, section 8), Italy was facing serious problems and needing substantial adjustments to its economic policy during the 1990s. For Italy, as for other EC countries, this became a dominant goal of her economic policy in the 1990s.

7. Spain and Portugal

A common characteristic for these two countries during the 1970s was their transformation from dictatorship to democracy. In Spain, this took place after the death of Franco in November 1975, which was followed by the proclamation of king Juan Carlos. Eighteen months earlier, the transition to democracy had been accomplished in Portugal, as the result of a peaceful coup d'etat, later to be known as the Revolution of the Carnations. In both countries, a period of economic turbulence followed. The major economic event of the period for both Spain and Portugal was their admission to the EC in 1986.

Throughout the 1960s and early 1970s, *Spain* had experienced average growth rates of around 7 per cent, primarily due to the prosperous tourist industry. Described on the basis of macro-economic indicators, Spain experienced growth rates in 1973-93 that were similar to those in OECD Europe, including the tendency towards a decrease over time. Between OPEC I and II, the annual rise of the GDP deflator was as high as 20 per cent, and it remained at around 10 per cent until the middle of the 1980s, clearly above most of Western Europe. Unemployment figures were even more exceptional. From a low 3 per cent of the labour force in 1973, modest increases took place until 1980. From then on, the unemployment rate accelerated from 11 per cent to 21 per cent in 1985, thus making Spain the country in Western Europe with by far the highest rates. It is remarkable that this development was accompanied by annual wage increases of 10 per cent. By the end of the 1980s, a reduction in the unemployment occurred. However, in 1993, unemployment again passed the 20 per cent mark. The first election following the end of the Franco period was held in 1977 and resulted in a right-wing government. In 1982, a Socialist government came into power. It was during this government that the unemployment rate skyrocketed in spite of expressed plans to the contrary. Part of the explanation for the growing unemployment was increased competition for the Spanish tourist industry from Greece and Turkey, new patterns of travel, and overseas competition for Spanish steel, shipbuilding and textile industries. To this must be added the existence of a traditional, seasonal unemployment in Spanish agriculture.

In 1979, Spain – and Portugal – applied for membership of the EC and both were admitted in 1986. The outcome of the negotiations has since been criticised as being less satisfactory for Spain. According to the rules of accession, the original EC countries were not obliged to open their markets up for Spanish fruit and vegetables for the first ten years, whereas Spain had to open its market to industrial products and accept the lowering of its external customs duties to the level of the EC-tariff within a period of seven years.

The economic development in *Portugal* since OPEC II resembles that of Spain, although Portugal experienced even greater changes to her economic development.

As far as the political climate is concerned, the fall of the regime in 1974 caused a fast and sharp swing to the left. Under a new constitution, extensive nationalisations within banking and manufacturing industries took place. This was supplemented by a policy aiming at a change in the distribution of incomes in favour of wage earners. The total wage bill, previously as low as around 50 per cent of total incomes, increased to 60 per cent within a few years. This took place in the aftermath of OPEC I, contributing to a strong inflationary pressure. While the rise of the GDP deflator had been as low as 3 per cent per year throughout the 1960s, it went as high as 20-25 per cent during the years 1977-86.

The change of the system, including the shift to the left, involved other macro-economic problems as well. Portugal was, as might be expected, confronted with a BoP problem, partly met by an assistance scheme by the IMF, which included a devaluation of the escudos. The plan involved a tight monetary and fiscal policy and brought down the BoP deficit close to zero. In 1982, another constitutional reform took place involving the privatisation of some of the previously nationalised undertakings. The early 1980s were characterised by renewed serious BoP problems, once again prompting the assistance of the IMF. Portugal's admittance to the EC in 1986 marked a change and was followed by a restructuring of the Portuguese economy, taking advantage of its comparatively low wage level as a member of the Common Market.

8. The USA

The economic policy of the USA throughout the 1970s and 1980s seems paradoxical on a close examination. According to the political rhetoric, periods with Republican administration ought to be characterised by classical virtues like balanced public budgets and stable prices. This, however, was not the case after the inauguration of Richard Nixon in 1969. And it did not happen either when Ronald Reagan (1911–) followed the Democrat Jimmy Carter (1924–) in 1981, in spite of the fact that the Reagan election campaign explicitly referred to such intentions. On the contrary, the pressure on the federal budgets was increased when the Reagan administration simultaneously had to fulfil promises to ensure tax cuts and strengthen the USA's defence. A tightening was seen in social security; but not in the overall fiscal policy.

If a line of demarcation were to be drawn, it would have to be in 1979 during the presidency of Jimmy Carter. The USA's central bank, the Federal Reserve System, changed its policy in autumn 1979. Whereas before it placed its major emphasis on the level of the interest rate, it now concentrated on the development of the money supply with the outcome that the interest rate under OPEC II rose above 10 percent; a most unusual situation according to recent American standards.

Part of the explanation of why the change of administration in 1981 did not cause deeper changes to the economic policy may be found in the fact that the Republicans did not have a majority in the Congress. While Margaret Thatcher, as the new, contemporary British prime minister, had a solid majority behind her, Reagan had to govern partly on the basis of the powers vested in the presidency alone. He could use those powers to intervene in the business of trade unions, as when he brought a long-lasting strike among commercial pilots to a halt, and when he carried out "decontrol", terminating systems of concessions and regulations in business. But the laying down of the central fiscal policy itself was dependent on Congress. In table 20.2, some central macro-economic indicators are presented for the USA, Japan and OECD Europe in selected years from 1960 to 1993. The table gives an idea of the relationship between the internal and external balance problems of the USA. During the period 1981 to 1993, an increase in the deficits in the government sector took place without being com-

Table 20.2: Central macroeconomic indicators for USA, Japan and OECD Europe. Selected years 1960-93.

Per cent of GDP		1960	1968	1974	1981	1993
Public expenditures	USA	27.2	30.7	32.1	34.1	37.3
	Japan	17.5	19.2	24.5	33.5	34.9
	OECD Europe	31.3	36.3	40.0	48.9	52.2
Public social transfers	USA	5.0	6.4	9.5	11.1	13.2
	Japan	3.8	4.5	6.2	10.6	12.1
	OECD Europe	9.5	12.0	13.2	18.1	19.2
Public net-borrowing	USA	-0.4	0.7	0.3	1.1	4.4
	Japan	-1.7	-0.8	-0.4	3.8	1.4
	OECD Europe	-0.8	0.7	1.8	4.4	6.3
Fixed gross-investments	USA	18.0	18.4	18.9	18.6	16.2
	Japan	29.0	33.2	34.8	30.7	29.8
	OECD Europe	22.3	23.2	24.3	20.6	19.3
Gross-savings	USA	19.9	19.6	20.2	19.8	14.9
	Japan	32.9	37.1	36.3	31.1	32.5
	OECD Europe	24.7	24.6	24.1	19.5	18.8
Export of goods and services	USA	5.2	5.3	8.6	9.7	10.3
	Japan	10.7	10.1	13.6	14.8	9.5
Import of goods and services	USA	4.4	5.2	8.7	10.3	11.6
	Japan	10.2	9.0	14.3	14.0	7.2
Position of BoP, current account	USA	0.6	0.2	0.5	0.3	-1.5
	Japan	0.5	0.8	-1.0	0.5	3.2

Source: OECD, Historical Statistics 1960-93. For 1981, the edition covering 1960-85.

pensated by a corresponding increase in savings in the private sector. In 1993, savings of only 14.9 per cent of GDP met fixed gross investments of 16.2 per cent of GDP. The difference between the two is found (almost) at the bottom of the table, as a deficit of the BoP corresponding to 1.5 per cent of GDP.[13] In Japan, the situation was just the opposite, with surplus savings of nearly 3 per cent of GDP making up a BoP surplus of 3 per cent.

Those two pairs of figures might lead to two entirely different conclusions concerning the American economy and economic policy. One might be based on the view that the American market was being flooded with Japanese cars, consumer electronics, etc., while the Japanese simultaneously put up all sorts of barriers to US exports. A solution here could be to introduce trade restrictions against Japanese goods, or at least threaten to do so. The other conclusion concentrates on the existence of the American savings deficit. Here, the appropriate corrective measures might then be tax favours to promote private sector saving or a tightening of fiscal policy – all depending on the political viewpoint.

As will be seen, the American export quota[14] doubled between the 1960s and the 1990s from 5 to 10 per cent. The US economy is not as closed as it used to be. The export of goods and services is not an unimportant part of the total demand for American products, which seems to have balanced the protectionist forces in US trade policy.[15]

In the development of public expenditure, including public social transfers, the US figures are still far below those for OECD Europe. However, it should be noted that the figures for the USA have been increasing. The figures for public social transfers as a fraction of GDP are now as high in the USA as they were in OECD Europe in 1974. It seems justifiable to state that the USA, as far as its public sector is concerned, is approaching European conditions.

During the last twenty to thirty years, a new relationship between the American and European economies has emerged. In American literature, increased competition from European firms and their affiliates in the USA is a recurring theme. This may be proof of the development Europe has gone through since the days of the Dollar gap and the Marshall aid at the end of the Second World War.

---

13. The difference between the two deficits may be due to changes in stocks.
14. Exports as a percentage of GDP. Note that the figures of table 20.2 include the export of services.
15. The "external" export quota of the 12 EC countries (not including their internal trade) which were members in 1993 were (goods only) 9 per cent, compared to a corresponding figure for the USA of 7 per cent. As will be seen, the dependence on external, non-EU trade was nearly at the same level for the two areas. Eurostat Yearbook, 1995.

9. Japan

During the period 1951-73 Japan experienced average growth rates above 9 per cent, compared to 4-6 per cent for the countries of Western Europe. This gives rise to the question of whether Japan could continue to have growth rates considerably higher than those of Western Europe and the USA. The answer seems to be positive – but only for a time. During the period 1973-93, the average growth rates for Japan were 3.6 per cent compared to 2.2 per cent for OECD Europe and 2.3 per cent for the USA. These indicate that Japan not only was catching up, but on her way to passing her rivals. However, the difference between the growth rates was diminishing and during the 1990s the Japanese growth rates actually fell behind both those of Western Europe and the USA.[16]

The economy of Japan has, on the whole, seen the same sort of ups and downs as the rest of the OECD countries, but, as explained, at a higher level of growth until the early 1990s. Japan first experienced a major setback in 1974-75, caused by the dependence on imported energy. The country faced strong internal pressure on costs, reflected in a rise of the GDP-deflator of 20 per cent in 1974,[17] surpassing even the Italian inflation. At the same time, the BoP ran a deficit, which was, all in all, a most unusual situation for Japan. This may explain Japan's reluctance to participate in a coordinated action to sustain the international economy. In this, Japan behaved like another potential great economic locomotive, Germany. The second oil crisis, OPEC II, had far less impact on Japan. The rise in the GDP deflator was below 4 per cent this time; half the rise experienced in Western Europe and only one fifth of that in 1974.

With reference to table 20.2, some major aspects of the Japanese economy since 1973 are to be pointed out. When considering the figures in the table, it should be kept in mind that the years 1974 and 1981, as already mentioned, have special characteristics. This is especially true for 1974, particularly in regard to the import figures. The

---

16. For the years 1992-99 on average for Japan 0.7 per cent, compared to 2.0 per cent for the EC and 3.2 per cent for the USA.
17. In 1973, oil imports made up 22 per cent of the value of the total goods imported by Japan. Because of oil price increases of 3-4 times, the share in the short run increased to more than 50 per cent. In 1980, after OPEC II, the share was exactly 50 per cent. B. Balassa and M. Noland, (1988, 27). It may be proper to remind the reader that it was fear of an oil embargo that was the direct cause of Japan's attack on the US naval base at Pearl Harbor in December 1941.

deficits on the BoP are neither representative of the 1970s nor the 1980s.[18] A striking feature of the table – reflected in the BoP-figures – is the high level of savings in Japan. In 1993, savings as a fraction of GDP exceeded investments by 3 per cent. The equivalent to this is found at the bottom of the table as a surplus on the current account of the BoP (see the discussion in the previous section concerning the corresponding deficit in the USA). In 1981-82, a drop in the exchange rate of the Yen took place causing an increase in the Japanese BoP surplus, just when the opposite was being hoped for in USA and other deficit countries of the OECD.

The critique of the Japanese economic policy has taken several directions. The industrial and trade policies were criticised for all sorts of protective measures, including export subsidies and hidden obstacles to imports, NTBs. Against this it could be argued that Japan's advantage lay in its high productivity rates in the production of cars and household electronics, but seen from the point of view of its trade partners there was a general need for Japan to increase its internal demand. One area that was subjected to criticism was Japanese housing and construction policy. The shortage of building land fit for residential development has caused prices to skyrocket with the result that rents are extremely high, dwellings small and building activities low compared to the size of the population. This again meant that a comparatively modest home by western standards was very expensive and required many years of savings to pay for it. This, combined with other factors, led to low levels of activity in the building and the furnishing industries.

During the post-war years of high growth, an increase in the relative importance of the manufacturing industries had taken place. However, compared with the advanced OECD countries, the growth in the service sector has been rather modest. This might have been due to the structure of the firms, which were either very big or rather small and provided services for themselves. Over many years, more specifically during the 1960s and 1970s, the composition of Japanese exports has changed from consisting mainly of less advanced products like steel and steel products and labour intensive products based on cheap, unskilled labour producing textiles, textile goods and leather manufac-

18. In the period 1974-79, there was a total surplus of 0.3 per cent of GDP and in 1980-89 of 2.1 per cent of GDP. The Corresponding figures for Germany were 1.0 and 2.0 per cent.

tures. Exports have switched to advanced products from the metallurgy industry, and employing a highly skilled labour force. From here on, the development continued, though based by then on a high rate of R&D, much of which takes place at industry level.

Table 20.3: Japanese production, export and import of passenger cars and US production, 1960-90. In 1000 units.

1000 units.	1960	1970	1980	1990
Production	250	3.179	7.038	9.948
Export	n.a.	789	4.352	5.026
Import	n.a.	19	46	254
World production	11.580	22.560	29.006	35.316
US production	5.543	6.547	6.376	6.081

Source: Statistical Yearbook. Separate volumes, Danish Statistics.

The greatest export success story belongs to the automobile industry. From a modest beginning in the 1950s, production counted by number of units grew by more than ten times during the 1960s, with continued growth in the 1970s and 1980s. In 1980, Japan had passed the USA, calculated on the basis of the number of cars produced. This difference further widened in the decade that followed. In 1990, Japan accounted for nearly 30 per cent of world car production. A remarkable, not to say astonishing, feature is the low number of cars imported by Japan. This lack of balance has been used by other car producing countries as an argument for restrictions on the imports of Japanese cars. In response to British wishes, Japan agreed to keep its export of cars to the British market down at a level corresponding to 11 per cent of the total sale of new cars in Britain. A corresponding agreement with France kept the level as low as 3 per cent. A similar agreement with Italy set the figure at 3.000 cars a year![19] To escape those restrictions, Japanese car manufacturers have set up production subsidiaries within the EC, raising the question of whether their output ought to be considered as having been "produced" within the customs union and therefore entitled to treatment as such. In 1993, an agreement was reached between the EC Commission and the Japanese Ministry of Trade, MITI, according to

19. D.Dyker, ed., (1992a, 200).

which MITI undertook the ongoing administration involved in controlling the export of cars.[20]

Seen in a wider context, and just as in other Newly Industrializing Countries in the Far East, the developments within Japanese car manufacture and its electronics industry point to a far wider field of problems concerning the renewal of the trades and industries of the "old" industrial countries. This topic will be dealt with in the next chapter in relation to the establishment of the EC's internal market at the end of 1992 and the revival of its dynamism.

20. D.Dyker, ed. (1999, 233f).

Chapter 21

European Integration 1973 –
Slowing down and movement again

The development of European integration since 1973 consists of two distinct parts separated by the period 1983-85, which was marked by the meetings of the heads of state and government held in Stuttgart in 1983, Fontainebleau in 1984 and Milan in 1985. Prior to these meetings, a number of initiatives had been taken from the start of the 1970s, all of which proved fruitless due to various problems of the day such as the energy crises, agricultural policy, budgetary matters, rising inflation, unemployment and so on. These problems were further aggravated by the second oil crisis of 1979-80 when Community members experienced a prolonged recession with growth rates down around zero and inflation and unemployment up in the region of 10 per cent (tables 19.1 and 19.5).

By comparison with these signs of European weakness, the growth rates of the newly industrialized countries were virtually unaffected by the energy crises. The combination of internal stagnation and growth overseas confronted the EC member states with the following question: *Has Western Europe had its day?* Just as external political pressure in the late 1940s and 1950s had contributed to the process of integration, external economic pressure was now having the same effect. A need made itself felt to replace national answers and solutions to the economic crisis with mutual solutions through the process of integration. The result of the initiatives taken in the mid-1980s was a decision to call an inter-governmental conference aimed at the reform of both economic and political cooperation within the EC. It was this decision which resulted in 1986 in the drawing up of the Single European Act (SEA), followed by its ratification and entry into force in July 1987.

The Single Act contained both institutional and economic reforms, it scheduled the creation of the "internal market" as well as preparations for a coming *Economic and Monetary Union*, EMU. With a view to bringing this about, a study group was set up in 1988 under the chairmanship of Jacques Delors in order to produce concrete suggestions concerning EMU. The next step was taken in calling two inter-governmental conferences dealing with economic and political cooperation respectively. These conferences resulted in the signing of the Maastricht Treaty in February 1992 followed by its coming into force in November 1993 after a highly dramatic process of ratification.

In parallel with this development, upheavals took place within the Soviet bloc and the USSR from 1989 onwards. 1989-90 saw the reunification of Germany followed in 1991 by the collapse of the USSR and the remainder of the Soviet bloc. This train of events led to a number of countries knocking on the door of the EC. From an economic point of view, Austria, Finland and Sweden, along with Switzerland and Norway, were ready for membership, but it was decided to postpone any decisions until the Maastricht Treaty came into force, while other potential applicants had to wait for a later opportunity.

1. The slowdown and the forces behind

The December 1969 meeting in The Hague signalled important developments within the Communities: enlargement of the EC by the earlier applicants headed by Great Britain and the strengthening of both economic and political cooperation between member countries. Of these three goals, only the first was to be realized at that time.

A report on the establishment of an economic and monetary union was presented in October 1970. It was to be known as the *Werner report* after Pierre Werner, chairman of the committee that prepared the report and prime minister of Luxembourg. According to the report, an economic and monetary union was to be achieved by 1980. There was a specific timetable, though, in retrospect, the whole approach seems to have been far too ambitious, if not unrealistic.

In the meantime another committee chaired by the Belgian diplomat, Étienne Davignon, had been at work preparing a report on cooperation within foreign policy. The *Davignon report* proposed a strengthening of common foreign policy, though in such a way that it would conform to French ideas by taking place outside Community structures; in other words, traditional, inter-governmental or confederal cooperation.

In March 1971, the Council adopted a resolution outlining the creation of an Economic and Monetary Union as well as the start of a first stage of a transitional period. In October 1972, at a meeting of the heads of state and government leaders, this decision was confirmed. After that nothing more was heard of the plan at governmental level for the next ten to fifteen years! To understand why the Werner plan was ill-fated, the following contemporary economic problems should be taken into consideration:

a. since 1969 the Bretton Woods system with its fixed exchange rates was in trouble, and turbulence in international money markets was a hindrance at the time to the creation of a monetary union,

b. increasing oil prices in 1973 gave rise to balance of payments deficits in the oil importing countries accompanied by rising unemployment; a situation met by national measures instead of coordinated measures at Community level,

c. the widening of the EC at the start of 1973 slowed down the potential deepening of cooperation. Great Britain wanted a renegotiation of her conditions of entry and her wishes tended toward a reduction in the scope of cooperation, not its deepening, with the British being supported in this by Denmark,

d. the CAP and budgetary problems were causing increasing problems in the day-to-day business of the Community. Just maintaining what had already been accomplished was proving difficult, so further achievements were put on hold for the time being.

As a summary of points a to d, the following lines are apropos from the Delors report which looked back at the 1970s and early 1980s: "...by the mid-1970s, the process of integration had lost momentum under the pressure of divergent policy responses to the economic shocks of the period".[1]

---

1. Committeee for the Study of Economic and Monetary Union. Report on Economic and Monetary Union in the European Community. 1989, section 1 point I.2.

2. Institutional changes

In chapter 16 the distinction between traditional inter-governmental cooperation and supra-national cooperation was touched upon (confederal versus federal cooperation) as was the distinction between sectoral and general cooperation where the latter includes foreign policy and security issues.

If the EC is to be categorized according to these criteria, then for the first twelve years of its existence, 1958-70, it was a *sectoral, federal cooperation*. This corresponds with what was stated in the Treaty of Rome: that the supreme body of the Community should have the power to make decisions in the form of regulations that were directly binding *in* the member states and that, to an increasing degree, this was to be accomplished through the use of majority decisions. This latter point had, however, been softened through the Luxembourg compromise due to French pressure. The overall impression left by the transitional period was one of development towards sectoral, federalist cooperation which was acceptable even to the French because of the economic advantages attached to the realization of the Treaty of Rome.

At the end of the transitional period, after the Hague meeting in December 1969, a new situation prevailed. If cooperation was to be extended to new fields such as monetary and fiscal policy, foreign policy and security issues, then adjustments would have to be made to the treaties. This in turn, however, would mean inaugurating a debate about the very nature of cooperation: federal or confederal? The fact that the Treaty of Rome had indicated federal, sectoral cooperation as the way to proceed initially did not mean that any extension of the process of integration had to take place along exactly the same lines. At this point, it is worth remembering that the inclusion of Great Britain and Denmark meant that the confederalist wing was reinforced.

In the Assembly, however, renamed the European Parliament in 1993, activist forces were represented. These were forces working towards development along federalist lines that wanted the Assembly to acquire increased influence at the expense of the Council, national governments and national parliaments. In this fashion, a source of tension arose between the Assembly and the Council, to which should be added the interest of the Commission in retaining its right to take initiatives and present proposals to the Council.

The initiative to call a meeting at The Hague in December 1969 was taken be the newly elected French president, Georges Pompidou, and the meeting proper took place outside the aegis of EC institutions, although some of its decisions had to be confirmed at a subsequent meeting of the Council. The Hague meeting was noteworthy as it introduced the new idea of convening special meetings between heads of state and government leaders.[2]

The next meeting of this type took place in Paris in October 1972, once again due to a French initiative. The participants this time included the newcomers to the Community: Great Britain, Ireland and Denmark. A resolution was passed at this meeting stating that the participants would aim at the creation of a European union before the end of the decade. The Danish prime minister had a hard time explaining what this meant upon his return to Denmark. The next step in the development of this "non-Community cooperation" – called *"summits"* – between the EC countries was another Paris meeting in December 1974 when it was decided that these summits from then on were to be held on a regular basis, three times a year. This was, however, later changed to twice a year, and so that the chairmanship of these meetings would follow that of the EC Council. In order to distinguish this new body from the *Council*[3] (of the EC), the gatherings at the summits were named *the European Council* and, just to make the confusion all the more complete, it should be noted the body which resides in Strasbourg and has held its meetings there since 1949 is called the *Council of Europe.*

The scope of the meetings in the European Council was not restricted to matters dealt with in the EC treaties. In this sense, a new European institution had been created where matters such as policy towards refugees and foreign policy could be dealt with. It should be noted, however, that decisions were not binding on the participants, though the regular summits might be used to make decisions that would afterwards be confirmed in the Council (of the EC) in order to classify them as part of the formal EC cooperation. An example of this was the decision taken in December 1978 to establish the European Monetary System, the EMS.

As will be seen, the overall picture of the development of integration during this period was blurred. It seems fair, nevertheless, to conclude

2. It should be noted here that only France is represented by its head of state, the president, at these meetings while the other countries are represented by their prime ministers.
3. Often referred to as the *Council of Ministers.*

that the initiative was moving away from the EC institutions in Brussels to the capitals of the member states – meaning that development was moving in the direction of a general, confederalist cooperation.

3. CAP and the budget

3.1. Increasing surplus production

A major aim of the CAP was to secure decent incomes for the farmers and in order to bring this about a system of guaranteed prices had been established. It was hoped that this could be done without substantial net costs to the Community, and that the costs incurred by the occasional instances of surplus production would be covered by the revenue of the variable import levies and the common tariff. The prerequisite for this was that the EC, considered as a whole, was a net importer of agricultural products.

This was where things started going wrong. As expected, there was a decline in the number of farms and farmers, but the productivity of those who remained in business grew much faster than consumption. So, as the various schemes were based on levels of self-sufficiency below one hundred per cent, when self-sufficiency exceeded the one hundred per cent level, this posed a major problem for the economy of the Community.

The central steering instrument of the CAP at this stage was its policy of guaranteed prices for producers, which were normally agreed upon for a period of a year at meetings of the ministers of agriculture. These schemes were, in a way, based on market forces to the extent that producers and consumers made their decisions on the basis of prices – in the early days, no use was made of production quotas. The prices, however, were not the result of market forces, but of late-night meetings of the Council of Ministers, followed in the corridors with keen interest by various pressure groups from their home countries.

According to the schemes, individual farmers benefitted from the price increases according to the size of their production. This produced the odd result that when prices were raised in order to assist smallholders working under unfavourable conditions, perhaps in mountainous areas, it was the farmers with the largest farms, mainly in the northern parts of the EC, who benefitted the most.

A few figures will illustrate the degree of EC self-sufficiency from the late 1960s to the 1980s. They also show the rate of development and what went wrong. The degree of self-sufficiency is indicated in percentage terms for the years 1968/69, 1973/74 and 1986/87 respectively; for grain: 86, 98 and 111; sugar: 82, 100 and 127; butter: 92, 98 and 105; beef: 95, 96 and 108.[4]

The swift growth of the expenses involved with the CAP made a newcomer to the summits in 1979, the new British prime minister, Margaret Thatcher, announce to her European colleagues that "I want my money back", though the legitimacy of this statement is debatable. There can be no doubt that the British were large net-payers for a policy that had failed to fulfil its original purpose, but they had, however, in joining the EC accepted the CAP as part of the EC system. The CAP and the budget were to remain a constant problem for Britain – and the EC – throughout the 1980s.

3.2. Budget crises

In 1978, CAP expenditure levels reached 80 per cent of total EC expenditure and, despite the fact that the Community had been granted the income of a new value-added tax, VAT, the total expenditure of the Communities now exceeded total income. It was only through the use of creative bookkeeping involving the transfer of expenses to the following fiscal year that the EC was able to stay out of the red. This general state of affairs where the EC was teetering on the brink of general deficit, not to say bankruptcy, continued until the mid-1980s by which time it was not only the British who were protesting.

After enlargement to the South; Greece in 1981, Portugal and Spain in 1986, there were, with Italy, four countries of Southern Europe which wanted the expenditure of the EC to be changed in favour of regional development programmes to be paid for through the regional development funds. At this time, CAP costs still amounted to almost two-thirds of total Community expenditure, corresponding to 0.7 per cent of the total GDP of the EC area. Generally speaking, subsidies represented 50 per cent of the farmers' total revenue or turnover. Another point of criticism was the 1 per cent of VAT paid to the EC. In this instance, it was argued that the basis for calculating VAT, private

---

4.   Figures reproduced from the Danish Ministry of Trade. Erhvervspolitisk redegørelse. 1993. P. 303.

consumption, made up a larger proportion of GDP in those countries with lower per capita incomes. In order to compensate for this effect, a new source of income based on the size of GDP was introduced. Accordingly, such a contribution, within EC called the wealth tax, was introduced in 1988. In 1993, the EC income situation was as follows: original income i.e. revenue of customs duties and variable import levies, amounted to 20 per cent of total income, VAT to 55 per cent and the new wealth tax, 25 per cent.[5]

3.3. Changing the Common Agricultural Policy

A major theme of the budget crisis was a reform of the CAP that included a ceiling on CAP expenditure. The solution involved the basic principle of the system, that producer prices were the steering instrument. In breach of the policy, and under the shadow of the "butter mountain", quotas for milk production were introduced in 1984. In the wake of this, the Commission presented a plan in 1985 which led to a reform of the CAP along the following lines:

a. a reduction in the price of grain and oil seed according to which grain prices were to fall by 35 per cent over a period of three years. This reduction was to be compensated for in part by premiums paid for arable land that was allowed to lie fallow, the so-called "set aside" land which had to comprise at least 15 per cent of any given farm for the money to be paid out,

b. a change from price support to direct subsidies, see above, including special transfers to farmers with low incomes,

c. in principle, the subsidies were to be based on factor input instead of the size of production, the intention being to diminish the incentive to increase production.

Since then, there has been a tendency towards a reduction of the proportion of total EC expenditure represented by the CAP. Whereas, in 1988, the price support schemes, administered through the Guarantee Fund, accounted for 65 per cent of EC expenditure, by 1993 the share was down to 52 per cent, while the funds for structural support in-

5.   Eurostat. Yearbook 95, p. 402.

creased slightly from 2.7 to 4.6 per cent. In accordance with the wishes of the new member countries, supported by Great Britain and Ireland, the share of the Regional Development Fund increased from 7 to 14 per cent and the share of the Social Fund from 5 to 8 per cent of total expenditure.[6] It should, however, not be forgotten that the EC budget, by comparison with the GDP of the member states, still seemed modest. In 1985, total income corresponded to 0.8 per cent of member states' GDP, though by 1993 this had risen to 1.2 per cent.[7]

Fig. 19: French farmers driving their tractors slowly on the Strasbourg-Paris motorway in February 1999. The farmers were protesting against reforms of the CAP in preparations for the anticipated enlargement of the EU.

6.   Eurostat. Yearbook 95, p. 403
7.   Eurostat. Yearbook 96, pp. 208 and 420

4. Exchange rate policy

4.1. A period of turbulence

As far as exchange rate policy was concerned, the Treaty of Rome confined itself to stating that each member state considered its exchange rate policy to be *a matter of common interest* (art. 107, section 1), followed by a vague statement concerning the possibilities open to the Commission to prevent the relative competitiveness of the member states from changing substantially due to exchange rate fluctuations. As exchange rates were rather stable until the late 1960s, no need was felt at that time to take initiatives in this area at Community level.

A related matter was the question of freeing the movement of capital, the point of departure being the existence of restrictions on the free movement of capital in the 1950s and the early 1960s. The Treaty of Rome stated that the member states had to abolish restrictions insofar as they affected persons living within their borders to the extent necessary for the Common Market to function (Art. 67, section 1). This particular area did not give rise to any substantial problems during the 1960s either. Liberalization of capital movements was taken care of first by the OEEC, then by the OECD, and tended to take place at a global level. As a general rule, it can be said that the movements of long-term capital were the first to be liberalized and, after some delay, were followed by those of short-term capital.

A change in the stability of exchange rates took place in the late 1960s which involved occasional pressure on the US dollar and sterling, along with the strengthening of the yen and the mark. By the early 1970s, the Bretton Woods system had broken down. The margins for exchange rate movement had increased and floating currencies made their appearance. In March 1973, West Germany decided to let the mark float vis-à-vis the US dollar as well as other currencies. The background for this action was sustained speculation against the dollar. At this point in time, the German Bundesbank stopped buying US dollars in order to protect itself against potential losses if the value of the dollar felt permanently. The situation for the EC countries was such that there were no formal arrangements concerning exchange rates within the Community. In practice, this led to the creation of a system of block floating of EC currencies in the wake of the flotation of the mark, with occasional adjustments of exchange rates vis-à-vis the mark. Great Britain pursued a policy of her own and experienced a great fall in the value of sterling in the mid-1970s, which caused a number of problems in the functioning of the Community.

This was felt most strongly in relation to the workings of the CAP as the guaranteed prices were fixed according to a special accounting unit that corresponded to the value of a "gold dollar". Exchange rate adjustments in the EC countries meant reduced or increased prices in local currencies for farmers of countries that were respectively devaluing or revaluing. Just reaching an agreement on the prices of agricultural products was already sufficiently complex without the added difficulty of allowing for exchange rate fluctuations. Special *green exchange rates* were introduced for calculating the prices paid to farmers, and these were supplemented by special internal levies to adjust for price differences between member states.

EC income and expenditure posed another set of problems. A common accounting unit corresponding to a gold dollar was used in fixing the budget and the transfer of contributions from member states, but fluctuating exchange rates led to the application and use of a multi-exchange rate system. So, both for more narrow, practical reasons as well as wider, economic and political reasons, a need was felt to introduce a more stable exchange rate system.

4.2. The European Monetary System, EMS

When the values of the currencies of two countries that are otherwise working closely together move against one another, which country should then adjust its economic policy? Should the country whose currency is gaining in international value initiate an expansionist policy so as to bring the rise in value to a halt? Or should the country with the weak currency conduct a contractive economic policy in order to stop the depreciation? Or should both countries contribute to a solution through a combination of both kinds of policy? The third case would be one of *symmetric* adjustment, whereas the first two would be examples of *asymmetric* adjustment. If the two hypothetical countries correspond to West Germany and the remaining EC countries, then the policies of the 1970s could be characterized as being asymmetric; West Germany pursued its policy of keeping a lid on price rises and of running a healthy surplus on the balance of payments, leaving it to the rest of the EC members to adjust their exchange rates vis-à-vis the mark. In this way, the German central bank, the Bundesbank, decided the monetary and exchange rate policies of the EC.

By the late 1970s, there was a general feeling that the EC countries would have to stabilize their internal exchange rates, though even if this were to be accomplished, there would have to be the possibility of making occasional adjustments. At the same time, there was a feeling that Germany ought to follow a looser economic policy; in other words, participate in a symmetric policy. Among the set of goals defined at the time was, *first*, the creation of a zone of countries within the EC having stable, though adjustable exchange rates, *second*, the execution of a symmetric policy where countries with surpluses and those with deficits contributed to the balancing of the national economies and, *third*, to enter arrangements which limited the dangers of speculation against the currencies of individual member states. With a view to all this, the *European Monetary System*, the *EMS*, was established.

The *European Currency Unit, the ECU* was at the heart of the system. It consisted of a "basket" containing a well-defined amount of member state currencies including sterling, although Britain did not participate. At *a given time*, the value of the basket, stated in the form of each of the participating currencies, was calculated on the basis of current exchange rates; the price of the basket in a given currency was then considered to be the *central exchange rate* of that currency. From that point on, limits were fixed for the movements of the currencies, firstly against the central exchange rate and, secondly, against one another. Member states were now obliged to take measures in order to remain within a certain proximity to the central exchange rate and to assist one another should the distance between two currencies become too large.

Details of how the system functioned are beyond the scope of this work. The system came into force in March 1979 and within it there was a general tendency towards a strengthening of the D-mark and a weakening of the Italian lira and, at the beginning, the French franc. On the whole, in spite of the original intentions, the system remained asymmetric in the sense that the participants still had to adjust to German leadership, which in practice meant that the members adjusted to German policy when formulating their own economic policies.

In the early years of the EMS a number of adjustments were made to central exchange rates though, from the mid-1980s onwards, this activity tapered off. The background to this was a convergence of economic policies as well as convergence in the rates of inflation. This system suffered its final blow in 1993, by which time the EMU and the Euro was under way, bringing with it a new pattern for European monetary policy.

5. The European Parliament

By comparison with national parliaments, the European Parliament, known until 1993 as the Assembly, has only a limited remit. A central task of an ordinary parliament is reflected in the power to raise taxes. This power is often exclusive and in this way a parliament – whose origins are usually traced back to the English Parliament – holds supreme power over a government and its administration. In this respect, the European Parliament is almost powerless as the right to make decisions concerning the income – and most of the expenditure – of the Community rests with the Council. Most EC expenditure is obligatory in the sense that it derives from the outcomes of decisions made by the Council, like expenditure on the CAP, and over which the Parliament does not have any influence. During the 1980s, non-obligatory expenses amounted to only 20 per cent of total expenditure, but this portion, however, has been on the increase since then due mainly to the growth of the regional funds and of the Social Fund.

That said, it should be pointed out that the European Parliament has increased its possibilities to influence the budget on several occasions. In 1977 it was granted the power to refuse to approve the budget. Although this would normally give the body in question a more powerful position, this was not quite the case in this instance. Should the EC ever be left without a budget, it would automatically receive a monthly allowance corresponding to one twelfth of the means granted to it in the previous year. A refusal to approve the budget would mean a stagnation in expenditure and, as the aim of the Parliament is usually to increase those means, a refusal would have the opposite effect. In 1986, as part of the Single European Act, the Parliament was further granted the power to make some changes to the budget, though only within its given, total size and only insofar as non-obligatory expenses were concerned.

The primary function of the Parliament is that of a listening institution. In this respect, its position was reinforced as part of the Single European Act when Parliament was then given the power to reject proposals for regulations and the like from the Council. These then have to be adopted by the Council unanimously in their original form to enter into force. This "procedure of cooperation" opened up new possibilities for the Parliament to influence the work of the Community.

Originally, the members of the Assembly were elected among the members of parliament from the member states. However, in the Treaty of Rome, an article was found which opened up the possibility of having direct elections among the electorates of the EC countries. In 1974-76, the summits of the European Council spoke in favour of this reform, although Great Britain and Denmark were opposed. Nonetheless, the outcome was the introduction of this reform which led to the first direct elections in 1979 for the Assembly as it was still then known.

The increased powers of the European Parliament represent a movement towards a strengthening of the federalist elements of the Community, not so much through the direct influence given to the Parliament as through its ability to take initiatives and start debate about new areas of cooperation to be included in the process of integration.[8]

6. The Single European Act (SEA) and the internal market

The origins of the SEA may be traced back to meetings of the European Council in 1983 (Stuttgart), 1984 (Fontainebleau) and 1985 (Milan). In 1983, a solemn declaration concerning a European union covering both economic and wider political subjects was agreed upon. In 1984, it was decided to appoint a committee to prepare institutional reforms and the realization of an internal market. The outcome of this was a report presented by the Commission in June 1985 entitled: "Completing the Internal Market, a White Paper from the Commission to the European Council".

The report noted explicitly that: "...momentum was lost..."and went on to state that:"...each Member State endeavoured to protect what was in its short term interests – not only against third countries but against fellow member states as well." After citing further exam-

---

8. In spring 1999, the European Parliament made use of its powers to censure the Commission, and this may be seen as a further step towards increased powers for the Parliament.

ples of lack of development and cooperation within the Community, the description of the situation concludes: "Disgracefully, that remains the case"! After this sad, but realistic, description of the "state of the union" there followed a detailed survey of existing hindrances to the process of integration: physical and technical barriers and all sorts of hindrances due to internal taxes and duties. As far as goods and persons were concerned, the aim was to bring about a situation where any need for border controls fell away and to secure the free, unfettered mobility of capital and services. With a view to this, the report contained a list of well over three hundred directives that the Council could start looking at. It may be added that the realization of "1992", as the entry into force of the internal market was called, dealt with matters such as public procurement and the strengthening of the policy on competition as well.

In 1985, an inter-governmental conference was convened to prepare changes in existing treaties, and the result was the *Single European Act, the SEA,* finished in early 1986 and which entered into force in July 1987 after ratification.

Its main points were:

a. the establishment of an internal market before the end of 1992,

b. increased cooperation concerning economic and monetary policy,

c. increased access for the use of the majority vote in the Council with a view to promoting the realization of the internal market by means of the adoption of the necessary regulations and directives,

d. the strengthening of the European Parliament vis-à-vis the Council through the procedure of cooperation,

e. the formalization of the existence of the European Council and of a description of European cooperation within foreign policy, though this was thought to be *outside* the Community sphere.

The SEA defines the internal market as an area without internal frontiers, with free movement of goods, persons, services and capital, corresponding to the conditions stated in this treaty (the SEA). After this there is a paragraph which states that the internal market is to be achieved by the end of 1992. As will become apparent, the definition of the internal market did not go far beyond the definition of the common market spelled out in the Treaty of Rome where the "four freedoms" were also mentioned, although their implementation had come to a halt, if not gone into reverse.

For Great Britain and Denmark, the SEA presented the dilemma that it offered both negative and positive elements. The positive aspects included dragging out hidden protectionism into the light of day, but the negative aspects comprised the increased use of the majority vote along with vague, though alarming, hints at a coming economic and monetary union. For Great Britain and its Conservative government, much trouble was caused by a section concerning increased co-operation in the area of social security, especially as the signatories of the SEA were encouraged to work together with trade unions at a time when the Thatcher government was fighting the influence of the trade unions in Britain.

For the remaining EFTA countries, "1992" and the creation of the internal market was bound to give rise to speculation and fears. The creation of such a market placed demands and made requirements of its participants that went well beyond those necessary for participating in a free trade area. With all this in mind, the Scandinavian EFTA countries took the initiative in 1987-88 and started negotiations between the EFTA and EC countries about an agreement on economic cooperation. These negotiations went on throughout 1989 and 1990 and resulted in the creation of the framework of a *European Economic Area,* the *EEA.* Part of this arrangement was an agreement that the EFTA countries should adapt their legislation so that it was in line with EC directives and that they, being among the more prosperous nations of Western Europe, should contribute to the EC's development funds. The final agreement was ready by October 1991, by which time events in the USSR and Eastern Europe had overtaken it while opening up new possibilities for enlarging the Community.

The SEA contained (see point b) a vague reference to the creation of an economic and monetary union. According to a resolution of the European Council of June 1988, this point was referred to a committee under the chairmanship of Jacques Delors whose results were presented in April 1989. Despite the modest wording on the subject in the SEA, the Delors Report contained far-reaching recommendations.

7. The breakdown of the Soviet Bloc

From summer 1989 onwards, a number of dramatic events occurred in Eastern Europe and the Soviet bloc. These included the transformation of the regime in the USSR, the reunification of Germany, the August 1991 coup attempt in Moscow followed by the collapse of the Soviet Union and the final breakdown of the Soviet bloc.

In terms of European integration, these new and unexpected developments raised two fundamental problems. *Firstly*, the end of the East-West conflict, was expected to lead to requests from the former neutral states and the Eastern bloc countries to join the Community, which meant that the present members had, from then on, to consider the entire problem of European integration in a new context comprising countries with a different economic and political background. *Secondly*, German reunification meant that Germany had become by far the strongest member of the EC. The geographical position of Germany as a neighbour to the new, probable applicants gave her a position as the country potentially at the centre of the Community – one hitherto held by France.

Four or five countries, which could not be denied access to the Community on the grounds of having backward economies, were expected to submit their applications soon: Besides the four neutrals – Austria, Finland, Sweden and Switzerland – Norway was expected to give in a new application for membership. Of the former Eastern bloc countries, it was expected that Poland, Hungary and Czechoslovakia might apply soon. For many reasons it was impossible to conduct negotiations concerning the accession of five to ten applicants while at the same time negotiating reforms of the treaty itself amongst the present members of the Community. The existing members had to settle their differences and internal problems first. This corresponded with the procedure used hitherto when applicants such as Great Britain and Denmark had to learn the lesson: "we take the treaty as it stands".

The result was a decision to accelerate the revision of the treaties. Furthermore, Germany wished to calm the fears of its EC partners by expressing a wish to complete the revision of the treaties as soon as possible and bring about a deepening of the cooperation to include foreign policy and security issues.

8. The Maastricht Treaty

In December 1989, a month after the fall of the Berlin Wall, the European Council decided to call an inter-governmental conference about the establishment of an Economic and Monetary Union, the EMU. In April and June 1990, this was supplemented by decisions to call a parallel conference about the establishment of a political union. As the British historian, Derek Urwin, writes: "It was the course of events in Eastern Europe which had made Delors and others even more determined in 1990 to push harder for a European Union."[9] The two conferences started in December 1990 and finished in Maastricht in December 1991. They were followed by the signing of the documents in February 1992: once again, external events had pushed European integration forward.

The use of the words "European Union" in the title of the Maastricht Treaty was new. The text itself was rather confusing in that it consisted of additions to earlier treaties, in themselves additions to other texts, and minor and major subjects were jumbled up together. An introduction to the treaty (Part I) presents the establishment of a European Union, describes its goals and mentions the European Council. After this follow changes to the treaties concerning the three communities, the EEC, the ECSC and Euratom (Parts II – IV); provisions concerning foreign policy and security issues (Part V); provisions concerning judicial and internal matters (Part VI) and concluding provisions including those concerned with the entry into force of the Treaty (Part VII). As far as the institutions were concerned, the outcome can be characterized as a continuation of the SEA with, however, the addition that the Commission was now directly involved in the work of the European Council concerning foreign policy and security matters. Furthermore, the Parliament was given a limited right to submit proposals to the Council and to block the latter's decisions.

Cooperation under the Maastricht Treaty is referred to as consisting of three pillars. *Pillar 1* consists of the economic cooperation mentioned above in reference to Parts II to IV (EC-matters or Community sphere). *Pillar 2* concerns foreign policy and security issues while *Pillar 3* deals with judicial and internal matters. The connection between the three pillars (Part I) consists of the provisions common to the different parts, including provisions concerning the rôle of the European Council as the

9.   D.Urwin, 1995, pp. 250-251.

superior, common body of the Union. All in all, the Maastricht Treaty marked a substantial increase in the scope of cooperation within the area of foreign policy. It should, however, be noted that the cooperation within pillars 2 and 3 is kept outside the legislative framework of the EC and has, in this manner, maintained its confederal or inter-governmental nature. Pillar 3 deals with questions such as asylum policy, immigration policy, cooperation on law enforcement, etc., all subjects related to the breakdown of the internal borders of the Community; so, initiatives have to be taken to move parts of this to Pillar 1, the Community sphere. In Pillar 1, among the novelties were the provisions concerning the social dimension and the establishment of the EMU. The social dimension was an addition to the SEA provision concerning the labour market and was strongly opposed by Britain. The outcome was that Britain declared that she would opt out of this part of the Maastricht Treaty.

The greatest innovation by far of the Maastricht Treaty was, however, contained in those provisions concerning a forthcoming Economic and Monetary Union, the EMU. The concrete measures of the proposal can be traced back to the Delors Report of 1989 and even further back to the Werner Plan of the early 1970s. In June 1989, the European Council confirmed its ideas of a gradual creation of the EMU and it was decided that the Community should enter a first stage of transformation on 1st July 1990. The result as described in the Maastricht Treaty was a plan similar to that outlined in the Delors Report. The second stage was to begin in January 1994 and was to be spent harmonizing the economies of the various participants with a view to starting the third and final stage where exchange rates were to be frozen. To what extent the individual countries of the European Union fulfilled the conditions for entering the third stage was to be monitored through the *convergence criteria* which presumed the following:

a. a high degree of price stability,

b. sustainable public finances, to be observed from the size of the overall net budget position of the government and total public debt relative to the GDP of the country,

c. a high degree of exchange rate stability within the EMS and, finally,

d. a comparatively low long-term interest rate.

A special protocol was attached to the conditions set out above which specified them in greater detail. It was said of the transition from stage 2 to stage 3, the final stage, that it might take place as early as the beginning of 1997, though no later than early 1999 which is what in fact happened.

The transition to the last stage would mean a final freezing of the internal exchange rates, the introduction of a common currency, later to be named the *Euro*, and the introduction of a common monetary and exchange rate policy with price stability as a leading objective. To bring all this about required the creation of a European Central Bank, the *ECB*, which would conduct the common monetary policy. In consequence, the ECB was granted a monopoly of the issue of banknotes within the EMU. One point which has encountered scepticism is the high degree of importance attached to the question of price stability, a priority inherited from the German Bundesbank and traditional German policy. The British and Danish governments announced in protocols that they did not feel obliged to proceed to the third and final stage of the EMU. Of the fifteen members of the EU, four remained outside the EMU from the outset. These were Great Britain, Denmark, Sweden and Greece.

9. Ratification with impediments

After the signing of the Maastricht Treaty in February 1992, the process of ratification was started and it turned out to be a lengthy and dramatic affair with Denmark, France and Germany assuming central rôles.

The first problem – and surprise – was provided by *Denmark*. For constitutional reasons the ratification had to be confirmed by a referendum, to be held in June 1992. The outcome of this was that a narrow majority of 50.7 per cent voted against. As a result, the Maastricht Treaty had in principles been rejected not just in Denmark, but throughout the entire EU because of the provisions concerning its entry into force. Attempts were made, however, to allay the scepticism of the Danish electorate and, at a meeting in Edinburgh of the European Council in December 1992, a solution was reached according to which Denmark, through an exchange of letters of agreement, was relieved of some of the Treaty obligations. These were judicial cooperation, defence, the EMU, union citizenship and some of the declarations of intent. A new referendum was held May 1993 and this time the result was positive, supported by 56.8 per cent of votes cast. Thus the Danish problem was solved – for a while at least.

In *France*, the ratification of the Maastricht Treaty required a change in the constitution because of the rules governing union citizenship (representatives of local assemblies elect members to the French Senate); and some of the provisions concerning the European Central Bank (ECB) also required adjustments. After the necessary decisions had been taken by the National Assembly, President Mitterrand announced that a referendum would be held in September 1992. The winning margin was very small, the number of "yes" votes only representing 51.05 per cent of the total. As that of Denmark, this meagre result no doubt came as a great surprise and indicated that support for the European Union in its current shape was limited, even in one of the original Six.

Germany also had to change its constitution because of both the ECB provisions and the rights of individual states within the Federal Republic of Germany. No solution to those problems was found until autumn 1993. After Germany had ratified the Treaty as the last of the twelve countries, the Maastricht Treaty finally came into force on 1st November 1993.

10. From Maastricht to Amsterdam

The Maastricht Treaty contained a provision[10] according to which a new inter-governmental conference was to be called in 1996. The topics of that conference, however, were not indicated with any degree of precision; though it was stated that a report concerning foreign policy matters was to be presented with a view to possible revision of the EU Treaty, i.e. the treaties of the EC plus the Maastricht Treaty.

On 1st January 1995, the EU was enlarged from twelve to fifteen members, the newcomers being Austria, Finland and Sweden. Referendums held in the two latter countries produced "yes" votes of 56.9 and 52.1 per cent respectively, while once again in Norway 52.5 per cent voted against joining. In the wake of this, a revision of the number

10. Art. N, point 2.

of members of Community institutions took place, including an enlargement of the Commission to twenty members. At the same time,
growing pressure was felt from the countries of Eastern and Central
Europe due to their keen interest in joining the EU.

At the time of the new inter-governmental conference, there was a
widespread feeling that the question of enlargement was going to be a
major theme. Here, however, great difficulties arose. The number of
potential applicants was as high as eleven which meant, if they were all
accepted, that fundamental changes in the institutions and procedures
of the EU were necessary. This involved matters such as the size and
the composition of the Commission, votes in the Council, the balance
of votes between the smaller and the larger member states, increased
use of majority voting, the distribution of influence between Southern
and Northern Europe, the redistribution of regional assistance, reform
of the CAP, etc.

In May 1996 the inter-governmental conference was opened and
lasted until June 1997, after which its results were endorsed when the
Amsterdam Treaty was signed in October 1997. The outcome seems,
however, to be a temporary solution, though the five large member
states agreed to the interim reduction of their representation in the
Commission from two to one representative each. When the number of
member countries exceeds twenty, a conference will be called in order
to revise the institutional provisions of the Community. Poland, the
Czech Republic, Hungary, Slovenia, Estonia and Slovakia were desig-
nated as first rank applicants. It is clear that the final solution to the
fundamental problems related to a coming enlargement of the European Union has so far only been postponed.

11. Putting the EMU into practice

1992-3 saw substantial instability in the international monetary markets,which has been partly explained by the increasing difficulties of
some of the EU countries in keeping down costs which caused a real
appreciation of their currencies (Great Britain, Italy, Spain, Belgium
and others) and partly by growing doubts throughout 1992-3 as to
whether the EMU could be achieved.

Throughout the late 1980s and early 1990s there were only very few
realignments within the EMS; Italy in 1990 being one instance. In

practice this meant an appreciation in real terms of a number of currencies causing increased expectations of forthcoming adjustments, and to this may be added doubts concerning the future of the EMU. The referendums in Denmark in June 1992 and in France in September 1992 had shown that there was great popular resistance to the EMU, so doubts were emerging in the markets as to the will of the countries to fulfil the convergence criteria including the provisions concerning stable exchange rates. Furthermore, member countries including France were opposed to the strict policy of the Bundesbank which resulted in high interest rates at a time of virtually zero growth and rising unemployment. The result was recurrent waves of speculation against the currencies of several member countries, including the French franc, in summer 1993. In August 1993, the EMS was in reality suspended when the limits for exchange rate adjustments were enlarged from 2.25 per cent to 15 per cent.

Table 21.1: Real GDP. Annual growth rates. 1990-98. Selected areas and countries.

	90	91	92	93	94	95	96	97	98
OECD	3.0	1.4	2.2	1.3	3.1	2.5	3.3	3.5	2.4
EU 15	3.0	1.8	1.2	-0.4	2.7	2.4	1.6	2.5	2.7
Germany	5.7	5.0	2.2	-1.1	2.3	1.7	0.8	1.5	2.2
France	2.6	1.1	1.4	-1.0	1.8	1.8	1.2	2.0	3.4
Italy	2.0	1.4	0.8	-0.9	2.2	2.9	0.9	1.5	1.3
UK	0.6	-1.5	0.1	2.3	4.4	2.8	2.6	3.5	2.2
Austria	4.6	3.4	1.3	0.5	2.4	1.7	2.0	2.5	3.3
Belgium	2.7	2.0	1.6	-1.5	3.0	2.6	0.9	3.2	2.9
Netherlands	4.1	2.3	2.0	0.8	3.2	2.3	3.0	3.8	3.7
Switzerland	3.7	-0.8	-0.1	-0.5	0.5	0.5	0.3	1.7	2.1
Denmark	1.2	1.4	1.3	0.8	5.8	3.7	2.8	3.1	2.7
Finland	-0.5	-5.9	-3.2	-0.6	3.7	3.9	4.1	5.6	5.6
Norway	2.0	3.1	3.3	2.7	5.5	3.8	4.9	4.3	2.1
Sweden	1.6	-1.1	-1.6	-2.4	4.0	3.7	1.3	1.8	2.6
USA	1.7	-0.2	3.3	2.4	4.0	2.7	3.7	4.5	4.3
Japan	5.1	3.8	1.0	0.3	0.6	1.5	5.1	1.4	-2.8

Source: OECD Econ. Outlook no. 66, December 1999. Annex Table 1.

According to the Maastricht Treaty, the third and final stage of the EMU could start at the earliest at the beginning of 1997, though no later than the beginning of 1999, which is what happened. It was clear from the outset that the participants needed time to adjust to the convergence criteria such as price stability, sustainable public finances, exchange rate stability and low long–term interest rates. The adjustments of the national economies to the criteria was to take place in the second stage which had started in January 1994. In order to meet these criteria, EC countries, on the whole, had pursued strict economic policies in this period, thus increasing the average level of unemployment for the EU from 9.3 per cent in 1991 to 11.2 per cent in 1993; at which level it remained until 1998.

In December 1995, the European Council decided at its meeting in Madrid that the EMU should come into force by January 1999. This was followed in December 1996 by a decision to set up a so-called *Stability Pact* which had more precise rules guiding the economic policies of the participating countries as well as their budget policy. The core of this was the imposition of fines on countries having a budget deficit over 3 per cent of GDP, where the maximum fine was fixed at 0.5 per cent of GDP to be paid to the EU. This decision was confirmed as a resolution of the European Council at its meeting in Amsterdam in June 1997.

At that time, increased unemployment had caused growing problems for member countries and a need was felt to express concern for the future of unemployment and economic growth. Consequently a resolution was added to the Stability Pact concerning employment, as well as a declaration that the issue of unemployment would constantly be at the top of the agenda of the European Council. The resolution contains little of a more concrete nature. Correspondingly, a declaration of intent was added to the Amsterdam Treaty which was finalized at the same meeting of the European Council. It seems fair to say that this does not, in any significant manner, change the balance of economic goals of the EU as price stability still receives top priority.

A detailed timetable for the introduction of the third stage of the EMU had been agreed upon at Madrid in December 1995. It included, in accordance with the Maastricht Treaty, the setting up of the European Central Bank (ECB) in January 1999 and a freezing of the exchange rates of the participating countries. The common currency was to be called the Euro, one Euro consisting of 100 cents, and it was to be put into circulation from 2002. The Commission was instructed to evaluate whether the member countries fulfilled the criteria. Rules were set up concerning relations with non-participant member countries, and these rules are similar to the former EMS and are known as ERM 2.[11]

In January 1999, eleven of the fifteen member states entered the third stage of the EMU. That eleven countries, including Belgium, Spain, Portugal and Italy which were having great difficulties in meeting the convergence criteria, were accepted by January 1999 may be viewed as a result of a mild interpretation of the governing rules, including the way in which the size of net public debt was calculated. Of the four countries so far staying outside, Greece has been accepted by January 2001, Denmark has voted "no" by 53.1 per cent[12] at a referendum September 2000 and Great Britain and Sweden still have to decide when to have a referendum.

All in all, the period of seven years between the signing of the Maastricht Treaty in January 1992 and the entry into force of the of the third and final stage of the EMU in January 1999 stand out as a period of turbulence in the process of European integration. There was, first, the uncertainty about the approval of the Maastricht Treaty followed by the crisis of the EMS, in turn followed by the bold attempts to bring about the final stages of the EMU. Looking back, once again it seems that the declaration in the preamble to the Treaty of Rome proclaiming the intention to create "an ever closer union..." has emerged victorious.

11. So named as it replaced the Exchange Rate Mechanism under the former EMS.
12. With a turn out of 87.6 per cent of the electorate.

A brief guide to literature

The number of books on economic history is immense. However, textbooks which cover a wide range of countries over an extended period of time are rare. An extended period of time stretches in this context from the end of the Middle Ages to the present day and a wide range of countries comprises at least Western Europe, the USA and, more recently, Japan. A leading example of this broad exposition is provided by Rondo Cameron's *A Concise Economic History of the World* (1997). As indicated by its title, this book also covers overseas, non or late industrialized areas although most of the book is devoted to Western Europe and North America; the exposition focuses on the larger states: Great Britain, France, Germany and the USA supplemented in the early stages by the Italian city states, Spain, Portugal and the Netherlands. Only thirty pages out of a total of four hundred deal with the period after the Second World War. This book does contain a most useful annotated bibliography, besides references to broad expositions and leading periodicals, it also contains specific references relating to individual chapters as well as the periods dealt with therein. While the descriptions and analyses in this book are only quantified to a modest extent, it does use political science methods to explain the dominant position of Western Europe and the USA in the world economy.

A somewhat older, single volume exposition of a similar nature is *Economic Development of the North Atlantic Community* by Dudley Dillard published in 1967. As its title suggests, the scope of this work is not as extensive as that of Cameron's book. This and its over seven hundred pages means that it does contain more detail; this is especially noticeable in the account of the development of economic legislation, special chapters on the development of the American economy as well as the relationship between the economies on the two sides of the North Atlantic.

The Fontana Economic History edited by Carlo M. Cipolla appeared as a nine-volume paperback edition published from 1972 to 1976. A special edition for libraries was also produced. This work covers a wide range of countries: the Benelux countries, France, Germany, Great Britain, the Habsburg Monarchy, Italy, the Nordic countries, Russia and the Soviet Union, Spain and Switzerland. Besides the description of individual countries, this work contains chapters specifically devoted to themes such as agricultural development, technology, manufacturing industry, trade, banking and finance. The work is divided in to six parts: (1) The Middle Ages, (2) The Sixteenth and Seventeenth Centuries, (3) The Industrial Revolution, (4) The Emergence of Industrial Societies, (5) The Twentieth Century and (6) Contemporary Economies. As a general exposition, it is far too large for the purposes of an introductory course, however, those readers who are interested in specific features of European economic history will find this work most useful.

An even more extensive work is *The Cambridge Economic History of Europe*, the publication of which began before the Second World War. This work consists of eight volumes, the first of which have since been revised and published again as new editions. Like the Fontana Economic History it is organized according to both general subject matters and individual countries. Whereas the three previously mentioned works were written as textbooks, this work is intended for advanced studies. Another similarly broad scope work is now being edited under the title of *The Economic Development of Modern Europe Since 1870*. In the individual volumes, the words "Modern Europe" have been replaced by the name of the particular country in question just as those mentioned below edited by K. G. Persson and J.L. van Zanden, each volume consisting of a collection of articles. These volumes are rich in information. They are, however, not intended to provide the reader with a general overview of the reviewed countries' economic development. This work will eventually comprise France, Denmark and Norway, Italy, Austria, Ireland, the Netherlands, Belgium, Germany, the United Kingdom, Sweden and Spain besides the European Community.

An account combining political and economic history is found in Paul Kennedy's *The Rise and Fall of the Great Powers* published in 1987, a paperback edition appearing in 1989. The author of this noted best-seller then felt inclined to write a successor tome dealing with the problems of the present-day titled *Preparing for the Twenty-first Century* which was published in 1993, a paperback edition appearing the next year. David S. Landes, of which more below, has recently published *The Wealth and Poverty of Nations*. This 1998 publication has the subtitle "Why Some are So Rich and Some So Poor"; the lively style of this book is characteristic of the author.

Among works devoted to specific themes over extended periods of time is *The Unbound Prometheus* also by Landes, first published in 1969 with many subsequent reprints. It has the subtitle "Technological Change and Industrial Development in Western Europe from 1750 to the present" and is a definite must for those students who are interested in the history of technology. The history of modern international trade is covered by James Foreman Peck in his *A History of the World Economy: International Economic Relations Since 1850* (second edition, 1995). A. G. Kenwood and A.L. Lougheed have produced another textbook on this subject, *The Growth of the International Economy: An Introductory Text* (third edition, 1992). Then there is William Ashworth's *A Short History of the International Economy Since 1850* (fourth edition, 1987) which is divided up between a description of long-term trends in specific fields such as technology, business management, labour, government and a description of the development of international economic relations, the main emphasis resting on the period before the Second World War. An extensive account of the history of financial and monetary matters is to be found in Charles P. Kindleberger's *A Financial History of Western Europe* published in 1993. A striking feature of development after the Second World War has been the growth in international organization. Readers are referred to David Armstrong's *The Rise of the International Organisation: A Short History* published in 1982 and subsequently reprinted as well as a work which is more narrow in scope, G. J. Lanjouw's *International Trade Institutions* which appeared in 1996.

The pre-industrial period is dealt with by Carlo M. Cipolla in his *Before the Industrial Revolution. European Society and Economy 1000-1700* (third edition, 1993). Two somewhat older though fascinating accounts are *The Birth of Europe* by R.S. Lopez published in 1966 as well his *The Commercial Revolution of the Middle Ages, 950-1350* which appeared in 1971. A classic on the industrial breakthrough in Britain is *The First Industrial Revolution* by Phyllis Deane first published in 1965 and reprinted many times since. As for the spread of industry beyond the English Channel, the general introductory works are recommended, especially the work on the history of technology by David Landes. W. Arthur Lewis' *Economic Survey 1919-39* is a classic which was first published in 1949, subsequently reprinted and still worth reading. A more recent title is *Crisis, Recovery and War. An Economic History of Continental Europe 1918-45* by Roger Munting and B. A. Holderness published in 1991. A further work covering both the interwar and postwar years is the *European Economy 1914-90* by Derek H. Aldcroft (third edition, 1993). *Western Europe: Economic and Social Change Since 1945* edited by Max Stephan Schulze, published in 1999, is in three parts; part one dealing with specific trends of the postwar years, part two with long-term forces in economic and social change and part three, the national economic policies of the Benelux countries, Great Britain, France, Germany, Italy, Scandinavia and Spain. *The National Economies of Europe* edited by David A. Dyker, published in 1992, provides in separate chapters descriptions of the development of France, West Germany, Italy, the United Kingdom, the Benelux countries, Sweden, Spain, Hungary, Poland, Yugoslavia and the Soviet Union; as it is apparent, this work does not cover the period of reforms after the breakdown of the Soviet bloc.

Two major themes of economic history writing in recent years have been the exceptionally high growth rates after the Second World War and progressive European integration which culminated in the form of the Economic and Monetary Union which was put into force at the close of the century.

A pioneering work in the field of growth calculations is Edward Denison's *Why Growth Rates Differ. Postwar Experience in Nine Western Countries* of 1967. A more recent study along similar lines is Angus Maddison's *Dynamic Forces in Capitalist Development, A Long-Run Comparative View* of 1991. As the title indicates, the book contains comparisons between the growth rates of different periods for different countries going back to the early nineteenth century. This book is a rich source of historical statistics, including figures on the development of the gross national product and gross domestic product of OECD member countries as at the end of the 1980's. *Monitoring the World Economy 1820-1992* by the same author and published by the OECD covers a wider range of countries in that Eastern Europe, Africa, Asia and South America are represented. Another recent comparative study, *Economic Growth in Europe Since 1945* edited by Nicholas Crafts and Gianni Toniolo, was published in 1996. Its first five chapters deal with general aspects of postwar economic growth and the remaining twelve cover the development in individual countries: Great Britain, Belgium, France, Sweden, the Netherlands, Portugal, Spain, Ireland, Italy, West Germany, East Germany and Denmark. This book contains a vast number of references to recent literature on economic growth. The work edited by Schulze mentioned above contains chapters dealing specifically with postwar growth as well. A leading source of macroeconomic statistics is the OECD whose most recent publication entitled *OECD Historical Statistics 1960-97* was published in 1999. Besides this, the OECD regularly publish special volumes entitled *National Accounts*. The *OECD Economic Outlook*, a semi-annual publication which also contains chronological data has now been published for over thirty years. Special reports on individual OECD countries are published under the title *Economic Survey* of a given country. Under the title *Eurostat Yearbook*, the EU has recently started to publish its own statistics including ten-year time series for individual member states and the EU as a whole on demography, trade, EU budgets et alia. This publication is produced in the languages of the member states. *International Historical Statistics. Europe. 1750-1988* by B.R. Mitchell, published in 1992, is by far the largest single volume publication on the subject totalling nearly 950 pages. This book contains useful references to national statistics.

Most books on European integration may be characterized as either descriptions of the present state of affairs or as contributions to the debate concerning the future of the Community. Literature on the history of European integration tends to divide itself into two groupings dealing either with the political aspects of the process, including foreign policy and security issues, or with the economic aspects. *The Community of Europe. A History of European Integration Since 1945* by D. W. Urwin (second edition, 1995) does cover both fields albeit with the main emphasis on the political aspects. This work consists mainly of excerpts from his earlier work *Western Europe Since 1945; a political history* of 1989, subsequently reprinted, which includes the wider political environment of the Community. The work mentioned first includes an extensive guide for further reading. *The European Union. Readings on the Theory and Practice of European Integration* edited by Brent F. Nelsen and Alexander G. Stubb, published in 1994, reproduces a number of central texts and documents in the history of European integration; it also contains excerpts from documents concerning the theory and strategy of integration which discuss the concepts of federalism, functionalism and neo-functionalism. Excerpts and analysis are also to be found in *Peter M. R. Stirk and David Weigall (ed.), The Origins and Development of European Integration. A Reader and Commentary* published in 1999; this work covers the period all the way back to 1918. An authoritative description of the early years of the EC is found in *The European Community. The Formative Years* by Hans von der Groeben, published in 1987, it has the subtitle "The struggle to establish the Common Market and the Political Union, 1958 – 1966". The author was a member of the EEC Commission from its very outset in 1958 and the book is characterized by the eyewitness nature of the account of this dynamic period of Community history. Another account and further analysis of the background and early years of the EC are to be found in *The European Rescue of the Nation State* by Allan S. Milward published in 1992. *The European Economy* edited by David A. Dyker (second edition, 1999) provides an up-to-date account of recent developments within European integration including the relations of the EC/EU with the former members of the Soviet bloc as well as to Third World countries.

List of Selected Literature

The following list only contains that literature which has been directly drawn upon. Most of the references to literature in Scandinavian languages have been excluded.

Aldcroft, D. H., *The European Economy 1914-1990*. 3rd ed. 1993.

Angresano, J., *Comparative Economics*. 2nd ed. 1996.

Armstrong, d., *The Rise of the International Organisation. A Short History*. 1982. Reprints.

Ashley, P., *Modern Tariff History. Germany-United States-France*. 3. ed. 1920.

Ashworth, W., *A Short History of the International Economy Since 1850*. 4th ed. 1987.

Bairoch, P., *Economics and World History. Myths and Paradoxes. 1993*.

Balassa, B. and M. Noland, *Japan in the World Economy*. 1988.

Barnett, C., *The Pride and the Fall. The Dream and Illusion of Britain as a Great Nation*. 1986.

Batchelor, R. A., et. al., *Industrialisation and The Basis for Trade*. 1980.

Bath, B. H. Slicher van., *The Agrarian History of Western Europe, A.D. 500-1850*. 1963.

Bolin, S., *The Agrarian Life in the Middle Ages*. The Cambridge Economic History of Europe. Vol I. 2nd ed. 1966.

Cameron, R., *A Concise Economic History of the World. From Paleolithic Times to the Present*. 1989.

Carus-Wilson, E., *The Woollen Industry*. Cambridge Economic History. Vol. II, Chap. IX. 1987.

Chandler J., A. D., *The Railroads: The first modern business enterprises, 1850s-1860s*. As reproduced in R. Whaples (ed), Historical Perspectives on the American Economy. Selected Readings. 1995.

Cipolla, C. M., ed., *The Fontana Economic History*. 1972-76.

Cipolla, C. M., *Guns, Sails and Empires. Technological Innovation and the Early Phases of European Expansion 1400-1700*. 1965, reprint 1985.

Cipolla, C. M., *Before the Industrial Revolution. European Society and Economy 1000-1700*. 1993.

Claude Jr., I. L., *Swords into Plowshares. The Problems and Progress of International Organization*. 1963 or later.

Crafts, N. and G. Toniolo ed., *Economic Growth in Europe Since 1945*. 1996

Craig, L. A., and D. Fisher, *The Integration of the European Economy, 1850-1913*. 1997.

Dansgaard, W., *Klima, vejr og mennesker*. 1987.

Deane, P., *The First Industrial Revolution*. 1965. Reprints.

Denison, E. F., *Why Growth Rates Differ. Postwar Experience in Nine Western Countries*. 1967.

Dillard, D., *Economic Development of the North Atlantic Community*. 1967.

Dyker, D. A., ed., *The National Economies of Europe*. 1992.

Dyker, D. A., ed., *The European Economy*. 2nd. ed. 1999.

Dyrvik, S. et.al., *Norsk økonomisk historie 1500-1970*. Band 1, 1500-1850. 1979.

European Communities, The., Committee for the Study of Economic and Monetary Union, *Report on Economic and Monetary Union in the European Community*. (The "Delors-report"). 1989.

Feldbæk, O., *Danmarks økonomiske Historie 1500-1840*. 1993.

Forfatningskommissionen, *Betænkning afgivet af Forfatningskommissionen af 1946*. 1953.

Foreman-Peck, J., *A History of the World Economy. International Economic Relations Since 1850*. 2nd. ed. 1995.

Griffiths, R. T., *The Economic Development of the EEC*. 1997.

Groeben, H. von der, *The European Community. The Formative Years. The struggle to establish the Common Market and the Political Union (1958-66)*. Edited by the EC-Commission. 1987.

Harrod, R. F., *The Life of John Maynard Keynes*. 1951. As Pelican Book 1972.

Hecksher, E. F., *Mercantilism*. 2nd. English ed. 1965.

Hicks, J. R., *A Theory of Economic History*. 1969

Hvidt, K., *Flugten til Amerika eller Drivkræfter i masseudvandringen fra Danmark 1868-1914*. 1971.

Kennedy, P., *The Rise and Fall of the Great Powers*. 1987.

Kenwood, A. G. and A. L. Loughead, *The Growth of the International Economy. An Introductory Text*. 3rd ed. 1992.

Kindleberger, C. P., *Europes Postwar Growth: The Role of Labour Supply*. 1967.

Kindleberger, C. P., *The World in Depression*. 2nd ed. 1986.

Kindleberger, C. P., *The Marshall Plan seen from The United States 1947 and 1987*. Økonomi og Politik, 60th vol. 1987 no. 7.

Kindleberger, C. P., *Historical Economics. Art or Science?* 1990.

Kindleberger, C. P., *A Financial History of Western Europe*. 2nd ed. 1993.

Kissinger, H., *Diplomacy*. 1994.

Kjeldsen-Kragh, S., *International Trade Policy*. 2000.

Kjærgaard, Th., *The Danish Revolution – an ecohistorical interpretation*. 1994.

Krag, J. O. and K. B. Andersen, *Kamp og Fornyelse. Socialdemokratiets indsats i dansk politik 1955-71*. 1971.

Kuznets, S., *Economic Growth of Nations. Total Output and Production Structure*. 1971.

Landes, D. S., *The Unbound Prometheus. Technological Change and Industrial Development in Western Europe from 1750 to the Present*. 1969 (several reprints).

Landes, D. S., *The Wealth and Poverty of Nations*. 1998.

Lanjouw, G. J., *International Trade Institutions*. 1995.

Lewis, W. A., *Economic Survey 1919-1939*. 1949.

Lindbeck, A., *Swedish Economic Policy*. 1975.

Lopez, R. S., *The Commercial Revolution of the Middle Ages 950-1350*. 1971.

Lopez, R. S., *The Birth of Europe*. 1966.

Maddison, A., *Economic Growth in the West. Comparative Experience in Europe and North America*. 1964.

Maddison, A., *Phases of Capitalist Development*. 1982.

Maddison, A., *Dynamic Forces in Capitalist Development. A Long-Run Comparative View*. 1991.

Maddison, A., *Monitoring the World Economy 1820-1992*. Edited by OECD. 1995.

Malthus, T.R., *Essay on Population*. 1798. Several editions. Here from the 7th ed.

Milward, A. S., *The Development of the Economies of Continental Europe 1850-1914*. 1977.

Milward, A. S., *The European Rescue of the Nation State*. 1992.

Mitchell, B. R., *International Historical Statistics. Europe 1750-1988*. 1992.

Monnet, J., *Ma Vie*. 1976.

Munting, R. and B. A. Holderness, *Crises, Recovery and War. An Economic History of Continental Europe 1918-1945*. 1995.

Nelsen, B. F. and A.-G. Stubb (ed.), *The European Union. Readings on the Theory and Practice of European Integration*. 1994.

North, D. C. and R. P.Thomas, *The Rise of the Western World. A New Economic History*. 1973.

North D. C., *Institutions, Institutional Change and Economic Performance*. 1990. Reprints.

OECD, *Economic Outlook*. Several editions.

OECD, *Historical Statistics*. Several editions.

OECD, *National Accounts*. Several editions.

OECD, *The Aims and Instruments of Industrial Policy. A Comparative Study*. 1975.

OECD, *Selected Industrial Policy Instruments. Objectives and Scope*. 1978.

OECD, *Positive Adjustment Policies. Managing Structural Change*. 1983.

OECD, *Economies in Transition. Structural Adjustment in OECD Countries*. 1989.

Ogg, F. A. and W. R. Sharp, *Economic Development of Modern Europe*. Rev. ed. 1949.

Overy, R. J., *The Nazi economic recovery 1932-38*. 2nd ed. 1996.

Parker, G., *The Emergence of Modern Finance in Europe 1500-1730*. The Fontana.

Persson, K. G., *The Economic Development of Denmark and Norway since 1870*. 1993.

Pollard, S., *European Economic Integration 1815-1970*. 1974.

Pope, R., *The British Economy Since 1914. A Study in Decline?* 1998.

Porter, M., *The Competitive Advantage of Nations*. 1990.

Postan, M., *Trade and Industry in the Middle Ages*. The Cambridge Economic History of Europe from the Decline of the Roman Empire. Vol. II. 2nd ed. 1987.

Ross, A., *Dansk Statsforfatningsret I*. 1959.

Scheiber, H. N., H. G. Vatter and H.U. Faulkner, *American Economic History*. 9th ed. 1976.

Schulze, M.-S., ed., *Western Europe: Economic and Social Change Since 1945*. 1999.

Smith, A., *The Wealth of Nations*. 1776.

Sorensen, T., *Kennedy*. 1965.

Stewart, M., *The Jekyll and Hyde Years. Politics and Economic Policy since 1964*. 1977.

Stirk, P. M. R. and D. Weigall, *The Origins and Development of European Integration. A Reader and Commentary*. 1999.

Sæter, M., *Det europeiske Fellesskap. Institusjoner og politikk*. 1993 or later.

Tipton, F. B. and R. Aldrich, *An Economic and Social History of Europe 1890-1939*. 1987. Reprints.

Tipton, F. B. and R. Aldrich, *An Economic and Social History of Europe from 1939 to the Present*. 1987. Reprints.

Trevelyan, G. M., *English Social History*. Pelican Books, 1967.

Tsuru, S., *Japan's capitalism: Creative defeat and beyond*. 1993.

Urwin, D. W., *Western Europe Since 1945, a political History*. 1989.

Urwin, D. W., *The Community of Europe. A History of European Integration since 1945*. 2nd ed. 1995.

Viner, J., *The Customs Union Issue*. 1950.

Walters, F. P., *A History of the League of Nations*. 1952.

Wigforss, E., *Minnen III. 1932-49*. 1954.

Young, J. W., *Britain and European Unity, 1945-1992*. 1993.

Zanden, J. L. van, *The Economic Development of the Netherlands since 1870*. 1996.

Zeuthen, F., *Social Sikring. Socialpolitik, II bind*. 1948.

Index